MODERN STUDIES IN PHILOSOPHY

DESCARTES

A Collection of Critical Essays

EDITED BY WILLIS DONEY

UNIVERSITY OF NOTRE DAME PRESS

NOTRE DAME   LONDON

First Hardbound Edition: 1968

University of Notre Dame Press

Notre Dame, Indiana 46556

Printed by special arrangement with Doubleday & Company, Inc.

Anchor Books Edition: 1967
Doubleday & Company, Inc.
Garden City, New York

Manufactured in the United States of America

CONTENTS

Modern Studies in Philosophy is a series of anthologies presenting contemporary interpretations and evaluations of the works of major philosophers. The editors have selected articles designed to show the systematic structure of the thought of these philosophers, and to reveal the relevance of their views to the problems of current interest. These volumes are intended to be contributions to contemporary debates as well as to the history of philosophy; they not only trace the origins of many problems important to modern philosophy, but also introduce major philosophers as interlocutors in current discussions.

Modern Studies in Philosophy is prepared under the general editorship of Amelie Rorty, Associate Professor of Philosophy at Douglass College, Rutgers University.

WILLIS DONEY, who received his Ph.D. from Princeton University, is Professor of Philosophy at Dartmouth College, with which he has been associated since 1958. In addition to editing the present volume on Descartes, he has written articles on Descartes for philosophical journals.

INTRODUCTION

With two exceptions, the studies of Descartes and Cartesian problems that are assembled here were written in English or by British or American philosophers. All of them were written after 1925, most of them fairly recently, and some have not been published before. The two exceptions are Émile Bréhier's "La Création des vérités éternelles dans le système de Descartes" and P. H. J. Hoenen's account of Descartes's Mechanicism in his *Cosmologia*. Both, which appear here in translation, contain interpretations that, to the best of my knowledge, are not represented in the rapidly growing literature on Descartes in English. They also have an important bearing on problems that are now being discussed. The discussions in general are directed toward views and arguments in Descartes that have been of special concern to philosophers whose interest in Descartes has been related to, or has been conjoined with, their interest in the theory of knowledge and adjoining problems in metaphysics. The theory of knowledge or epistemology has occupied—on some estimates preoccupied—a great many philosophers in English-speaking countries. Since there is little doubt about the paternity of modern theory of knowledge, it is not surprising that many have turned to Descartes for the statement of views and arguments that they wished to examine and very often nowadays to criticize. In recent years, interest in Descartes and Cartesian problems appears to have increased, and the number of papers that have been written in English alone is, as indicated in the Bibliography, very considerable.

This is in part, I believe, the result of a changing picture of the history of modern philosophy and a clearer recognition of our indebtedness to Descartes. For some time, in surveys of the history of modern philosophy and in titles of courses and seminars, the terms "Rationalism" and "Empiricism" have been used to separate Descartes from Locke and his Empiricist successors Berkeley and Hume. But the picture of divergent streams—or of warring camps—in modern philosophy now appears badly distorted, or at least very greatly oversimplified. It is clear that, in many important respects, Locke, though he represented himself as taking issue with his predecessors on the important (and complex) issue of the origin of ideas and principles, was in fact a Cartesian. Underlying views and basic notions that he shared with Descartes have been referred to recently as an "official doctrine," and it has been suggested that philosophy as practiced in English has been basically Cartesian. But the "official doctrine" has, as a whole and in parts, been under attack recently; and it would not be incorrect to speak of an anti-Cartesian movement in contemporary British and American philosophy. As a consequence, some of the studies presented here are openly critical of Cartesian ideas. Others, however, contain more neutral exegesis, and in some Descartes is defended against interpretations and criticisms that appear to be mistaken. In all the discussions the authors pay tribute to Descartes by taking his views—right or wrong—very seriously; that is, as views that are not merely of historical interest but of philosophical importance and to be treated and judged as such.

Though there are differences of opinion and of outlook expressed in the discussions, they are by no means representative of all the Cartesian studies that have appeared in recent years, and omissions should be noted. With the exception of Bréhier's paper, nothing is included of the many excellent studies of Descartes by French scholars. I might mention in particular the writings of Ferdinand Alquié, Étienne Gilson, Henri Gouhier, Martial Gueroult, Jean Laporte, and Geneviève Rodis-Lewis. Even within the literature in English, it was necessary to adopt rather restrictive principles of selection. I have not, for instance, included parts of books now available on Descartes, nor any of the exceedingly interesting articles that have begun to appear on Descartes's scientific work. Nor indeed have I been able to include all the important articles in English relating to his theory of knowledge and metaphysics. The discussions that are included—on topics currently discussed by philosophers with certain interests—deal with six major aspects or parts of Descartes's "first philosophy." To introduce them, I shall say something about the views in the *Meditations on First Philosophy* that form the bases of the discussions.

1

The question that Descartes raises in the First Meditation —are any of one's opinions entirely certain and without doubt? —has been a standard and perhaps the fundamental question in the theory of knowledge. It has often been assumed, as Descartes does, that knowledge must have a foundation in absolute certainty and that if an opinion or belief cannot stand on its own as absolutely certain yet is to qualify as knowledge, it must be shown to be related in an acceptable way to certainties that are, so to speak, self-sufficient and basic. Not all of Descartes's successors have insisted on the same kind of logical relations or ordering within the structure of knowledge, but it has been a widespread notion that there must be a structure and that the philosopher's task is to locate the basic certainties and show how they are, or can be, the foundations of the edifice of human knowledge. As in the First Meditation, various kinds of statements or beliefs have been singled out as candidates for the roles of basic certainties, and their *prima facie* certainty has been examined and tested. In the First Meditation, Descartes distinguishes two kinds of opinions that seem to him to be most certain: those received "from the senses or by way of the senses" and opinions about "the simplest and most general matters." Among the latter, he includes simple mathematical judgments, e.g. "Two plus three equals five" and "A square has four sides." In order to test their certainty, he m: kes use of a variety of skeptical arguments, some of them i aving their origin with the Greek skeptics; and, in the course of his "methodic doubt," he reaches the conclusion that opinions of neither sort are entirely certain and indubitable. Since these

opinions seemed to him to be the most certain of all his
former opinions, he concludes in the First Meditation that
there is no one of his former opinions that is not subject to
doubt.

The skeptical arguments that Descartes employs here have
been of urgent concern to philosophers who have been unable to follow him in his escape from skepticism in the succeeding Meditations, and have felt that if these arguments
are conceded, 'the tentative skepticism of the First Meditation may very well have to be the final answer. Some of the
discussions here are about Descartes's doubts about "the simplest and most general matters" and his attempt to allay
these doubts in the Meditations that follow. The first two
papers, however, are about the certainty, in Descartes's terms,
of what is received "from the senses or by way of the senses."
Both papers take account of a very powerful and persuasive
argument that he presents in the First Meditation to question
the certainty of perceptual judgments—that is, the skeptical
argument from the possibility of dreaming.

In "Certainty," his posthumously published Howison lecture, G. E. Moore does not refer to Descartes by name, but
the very examples that he uses call the First Meditation to
mind. Moore begins his famous lecture by making a number
of assertions:

> I am at present, as you can all see, in a room and not in
> the open air; I am standing up, and not either sitting or
> lying down; I have clothes on, and am not absolutely
> naked; I am speaking in a fairly loud voice, and am not
> either singing or whispering or keeping quite silent; I
> have in my hand some sheets of paper with writing on
> them; there are a good many other people in the same
> room in which I am; and there are windows in that wall
> and a door in this one.

These assertions, whose certainty Moore proceeds to examine,
are some of them of an exact kind with the opinions derived
"from the senses or by way of the senses" that Descartes considers in the First Meditation, and the questions that Moore
raises are clearly the descendants of Descartes's; namely,

whether any of the propositions that he asserted at the beginning of his lecture were known to be true and whether they were "absolutely certain." Both Moore and Descartes take it to be the case that if the opinions or assertions to which they refer were not absolutely certain, then no opinion or assertion about "corporeal things" or an "external world" (in Descartes's case, to be exact, no specific or particular opinion) would be absolutely certain. And, for both of them, the certainty of opinions or assertions like these is taken to depend on whether or not it is possible that what is believed or asserted is false.

But here the agreement ends, for Moore, unlike Descartes in the First Meditation, is not prepared to conclude that the propositions that he asserted were not absolutely certain. He maintains that from the mere fact that his assertions might have been false and were assertions of contingent propositions, it does not follow that these propositions were not known to be true, or that they were not absolutely certain. This would have to be shown, and Moore turns to one kind of argument that has been proposed to show it—that is, to the argument from the possibility of dreaming. Pointing out difficulties in certain formulations of the argument—difficulties that seem to tell against Descartes's formulation—Moore states an argument that is not subject to just these objections. But persuasive as this argument is, he is not in the end prepared to accept it. His reason for not accepting it is based in part on his uncertainty as to whether indeed it is "logically possible that I should *both* be having all the sensory experiences and the memories that I have and *yet* be dreaming"; for it seems to Moore that the conjunction of his "memories of the immediate past" with his present sensory experiences *may* be enough to enable him to know with certainty that he is not dreaming. It is interesting to note that when Descartes in the Sixth Meditation returns to the problem raised in the First Meditation about the possibility of dreaming and attempts to dispose of his earlier doubts, he, too, refers to memory. In the Sixth Meditation he declares: "Dreams are never connected by memory with all the other events of life, as are the things that happen while we are awake."

In "Dreaming and Skepticism," Norman Malcolm examines this statement and also certain assertions that Descartes makes in presenting his argument in the First Meditation; namely, that he has "in sleep been deceived by similar illusions" and that "there are no certain marks distinguishing waking from sleep." Concerning the first assertion, Malcolm contends that if by "sleep" Descartes means "sound sleep," he is in error; for a necessary condition of being "deceived" is having thoughts, and being *sound* asleep—Malcolm argues—precludes the possibility of having thoughts. It is also a mistake, according to Malcolm, to say that a person cannot tell whether he is awake or sound asleep and dreaming. To say this would be to imply, among other things, that a person might *think* that he is awake while he is sound asleep; and according to Malcolm's argument, it is impossible for a person both to be sound asleep and also to think. But it would also be incorrect to say, as Descartes suggests in the Sixth Meditation, that there *is* a way of distinguishing waking from sound sleep; and so it seems that Descartes's solution in the Sixth Meditation of the problem raised in the First Meditation is destroyed along with the problem itself. In his criticisms of Descartes's assertions about dreaming, Malcolm points out certain general views of Descartes's about the nature of thought and of the mind, and the discussion of these views, as well as of the argument itself, is very illuminating. The critical points that he makes here and in his book *Dreaming* have provoked a great deal of controversy, and some of the papers listed in the Bibliography support Cartesian views against Malcolm's criticisms. There seems to be general agreement, however, among Malcolm and his critics that Descartes, in stating the argument from the possibility of dreaming in the First Meditation, carried out his intention of putting the case for skepticism concerning the senses in the strongest possible way.

2

In the Second Meditation, when Descartes represents himself as emerging from his seemingly universal doubt and discovering an indisputably certain first principle in his own existence, he does not, as is sometimes assumed, express his famous insight in the words *cogito ergo sum.* In the parallel passage in the *Discourse on Method,* he uses the French equivalent *je pense, donc je suis;* and, in his Replies to Objections appended to the *Meditations,* he employs a fuller locution: *ego cogito, ergo sum, sive existo.* The term *cogito* is commonly used, however, to refer to the insight expressed in the Second Meditation and in general to the way in which, according to Descartes, a person attains certainty about his own existence. To philosophers concerned with the theory of knowledge, the *cogito* has been a subject of great interest in part because the statements associated with it—*Cogito,* read as "I am thinking" or "I am conscious," and *Sum,* "I am" or "I exist"—have been taken to be statements ostensibly about matters of fact that are without question indubitable. In recent discussions a complex question raised by Descartes's contemporaries has been reopened with a view to a better understanding of the nature of these statements and the certainty that attaches to them. The question is whether Descartes regarded the *cogito* as an inference; that is, whether he thought of *Sum* as a conclusion deduced from *Cogito* as a premise. The locutions that he uses in expressing his insight—e.g. ". . . *ergo* . . ." and ". . . *donc* . . ."—seem to show conclusively that he did think of the *cogito* as an inference. But certain statements of and about the *cogito* give the reader pause. Descartes claims, for instance, that the first principle of his philosophy can be intuited as self-evident; and he clearly denies that *Sum* is deduced by attending to *Cogito* in conjunction with a major premise, "Everything that thinks exists."

Because of statements like these, the questions have been raised whether Descartes consistently thought of the *cogito* as an inference and also in exactly what sense or senses of "inference" he did think of it as an inference. In recent discussions, textual evidence has been brought to bear on closely related questions—for instance, his distinction of deduction from intuition and the status assigned to the general principle, "Everything that thinks exists." But considerations of a logical as well as of a textual sort have entered into the discussions. Questions have been raised that depend in no way on an appeal to the Cartesian *corpus*; for example, whether the *cogito*, construed as an inference, is a logically acceptable argument. An assumption or principle of interpretation that seems to have been at work, for instance, in Jaakko Hintikka's extremely interesting discussion, is that if a certain view or argument can be shown to be indefensible and if it is reasonable to suppose that Descartes was in a position to see this, there is some reason to think that he did not at any rate clearly accept the view or argument in question.

The first discussion of the *cogito* is by A. J. Ayer and is part of a chapter in *The Problem of Knowledge* in which he discusses the "quest for certainty" and the attempt—by Descartes and many others—to find statements or kinds of statements that are "immune from doubt." A conclusion that he reaches in this chapter is that neither necessary statements nor descriptive statements of any sort are immune from doubt, and that the only statements that satisfy the Cartesian demand for certainty are "degenerate" statements such as those associated with the *cogito*. Although Ayer implies that Descartes did in fact think of the *cogito* as an inference, he maintains that "there was . . . no need for Descartes to derive '*sum*' from '*cogito*' . . ."; and he undertakes to explain the peculiar nature of both statements neither of which is a "truth of logic" nor a "descriptive statement." To show that they are not necessary truths, he argues that if a person says "I am not thinking" or "I do not exist," what he says, though it "must be false," nonetheless "might not have been false" and hence is not self-contradictory. Nor, according to Ayer, are "I am conscious" and "I exist" used to make descriptive statements; for when we use them, the demonstrative "I" does all the work and the ostensible predicates are "sleeping partners."

Bernard Williams, in his very interesting study of the *cogito*, is concerned with the interpretation of certain puzzling passages and also with the logic of the *cogito*. He agrees with Ayer that the statements associated with the *cogito* are not logical or necessary truths, but he points out a difficulty in attempts like Ayer's to make this point. On the question whether Descartes thought of the *cogito* as an inference, Williams introduces a number of important distinctions. He maintains that, from a logical as well as a psychological point of view, Descartes was (at least for the most part) of the opinion that the *cogito* is not a *syllogistic* inference. But he contends that Descartes did think of it as an inference of a certain kind—of a kind that Williams, calling attention to recent work on the notion of presupposition, e.g. by P. T. Geach and P. F. Strawson, tries to specify. In his discussion he raises questions about the principle that seems to underlie the *cogito*, "Everything that thinks exists." One question of great importance from a critical point of view is whether existence is, as Descartes evidently thought, an attribute or a predicate. From considerations involving this question, Williams is led to ask about the content of *Sum* as it appears in the context of the Second Meditation; but he is not prepared to conclude that it is, as for Ayer, "purely demonstrative" and "degenerate," nor that, in its logical form, Descartes's conclusion is "strictly speaking, incorrect."

On certain points Hintikka's interpretation of the *cogito* is opposed to Williams'. Although he acknowledges that some of Descartes's statements of and about the *cogito* indicate that he did at times think of it as an inference, he argues on textual grounds and also on points of logic that Descartes, "albeit dimly" or "however implicitly," also thought of the *cogito* as something other than an inference—that is, as a "performance." According to this reading, Descartes realized to some extent that the certainty of *Sum* derives, not from being deduced from an indubitable proposition *Cogito*, but from the "existentially inconsistent" or "self-defeating" character of the attempt to think its contrary. Hintikka contends that the sentence "Everybody who thinks exists" cannot serve as a general truth from which *cogito ergo sum* can be inferred and that when we try to construe the *cogito* as a logical inference, we encounter formidable difficulties. This important paper has been widely discussed. (See the articles by Carney, Weinberg, and Frankfurt listed in the Bibliography, and also Malcolm's "Descartes's Proof that His Essence is Thinking," pp. 312–337.) These discussions of the *cogito* testify to the richness and also to the complexity of Descartes's famous insight.

3

A third group of papers deal with problems arising from the doubts that Descartes expresses in the First Meditation about "the simplest and most general matters." In the Third Meditation, reflecting on his initial certainty, Descartes proposes his so-called Rule of Truth: "Everything that I very clearly and distinctly perceive is true." In view of his initial doubts, it seems that he tries to validate this Rule by *proving* that what he very clearly and distinctly perceives is true. But it also seems that in attempting to validate the Rule he makes use of it and is guilty of begging the question and of circular reasoning. This kind of objection, which has given to his reasoning here the prejudicial name "Cartesian circle," was raised by Descartes's contemporaries; and, in his Replies to Objections, he defends his procedure in the *Meditations* against the imputation of circularity. It is not clear, however, that he succeeds—at any rate without withdrawing from positions taken in the *Meditations*; nor is it clear exactly how he thinks he answers his critics' objections. There are also problems about the use of this Rule as a test or a criterion of knowledge, as Descartes seems at times to have thought of it. Can a person, for instance, be mistaken in thinking that he clearly and distinctly perceives something? Either answer seems to bring unwelcome consequences. And further difficulties arise when the question is asked whether, in order to know that a proposition is true, a person must not only clearly and distinctly perceive it but also know in addition that his state is one of clear and distinct perception.

In his posthumously published lectures on the history of the theory of knowledge, H. A. Prichard raises these difficulties and points out wherein he thinks Descartes went astray. His approach to the *Meditations* in these lectures is clearly stated:

> My idea is to take the book as it stands and ask whether it is true or false. In doing this, however, it is necessary to distinguish the wheat from the chaff. It will strike you —or must have struck you—in reading the book, that it is extraordinarily unequal. Some parts will seem to you to deal with what is important and very much to the point, and others as being very artificial and unconvincing. And the proper attitude for the reader and the commentator is to concentrate attention on what seem the important parts and to bother very little about the rest. [P. 72, *Knowledge and Perception*, in a section preceding what is included here.]

Prichard's attitude toward the *Meditations* may disaffect conventional historians of philosophy. This is one way, however, in which philosophers have turned to the *Meditations*; and Prichard's reading of them not only is philosophically very exciting but also gives us a deeper insight into the problems with which Descartes was concerned. Concerning the alleged "Cartesian circle," Prichard finds Descartes guilty, for he thinks that once Descartes seriously entertains doubts about the competence of his intelligence, he should at that moment stop. But Descartes of course does not stop, and Prichard presents an exceedingly ingenious explanation of why this is so. His understanding of Descartes's problems and of his conflicting tendencies in the face of them make this an exceptionally rewarding study.

In A. K. Stout's "The Basis of Knowledge in Descartes" and in Harry G. Frankfurt's "Descartes' Validation of Reason," problems relating to the alleged Cartesian circle are considered in some detail and with very different results. These questions are also alluded to in Bréhier's "The Creation of the Eternal Truths," and a highly original solution is suggested. The papers as a group offer three major answers to the question why Descartes did not think that his procedure in the *Meditations* was, as his critics claimed, circular. Stout presents what has been called the "developmental hypothesis." His contention is that Descartes, having intended (though not presumably exclusively or altogether clearly) to question and then to validate clear and distinct perceptions in the *Meditations,* "imperceptibly transferred the doubt from clearness and distinctness to memory" when he was faced with objections and was, as it were, under fire. According to this interpretation, what is questioned and validated on Descartes's amended or considered view is the accuracy of memory impressions of having clearly and distinctly perceived something and not clear and distinct perceptions themselves; in particular, not those perceptions used to establish the existence of a nondeceptive God and the reliability of memory.

In "The Creation of the Eternal Truths," Bréhier maintains that the doubts that Descartes expresses and attempts to overcome about "the simplest and most general matters" are not about the reliability of memory nor about the present truth of what is intuited. Rather, the question with which he is concerned is whether what is intuited at a certain time—admittedly true at that time—is true at all times or is an "eternal truth." To be assured of this, Descartes needs to know that the essences that he intuits are permanent and not subject to change from time to time by a deceitful demon; and Bréhier suggests in his paper that Descartes can be assured of this without at any rate flagrantly begging the question. In the third paper, Frankfurt attributes to Descartes an answer to the skeptic's doubts about reason similar to the one that we find in Spinoza. His contention is that Descartes's "reasoning in the *Meditations* is designed not so much to prove that what is intuited is true as to show that there are no reasonable grounds for doubting this" and that Descartes can do this without being guilty of the kind of circular reasoning with which he has often been charged. It is worth noting that Spinoza, although his answer to the skeptic is like the one that Frankfurt attributes to Descartes, does not attribute an answer of this kind to Descartes. And it does seem difficult at any rate to reconcile Frankfurt's interpretation with Descartes's claim that the *cogito* is certain prior to, and independently of, his certainty of the existence of God. In a recent paper about the *cogito*, Frankfurt in effect tries to answer this objection by maintaining that, in the Second Meditation, Descartes is not in fact concerned to establish that *Sum* is true.

4

In the Third Meditation, Descartes introduces a term that plays an enormously important role in the statement of his views. The term is *idea*; and though Descartes is aware that he is using the word in a novel way, his explanation in the Third Meditation is brief, and he leaves a number of important questions unanswered. Throughout his works, moreover, we find statements about the nature of ideas and about their origin that seem to conflict, and it is difficult to say just what Descartes means by this difficult and, for his philosophy, crucial term. In "Descartes on Ideas," Anthony Kenny points out a number of ambiguities in Descartes's use of the term. He finds that he uses it sometimes to refer to episodes and sometimes to capacities, sometimes for acts of thinking and sometimes for objects of thought, and that Descartes's ideas have some of the characteristics of material pictures but also characteristics of mental images and of concepts. Concerning the arguments in which Descartes uses this word, Kenny asks us to consider the very important question "whether the premises of his argument are true and whether his conclusion follows if the interpretation of 'idea' is held constant throughout." Like some of Descartes's early critics, Kenny, following his admonition, detects certain confusions and bad arguments. In Descartes's discussion of the "objective existence" of ideas, for instance, he notes a confusion and claims that here "an extra entity has been spirited into existence." He also finds a confusion in the famous account that Descartes gives of clarity and distinctness in the *Principles of Philosophy*. His analyses of the passages in the *Principles*,

and also of Descartes's perplexing statements about innate
ideas and about "materially false" ideas, are extremely perceptive and acute; and his objections to Descartes's views and
arguments involving the term "idea" are based on a meticu-
lous examination of the important passages in which Descartes indicates or tries to explain what he means by this key
term in his philosophy.

In "Clearness and Distinctness in Descartes," Alan Gewirth
is also concerned with Descartes's conception of ideas and
with the characteristics—clarity and distinctness primarily,
but also completeness, adequacy, and material truth and falsity—that he assigns to them. Some of Gewirth's conclusions
are in direct opposition to Kenny's. For both, an important
question is: how, according to the definitions of clarity and
distinctness in the *Principles,* can an idea fail to be clear
and distinct? Unlike Kenny, who suggests that Descartes cannot in the end give a consistent and entirely satisfactory answer to the question, Gewirth sees the answer in the notion
that he attributes to Descartes of the "interpretive content"
of an idea—the interpretive content being distinguished, on
the one hand, from the "direct content" and, on the other,
from a judgment relating to the idea. According to this interpretation, an idea is clear and distinct if, and only if, there
is "equality" between direct content and interpretive content. A number of examples are given of "equality," and also
of lack of equality, i.e. obscurity or confusion. In the discussion of these examples, there are very astute remarks, for instance, about Descartes's "analysis" of the piece of wax in
the Second Meditation and about his conception of method
both in general and as it is to be exercised in mathematics
and physics. This paper and Gewirth's "The Cartesian Circle" and "Experience and the Non-Mathematical in the Cartesian Method" comprise an extremely interesting interpretation and a defense of Descartes's views against objections
that have often been raised. Whether Kenny or Gewirth is
right about the passages in the *Principles* is a very difficult
question, which the reader is left to answer.

5

Descartes's a priori or ontological argument for the existence of God in the Fifth Meditation has been of interest to philosophers concerned with the theory of knowledge, not or not just for historical or for religious reasons nor because Descartes seems to think of it as a means for removing doubts about reason, but because this seemingly simple but really very complex argument raises problems about existence, reference, and necessity of very great interest in their own right. Several recent papers have dealt particularly with Anselm's argument (or arguments) in the *Proslogion*, and there are questions to be raised about the historical and also the logical relations of Descartes's attempted proof in the Fifth Meditation and Anselm's. In a characteristically ahistorical remark, when Descartes's attention was called to the apparent similarity of his argument and Anselm's, he replied that he would look at St. Anselm at the first opportunity; and in the Replies to Objections he denies that the argument criticized by Aquinas is his, and gives the impression of siding with Aquinas against Anselm. Whatever we are to make of the relations between Anselm's and Descartes's proofs, in the papers that have appeared on Anselm attention is given to the standard objection that existence is not a predicate, and, since Descartes states or implies in the various formulations of his a priori argument that existence—in some sense or of some kind—is a "perfection" and hence presumably a predicate, the papers on Anselm are relevant to Descartes as well. Of these, there have been a great many, some defending Anselm's or Descartes's proof against the standard objections, others devising new and more effective refutations.

In "The Ontological Argument Revisited," William P. Alston argues very persuasively that the standard argument for denying that "exists" is a predicate is defective and cannot be used in a refutation of the ontological argument. We may distinguish, he points out, "modes of existence," e.g. Anselm's "existence in the understanding"; and, accepting this distinction, we do not find in the standard argument any reason for denying that existence can be predicated of something—for instance, a supremely perfect being, that is presupposed to exist in some "nonreal mode," for instance, in the understanding. (Though Alston does not make this point, it might be said that, in the Fifth Meditation, Descartes's "supremely perfect being" is assumed, like "the triangle," to be a Meinongian *res* capable of existing both in reality and in the understanding.) But Alston does not conclude that "exists" is a predicate. Arguing in a way that is reminiscent of one of Aquinas' criticisms, he draws a distinction between the "real correlate" and the "real archetype" of what exists in the understanding and constructs a "revised proof" that "exists" is not a predicate and a revised refutation of the ontological argument. Alvin Plantinga, in a section from a forthcoming book, maintains that two premises of Alston's refutation are open to serious objections. In earlier sections of his study, Plantinga takes exception to other attempts to refute the ontological argument by way of showing that "exists" is not a predicate. The conclusion that he reaches in this chapter is that neither Alston nor his predecessors have succeeded in giving a general refutation of the argument. It is clear from these discussions that Descartes's a priori argument cannot be dismissed or easily refuted.

6

Norman Malcolm's "Descartes's Proof that His Essence is Thinking" and "Descartes' Myth," the opening chapter of Gilbert Ryle's *The Concept of Mind,* are concerned with Descartes's most renowned doctrine, "Cartesian dualism" of mind and body. In "Descartes' Myth," Ryle refers to an "official doctrine" deriving from Descartes and explains what in general he thinks is wrong with it. In the chapters that follow, he examines many more particular features of the "myth" and supports his initial claims with a wealth of arguments. The first chapter is of interest by itself, however, for it shows both the clear recognition of a Cartesian tradition in philosophy and (in an extreme form) the reaction to Cartesian views that has taken place. In "Descartes's Proof that His Essence is Thinking," Malcolm distinguishes three arguments that Descartes presents in support of his contentions that his essential nature is thought and that his mind is "really distinct" from his body. Each of them taken by itself seems fallacious, but Malcolm thinks that, supporting Descartes's conclusion, there is a very persuasive argument that is not made explicit but is involved in Descartes's thinking when he makes the transition in the Second Meditation from the *cogito* to *sum res cogitans*. Though Malcolm thinks that this argument accounts for the transition and can bear the weight that Descartes places on his conclusion, he also thinks that the proof fails and that in the *Meditations* there is, neither implicitly nor explicitly, solid ground for Descartes's most celebrated conclusion.

The last discussion is "Descartes's Mechanicism" by P. H. J. Hoenen. From a very different point of view, Hoenen considers another aspect of Descartes's dualism of mind and body contained in his assertion that matter is extension and in his denial of intrinsic change to bodies and, closely related to this, his denial of "real qualities" and "substantial forms." In this selection and also in an earlier section of his book, Hoenen relates the distinction of "primary" and "secondary" qualities to the problem raised by Parmenides about "becoming." The problem, on this account, was solved in Aristotelian philosophy, but Descartes misunderstood Aristotle and his followers and presented his Mechanicism as a solution of the problem. Hoenen also points out some common misconceptions about Descartes—notably, the view that Descartes, like some of the Occasionalists, denies that there is force or activity in bodies.

For valuable suggestions about the contents of this volume, I am indebted to Harry Frankfurt, Jaakko Hintikka, Anthony Kenny, Norman Malcolm, Maurice Mandelbaum, Amelie Rorty, and W. H. Walsh. I should like to thank P. J. Crittenden for his translation of the section on Mechanicism in

Hoenen's *Cosmologia* and Anne and David Sanford for a translation of Bernard Williams' paper, which appeared originally in French. My chief indebtedness is of course to the philosophers whose discussions are included here.

DESCARTES

CERTAINTY

G. E. MOORE

I am at present, as you can all see, in a room and not in the open air; I am standing up, and not either sitting or lying down; I have clothes on, and am not absolutely naked; I am speaking in a fairly loud voice, and am not either singing or whispering or keeping quite silent; I have in my hand some sheets of paper with writing on them; there are a good many other people in the same room in which I am; and there are windows in that wall and a door in this one.

Now I have here made a number of different assertions; and I have made these assertions quite positively, as if there were no doubt whatever that they were true. That is to say, though I did not expressly say, with regard to any of these different things which I asserted, that it was not only true but also *certain*, yet by asserting them in the way I did, I *implied*, though I did not say, that they were in fact certain —implied, that is, that I myself knew for certain, in each case, that what I asserted to be the case was, at the time when I asserted it, in fact the case. And I do not think that I can be justly accused of dogmatism or over-confidence for having asserted these things positively in the way that I did. In the case of some kinds of assertions, and under some circumstances, a man can be justly accused of dogmatism for asserting something positively. But in the case of assertions such as I made, made under the circumstances under which I made them, the charge would be absurd. On the contrary, I should have

From George Edward Moore, *Philosophical Papers* (London: George Allen & Unwin, Ltd., 1959, and New York: Humanities Press, Inc.), pp. 227–251. Reprinted by permission of George Allen & Unwin, Ltd., and Humanities Press, Inc.

been guilty of absurdity if, under the circumstances, I had *not* spoken positively about these things, if I spoke of them at all. Suppose that now, instead of saying 'I am inside a building', I were to say 'I *think* I'm inside a building, but perhaps I'm not: it's not *certain* that I am', or instead of saying 'I have got some clothes on', I were to say 'I think I've got some clothes on, but it's just possible that I haven't'. Would it not sound rather ridiculous for me now, under these circumstances, to say 'I *think* I've got some clothes on' or even to say 'I not only think I have, I know that it is very likely indeed that I have, but I can't be quite sure'? For some persons, under some circumstances, it might not be at all absurd to express themselves thus doubtfully. Suppose, for instance, there were a blind man, suffering in addition from general anaesthesia, who knew, because he had been told, that his doctors from time to time stripped him naked and then put his clothes on again, although he himself could neither see nor feel the difference: to such a man there might well come an occasion on which he would really be describing correctly the state of affairs by saying that he *thought* he'd got some clothes on, or that he knew that it was very likely he had, but was not quite sure. But for me, now, in full possession of my senses, it would be quite ridiculous to express myself in this way, because the circumstances are such as to make it quite obvious that I don't merely think that I have, but know that I have. For me now, it would be absurd to say that I *thought* I wasn't naked, because by saying this I should imply that I didn't know that I wasn't, whereas you can all see that I'm in a position to know that I'm not. But if *now* I am not guilty of dogmatism in asserting positively that I'm not naked, certainly I was not guilty of dogmatism when I asserted it positively in one of those sentences with which I began this lecture. I knew then that I had clothes on, just as I know now that I have.

Now those seven assertions with which I began were obviously, in some respects, not all of quite the same kind. For instance: while the first six were all of them (among other things) assertions about myself, the seventh, namely that there were windows in that wall, and a door in this one, was not about myself at all. And even among those which were about myself there were obvious differences. In the case of two of these—the assertions that I was in a room, and the assertion that there were a good many other people in the same room with me—it can quite naturally be said that each gave a partial answer to the question what sort of *environment* I was in at the time when I made them. And in the case of three others—the assertions that I had clothes on, that I was speaking in a fairly loud voice, and that I had in my hand some sheets of paper—it can also be said, though less naturally, that they each gave a partial answer to the same question. For, if I had clothes on, if I was in a region in which fairly loud sounds were audible, and if I had some sheets of paper in my hand, it follows, in each case that the surroundings of my body were, in at least one respect, different from what they would have been if that particular thing had not been true of me; and the term 'environment' is sometimes so used that any true statement from which it follows that the surroundings of my body were different, in any respect, from what they might have been is a statement which gives *some* information, however little, as to the kind of environment I was in. But though each of these five assertions can thus, in a sense, be said to have given, if true, *some* information as to the nature of my environment at the time when I made it, one of them, the assertion that I was speaking in a fairly loud voice, did not *only* do this: it also, if true, gave some information of a very different kind. For to say that I was speaking in a fairly loud voice was not only to say that there were audible in my neighbourhood fairly loud sounds, and sounds of which it was also true that they were words; it was also to say that some sounds of this sort were *being made by me*—a causal proposition. As for the sixth of the assertions which I made about myself—the assertion that I was standing up—that can hardly be said to have given any information as to the nature of my environment at the time when I made it: it would be naturally described as giving information only as to the posture of my body at the time in question. And as for the two assertions I made which were not about myself at all—the assertions that there were windows in that wall

and a door in this one—though they were, in a sense, assertions about my environment, since the two walls about which
I made them were, in fact, in my neighbourhood at the time;
yet in making them I was not expressly asserting that they
were in my neighbourhood (had I been doing so, they would
have been assertions about myself) and what I expressly asserted was something which might have been true, even if
they had not been in my neighbourhood. In this respect they
were unlike my assertion that I was in a room, which could
not have been true, unless some walls had been in my neighbourhood. From the proposition that there is a door in that
wall it does not follow that that wall is in my neighbourhood; whereas from the proposition that I am in a room, it
does follow that a wall is in my neighbourhood.

But in spite of these, and other, differences between those
seven or eight different assertions, there are several important
respects in which they were all alike.

(1) In the first place: All of those seven or eight different
assertions, which I made at the beginning of this lecture, were
alike in this respect, namely, that every one of them was an
assertion, which, though it wasn't in fact false, yet *might have
been false*. For instance, consider the time at which I asserted
that I was standing up. It is certainly true that at that very
time I *might* have been sitting down, though in fact I wasn't;
and if I *had* been sitting down at that time, then my assertion that I was standing up would have been false. Since,
therefore, I might have been sitting down at that very time,
it follows that my assertion that I was standing up was an
assertion which *might have been false*, though it wasn't. And
the same is obviously true of all the other assertions I made.
At the time when I said I was in a room, I might have been
in the open air; at the time when I said I had clothes on, I
might have been naked; and so on, in all the other cases.

But from the fact that a given assertion might have been
false, it always follows that the negation or contradictory of
the proposition asserted is not a self-contradictory proposition. For to say that a given proposition might have been
false is equivalent to saying that its negation or contradictory
might have been true; and from the fact that a given prop-

osition might have been true, it always follows that the proposition in question is not self-contradictory, since, if it were, it could not possibly have been true. Accordingly all those things which I asserted at the beginning of this lecture were things of which the *contradictories were not self-contradictory*. If, for instance, when I said 'I am standing up' I had said instead 'It is not the case that I am standing up', which would have been the contradictory of what I did say, it would have been correct to say 'That is not a self-contradictory proposition, though it is a false one'; and the same is true in the case of all the other propositions that I asserted. As a short expression for the long expression 'proposition which is not self-contradictory and of which the contradictory is not self-contradictory' philosophers have often used the technical term 'contingent proposition'. Using the term 'contingent' in this sense, we can say, then, that one respect in which all those seven propositions which I asserted at the beginning of this lecture resembled one another was that *they were all of them contingent*.

And before I go on to mention some other respects in which they were all alike, I think I had better now at once say some things about the consequences of this first fact that they were all of them contingent—things which are very relevant to a proper understanding of the use of the word which forms the title of this lecture, the word 'Certainty'.

The first thing I want to say about the consequences of the fact that all those propositions were contingent is this: namely, that from the mere fact that they were all of them contingent, it does not follow that they were not all *known to be true*—nay more, it does not follow, in the case of any particular person whatever, that *that* person did not know them to be true. Some philosophers have in fact suggested that no contingent proposition is ever, as a matter of fact, known to be true. And I am not *now* disputing that suggestion, though I do in fact hold it to be false, and intend, in the course of this lecture to dispute it. All that I am asserting *now* is that, even if it is a fact that no contingent proposition is ever known to be true, yet in no case does this *follow* from the mere fact that it is contingent. For instance, that I am

now standing up is a contingent proposition; but from the
mere fact that it is so, from that fact *alone*, it certainly does
not *follow* that I do not know that I am standing up. If it is
to be shown—as many philosophers think they can show—
that I do *not* know now that I am standing up, some other
argument must be brought forward for this contention, over
and above the mere fact that this proposition is contingent;
for from this fact, by itself, it certainly does not *follow* that
I don't know that I am standing up. I say that this is certain,
and I do not know that anyone would dispute it. But if I
were asked to defend my assertion, I do not know that I
could give any better defence than merely to say that the
conjunctive proposition 'I know that I am at present standing
up, and yet the proposition that I am is contingent' is certainly not itself self-contradictory, even if it is false. Is it not
obvious that if I say 'I know that I am at present standing
up, although the proposition that I am is contingent', I am
certainly not contradicting myself, even if I *am* saying something which is false?

The second thing I want to say about the consequences of
the fact that all those seven propositions were contingent is
something which follows from the first: namely that from the
fact that they were contingent it does not follow, in the case
of any single one among them, that it was *possible* that the
proposition in question was false. To take, for instance, again,
the proposition that I was then standing up: from the fact
that this proposition was contingent, it does not follow that,
if I had said 'It is possible that it is not the case that I am
standing up', I should have been saying something true. That
this is so follows from my former contention that the contingency of the proposition in question does not entail that
it was not known to be true, because one, at least, of the
ways in which we use expressions of the form 'It is possible
that p' is such that the statement in question cannot be true
if the person who makes it knows for certain that p is false.
We very, very often use expressions of the form 'It is possible
that p' in such a way that by using such an expression we are
making an assertion of our own ignorance on a certain point
—an assertion namely that we do not *know* that p is false.

This is certainly one of the very commonest uses of the word 'possible'; it is a use in which what it expresses is often expressed instead by the use of the word 'may'. For instance, if I were to say 'It is possible that Hitler is dead at this moment' this would naturally be understood to mean exactly the same as if I said 'Hitler *may* be dead at this moment'. And is it not quite plain that if I did assert that Hitler *may* be dead at this moment part at least of what I was asserting would be that I personally did not know for certain that he was not dead? Consequently if I were to assert now 'It is possible that I am not standing up' I should naturally be understood to be asserting that I do not know for certain that I am. And hence, if I do know for certain that I am, my assertion that it is possible that I'm not would be false. Since therefore from the fact that 'I am standing up' is a contingent proposition it does not follow that I do not know that I am, it also does not follow from this fact that it is possible that I am *not*. For if from the contingency of this proposition it did follow that it is possible that I am not standing up, it would also follow that I do not know that I *am* standing up: since from 'It is possible that I am not standing up' there follows 'I do not know that I am standing up'; and if *p* entails *q*, and *q* entails *r*, it *follows* that *p* entails *r*. Since, therefore, our *p* ('the proposition "I am standing up" is contingent') does not entail our *r* ('I do not know that I am standing up'), and since our *q* ('It is possible that I am not standing up') *does* entail our *r*, it follows that our *p* does not entail our *q*: that is to say, the fact that the proposition 'I am standing up' is contingent does not entail the consequence that it is possible that it is false that I am standing up. In no case whatever from the mere fact that a proposition *p* is contingent does it *follow* that it is *possible* that *p* is false. But this, of course, is not to deny that it may, *as a matter of fact*, be true of every contingent proposition that it is possible that it is false. This *will* be true, if no contingent proposition is ever known to be true. But even if this is so, it still remains true that from the mere fact that a proposition is contingent it never *follows* that it *may* be false; this remains true because from the mere fact that a proposition is contingent it never follows that it is not known to be true, and never follows, either, in the case of any particular person, that that person does not know it to be true.

In the above paragraph I confined myself to saying that there is at least one common use of expressions of the form 'It is possible that p', such that any person who makes such an assertion is asserting that he personally does not know that p is false; and hence the only conclusion to which I am so far entitled is that the mere fact that a given proposition p is contingent does not entail the consequence that what is expressed by 'it is possible that not-p' will be true, *when 'possible' is used in the way in question.* And it may be thought that there is another use of 'possible' such that from 'p is contingent' there does follow 'it is possible that p is false'. The fact is that the expression 'logically possible' has often been used by philosophers in such a way that many might be tempted to think that it is a mere synonym for 'not self-contradictory'. That it is not a mere synonym for this can, I think, be seen from the fact that the expression 'it is not self-contradictory that I am not standing up' is not English at all, whereas the expression 'It is logically possible that I am not standing up' certainly is English, though it may be doubted whether what it expresses is true. If, however, we consider the expression 'the proposition that I am not standing up is not self-contradictory' I think it would not be incorrect to say that the words 'logically possible' are so used that *in this expression* they could be substituted for 'not self-contradictory' without changing the meaning of the whole expression; and that the same is true whatever other proposition you might take instead of the proposition that I am not standing up. If this be so, then it follows that, in the case of any proposition whatever, from the proposition that that proposition is not self-contradictory it will follow that the proposition in question is also logically possible (and *vice versa*); in other words, for any p, 'p is not self-contradictory' entails 'p is logically possible'. But this being so, it is very natural to think that it follows that you can also take a further step and say truly that, for any p, 'p is not self-contradictory' entails 'It is logically possible that p'; for surely from 'p is logically possible' it must follow that 'it is logically possible that p.' Certainly it is very natural to think this; but for all that, I think it is a mistake to think so. To think that 'p is logically possible' must entail 'It is logically possible that p' is certainly a mere mistake which does not do justice to the subtlety of the differences there may be in the way we use language. And I think it is actually a mistake to say that 'p is not self-contradictory' entails 'It is logically possible that p', even though it does entail 'p is logically possible'. Consider the following facts. 'It is logically possible that I *should have been* sitting down now' certainly does entail 'The proposition that I am sitting down now is not self-contradictory'. But if this latter proposition did entail 'It is logically possible that I *am* sitting down now' then it would follow that 'It is logically possible that I *should have been* sitting down now' entails 'It is logically possible that I *am* sitting down now'. But does it? Certainly it would be quite unnatural for me, who know that I am standing up, to say the latter, whereas it would be quite natural for me to say the former; and I think perhaps we can go further and say that if I said the latter I should be saying something untrue, whereas if I said the former I should be saying something true; just as if I said 'I *might have been* sitting down now', I should be saying something true, whereas if I said 'I *may* be sitting down now', I should be saying something false. In short I think that even the expression 'It is *logically* possible that so-and-so *is* the case' retains the characteristic which we have seen to belong to one ordinary use of the expression 'It is possible that so-and-so *is* the case', namely that it can only be said *with truth* by a person who does not know that the so-and-so in question is *not* the case. If I were to say now 'It is logically possible that I am sitting down' I should be implying that I don't know that I'm not, and therefore implying something which, if I do know that I'm not, is false. I think that perhaps philosophers have not always paid sufficient attention to the possibility that from the mere fact that a given proposition, p, is not self-contradictory, it perhaps does not follow that any person whatever can say with truth 'It is logically possible that p *is* true'. In the case of a non-self-

contradictory proposition such as the proposition that I am at
present sitting down, if there be a person, for instance some
friend of mine in England, who does not know that this proposition is false, then, in his case, from the *conjunction* of the
fact that the proposition is not self-contradictory with the
fact that he does not know it to be false, it does follow that
he could say with truth 'It is logically possible that Moore
is at present sitting down'; but if there be another person,
myself for instance, who does know that the proposition is
false, it is by no means clear that from the mere fact that the
proposition is not self-contradictory—from that fact *alone*—it
follows that *I* can truly say 'It is logically possible that I am
at present sitting down'. From the conjunction of the fact
that the proposition is logically possible with the fact that I
know it to be false, it does follow that I can truly say 'It is
logically possible that I *should have been* sitting down at this
moment'; but from the fact that I can truly say this, it certainly does not follow that I can *also* truly say 'It is logically
possible that I *am* sitting down'; and it is certain that in fact
the two are incompatible: that, if I can truly say 'It is logically
possible that I *should have been* sitting down now' then it
follows that I *cannot* truly say 'It is logically possible that I
am sitting down now'. Perhaps, however, our use of the expression 'It is logically possible that so-and-so *is* the case' is
not clearly enough fixed to entitle us to say this. What is important is to insist that if 'It is logically possible that *p is*
true' is used in such a way that it does follow from '*p* is not
self-contradictory', *by itself*, then from 'It is logically possible
that *p is* true', it does not follow that *p* is not known to be
false. And if a philosopher does choose to use 'It is logically
possible that *p* is true' in such an unnatural way as this, there
will be a danger that he will sometimes forget that that is
the way in which he has chosen to use it, and will fall into the
fallacy of thinking that from 'It is logically possible that *p
is* true' there *does* follow '*p* is not known to be false'.

The third thing which I wish to say about the consequences
of the fact that those seven assertions with which I began this
paper were assertions of contingent propositions, is this: that
this fact is quite compatible with its being true that every

one of those seven things that I asserted was not only true but *absolutely certain*. That this is so again follows from the fact that the mere contingency of a given proposition, *p*, never entails, in the case of any person whatever, that that person does not know *p* to be true. It follows from this fact, because if any person whatever does at a given time know that a given proposition *p* is true, then it follows that that person could say with truth at that time 'It is absolutely certain that *p*'. Thus if I do know now that I am standing up, it follows that I can say with truth 'It is absolutely certain that I am standing up'. Since, therefore, the fact that this proposition is contingent is compatible with its being true that I know that I am standing up, it follows that it must also be compatible with its being true that it is absolutely certain that I am standing up.

I think that possibly some people might be inclined to object to what I have just said on the following ground. I have just said that if a person can ever say with truth, with regard to any particular proposition *p*, 'I know that *p* is true', it follows that he can also truly say 'It is absolutely certain that *p* is true'. But an objector might perhaps say: 'I admit that if a person could ever truly say "I know *with absolute certainty* that *p* is true" then it would follow that he could also truly say "It *is* absolutely certain that *p* is true". But what you said was not "know with absolute certainty" but "know"; and surely there must be some difference between "knowing" and "knowing with absolute certainty", since, if there were not, we should never be tempted to use the latter expression. I doubt, therefore, whether a mere "I know that *p*" does entail "It is absolutely certain that *p*".' To this objection I should reply: I do not think that the only possible explanation of the fact that we sometimes say 'I know with absolute certainty that so-and-so' and sometimes merely 'I know that so-and-so' is that the latter can be properly used to express something which may be true even when what is expressed by the former is not true: I doubt therefore whether 'I know that *p*' does not always entail 'I know with absolute certainty that *p*'. But even if 'I know that *p*' can be sometimes properly used to express something from which 'I know with absolute

certainty that p' does *not* follow, it is certainly also sometimes used in such a way that if I don't know with absolute
certainty that p, then it follows that I don't know that p.
And I have been and shall be only concerned with uses of
'know' of the latter kind, i.e. with such that 'I know that
p' does entail 'I know with absolute certainty that p'. And
similarly, even if there are proper uses of the word 'certain',
such that a thing can be 'certain' without being 'absolutely
certain', there are certainly others (or at least one other) such
that if a thing is not absolutely certain it cannot be truly said
to be certain; and I have been and shall be concerned only
with uses of 'certain' of this latter kind.

Another comment which might be made upon what I have
said is that, even if there is *one* use of 'absolutely certain'
such that, as I said, it is never logically impossible that a
contingent proposition should be absolutely certain, yet there
is another use of 'absolutely certain' such that this *is* logically
impossible—a sense of 'absolutely certain', that is to say, in
which only propositions whose contradictories are self-contradictory can be absolutely certain. Propositions whose contradictories are self-contradictory have sometimes been called
'necessary truths', sometimes 'a priori propositions', sometimes 'tautologies'; and it is sometimes held that the sense in
which such propositions can be 'certain', and therefore also
the sense in which they can be 'known to be true', must be
different from the sense (if any) in which contingent propositions are sometimes 'certain' and 'known to be true'. That
this may be so, I do not wish to deny. So far as I can see, it
may be the case that, if I say, 'I know that' or 'It is certain
that' 'it is not the case that there are any triangular figures
which are not trilateral', or 'I know that' or 'It is certain
that' 'it is not the case that there are any human beings
who are daughters and yet are not female', I am using 'know
that' and 'it is certain that' in a different sense from that
in which I use them if I say 'I know that' or 'It is certain
that' 'I have some clothes on'; and it may be the case that
only necessary truths can be known or be certain in the
former sense. Accordingly, my statements that from the fact
that a given proposition, p, is contingent it does not fol-

low that p is not known and is not certain, should be understood to mean only that there is at least one sense in which 'known' and 'certain' can be properly used, such that this does not follow; just as all that I asserted positively before about the phrase 'It is possible that' was that there is at least one sense in which this phrase can be properly used, such that 'p is contingent' does not entail 'It is possible that p is false'.

Finally, there is one slightly puzzling point about our use of the phrases 'it is possible that' and 'it is certain that', which might lead some people to suspect that some of the things I have been saying about the consequences which follow from the fact that a given proposition is contingent are false, and which therefore I think I had better try to clear up at once.

There are four main types of expression in which the word 'certain' is commonly used. We may say 'I feel certain that . . .', or we may say 'I am certain that . . .', or we may say 'I know for certain that . . .', or finally we may say 'It *is* certain that . . .'. And if we compare the first of these expressions with the two last, it is, of course, very obvious, and has been pointed out again and again, that whereas 'I feel certain that p' may quite well be true in a case in which p is not true—in other words that from the mere fact that I feel certain that so-and-so is the case it never follows that so-and-so is in fact the case—there is at least one common use of 'I know for certain that p' and 'It is certain that p' such that these things can't be true unless p is true. This difference may be brought out by the fact that, e.g., 'I felt certain that he would come, but in fact he didn't' is quite clearly not self-contradictory; it is quite clearly logically possible that I should have felt certain that he would come and that yet he didn't; while, on the other hand, 'I knew for certain that he would come, but he didn't' or 'It was certain that he would come but he didn't' are, for at least one common use of those phrases, self-contradictory: the fact that he didn't come *proves* that I didn't *know* he would come, and that it wasn't certain that he would, whereas it does not prove that I didn't *feel* certain that he would. In other words, 'I feel certain that p' does not *en-*

tail that *p* is true (although by saying that I feel certain that
p, I do *imply* that *p* is true), but 'I know that *p*' and 'It is
certain that *p*' do entail that *p* is true; they can't be true, unless it is. As for the fourth expression 'I *am* certain that . . .'
or 'I am quite sure that . . .' (it is perhaps worth noting
that in the expressions 'I feel certain that . . .' and 'I am
certain that . . .' the word 'sure' or the words 'quite sure'
can be substituted for the word 'certain' without change of
meaning, whereas in the expressions 'I know for certain
that . . .' or 'it is certain that . . .' this is not the case)
these expressions are, I think, particularly liable to give rise
to fallacious reasoning in philosophical discussions about certainty, because, so far as I can see, they are sometimes used
to mean the same as 'I feel certain that . . .' and sometimes,
on the contrary, to mean the same as 'I know for certain that'.
For instance, the expression 'I was quite sure that he would
come, but yet he didn't' *can*, it seems to me, be naturally
used in such a way that it is not self-contradictory—which can
only be the case if it is in that case merely another way of
saying 'I felt quite sure that he would come . . .'; but if on
the other hand a philosopher were to say to me now (as many
would say) 'You can't be quite sure that you are standing
up', he would certainly not be asserting that I can't *feel* certain that I am—a thing which he would not at all wish to
dispute—and he certainly would be asserting that, even if I
do feel certain that I am, I don't or can't *know for certain*
that I am.

There is, therefore, a clear difference in meaning between
'I feel certain that . . .' on the one hand, and 'I know for
certain that . . .' or 'It is certain that . . .' on the other. But
the point with which I am at present concerned is whether
there is not also a difference of importance between each of
these expressions 'I feel certain that . . .', 'I am certain
that . . .', and 'I know for certain that . . .', on the one
hand, and 'It *is* certain that . . .' on the other. The first
three expressions are obviously, in spite of the important
difference I have just pointed out between the first and the
last of them, alike in one important respect—a respect which
may be expressed by saying that their meaning is relative to

the person who uses them. They are alike in this respect, because they all contain the word 'I'. In the case of every sentence which contains this word, its meaning obviously depends on who it is that says that sentence; if I say 'I am hot', what I assert by saying this is obviously something different from what any other person would be asserting by saying exactly the same words; and it is obvious that what I assert by saying so may quite well be true even though what another person asserts by saying exactly the same words at exactly the same time is false. 'I am hot' said by me at a given time, does not contradict 'I am not hot' said by you at exactly the same time: both may perfectly well be true. And in the same way, if I say 'I feel certain that there are windows in that wall' or 'I know for certain that there are windows', I, by saying this, am making an assertion different from, and logically independent of, what another person would be asserting by saying exactly the same words at the same time: from the fact that I feel certain of or know for certain a given thing it *never* follows, in the case of any other person whatever, that he feels certain of or knows the thing in question, nor from the fact that he does does it ever follow that *I* do. But if we consider, by contrast, the expression 'It *is* certain that there are windows in that wall', it looks, at first sight, as if the meaning of this expression was *not* relative to the person who says it: as if it were a quite impersonal statement and should mean the same whoever says it, provided it is said at the same time and provided the wall referred to by the words 'that wall' is the same. It is, indeed, obvious, I think, that a thing can't be certain, unless it is *known*: this is one obvious point that distinguishes the use of the word 'certain' from that of the word 'true'; a thing that nobody knows may quite well be true, but cannot possibly be certain. We can, then, say that it is a necessary condition for the truth of 'It is certain that *p*' that somebody should know that *p* is true. But the meaning of 'Somebody knows that *p* is true' is certainly not relative to the person who says it: it is as completely impersonal as 'The sun is larger than the moon', and if two people say it at the same time, then, if the one by saying it is saying something true, so must the other be. If, therefore, 'It is certain that p' meant merely 'Somebody knows that p is true', then the meaning of 'It is certain that p' would *not* be relative to the person who says it, and there would then be an important difference between it, on the one hand, and 'I feel certain that p' or 'I know for certain that p' on the other, since the meaning of these two *is* relative to the person who says them. But though 'Somebody knows that p is true' is a necessary condition for the truth of 'It is certain that p', it can be easily seen that it is *not* a sufficient condition; for if it were, it would follow that in any case in which somebody did know that p was true, it would always be false for anybody to say 'It is not certain that p'. But in fact it is quite evident that if I say now 'It is not certain that Hitler is still alive', I am not thereby committing myself to the statement that nobody knows that Hitler is still alive: my statement is quite consistent with its being true that Hitler is still alive, and that he himself and other persons know that he is so. The fact is, then, that all that follows from 'Somebody knows that p is true' is that *somebody* could say with truth 'It is certain that p': it does not follow that more than one person could; nor does it follow that there are not some who could say with truth 'It is *not* certain that p'. Two different people, who say, at the same time about the same proposition, p, the one 'It is certain that p is true', the other 'It is not certain that p is true', may both be saying what is true and not contradicting one another. It follows, therefore, that, in spite of appearances, the meaning of 'It *is* certain that p' *is* relative to the person who says it. And this, I think, is because, as I have implied above, if anybody asserts 'It is certain that p' part of what he is asserting is that he himself knows that p is true; so that, even if many other people do know that p is true, yet his assertion will be false, if he himself does not know it. If, on the other hand, a person asserts 'It is *not* certain that p' his assertion will not necessarily be true merely because he personally does not know that p is true, though it will necessarily be false if he personally does know that p is true. If *I* say 'It is certain that p', that *I* should know that p is true is both a necessary and sufficient condition for the truth of my assertion. But if I say 'It is *not* certain that *p*', then that I should *not* know that *p* is true, though it is a necessary, is not a sufficient condition for the truth of my assertion. And similarly the expression 'It is possible that *p* is true' is, though it looks as if it were impersonal, really an expression whose meaning is relative to the person who uses it. If *I* say it, that I should not know that *p* is false, is a necessary, though not a sufficient, condition for the truth of my assertion; and hence if two people say it at the same time about the same proposition it is perfectly possible that what the one asserts should be true, and what the other asserts false: since, if one of the two knows that *p* is false, his assertion will necessarily be false; whereas, if the other does not know that *p* is false, his assertion may be, though it will not necessarily be, true. On the other hand, if it were right to use the expression 'It is *logically* possible that *p*' as equivalent to '*p* is not self-contradictory', then the meaning of 'It is *logically* possible that *p*' would *not* be relative to the person who says it.

To sum up this digression. What I have said about the consequences of the fact that all those seven propositions with which I opened this lecture were contingent, is firstly (1) that this fact does *not* entail the consequence that I did not, when I made them, know them to be true; (2) that it does *not* entail the consequence that I could then have said with truth about any of them 'It is possible that this is false'; and (3) that it does not entail the consequence that I could then have said with truth about any of them 'It is not absolutely certain that this is true'. It follows that by asserting that those seven propositions were contingent, I have not committed myself to the view that they were not known to be true or that it was not absolutely certain they were. But on the other hand, even if I am right in saying that these consequences do *not* follow from the mere fact that they were contingent, it, of course, does not follow from this that I *did* know them to be true, when I asserted them, or that they were absolutely certain. The questions whether, when I first said that I was standing up, I did know that I was, and whether, therefore, it was absolutely certain that I was, still remain completely open.

(2) A second respect, in addition to the fact that they were all of them contingent, in which all those seven propositions resembled one another, was this: In the case of every one of them part at least of what I was asserting, in asserting it, was something from which nothing whatever about the state or condition of my own mind followed—something from which no psychological proposition whatever about myself followed. Every one of them asserted something which might have been true, no matter what the condition of my mind had been either at that moment or in the past. For instance, that I was then inside a room is something which might have been true, even if at the time I had been asleep and in a dreamless sleep, and no matter what my character or disposition or mental abilities might have been: from that fact alone no psychological proposition whatever about myself followed. And the same is true of part at least of what I asserted in each of the other six propositions. I am going to refer to this common feature of all those seven propositions, by saying that they were all of them propositions which implied the existence of *an external world*—that is to say, of a world *external to my mind*. These phrases 'external world' and 'external to my mind' have often been used in philosophy; and I think that the way in which I am now proposing to use them is in harmony with the way in which they generally (though not always) have been used. It is indeed not obvious that my assertion that I was standing up implied the existence of anything external to *my body*; but it has generally been clear that those who spoke of a world *external* to any given individual, meant by that a world external to that individual's *mind*, and that they were using the expression 'external to a mind' in some metaphorical sense such that my body *must* be external to my mind. Accordingly a proposition which implies the existence of my body does, for that reason alone, with this use of terminology, imply the existence of a world *external to my mind*; and I think that the reason why it is said to do so is because from the existence of my body at a given time nothing whatever logically follows

as to the state or condition of my mind at that time. I think, therefore, that I am not saying anything that will be mis- leading to those familiar with philosophical terminology, if I say, for the reason given, that each of those seven assertions implied the existence of something external to my mind; and that hence, if I did know any one of them to be true, when I asserted it, the existence of an external world was at that time absolutely certain. If, on the other hand, as some philosophers have maintained, the existence of an external world is never absolutely certain, then it follows that I cannot have known any one of these seven propositions to be true.

(3) A third characteristic which was common to all those seven propositions was one which I am going to express by saying that I had for each of them, at the time when I made it, *the evidence of my senses*. I do not mean by this that the evidence of my senses was the *only* evidence I had for them: I do not think it was. What I mean is that, at the time when I made each, I was seeing or hearing or feeling things (or, if that will make my meaning clearer, 'having visual, auditory, tactile or organic sensations'), or a combination of these, such that to see or hear or feel those things *was* to have evidence (not necessarily *conclusive* evidence) for part at least of what I asserted when I asserted the proposition in question. In other words, in all seven cases, what I said was at least partly *based* on 'the then present evidence of my senses'.

(4) Fourth and finally, I think that all those seven asser- tions shared in common the following characteristic. Con- sider the class of all propositions which resemble them in the second respect I mentioned, namely, that they imply the ex- istence of something external to the mind of the person who makes them. It has been and still is held by many philoso- phers that no proposition which has this peculiarity is ever known to be true—is ever quite certain. And what I think is true of those seven propositions with which I began this lec- ture is this: namely, that, if I did not know them to be true when I made them, then those philosophers are right. That is to say, if those propositions were not certain, then nothing of the kind is ever certain: if *they* were not certain, then no proposition which implies the existence of anything external

to the mind of the person who makes it is ever certain. Take any one of the seven you like: the case for saying that I *knew* that one to be true when I made it is as strong as the case ever is for saying of any proposition which implies the existence of something external to the mind of the person who makes it, that *that* person knows it to be true.

This, it will be seen, is not a matter of logic. Obviously it is logically possible, for instance, that it should have been false then that I knew I was standing up and yet should be true now that I know I am standing up. And similarly in the other cases. But though this is logically possible—though the proposition 'I know that I am standing up now, but I did not know then that I was' is certainly not self-contradictory—yet it seems to me that it is certainly false. If I didn't know then that I was standing up, then certainly I know nothing of the sort now, and never have known anything of the sort; and, not only so, but nobody else ever has. And similarly, conversely (though this also is not a matter of logic), if I did know then that I was standing up then I certainly also know that I am standing up now, and have in the past constantly known things of the sort; and, not only so, but millions of other people have constantly known things of the sort: we all of us constantly do. In other words, those seven propositions of mine seem to be as good test-cases as could have been chosen (*as* good as, but also no better than thousands of others) for deciding between what seems to me to be the only real (though far from the only logically possible) alternatives—namely the alternative that none of us ever knows for certain of the existence of anything external to his own mind, and the alternative that all of us—millions of us—constantly do. And it was because they seemed to me to be as good test-cases as could be chosen for deciding this that I chose them.

But can we decide between these two alternatives?

I feel that the discussion of this question is frightfully difficult; and I feel sure that better and more decisive things could be said about it than I shall be able to say. All that I can do is to discuss, and that very inadequately, just one of the types of argument which have sometimes been alleged to show that nobody ever has known for certain anything about a world external to his mind.

Suppose I say now: 'I know for certain that I am standing up; it is absolutely certain that I am; there is not the smallest chance that I am not.' Many philosophers would say: 'You are wrong: you do not know that you are standing up; it is *not* absolutely certain that you are; there is *some* chance, though perhaps only a very small one, that you are not.' And one argument which has been used as an argument in favour of saying this, is an argument in the course of which the philosopher who used it would assert: 'You do not know for certain that you are not dreaming; it is not absolutely certain that you are not; there is *some* chance, though perhaps only a very small one, that you are.' And from this, that I do not know for certain that I am not dreaming, it is supposed to follow that I do not know for certain that I am standing up. It is argued: If it is not certain that you are not dreaming, then it is not certain that you are standing up. And that *if* I don't know that I'm not dreaming, I also don't know that I'm not sitting down, I don't feel at all inclined to dispute. From the hypothesis that I am dreaming, it would, I think, certainly follow that I don't *know* that I am standing up; though I have never seen the matter argued, and though it is not at all clear to me how it is to be proved that it would follow. But, on the other hand, from the hypothesis that I am dreaming, it certainly would not follow that I am *not* standing up; for it is certainly logically possible that a man should be fast asleep and dreaming, while he is standing up and not lying down. It is therefore logically possible that I should both be standing up and also at the same time dreaming that I am; just as the story, about a well-known Duke of Devonshire, that he once dreamt that he was speaking in the House of Lords and, when he woke up, found that he *was* speaking in the House of Lords, is certainly logically possible. And if, as is commonly assumed, when I am dreaming that I am standing up it may also be correct to say that I am *thinking* that I am standing up, then it follows that the hypothesis that I am now dreaming is quite consistent with the hypothesis that I am both thinking that I am standing up and also actually standing up. And hence, if, as seems to me to be certainly the case and as this argument assumes, from the hypothesis that I am now dreaming it *would* follow that I don't know that I am standing up, there follows a point which is of great importance with regard to our use of the word 'knowledge', and therefore also of the word 'certainty' —a point which has been made quite conclusively more than once by Russell, namely that from the conjunction of the two facts that a man thinks that a given proposition *p* is true, and that *p* is in fact true, it does *not* follow that the man in question *knows* that *p* is true: in order that I may be justified in saying that I know that I am standing up, something more is required than the mere conjunction of the two facts that I both think I am and actually am—as Russell has expressed it, true belief is not identical with knowledge; and I think we may further add that even from the conjunction of the two facts that I feel certain that I am and that I actually am it would not follow that I know that I am, nor therefore that it *is* certain that I am. As regards the argument drawn from the fact that a man who dreams that he is standing up and happens at the moment actually to be standing up will nevertheless not *know* that he is standing up, it should indeed be noted that from the fact that a man is dreaming that he is standing up, it certainly does not *follow* that he *thinks* he is standing up; since it does sometimes happen in a dream that we *think* that it is a dream, and a man who thought this certainly might, although he was dreaming that he was standing up, yet *think* that he was not, although he could not *know* that he was not. It is not therefore the case, as might be hastily assumed, that, if I dream that I am standing up at a time when I am in fact lying down, I am necessarily *deceived*: I should be deceived only if I thought I was standing when I wasn't; and I may dream that I am, without thinking that I am. It certainly does, however, often happen that we do dream that so-and-so is the case, without at the time thinking that we are only dreaming; and in such cases, I think we may perhaps be said to *think* that what we dream is the case *is* the case, and to be deceived if it is not the case; and therefore also, in such cases, if what we dream to be the case happens also to *be* the case, we may be said to be thinking truly that it is the case, although we certainly do not *know* that it is.

I agree, therefore, with that part of this argument which asserts that if I don't know now that I'm not dreaming, it follows that I don't *know* that I am standing up, even if I both actually am and think that I am. But this first part of the argument is a consideration which cuts both ways. For, if it is true, it follows that it is also true that if I *do* know that I am standing up, then I do know that I am not dreaming. I can therefore just as well argue: since I do know that I'm standing up, it follows that I do know that I'm not dreaming; as my opponent can argue: since you don't know that you're not dreaming, it follows that you don't know that you're standing up. The one argument is just as good as the other, unless my opponent can give better reasons for asserting that I don't know that I'm not dreaming, than I can give for asserting that I do know that I am standing up.

What reasons can be given for saying that I don't know for certain that I'm not at this moment dreaming?

I do not think that I have ever seen clearly stated any argument which is supposed to show this. But I am going to try to state, as clearly as I can, the premisses and the reasonings from them, which I think have led so many philosophers to suppose that I really cannot now know for certain that I am not dreaming.

I said, you may remember, in talking of the seven assertions with which I opened this lecture, that I had 'the evidence of my senses' for them, though I also said that I didn't think this was the only evidence I had for them, nor that this by itself was necessarily conclusive evidence. Now if I had *then* 'the evidence of my senses' in favour of the proposition that I was standing up, I certainly have *now* the evidence of my senses in favour of the proposition that I *am* standing up, even though this may not be all the evidence that I have, and may not be conclusive. But have I, in fact, the evidence of my senses *at all* in favour of this proposition? One thing seems to me to be quite clear about our use of this phrase, namely, that, if a man at a given time is only dreaming that

he is standing up, then it follows that he has *not* at that
time the evidence of his senses in favour of that proposition:
to say 'Jones last night was *only* dreaming that he was standing up, and yet all the time he had the evidence of his senses
that he was' is to say something self-contradictory. But those
philosophers who say it is possible that I am now dreaming,
certainly mean to say also that it is possible that I am *only*
dreaming that I am standing up; and this view, we now see,
entails that it is possible that I have *not* the evidence of my
senses that I am. If, therefore, they are right, it follows that
it is not certain even that I have the evidence of my senses
that I am; it follows that it is not certain that I have *the*
evidence of my senses for anything at all. If, therefore, I were
to say now, that I certainly have the evidence of my senses in
favour of the proposition that I am standing up, even if it's
not certain that I am standing up, I should be begging the
very question now at issue. For if it is not certain that I am
not dreaming, it is not certain that I even have the evidence
of my senses that I am standing up.

But, now, even if it is not certain that I have at this moment the evidence of my senses for anything at all, it is
quite certain that I *either* have the evidence of my senses
that I am standing up *or* have an experience which is *very*
like having the evidence of my senses that I am standing up.
If I am dreaming, this experience consists in having dream-
images which are at least very like the sensations I should be
having if I were awake and had the sensations, the having of
which would constitute 'having the evidence of my senses'
that I am standing up. Let us use the expression 'sensory
experience', in such a way that this experience which I certainly am having will be a 'sensory experience', whether or
not it merely consists in the having of dream-images. If we
use the expression 'sensory experience' in this way, we can
say, I think, that, if it is not certain that I am not dreaming
now, then it is not certain that *all* the sensory experiences I
am now having are not mere dream-images.

What then are the premisses and the reasonings which
would lead so many philosophers to think that all the sen-

sory experiences I am having now *may* be mere dream-images —that I do not know for certain that they are not?

So far as I can see, one premiss which they would certainly use would be this: 'Some at least of the sensory experiences which you are having now are similar in important respects to dream-images which actually have occurred in dreams.' This seems a very harmless premiss, and I am quite willing to admit that it is true. But I think there is a very serious objection to the procedure of using it as a premiss in favour of the derived conclusion. For a philosopher who does use it as a premiss, is, I think, in fact *implying*, though he does not expressly say, that he himself knows it to be true. He is *implying* therefore that he himself knows that dreams have occurred. And, of course, I think he would be right. All the philosophers I have ever met or heard of certainly did know that dreams have occurred: we all know that dreams *have* occurred. But can he consistently combine this proposition that he knows that dreams have occurred, with his conclusion that he does not know that he is not dreaming? Can anybody possibly know that dreams have occurred, if, at the time, he does not himself know that he is not dreaming? If he *is* dreaming, it may be that he is only dreaming that dreams have occurred; and if he does not know that he is not dreaming, can he possibly know that he is *not* only dreaming that dreams have occurred? Can he possibly know therefore that dreams *have* occurred? I do not think that he can; and therefore I think that anyone who uses this premiss and also asserts the conclusion that nobody ever knows that he is not dreaming, is guilty of an inconsistency. By using this premiss he implies that he himself knows that dreams have occurred; while, if his conclusion is true, it follows that he himself does not know that he is not dreaming, and therefore does not know that he is not only dreaming that dreams have occurred.

However, I admit that the premiss is true. Let us now try to see by what sort of reasoning it might be thought that we could get from it to the conclusion.

I do not see how we can get forward in that direction at all, unless we first take the following huge step, unless we say, namely: since there have been dream-images similar in important respects to some of the sensory experiences I am now having, it is logically possible that there should be dream-images *exactly like all* the sensory experiences I am now having, and logically possible, therefore, that all the sensory experiences I am now having *are* mere dream-images. And it might be thought that the validity of this step could be supported to some extent by appeal to matters of fact, though only, of course, at the cost of the same sort of inconsistency which I have just pointed out. It might be said, for instance, that some people have had dream-images which were *exactly like* sensory experiences which they had when they were awake, and that therefore it must be logically possible to have a dream-image exactly like a sensory experience which is *not* a dream-image. And then it may be said: If it is logically possible for some dream-images to be exactly like sensory experiences which are not dream-images, surely it must be logically possible for *all* the dream-images occurring in a dream at a given time to be exactly like sensory experiences which are not dream-images, and logically possible also for all the sensory experiences which a man has at a given time when he is awake to be exactly like all the dream-images which he himself or another man had in a dream at another time.

Now I cannot see my way to deny that it is logically possible that all the sensory experiences I am having now should be mere dream-images. And if this is logically possible, and if further the sensory experiences I am having now were the only experiences I am having, I do not see how I could possibly know for certain that I am not dreaming.

But the conjunction of my memories of the immediate past with these sensory experiences *may* be sufficient to enable me to know that I am not dreaming. I say it *may* be. But what if our sceptical philosopher says: It is *not* sufficient; and offers as an argument to prove that it is not, this: It is logically possible *both* that you should be having all the sensory experiences you are having, and also that you should be remembering what you do remember, and *yet* should be dreaming. If this *is* logically possible, then I don't see how to deny that

I cannot possibly know for certain that I am not dreaming: I do not see that I possibly could. But can any reason be given for saying that it *is* logically possible? So far as I know nobody ever has, and I don't know how anybody ever could. And so long as this is not done my argument, 'I know that I am standing up, and therefore I know that I am not dreaming', remains at least as good as his, 'You don't know that you are not dreaming, and therefore don't know that you are standing up'. And I don't think I've ever seen an argument expressly directed to show that it is not.

One final point should be made clear. It is certainly logically possible that I *should have* been dreaming now; I *might* have been dreaming now; and therefore the proposition that I *am* dreaming now is not self-contradictory. But what I am in doubt of is whether it is logically possible that I should *both* be having all the sensory experiences and the memories that I have and *yet* be dreaming. The conjunction of the proposition that I have these sense experiences and memories with the proposition that I am dreaming does seem to me to be very likely self-contradictory.*

* It should, I think, be mentioned that Moore was particularly dissatisfied with the last four paragraphs of this paper, and I believe that he was thinking primarily of these paragraphs when he wrote, in the Preface [to *Philosophical Papers*], that the paper contains bad mistakes.—Casimir Lewy.

DREAMING AND SKEPTICISM

NORMAN MALCOLM

In the *First Meditation,* Descartes represents himself as at first having the thought that surely it is *certain* that he is seated by the fire, and then as rejecting this thought in the following remark: "I cannot, however, but remind myself that on many occasions I have in sleep been deceived by similar illusions; and on more careful study of them I see that there are no certain marks distinguishing waking from sleep. . . ."[1] I believe that it is worth while reflecting on his assertion that he has often been *deceived* when asleep. In his reply to the objections against the *Meditations* raised by Hobbes, he repeats this assertion in the form of a rhetorical question: "For who denies that in his sleep a man may be deceived?"[2]

Descartes is clearly implying that while a man is asleep a certain thought may occur to him or he may come to believe something or to affirm something. And there is no doubt that he held this to be so.[3] In the *Fifth Meditation* he says that

The Philosophical Review, Vol. LXV, No. 1, January 1956, pp. 14–37. Reprinted with the permission of the author and *The Philosophical Review.*

[1] Norman Kemp Smith, *Descartes' Philosophical Writings* (London, 1952), p. 198; hereafter cited as DPW.

[2] E. Haldane and G. Ross, *The Philosophical Works of Descartes* (Cambridge, 1934), II, 78; hereafter cited as HR.

[3] Other philosophers have held it too. Aristotle, in a short paper on dreams, says: "It is . . . a fact that the soul makes . . . assertions in sleep" (*De Somnis,* in *The Basic Works of Aristotle,* ed. by R. McKeon [New York, 1941], p. 618). Kant, in *An Inquiry into the Distinctness of the Principles of Natural Theology and Morals,* says: "In deepest sleep perhaps the greatest perfection of the mind might be exercised in rational thought. For we have no reason for asserting the opposite except that we do not remember the idea when awake. This reason, however, proves nothing" (Immanuel Kant,

"once I have recognized that there is a God, and that all things depend on Him, and that He is not a deceiver, and from this, in turn, have inferred that all things which I clearly and distinctly apprehend are of necessity true," then no grounds remain for doubting any of the things that he remembers as having been previously demonstrated—for example, the truths of geometry. He continues:

> Will it be said that perhaps I am dreaming (an objection I myself raised a little while ago), that is, that all the thoughts I am now entertaining are no more true than those which come to me in dreams? Even so, what difference would that make? For even should I be asleep and dreaming, whatever is present to my understanding in an evident manner is indisputably true. [*DPW*, 247]

Descartes thinks that a man might have thoughts and make judgments while sleeping, and if those thoughts are "clear and distinct" they are true, despite the fact that he is sleeping. This doctrine is plainly set forth in his reply to the Jesuit, Bourdin: ". . . everything which anyone clearly and distinctly perceives is true, although that person in the meantime may doubt whether he is dreaming or awake, nay, if you want it so, even though he is really dreaming or is delirious" (HR II, 267). In Part IV of the *Discourse*, Descartes remarks that "whether awake or asleep, we ought never to allow ourselves to be persuaded save on the evidence of our reason" (*DPW*, 146). Here he implies that a man can reason, can be persuaded, and can resist persuasion—though all the while he is asleep!

His view is that when we sleep the same *kinds* of mental states and mental occurrences are present in us as when awake; the difference is that, as a general rule, our minds don't work as well when we are asleep.[4] But they work. Indeed, they *must* do so; for the "essence" or "principal attri-

---

Critique of Practical Reason and Other Writings in Moral Philosophy, ed. by L. W. Beck [Chicago, 1949], p. 275).

[4] As Gilson puts Descartes' view: "Sleep does not constitute in itself a state of error, but simply, because of physiological conditions, a state less favorable than waking to the free exercise of thought" (E. Gilson, *René Descartes: Discours de la Méthode: Texte et commentaire* [Paris, 1930], p. 366).

bute" of mental substance is consciousness, and so long as a mind exists there must exist "modes" of that essence, i.e. states of consciousness, mental occurrences, mental acts. As Descartes says in a letter:

> I had good reason to assert that the human soul is always conscious in any circumstances—even in a mother's womb. For what more certain or more evident reason could be required than my proof that the soul's nature or essence consists in its being conscious, just as the essence of a body consists in its being extended? A thing can never be deprived of its own essence.[5]

Descartes conceives of a dream as being a part of this continuous mental life. The thoughts of a dream are real thoughts. The feelings in a dream are real feelings. Descartes holds that to be frightened in a dream is to be frightened in the *same* sense as that in which I should be frightened now if half of the ceiling were suddenly to fall. He holds that the proposition "In my dream last night I was frightened" *entails* the proposition "Last night I was frightened." He holds that if in my dream I thought someone was at the door, then I had this thought, while asleep, in the very same sense as that in which I should have it now were I to hear the doorbell. It is only because Descartes conceives of a dream as composed of thoughts and sensations, in the same sense that a period of waking life is, that he is able, in the *First Meditation*, to derive a ground for doubting his senses from the fact that sometimes he dreams. According to his conception, the identical thoughts and sensations that you had when you were wide awake could have occurred to you when you were asleep. The *content* of a dream and of a waking episode could be the same. From this it follows "that there are no certain marks distinguishing waking from sleep." I will try to show that this conception is mistaken.

[5] C. Adam and P. Tannery, *Œuvres de Descartes* (Paris, 1899), III, 423; translation by E. Anscombe and P. Geach, *Descartes: Philosophical Writings* (Edinburgh, 1954), p. 266.

I

To begin with, I should like to call attention to the familiar distinction between being *sound* asleep and being *half* asleep. It is noteworthy that in American colloquial speech the phrase "dead to the world" is a synonym of the phrase "sound asleep" and not, of course, a synonym of the phrase "half asleep." If a man is half asleep he is also partly awake but not "clear" awake. Many different degrees of being asleep fall under the heading "half asleep." The criteria we commonly use for determining whether another person is or was sound asleep are different from the criteria we use for determining whether he is or was half asleep. It would seem that the former criteria are of two sorts: (1) a "present-tense" criterion, and (2) a "past-tense" criterion. We use the "present-tense" criterion to determine whether someone *is* (not was) sound asleep. It consists of things of this kind: that his eyes are closed, his body inert, his breathing rhythmical, and (more important) that he is unresponsive to questions, commands, and stimuli of moderate intensity. (Example: The sleeper does not react in any way when the carpenter begins hammering in the next room. In contrast, he might have rolled over and muttered a sleepy protest against the noise.) The "past-tense" criterion is used to determine whether a person *was* (not is) sound asleep, and it can be satisfied only when he is awake. It applies when the present-tense criterion has not been fulfilled in such a way that all question is removed as to whether the person is or is not sound asleep. We wait until he is awake and then find out whether he has any knowledge of what transpired in his vicinity while he was asleep: if he has none it is confirmed that he was sound asleep. (Example: He is surprised to learn that there was hammering close by while he slept: he has no recollection of any noise.) These two sorts of criterion can combine or conflict in many ways. It is possible that there should be cases in which there is no correct answer to the question "Was he sound asleep?"

The criteria of someone's being half asleep would seem to
fall into the same two categories. The main difference between the present-tense criteria for being sound asleep and
for being half asleep is that if someone is merely half asleep
he will be in some degree responsive to questions, commands, and disturbances, although only sluggishly or groggily
so. The main difference in the past-tense criteria for these
two conditions is that if someone was only half asleep then
he will be able to produce, when fully awake, some account
of what took place in his immediate vicinity while he was
half asleep, an account that will, however, be hazy and incomplete.[6] (A refinement of this last difference, pertaining to
dreaming, is mentioned in footnote 9.)

II

In the next place, I wish to compare the following two
sentences:

(1) "I am sound asleep."
(2) "I was sound asleep."

Although (1) and (2) differ grammatically only in tense, (1)
is seen, straight off, to be a queer sentence, but (2) is not.
Wherein lies the oddity of (1)?

Let us say that when a person utters or writes a sentence
he can *use* the sentence to claim or affirm or assert something. It will depend on circumstances whether one has used
a sentence to claim something, or whether one has merely
uttered the sentence in order to call attention to the sentence itself, as I might utter (1) merely to call attention to
it. (Also, of course, a sentence may be used to give a com-
mand or to put a question, and so on.) Now it is obvious
that sentence (2), "I was sound asleep," can be and is used

[6] The psychoanalyst Lawrence Kubie remarks that "sleep is a psy-
chologically active state, and we are never completely asleep, nor
completely awake" (E. Hilgard, L. Kubie, and E. Pumpian-Mindlin,
Psychoanalysis as Science [Stanford, 1952], p. 95). One wonders
whether Kubie is so using the words that no one *could* be "completely awake" or "completely asleep."

to claim or affirm or assert something. I shall express this by saying that it can be "used as an assertion."

The question now is whether (1) can be used as an assertion. It is not hard to see that there would be an absurdity in attempting to so use it. Suppose that I am in bed and that you come and shake me and ask "Are you asleep?" and that I reply "I am sound asleep." It would be amusing if you took me as claiming that I am sound asleep and then concluded from this that I am sound asleep. ("He says that he is sound asleep, and he ought to know.") The absurdity that would lie in the use of the sentence "I am sound asleep" as an assertion consists in this: if a person *claims* that he is sound asleep then he is *not* sound asleep. Notice that "claims" is a stronger verb here than "says." There is *a* sense of "says" in which a person says whatever words come out of his mouth. In this sense a man who is sound asleep can say things: he may talk in his sleep. He could say, in this sense, "I am sound asleep"; but this would not prove that he is not sound asleep. He is not claiming that he is sound asleep.

The absurdity that I am trying to describe does not lie in my uttering the words "I am sound asleep" but in my claiming or affirming or asserting that I am sound asleep. Whether I make the claim by using spoken or written words or by any other audible or visible signs is, therefore, irrelevant. If I use no physical signs but merely affirm in my mind that I am sound asleep (as I might affirm in my mind that my companion is a bore), it follows that I am not sound asleep.

The matter can be put by saying that the *assertion* "I am sound asleep" would be, in a certain sense, self-contradictory. The sentence "I am sound asleep" does not express a self-contradiction in the way in which the sentence "A is taller than B and B is taller than A," expresses a self-contradiction. If the latter sentence were written down in front of you, you could straight off deduce a proposition of the form "*p* and not-*p*." You cannot do this with "I am sound asleep." But as soon as you bring in the notion of a person's *asserting* or *claiming* that he is sound asleep then you get a kind of self-contradiction. It would be an assertion of such a nature that *making* the assertion would contradict the *truth* of the assertion. The proposition "I am sound asleep" (if it can be called a "proposition") does not entail the proposition "I am not sound asleep." But if I am asserting that I am sound asleep then I am not sound asleep. If I am asserting that I am sound asleep someone else is entitled to say of me "He claims that he is sound asleep." And this latter proposition, "He claims that he is sound asleep" (if it can be called a "proposition"), entails the proposition "He is not sound asleep." Thus the first-person assertion "I am sound asleep" and the related third-person proposition "He claims that he is sound asleep" may each, with propriety I think, be called "self-contradictory," although in somewhat different senses. In neither case, of course, is it that "strict" kind of self-contradiction that is illustrated by my "taller" sentence: for the latter expresses something from which there follows a proposition of the form "*p* and not-*p*"; whereas neither from "I am sound asleep" nor from "He claims that he is sound asleep" does there follow any proposition of that form. The kind of self-contradiction is this: if someone claims that he is sound asleep then it follows that he is not what he claims. It is an assertion that would necessarily be false each time it was made.

Not only is there a kind of self-contradiction in claiming or affirming that one is sound asleep; there is the same kind of self-contradiction in wondering or conjecturing whether one is sound asleep, or in being in doubt about it. The proposition "He wonders whether he is sound asleep" is absurd in the same way that the proposition "He claims that he is sound asleep" is absurd. From either of them equally there follows the proposition "He is not sound asleep." So not merely is the *assertion* "I am sound asleep" self-contradictory: the *question* "Am I sound asleep?" is self-contradictory in the same sense. And if the *thought* should occur to you that you are sound asleep it would be a self-contradictory thought. And if you should be under the *impression* that you are sound asleep it would be a self-contradictory impression: for the proposition "He is under the impression (it seems to him) that he is sound asleep" entails the proposition "He is not sound asleep."

Finally, it should be mentioned that the proposition "He knows (he realizes, he is aware) that he is sound asleep" is a self-contradictory proposition in the "strict" sense. Therefore, a person who is sound asleep cannot know, realize, or be aware that he is.[7]

Of course, a person can *dream* that he is sound asleep and can *dream* that he *knows* that he is sound asleep. It can be said of a person who dreamt either of these things that "he knew in his dream" that he was sound asleep. What my argument proves is that knowing-in-your-dream that you are sound asleep is not knowing that you are sound asleep.

III

So far I have called attention to the fact that if a person affirms, doubts, thinks, or questions that he is sound asleep then he is not sound asleep—and also to the fact that a person who is sound asleep cannot know that he is. But now it is important to see that if a person affirms, doubts, thinks, or questions *anything whatever* (and not merely that he is sound asleep) then he is not sound asleep. No doubt all of those verbs have "dispositional" senses: for example, you can truly say of a man who is in fact sound asleep that he affirms that war will break out within the year. But it is not that sense of those verbs to which I am referring. If we take "He affirms that there will be a war" in the sense in which it means "At this very moment he is affirming that there will be a war," then it entails "He is not sound asleep." In this "non-dispositional" sense of those verbs, "He is affirming (doubting, thinking, questioning) that p" entails "He is not sound asleep," *regardless* of what proposition is substituted for "p." Surely it is obvious that if "He is claiming that he is sound

[7] A proposition of the form "He knows that p" differs from a proposition of the form "He claims (thinks, conjectures, doubts) that p," in the respect that the former entails "p," the latter not. Therefore, "He knows that he is sound asleep" is self-contradictory in the "strict" sense: for, like propositions of the latter form, it entails "He is *not* sound asleep"; and, unlike those of the latter form, it entails "He *is* sound asleep."

asleep" entails "He is not sound asleep," then also "He is claiming that someone is at the door" entails "He is not sound asleep." And likewise, if the thought has struck him that there might be someone at the door, or if he wonders whether there is, or if he doubts that there is, or if it seems to him that there is, or if he is afraid that there is—then he is not sound asleep. To state the principle for which I am arguing in its most general form: if a person is in *any* state of consciousness it logically follows that he is not sound asleep. The proposition with which I started my argument—namely, the proposition that "He claims that he is sound asleep" entails "He is not sound asleep"—is a special case of this general principle, which may be expressed in Cartesian terms as follows: *Cogito ergo non dormio.*

When Descartes declared, in the course of his *Reply* to Gassendi's objections to the *Meditations,* that "when we sleep we perceive that we are dreaming" (HR II, 212), he was mistaken if he meant that when we are *sound* asleep we perceive that we are dreaming.[8]

The fact is that if someone is in bed with his eyes closed, whatever serves as a criterion for saying that just now he is thinking that so-and-so is the case, or is wondering or doubting whether it is, or perceives that it is—also serves as a criterion for saying that he is not sound asleep.

And if one cannot have thoughts while sound asleep, one cannot be *deceived* while sound asleep.

IV

There will be a temptation to conclude that, if all the foregoing is true, then clearly a person cannot *dream* when sound asleep. But this would be a mistake. Our normal criterion for someone's having had a dream is that, upon awaking, he relates ("tells") a dream. Suppose that the present-tense and

[8] Note the following consequence drawn by Freud from his theory of dreams: "Throughout the whole of our sleep we are just as certain that we are dreaming as we are certain that we are sleeping" (*The Interpretation of Dreams,* in *The Basic Writings of Sigmund Freud,* ed. by A. A. Brill [New York, 1938], p. 513).

past-tense criteria of sound sleep were satisfied in the case of a certain person—i.e. his body was inert, his breathing was heavy and rhythmical (perhaps he even snored); he did not react to moderately loud noises or to occurrences in his immediate vicinity that would have provoked his lively interest had he known about them: furthermore, when he woke up he had no suspicion that those noises and incidents had occurred. Also suppose that on awaking he related a dream. It would have been established both that he slept soundly and that he dreamt.[9]

[9] The proposition "I was sound asleep" has, on my view, the nature of an inference. I *conclude* that I was sound asleep from things that I notice or learn after or as I wake up. For example, I find out that while I slept for the past hour a heavy tractor was making an uproar a hundred feet away, yet I have no recollection of hearing any noise. I infer that I was very soundly asleep.

I must mention here a complicating subtlety. Suppose, in the above example, I *dreamt* that I heard a roaring and clanking (like that of a nearby tractor) and dreamt that this noise was made by a dinosaur. I believe we should be inclined to say that I *heard* the tractor *in my sleep*, although I had no suspicion, upon awakening, that there had been such goings-on, until I was told. I think we should also be inclined to say that my sleep was not completely sound, that I was not utterly "dead to the world." I think that in general a certain degree of similarity between the events of a dream and the events occurring within normal perceptual range of the sleeper counts in favor of saying both that the sleeper faintly perceived the latter events and that his sleep was not an absolutely deep sleep. This would be so even if the sleeper had no idea, after awaking, that the events in question had occurred. I doubt that there is any way of specifying what the degree of similarity must be. I will comment briefly on two examples adduced by T. M. Yost, Jr., and Donald Kalish in their paper "Miss Macdonald on Sleeping and Waking" (*Philosophical Quarterly*, April 1955). One is of an asthmatic who dreams that he is suffocating and finds on awaking that he is suffocating. The right thing to say here, I think, is that his dream was partly a perception of the reality, and also that it was not a dream of perfectly sound sleep. The other example is that of a person in California who dreams that the Washington Monument is being painted blue. A dream with such a content would not count against the dreamer's having been sound asleep, even if the Monument were being painted blue at the time he slept. What would indicate that a dreamer's sleep was not a very deep one would not be that his dream was veridical, but that the content of the dream suggests that he was to some extent perceptive of things that he would probably have perceived clearly, located as he was, had he been awake.

V

I will anticipate, at this point, a very general sort of objection to the manner in which I argue. It will be said that I am assuming throughout that there are *criteria* for determining whether a person other than myself is or was thinking, or frightened, or awake, or asleep; i.e. I am assuming that I have criteria for the existence of particular sorts of mental occurrences and states of consciousness in other persons, those criteria being of such a nature that if they are fully satisfied the existence of those occurrences and states is established beyond question—whereas, the objection runs, there are no such criteria and could be none: at best I only have *evidence*, which makes the existence of those mental states and occurrences in others more or less probable. It is true that I make this "assumption." I believe that to deny it leads one to the view that each person *teaches himself* what fright, doubt, thinking, and all other mental phenomena are, by noting his own fright, doubt, etc.: each person "knows from his own case" what these things are. And this view leads to the untenable notion of a language that "I alone *can* understand." I will not attempt here to show either that the denial of the above "assumption" has this consequence or that it is untenable. I believe that both of these things have been established by Wittgenstein in his *Philosophical Investigations*. A rough guide to some of his thoughts on this topic may be found in my review of that book (*Philosophical Review*, October 1954).

VI

Let us consider again Descartes' famous remark: "I cannot, however, but remind myself that on many occasions I have in sleep been deceived by similar illusions; and on more careful study of them I see that there are no certain marks distinguishing waking from sleep." Of course, if by "sleep" he means sound sleep, then it is false that in sleep he could ever have been deceived by any illusions whatever. But I want to pay particular attention to the idea that there are no certain marks distinguishing waking from sleep, an idea that has been commonly entertained and accepted by philosophers. Socrates put to Theaetetus the question:

> What evidence could be appealed to, supposing we were asked at this very moment whether we are asleep or awake—dreaming all that passes through our minds or talking to one another in the waking state?

To which Theaetetus replied:

> Indeed, Socrates, I do not see by what evidence it is to be proved; for the two conditions correspond in every circumstance like exact counterparts. The conversation we have just had might equally well be one that we merely think we are carrying on in our sleep; and when it comes to thinking in a dream that we are telling other dreams, the two states are extraordinarily alike.[10]

Bertrand Russell says the following:

> I dreamed last night that I was in Germany, in a house which looked out on a ruined church; in my dream I supposed at first that the church had been bombed during the recent war, but was subsequently informed that its destruction dated from the wars of religion in the sixteenth century. All this, so long as I remained asleep, had all the convincingness of waking life. I did really have the dream, and did really have an experience intrinsically indistinguishable from that of seeing a ruined church when awake. It follows that the experience which I call "seeing a church" is not conclusive evidence that there is a church, since it may occur when there is no such external object as I suppose in my dream. It may be said that, though when dreaming I may *think* that I am awake, when I wake up I *know* that I am awake. But I do not see how we are to have any such certainty. . . . I do not believe that I am now dreaming, but I cannot

10 F. M. Cornford, *Plato's Theory of Knowledge* (London, 1935), p. 53.

prove that I am not. I am, however, quite certain that I am having certain experiences, whether they be those of a dream or those of waking life.[11]

This manner of comparing dreaming and waking inevitably results in the skeptical question: "How can I tell whether at this moment I am awake or asleep?" and in the skeptical conclusion: "I *cannot* tell." The conception that underlies the comparison is the following: "Take any sequence of sensations, thoughts, and feelings. That same sequence could occur either when you were awake or when you were asleep and dreaming. The two conditions, being awake and being asleep, can have the same *content* of experience. Therefore, you cannot tell from the sensations, thoughts, and feelings themselves, at the time you are having them, whether you are awake or asleep."

If, however, we state the problem in terms of *sound* sleep, and bear in mind my preceding argument, then we see at least one respect in which this conception is mistaken. When a person is sound asleep he cannot have any sensations, thoughts, and feelings at all; sound sleep cannot, in *this* sense, have any "content of experience." This is so regardless of whether or not the sleeper dreams. Therefore it is not true, but senseless, to say that sound sleep and waking are "indistinguishable" from one another, or that they are "exact counterparts." For the meaning of this philosophical remark is that identically the same sensations, impressions, and thoughts could occur to one in either condition. But one might as well assert that a house and the mental image of a house could have the same weight; it is as meaningless to attribute sensations, impressions, thoughts, or feelings to sound sleep as to attribute weight to a mental image.

It is undoubtedly an ordinary use of language to call a dream an "experience": one may say of an unpleasant dream "I hope that I won't have that experience again." In this sense a man can have experiences when sound asleep. But this use of the word "experience" should not mislead us. In his dream

11 B. A. W. Russell, *Human Knowledge* (New York, 1948), pp. 171–172.

a man may see, hear, think, feel emotion. To say that "in his dream" he thought his bed was on fire and was frightened, is equivalent to saying that he dreamt that he thought his bed was on fire and dreamt that he was frightened. The fallacy I am warning against is to conclude "He was frightened" from "He dreamt that he was frightened," and "He thought his bed was on fire" from "He dreamt that he thought his bed was on fire." The experience of thinking your bed is on fire and (if you are sound asleep) of thinking in your dream that your bed is on fire are "experiences" in different senses of the word.

VII

In the notion of the dream of sound sleep there is no foothold for philosophical skepticism. It is an error to say that a person *cannot tell* whether he is awake or sound asleep and dreaming. For this implies (a) that he might *think* he was awake and yet be sound asleep—which is impossible. And it implies (b) that he might think he was sound asleep and yet be awake. Now (b), unlike (a), is not impossible: but the thought that the man has—namely, that he is sound asleep— is self-contradictory (in the special sense that I explained), and a little reflection could teach him that it is. Whether or not a particular person would see this point of logic, in any case no general ground for skepticism is provided.

But it is also an error to say that a man *can* tell whether or not he is sound asleep. For this would imply that he had some criterion or test at hand for determining the matter, and there is an absurdity in this idea—for he could not even *use* a criterion unless he were *not* sound asleep, and so nothing could turn on the "outcome" of using it. Therefore, it is wrong to say *either* that you can tell or cannot tell (in the sense of *determine*) that you are sound asleep and dreaming, or that you are awake.

There is a temptation to object to the preceding argument in the following way: "even if I cannot have thoughts and sensations during sound sleep, yet when I dream during sound

sleep it seems to me that I am having thoughts and sensations, and so there remains the problem of determining, at
any given time, whether I am having thoughts and sensations
or merely seeming to have them."[12] The pretty obvious answer to this is that to a person who is sound asleep, "dead to
the world," things cannot even *seem*. He cannot hear the
telephone ring nor can it seem to him that it rings. Suppose
that A is apparently sound asleep, but that B makes the following report to C: "It seems to A that he hears the telephone
ringing." C's natural reply would be: "Why, I thought that
he was sound asleep!" Whatever movements, gestures, or utterances of A's indicate that it seems to him that the telephone is ringing, also indicate, to an equal degree, that he is
not sound asleep.

Another objection to my argument is the following:
"Granted that while a person is sound asleep he gives no indication of having any thoughts or of being conscious of anything, nevertheless upon awaking he might testify that such
and such a thought had occurred to him while he slept. Likewise, nothing in the demeanor of the man who is quietly
smoking his pipe reveals that the thought of resigning his
government post has just occurred to him; but afterwards he
may declare that it did first occur to him then. You would
accept his testimony! Now, why shouldn't you accept it in
the other case too? Since the cases are similar it is merely
dogmatic and unreasonable to reject his testimony there while
accepting it here."

It is true enough that a man's declaration that a certain
thought passed through his mind on a particular occasion in
the very recent past is used by others as a criterion of that
thought's having passed through his mind on that past
occasion, even though his behavior at the time gave no indication of it. Similarly, someone who is calmly discussing something with you and giving no indication of physical discom-
fort, may later declare that he felt slightly ill just then; and

[12] Socrates in the *Republic* asks: "Does not dreaming, whether
one is awake or asleep, consist in mistaking a semblance for the reality
it resembles?" (F. M. Cornford, *The Republic of Plato* [New York,
1945], p. 183).

you will probably use his declaration as a criterion of his having felt slightly ill just then, even though he gave no sign of it. But note that we have said that he did not, in fact, give any sign of it. He *could* have done so. Whereas it is false that a man who is sound asleep could, while he is sound asleep, give any signs or indications that a certain thought was occurring to him or that he was experiencing some sensation.[13] For any sign of this would also be a sign that he was at least partly awake.

If a man were to get up from an apparently sound sleep and declare that while he was lying there a certain thought had occurred to him we might conclude that he was about to tell us something that he had dreamt; or we might conclude that, despite appearances, he had not been sound asleep; or we might conclude that he had awakened *with* that thought. Famous men testify to having solved difficult problems in their sleep. This can seem a paradox until we understand what it means: namely, that they went to sleep without a solution and woke up with one. But if a man, who knew English as well as anyone, declared that a certain thought had occurred to him while he was *sound* asleep, and insisted that he did not mean that he dreamt it or that he woke up with it, but that it had occurred to him in the same literal sense in which thoughts sometimes occur to him when he is drinking his coffee or weeding the garden—then I believe that in ordinary life we should not be able to make head or tail of his declaration.

[13] [Footnote added 1966] I was assuming here the following principle: If there is a certain state, S, such that it is *logically* impossible for a person in state S to give any *signs* of thinking or having experiences, then it is logically impossible for a person to think or to have experiences while in state S. Unfortunately this principle is not true. One can define a state (e.g. *total* paralysis) such that by definition a person in that state could not give any *signs* of thinking or experiencing: yet it would not follow that a person in that state could not think or have experiences. This problem is treated with greater sophistication in my monograph *Dreaming* (New York: Humanities Press, 1959). My argument there does not assume the foregoing false principle.

VIII

It will appear to some that there is a contradiction in maintaining, as I have, that it is true that someone who is sound asleep can in a dream think it is raining and in a dream seem to hear thunder, and yet that it is not true that he thinks it is raining or seems to hear thunder. One wants to argue: "In your dream you thought such-and-such. Dreams take place during sleep. Therefore, in your sleep you must have thought such-and-such." I have no objection to the conclusion if it merely means that I dreamt that I thought such-and-such: for this repeats the first premise and nothing is proved. It is only when the "argument" is taken, not as platitudinous and redundant, but as proving something, that I wish to attack it: when, that is, it is understood as proving that during a period of sound sleep I could have thoughts, sensations, impressions, and feelings in the *same* sense as that in which I have them during a half-hour of waking reverie.

Consider the second premise: "Dreams take place during sleep." Looked at in one way it is a tautology; looked at in another way it is a dubious proposition. It is a tautology in the sense that the inference from "He had a dream last night" to "He got at least some sleep last night" is valid. It is a dubious proposition when a dream is conceived of as an occurrence during sleep in the sense in which breathing is, or as an occurrence during the night in the sense in which a fright or a toothache can be. What is dubious about it? Well, let us take note of the fact that we have no way of determining *when* a dream occurred or *how long* it lasted. Of course it occurred "while he slept": but *when* while he slept? Some psychologists have conjectured that dreams occur, not during sleep, but during the period of *awaking* from sleep. Our feeling that it is impossible to decide whether this is so or not shows that we have no *criterion* for deciding it—shows that there is no sense in the question "When, while he slept, did he dream?" as there is in the questions "When, last night, did his headache begin?" or "When did his fright occur?"

There is a similar lack of any criterion with respect to the duration of dreams: when should you say of a sleeping person, "Now he has begun to dream," "Now he has stopped dreaming?" We know what it means to find out whether someone has had a dream: he tells us a dream on awaking, or tells us he had one. (This concept of verification does not apply, of course, to small children or dogs. Just how much sense is there in the familiar half serious "conjecture" that the dog whose feet are twitching is dreaming of rabbits? And where this concept does apply—namely, to people who can tell dreams—there is much indefiniteness; e.g. a man says, on awaking, "I don't know whether I had a dream or not: perhaps I did." Does it make any sense to insist that either he had a dream or he didn't have one, *regardless* of whether he knows anything about it?) In the way that we find out whether someone had a dream, we sometimes also find out that it was a long dream: i.e. he *says* it was a long dream. But what is the duration of a "long" or "short" dream in "objective" time?

We can imagine the discovery of a uniform correlation between the occurrence of a specific physiological process during sleep and the subsequent reporting of a dream.[14] This correlation might be so impressive that scientists would be tempted to adopt the occurrence of the physiological process as their criterion for the occurrence of a dream. Let us imagine that it even became the criterion in ordinary life. There would then be such a thing as *proving* that a man had dreamt, although on awaking he honestly reported that he had not; and the duration (three minutes, say) of the physiological

[14] There is some evidence in favor of there being a positive correlation between the occurrence of strong electrical currents in the bodies of sleeping persons and their subsequently reporting that they dreamt. The experiment in which this evidence was obtained is summarized in *Recent Experiments in Psychology*, by Crafts, Schneirla, Robinson, and Gilbert (New York, 1938), pp. 377–384. I quote: "In 33 cases, series of intense action currents . . . were recorded during sleep. After the action currents had been in progress a short time, but before they had disappeared, the subjects were awakened. In 30 of the 33 cases, subjects reported that they had just been dreaming" (p. 380).

process, and its time of occurrence, could be made the criterion of the duration and time of occurrence of the dream. It would even have sense to say of someone "He is halfway through his dream!" All of this would amount to the adoption of an extremely different use of the word "dreaming." Its meaning would have to be *taught* differently; and all sorts of remarks would make sense that at present do not.

As things are, the notions of duration and time of occurrence have no application in ordinary discourse to dreams. In *this* sense, a dream is not an "occurrence" and, therefore, not an occurrence during sleep. The proposition "Dreams occur during sleep" can now be seen to be a curious one. It is important to ask *why* we say such a thing. The answer, I believe, is not hard to find. When someone "tells" a dream he talks in the *past* tense: after sleeping he relates how he *did* this and *saw* that (none of which is true). It is this peculiar phenomenon of speaking in the past tense after sleep, the phenomenon called "telling a dream," that provides the sense of the proposition that dreams occur during sleep.

One would like to object here that a person who is telling a dream speaks in the past tense *because* he is reporting something that took place in the past while he slept, namely, his dream. The objection rests on the idea that his report corresponds to his dream in the same way that my report of yesterday's events corresponds to them. This is wrong. It is senseless to suppose that his dream differed from his report of it unless this means that he might change, add to, or contradict his report. No one knows what it would mean to "verify" his report. Others use his report as their criterion of what his dream was. In contrast, no one uses my report of the events of yesterday's robbery as his *criterion* of what actually happened: there are familiar ways of confirming or disconfirming my report, independently of my inclination or disinclination to amend or contradict it. If you take seriously the idea that the two reports correspond with reality, or fail to, in the *same* way, then you are confronted with the disturbing "possibility" that there are no dreams at all! I am guided here by Wittgenstein's remarks:

People who on waking tell us certain incidents (that they have been in such-and-such places, etc.). Then we teach them the expression "I dreamt," which precedes the narrative. Afterwards I sometimes ask them "did you dream anything last night?" and am answered yes or no, sometimes with an account of a dream, sometimes not. That is the language-game. . . .

Now must I make some assumption about whether people are deceived by their memories or not; whether they really had these images while they slept, or whether it merely seems so to them on waking? And what meaning has this question?—And what interest? Do we ever ask ourselves this when someone is telling us his dream? And if not—is it because we are sure his memory won't have deceived him? (And suppose it were a man with a quite specially bad memory?—)[15]

Perhaps when people give accounts of their dreams these accounts correspond to nothing at all! Perhaps it only *seems* to them on awaking that they dreamt!

I hope that I will not be misunderstood. I am not claiming that there are no dreams or that they do not occur in sleep— nor that these are genuine possibilities: of course they are not! If someone talks in a certain way after sleep then we say "He dreamt such-and-such while he slept." That is how the words are used! What I am trying to show is that *if* one thinks that a man's account of his dream is related to his dream just as my account of yesterday's happenings is related to them, one is in a hopeless difficulty: for then it *would* appear that our ostensible remembering that we dreamt such-and-such could be mistaken, not just once but all the time. If the report of the dream is "externally" related to the dream, then it may be that we are always only under the *illusion* of having had a dream, an illusion that comes to us as we awake. Trying to look at the matter in this way, we see that the notion that dreams really take place during sleep would become senseless: we should have no idea as to what would go to prove that they do.

We get out of this impasse only by realizing that there is

[15] *Philosophical Investigations* (New York, 1953), p. 184.

nothing to be proved. If after sleep a person relates that he thought and did and experienced such-and-such (all of this being false), and if he is not lying, pretending, or inventing, then we say "he dreamt it." "That is the language-game!" That he really had a dream and that he is under the impression that he had a dream: these are the same thing.

There is a sharp break between the concept of "remembering a dream" and the concept of remembering what happened downtown yesterday. If a man confidently relates that he witnessed such-and-such happen in the street the day before, it can turn out that it didn't happen that way at all: it merely seems to him that he remembers such-and-such. When he gives an account of his dream there is no sense in supposing that it merely seems to him that he dreamt such-and-such. In the case of remembering a dream there is no contrast between correctly remembering and seeming to oneself to remember—here they are identical! (It can even appear surprising that we should speak of "remembering" a dream.)

IX

I have put forward an argument intended to prove that a person who is sound asleep cannot have any thoughts or impressions or sensations. Many persons will not be convinced by this argument, which is perfectly sound, one reason being that they tend to misapprehend the concept of the dream. They think: You can dream in sound sleep (which is true enough); in your dream you can have various thoughts, impressions, sensations (also true); therefore, while you are sound asleep you can have thoughts, etc. (which is false, unless it is the redundant conclusion that *in the dream* you have in sound sleep there can be thoughts, etc.).

The inclination to draw the false conclusion comes from the mistake of thinking that someone's report that in his dream he was, say, afraid of snakes is a report that he was afraid of snakes *in the sense* in which his report that he was afraid of snakes when he was in the woods an hour ago is a report that he was afraid of snakes. But if his demeanor and behavior when he was in the woods expressed fearlessness of snakes, this would be in conflict with this report and would make its truth at least doubtful. Similarly, if in the woods he did show fear of snakes this would fit in with and confirm his report.

The logic of the matter is entirely different in the case of the report of a dream. If when he was in bed he had, by utterances and behavior, expressed a fear of snakes, this would have no tendency to confirm his report that he dreamt that he was afraid of snakes. Quite the opposite! It would tend to establish that he had *really* felt fear of snakes and not dreamt it at all! It would also tend to establish, in the same degree, that he had not been asleep, or at least not sound asleep, not "dead to the world." It is a logical impossibility that he should, when sound asleep, express fear or fearlessness or any other state of consciousness.

If a man declares that he was in a certain state of consciousness, what would count against his assertion would be evidence that he was, at the time referred to, either in an opposite state of consciousness or else not in any state of consciousness. Evidence that he was sound asleep would be evidence for the latter. His assertion that he dreamt last night that he was afraid of snakes (an assertion that could be true even though he slept soundly) does *not*, therefore, imply the proposition that in the night he was afraid of snakes, *in the sense* of this proposition in which it would be confirmed by his having manifested a fear of snakes in the night. And that is the normal sense of the proposition! When we say "He was afraid of snakes last night" we usually mean something that would be confirmed by the fact that during the night he expressed, by some demeanor or behavior of his, a fear of snakes. When we say "He dreamt last night that he was afraid of snakes" we do not mean anything of the sort. The latter proposition, therefore, does not imply the former one. In general, and contrary to Descartes, the proposition that a certain person had in his dream last night various thoughts, sensations, impressions, or feelings does not imply the proposition that last night he had those thoughts, sensations, impressions, or feelings, in the normal sense of the latter proposition.

X

So far I have discussed the notion of dreaming only in relation to sound sleep. The concept of dreaming when partly
awake is different. A person who is partly awake can have
thoughts (however groggy and confused) and so can be deceived. But he does not *have* to be deceived. He is not
"trapped in a dream." If it seems to him that he is sailing in
the air high over green meadows he can decide to investigate
—for example, to open his eyes and see where he is. The person who is sound asleep, in contrast, cannot *decide* to do anything; he can only dream that he decides; and, unlike the
man who is half asleep, he cannot *find out* anything but can
only dream that he does.[16] He who is sound asleep cannot

[16] A. Baillet, in his *Vie de Descartes* (Paris, 1691), Bk. II, ch. i,
pp. 81–86, gives an account of the famous three dreams that apparently had an important influence on Descartes' life. In the third
dream a man and a book appeared before him and then suddenly
disappeared. I quote: "What especially calls for remark is that in
doubt whether what he had just seen was dream or actual vision, not
merely did he decide in his sleep that it was a dream, but proceeded
to interpret the dream prior to his awaking" (translated by Norman
Kemp Smith, *New Studies in the Philosophy of Descartes* [London,
1952], p. 36). If my argument is correct either Descartes was not
sound asleep or else he *dreamt* that he decided and interpreted.

Miss Margaret Macdonald, in her paper "Sleeping and Waking"
(*Mind*, April 1953), observes that "it makes no sense to assert that
one could employ any confirming technique in a dream. For one
would but dream such employment" (p. 205); that a person who is
asleep cannot choose to do anything, e.g. to stop dreaming, for
"once asleep, a dreamer can only dream that he makes such a choice"
(p. 214); that if I saw the Hebrides in a dream it does not follow
either that I saw them or seemed to see them or thought I saw them
(p. 210); and that dreaming is neither a form of perception nor of
illusion (*passim*). Assuming that she refers to dreaming in sound
sleep, I am in agreement with these contentions although her method
of argument does not resemble mine. Unfortunately Macdonald seems
to have made a blunder. After noting important distinctions between
the concepts of sleeping and waking, she adds, "I suggest that these
differences destroy the need for Descartes' lament that 'there exist
no certain marks by which the state of waking may be distinguished

realize that he sleeps; but neither can he mistakenly think he is awake. He who is half asleep *can* mistake the sights and sounds that he "dreams" for real sights and sounds; but the concept of half sleep does not *require* that he make this mistake.

A consequence of my argument is that there is no room left for the skeptical question (a) "How can I know whether I am awake or sound asleep?"—for the question is absurd, since if I raise it I am not sound asleep. It is still possible, however, for a philosopher to be troubled by the question (b) "How can I know whether I am fully awake or only partly awake?" This cannot be disposed of in the same way, and I do not try to deal with it in this paper. I will only remark that it is in essence the same as the question (c) "How can I know whether I am having an hallucination?" That questions

---

from sleep.' For if what is said of one state is nonsensical when applied to the other, then this provides at least one certain mark by which to distinguish between them" (p. 215). From the fact that there are differences between the concepts of the two states it does not follow that I can tell whether I am in the one state or the other. I have argued (Sec. VII *supra*) that the notion of a person's determining whether he himself is awake or sound asleep is senseless. Macdonald is attacked on the above point by M. J. Baker ("Sleeping and Waking," *Mind*, October 1954).

Yost and Kalish (*op. cit.*) give an elaborate analysis of Macdonald's paper. Some of their critical remarks are in disagreement with what I have contended: e.g. "To say that one dreams is to say that one sees, hears, touches, etc., while asleep" (p. 120); "And as regards the so-called mental operations, we should maintain, with Descartes, that if anyone dreams that he believes, doubts, expects, desires, etc., then he really does" (p. 121); "People can really believe sentences to be true while they are dreaming" (*ibid.*); "A dreamer who is inspecting one dream-field could predict and expect certain later dream-fields; and when they occur he could recognize them to be or not to be the ones he predicted while inspecting earlier dream-fields" (p. 122). Apparently there is *a* sense of "dream" (dreaming when partly awake) in which it is possible for a dreamer to do the above things or at least some of them. But since there is another sense of "dream" (dreaming when sound asleep) in which none of them are possible, it follows that the general statements, "To say that one dreams is to say that one sees, hears, touches, etc., while asleep," and "If anyone dreams that he believes, doubts, expects, desires, etc., then he really does," are false.

(a) and (c) have a very different status is in itself a point of considerable interest.

XI

One result of the preceding treatment of the notions of sound sleep and dreaming is to show that Descartes' own solution of his problem of skepticism of the senses is untenable. In the *First Meditation* he observes that "there are no certain marks distinguishing waking from sleep." But after he has proved that God exists and is no deceiver, he goes on to declare, in the *Sixth Meditation*, that he ought

> to reject as hyperbolical and ridiculous all the doubts of these past days, more especially that regarding sleep, as being indistinguishable from the waking state. How marked, I now find, is the difference between them! Our memory can never connect our dreams with one another and with the whole course of our lives, in the manner in which we are wont to connect the things which happen to us while awake. If, while I am awake, someone should all of a sudden appear to me, and as suddenly disappear, as happens in dreams, and in such fashion that I could not know whence he came or whither he went, quite certainly it would not be unreasonable to esteem it a spectre, that is, a phantom formed in my brain, rather than a real man. When, on the other hand, in apprehending things, I know the place whence they have come, and that in which they are, and the time at which they present themselves to me, and while doing so can connect them uninterruptedly with the course of my life as a whole, I am completely certain that what I thus experience is taking place while I am awake, and not in dreams. And if after having summoned to my aid all my senses, my memory and my understanding, in scrutiny of these occurrences, I find that none of them presents me with what is at variance with any other, I ought no longer to entertain the least doubt as to their truth. God being no deceiver, it cannot be that I am here being misled. [*DPW*, 264–265]

Descartes is undoubtedly intending to point out a criterion for distinguishing waking from sleep (although I do not believe that he is rejecting what he *meant* when he said in the *First Meditation* that there is no criterion): and undoubtedly this is intended to be a criterion that will enable me to tell whether *I* am awake or asleep, and not merely to tell whether some other person is awake or asleep. In the sentence "Our memory can never connect . . ." he is surely implying that if I cannot "connect" the things that I experience with one another and with the whole course of my life then I ought to *conclude* that I am asleep and that these things belong to a dream. To this there is the conclusive objection that in regard to a person who is sound asleep (and sound sleep has to come into the question here) there is no sense in speaking of his making a connection or drawing a conclusion. Similarly, in the sentence "When, on the other hand . . . ," Descartes is implying that if I do not know where the things I apprehend come from and cannot connect them with the course of my life as a whole, then I am justified in *concluding* that I am asleep and dreaming. This involves the same absurdity. Descartes' criterion is identical with the principle of "coherence" or "consistency" that Leibniz,[17] Russell,[18] and others offer as a principle for distinguishing waking from sleeping. If my argument is correct, there cannot be such a principle.

[17] E.g. see Leibniz' paper "On the Method of Distinguishing Real from Imaginary Phenomena," *New Essays Concerning Human Understanding*, trans. by A. G. Langley (La Salle, Illinois, 1949), pp. 717–720, esp. pp. 718–719.
[18] E.g. see Russell's *Our Knowledge of the External World* (Chicago, 1914), p. 95.

'I THINK, THEREFORE I AM'

A. J. AYER

The attempt to put knowledge on a foundation which would be impregnable to doubt is historically associated with the philosophy of Descartes. But Descartes, though he regarded mathematics as the paradigm of knowledge, was aware that its *a priori* truths are not indubitable, in the sense that he required. He allowed it to be possible that a malignant demon should deceive him even with respect to those matters of which he was the most certain.[1] The demon would so work upon his reason that he took false statements to be self-evidently true. The hypothesis of there being such an arch-deceiver is indeed empty, since his operations could never be detected: but it may be regarded as a picturesque way of expressing the fact that intuitive conviction is not a logical guarantee of truth. The question which Descartes then raises is whether, of all the propositions which we think we know, there can be any that escape the demon's reach.

His answer is that there is one such proposition: the famous *cogito ergo sum*: I think, therefore I am.[2] The demon might perhaps have the power to make me doubt whether I was thinking, though it is difficult to see what this would come to; it is not clear what such a state of doubt would be. But even allowing that the expression 'I am doubting whether I am thinking' describes a possible situation, the doubt must be unwarranted. However much he can shake my confidence,

From *The Problem of Knowledge* (New York: St. Martin's Press, 1956), Ch. 2, S. iii, pp. 45–54. Reprinted by permission of St. Martin's Press, Inc.

[1] René Descartes, *Meditations on the First Philosophy*, Meditation I.

[2] *Vide* Meditation II and *Discourse on Method*, part IV.

the demon cannot deceive me into believing that I am thinking when I am not. For if I believe that I am thinking, then I
must believe truly, since my believing that I am thinking is
itself a process of thought. Consequently, if I am thinking, it
is indubitable that I am thinking, and if it is indubitable that
I am thinking, then, Descartes argues, it is indubitable that
I exist, at least during such times as I think.

Let us consider what this argument proves. In what sense
is the proposition that I think, and consequently that I exist,
shown to be indubitable? It is not a question for psychology.
The suggestion is not that it is physically impossible to doubt
that one is thinking, but rather that it somehow involves a
logical impossibility. Yet while there may be some question
about the meaning that one should attach to the statement
that I doubt whether I am thinking, it has not been shown
to be self-contradictory. Nor is the statement that I am thinking itself the expression of a necessary truth. If it seems to be
necessary, it is because of the absurdity of denying it. To say
'I am not thinking' is self-stultifying since if it is said intelligently it must be false: but it is not self-contradictory. The
proof that it is not self-contradictory is that it might have
been true. I am now thinking but I might easily not have
been. And the same applies to the statement that I exist. It
would be absurd for me to deny that I existed. If I say that
I do not exist, it must be false. But it might not have been
false. It is a fact that I exist, but not a necessary fact.

Thus neither 'I think' nor 'I exist' is a truth of logic: the
logical truth is only that I exist if I think. And we have seen
that even if they were truths of logic they would not for that
reason be indubitable. What makes them indubitable is their
satisfying a condition which Descartes himself does not make
explicit, though his argument turns upon it. It is that their
truth follows from their being doubted by the person who
expresses them. The sense in which I cannot doubt the statement that I think is just that my doubting it entails its truth:
and in the same sense I cannot doubt that I exist. There was
therefore no need for Descartes to derive '*sum*' from '*cogito*';
for its certainty could be independently established by the
same criterion.

But this certainty does not come to very much. If I start with the fact that I am doubting, I can validly draw the conclusion that I think and that I exist. That is to say, if there is such a person as myself, then there is such a person as myself, and if I think, I think. Neither does this apply only to me. It is obviously true of anyone at all that if he exists he exists and that if he thinks he thinks. What Descartes thought that he had shown was that the statements that he was conscious, and that he existed, were somehow privileged, that, for him at least, they were evidently true in a way which distinguished them from any other statements of fact. But this by no means follows from his argument. His argument does not prove that he, or anyone, knows anything. It simply makes the logical point that one sort of statement follows from another. It is of interest only as drawing attention to the fact that there are sentences which are used in such a way that if the person who employs them ever raises the question whether the statements which they express are true, the answer must be yes. But this does not show that these statements are in any way sacrosanct, considered in themselves.

Yet surely I can be certain that I am conscious, and that I exist. Surely my evidence for this could not be stronger than it is. But again it is not clear what is being claimed when it is said that these things are certain or that one can be certain of them. Perhaps only that I know that they are so, and of course I do. But these are not the only facts that I know, nor, as it sometimes appears to be suggested, is my knowing them a condition of my knowing anything else. It is conceivable that I should not have been self-conscious, which is to say that I should not know that I existed; but it would not follow that I could not know many other statements to be true. In theory, I could know any of the innumerable facts which are logically independent of the fact of my existing. I should indeed know them without knowing that I knew them, though not necessarily without knowing that they were known: my whole conception of knowledge would be impersonal. Perhaps this is a strange supposition, but it is not self-contradictory.

But while in the case of other facts which I may reasonably claim to know, it is at least conceivable that the evidence which I have for them should be even stronger than it is, surely the fact that I exist and the fact that I am conscious stand out for the reason that in their case the evidence is perfect. How could I possibly have better evidence than I do for believing that I am conscious, let alone for believing that I exist? This question is indeed hard to answer, but mainly because it seems improper in these cases to speak of evidence at all. If someone were to ask me How do you know that you are conscious? What evidence have you that you exist? I should not know how to answer him: I should not know what sort of answer was expected. The question would appear to be a joke, a parody of philosophical cautiousness. If it were seriously pressed, I might become indignant: What do you mean, how do I know that I exist? I am here, am I not, talking to you? If a 'philosophical' answer were insisted on, it might be said that I proved that I existed and that I was conscious by appealing to my experience. But not then to any particular experience. Any feeling or perception that I cared to instance would do equally well. When Hume looked for an impression of his self, he failed to find one: he always stumbled instead upon some particular perception.[3] He allowed that others might be luckier, but in this he was ironical. For the point is not that to have an experience of one's self is to perform a remarkably difficult feat of introspection: it is that there is nothing that would count as having an experience of one's self, that the expression 'having an experience of one's self' is one for which there is no use. This is not to say that people are not self-conscious, in the sense that they conceive of things as happening to themselves. It is that the consciousness of one's self is not one experience among others, not even, as some have thought, a special experience which accompanies all the others. And this is not a matter of psychology but of logic. It is a question of what self-consciousness is understood to mean.

If there is no distinctive experience of finding out that one is conscious, or that one exists, there is no experience at all

[3] David Hume, A *Treatise of Human Nature*, Book I, part IV, section VI.

of finding out that one is not conscious, or that one does not exist. And for this reason it is tempting to say that sentences like 'I exist', 'I am conscious', 'I know that I exist', 'I know that I am conscious' do not express genuine propositions. That Mr A exists, or that Mr A is conscious, is a genuine proposition; but it may be argued that it is not what is expressed by 'I exist' or 'I am conscious', even when I am Mr A. For although it be true that I am Mr A, it is not necessarily true. The word 'I' is not synonymous with 'Mr A' even when it is used by Mr A to refer to himself. That he is Mr A, or that he is identifiable in any other manner, is an empirical statement which may be informative not only to others, but also in certain circumstances to Mr A himself, for instance if he has lost his memory. It cannot therefore be reasoned that because one may succeed in expressing genuine propositions by replacing the 'I' in such sentences as 'I am conscious' or 'I exist' by a noun, or descriptive phrase, which denotes the person concerned, these sentences still have a factual meaning when this replacement is not made.

All the same it is not difficult to imagine circumstances in which they would have a use. 'I am conscious' might be said informatively by someone recovering from a swoon. If I had been presumed to be dead there might be a point in my proclaiming that I still existed. On recovering consciousness after some accident or illness, I might make this remark even to myself, and make it with a sense of discovery. Just as there are moments between sleep and waking when one may seriously ask oneself if one is awake, so there are states of semiconsciousness in which saying 'I exist' answers a genuine question. But what information does this answer give? If I have occasion to tell others that I exist, the information which they receive is that there exists a man answering to some description, whatever description it may be that they identify me by; it would not be the same in every case. But when I tell myself that I exist, I do not identify myself by any description: I do not identify myself at all. The information which I convey to myself is not that there exists a person of such and such a sort, information which might be false if I were mistaken about my own identity or character. Yet I am in fact a person of such and such a sort. There is nothing more to me than what can be discovered by listing the totality of the descriptions which I satisfy. This is merely an expression of the tautology that if a description is complete there is nothing left to be described. But can it not be asked what it is that one is describing? The answer is that this question makes sense only as a request for further description: it implies that the description so far given is incomplete, as in fact it always will be. But then if, in saying that I exist, I am not saying anything about a description's being satisfied, what can I be saying? Again it is tempting to answer that I am saying nothing.

Yet this would not be correct. Even when it is not doing duty for a description, nor coupled with one, the demonstrative 'I' may have a use. In the case which we envisaged, the case of a return to consciousness, it signals the presence of some experience or other. It does not, however, characterize this experience in any way. It merely points to the existence of whatever it is, in the given circumstances, that makes its own use possible. And since it is a contingent fact that any such situation does exist, the assertion which simply serves to mark it may be held to be informative. The sentence 'I exist', in this usage, may be allowed to express a statement which like other statements is capable of being either true or false. It differs, however, from most other statements in that if it is false it can not actually be made. Consequently, no one who uses these words intelligently and correctly can use them to make a statement which he knows to be false. If he succeeds in making the statement, it must be true.

It is, therefore, a peculiar statement; and not only peculiar but degenerate. It is degenerate in the way that the statements which are expressed by such sentences as 'this exists' or 'this is occurring now' are degenerate. In all these cases the verbs which must be added to the demonstratives to make a grammatical sentence are sleeping partners. The work is all done by the demonstrative: that the situation, to which it points, exists, or is occurring, is a condition of the demonstrative's use. It is for this reason that any statement of this sort which is actually expressed must be true. It is not neces-

sarily true, since the situation to which the demonstrative
points might not have existed; it is logically possible that the
condition for this particular use of the demonstrative should
not have obtained. It is, however, like an analytic statement
in that, once we understand the use of the demonstrative,
here functioning as subject, the addition of the predicate tells
us nothing further. Divorced from its context the whole statement has no meaning. Taken in context it is informative just
as drawing attention to whatever it may be that the demonstrative is used to indicate. It approximates, therefore, to a
gesture or to an ejaculation. To say 'I exist' or 'this is occurring now' is like saying 'look!' or pointing without words. The
difference is that, in the formulation of the indicative sentence, the existential claim is made explicit; and it is because
of this that the sentence may be said to express a statement,
whereas the ejaculation or the gesture would not: one does
not speak of ejaculations or gestures as being true or false.
But there is no difference in the information conveyed.

Thus we see that the certainty of one's own existence is
not, as some philosophers have supposed, the outcome of
some primary intuition, an intuition which would have the
distinctive property of guaranteeing the truth of the statement on which it was directed. It is indeed the case that if
anyone claims to know that he exists, or that he is conscious,
he is bound to be right. But this is not because he is then in
some special state of mind which bestows this infallibility
upon him. It is simply a consequence of the purely logical
fact that if he is in any state whatever it follows that he
exists; if he is in any conscious state whatever it follows that
he is conscious. He might exist without knowing it; he might
even be conscious without knowing it, as is presumably the
case with certain animals: there is at any rate no contradiction in supposing them to be conscious without supposing
them to be conscious of themselves. But, as we have seen, if
anyone does claim to know that he exists or that he is conscious, his claim must be valid, simply because its being valid
is a condition of its being made. This is not to say, however,
that he, or anyone, knows any description of himself, or his
state of consciousness, to be true. To know that one exists is

not, in this sense, to know anything about oneself any more than knowing that *this* exists is knowing anything about *this*. Knowing that I exist, knowing that this is here, is having the answer to a question which is put in such a form that it answers itself. The answer is meaningful only in its context, and in its context the condition of its being meaningful is its being true. This is the ground for saying that statements like 'I exist' are certain, but it is also the proof of their degeneracy: they have nothing to say beyond what is implied in the fact that they have a reference.

THE CERTAINTY OF THE *COGITO*

BERNARD WILLIAMS

I shall confine my discussion to the *cogito,* and to the formulation of some remarks about its certainty. I believe that
this question also has a connection with contemporary English philosophy. For one of the theses that have recurred most
frequently in discussions in Great Britain during the last half
century is that only logical truths are certain and any proposition that is not a logical truth but expresses some matter of
fact cannot be certain. This thesis, along with others, has
been subject to reappraisal; and a discussion centering on the
very special case of the *cogito* may, aside from its intrinsic
interest, throw some light on the more general problem: what
types of propositions may be taken to be certain.

I shall begin with one of the formulations of the *cogito:*

> And, observing that this truth "I think therefore I am"
> was so firm and so assured that the most extravagant
> suppositions of the skeptics could not shake it, I judged
> that I might accept it without scruple as the first princi-
> ple of the philosophy that I was seeking.[1]

I shall not enter into a discussion of all the disputed points
raised in Cartesian exegesis, which are more familiar to you
than to me.

Translation of a paper read at the Royaumont Conference on
Analytic Philosophy and published in *Cahiers de Royaumont, Philo-
sophie No IV: La Philosophie Analytique* (Paris: Les Éditions de
Minuit, 1962), pp. 40–57. By permission of the author and Les
Éditions de Minuit.

[1] *Discourse on Method,* Part IV, pp. 147–148. Quotations are
from the Pléiade edition (2nd ed.) with the page number(s) following.

There is one point, however, that cannot be avoided in a discussion bearing on the certainty of the *cogito*, or at least of the Cartesian *cogito*; namely, whether the proposition "I think therefore I am" is or is not an inference. The truth that emerges from the *cogito* and that Descartes takes as the foundation stone of the entire system he constructs is, most assuredly, "I exist"; but can we say that there is a logical relation between this proposition and the indubitable proposition "I think" such that Descartes, having reached the point where doubt can go no further, can, in formulating the latter, legitimately infer the former? Or is it, rather, the case that we cannot speak of a logical relation or a principle of inference leading from "I think" to "I exist" but that, in being forced to admit that I think, I am thereby forced to admit that I exist?—with the consequence that "I think therefore I am," in the misleading form of an inference, expresses in fact a single proposition, which is the exact point at which doubt is halted.

At first sight, the *cogito* certainly seems to be an inference, and Descartes indeed seems to speak of it as such. For example, there is the following sentence, a few lines farther on in the passage I quoted:

> [Seeing] that . . . from the very fact that I thought of doubting the truth of other things, *it followed* very evidently and very certainly that I was. . . .

Or again:

> . . . *to infer* that one exists from the fact that one doubts is something so simple and so natural of itself that anyone might have written it down.[2]

I am not unaware, however, that in other passages Descartes seems to deny that in the *cogito* we are concerned with an inference. On the authority of these texts, M. Gilson writes:

> Descartes's intention is not therefore in doubt, and it is usually not questioned. But critics and historians have

[2] Letter of 1640 (on St. Augustine). My emphasis in the two quotations.

often maintained that, no matter what Descartes's intention was, the *cogito* nonetheless was, and could not have been anything other than, an inference.[3]

But what exactly is being decided when someone says that the *cogito* is not an inference? The meaning of such a statement is perhaps not entirely clear. It may mean that the *cogito* is not a syllogistic inference—that it is not a syllogism with a major premise ("Everything that thinks exists") that is not expressed. This, I think, is what M. Gilson has in mind. But, even on this supposition, it would not follow that the *cogito* is not in any sense an inference. I shall defend the view that it is in fact a kind of inference, though not syllogistic in form. And I shall also contend that this is not just a plausible interpretation but Descartes's own understanding of the *cogito*.

Descartes was in fact concerned, on several occasions, to deny that the *cogito* is a syllogism with a suppressed major premise; notably, in this famous passage:

> When someone says, "I think, therefore I am, or I exist," he does not deduce his existence from his thinking by means of a syllogism but, by the mind's simple act of inspection, sees it as something that is self-evident. This is apparent from the fact that, if he deduced it by means of a syllogism, he would first have had to know the major premise, "Everything that thinks is or exists." But that, on the contrary, has been learned from the individual's awareness of himself—that he cannot be thinking unless he exists. For it is the nature of our mind to form general propositions from knowledge of particulars.[4]

It is significant that Descartes, in this passage, does not confine himself to denying that, from a *psychological* point of view, our access to the *cogito* is by a movement proceeding from major and minor premise to a conclusion. It is true that, in general, Descartes seems to consider the distinction between deduction and intuition as, at least in part, a distinc-

---

[3] *Discours de la Méthode, Commentaire,* p. 294.
[4] Replies to the Second Set of Objections, pp. 375–376.

tion that we should call psychological. Thus, in Rule III, he gives the impression of thinking that the question of knowing whether I can "determine the validity of a complex inference by intuition or by deduction" is tantamount to the question of knowing whether I can "conceive the whole chain of reasoning in a single act of the mind."[5] But here he clearly goes beyond the limits of psychology. For he indicates that, from a logical point of view, nothing would justify my using the supposed major premise in arriving at "I think therefore I am" since nothing would warrant my belief in the major premise if I did not already possess the certainty of the *cogito.*

Yet, if Descartes meant here that only after I have learned from my own case that my thinking involves my existence, can I then affirm the same of everything that thinks, his assertion would be a most peculiar one; and if we suppose that Descartes believed for one instant that, as a matter of logic, the proposition that everything that thinks exists can be established by *induction* from one's own case—and that he used this as an argument to deny that the *cogito* is a syllogism— we should be obliged to say that he was mistaken. Fortunately, this is not at all the case. Descartes says very clearly:

> When I said that the proposition "I think therefore I am" is the first and most certain to present itself to a person who conducts his thoughts in an orderly fashion, I was not thereby denying the necessity of prior knowledge of what thought, certainty, and existence are, and *that, in order to think, it is necessary to exist,* and other matters of this sort; but, because these notions are so simple that of themselves they do not give us knowledge of any existing thing, I did not think that they needed to be mentioned.[6]

Does this passage contradict the one I quoted before? Burman thought that it did and, in the course of his famous discussion, confronted Descartes with this objection. Descartes's reply offered little to reassure his interlocutor:

[5] Pp. 44–45.
[6] *Principles* I, 10, pp. 575. My emphasis.

Before reaching the conclusion "I think therefore I am," one can have knowledge of the major premise "Everything that thinks exists," since it is in reality prior to my conclusion and my conclusion depends on it. And this is the sense in which, in the *Principles*, the author says it precedes the conclusion, since implicitly it is always presupposed and prior. But I do not always have an express and explicit knowledge of its priority; and I do have prior knowledge of my conclusion in that I attend only to what I experience within myself, that is, to "I think therefore I am," while not attending, in similar fashion, to the general notion "Everything that thinks exists." We do not in fact, as I have pointed out, separate these propositions from particular things, but rather consider them in the particulars. It is in this sense that the passage cited must be understood.[7]

We might suppose that in this passage Descartes simply denies that on a psychological level the *cogito* takes the form of syllogistic reasoning. He seems, moreover, to have somewhat tempered his views on the relations between the general proposition and the singular proposition. We do not seem to be further along.

But surely the answer is to be found in the terms of the passage from the *Principles* quoted above, where he says that the notion that in order to think, it is necessary to exist does not give us "knowledge of any existing thing." This statement can be compared with another important passage in the *Principles*:

When we say that it is impossible for the same thing at the same time to be and not to be, that what has been done cannot be undone, that he who thinks cannot fail to be or exist while he thinks, and numerous other things of this sort, these are eternal truths and not things existing outside our thought. . . .[8]

In this passage Descartes quite unequivocally places the general principle of the *cogito* in the class of maxims or common notions—of eternal truths that we can know a priori to

[7] Conversation with Burman, pp. 1356–1357.
[8] *Principles* I, 49.

be true and that give us no knowledge of what exists nor indeed presuppose that something exists. Such is the status of the principle of the *cogito;* and it is precisely for this reason that the *cogito* is not a syllogism with a suppressed major premise. The major premise of an Aristotelian syllogism necessarily carries an existential presupposition; namely, that there exists at least one thing that falls under the definition of the subject term. To be in a position to assert that everything that thinks exists, I would, strictly speaking, have to know of the existence of at least one thinking thing. But this is just what I am supposed to discover in the *cogito,* and hence the difficulty of presupposing the general principle in using the *cogito.* The eternal truth "In order to think, it is necessary to exist" presupposes no existential proposition; but, by the same token, it cannot play the role of major premise in a syllogism.

It might be objected here that the major premise can be interpreted hypothetically as "If something thinks, it exists"; that is, as having a form compatible with its being an eternal truth. But do we really know exactly how this hypothetical proposition is to be understood? This question raises several difficulties that will help to show why, in a deeper sense, the *cogito* cannot be taken to be a syllogism or part of a syllogism. By contrast with what I believe is true of the preceding obstacle, there is no reason to assume here that Descartes was aware of these difficulties. They all turn on the idea that existence is not a predicate, and as there is every indication that Descartes thought the opposite, these difficulties would have had no meaning for him.

A rather mysterious remark of Kant's will perhaps help to explain this point. It is taken from a footnote in the Paralogisms, in the second edition of the *Critique of Pure Reason:*

> "I think" is, as I have said, an empirical proposition, and contains within itself the proposition "I exist." But I cannot assert: "Everything that thinks exists." For, in that case, the property of thought would make all beings that possess it necessary beings. The fact that I exist cannot therefore be inferred from the proposition "I think," as in Descartes's attempted demonstration—for it would

then have to be preceded by the major premise "Everything that thinks exists"—but the propositions in question are identical.[9]

Kant's interpretation of Descartes on this point seems to
be in every respect mistaken since, as we have just seen, it is
in exactly this sense that Descartes denies (or at least usually
denies) that the *cogito* is an inference. But what does Kant
mean by the remark that if we could say "Everything that
thinks exists," the property of thought would make all beings
that possess it necessary beings? Kant assumes, at the very
least, that the proposition "Everything that thinks exists" is
a necessary proposition; and, in a certain sense, he is quite
right. From this he infers that any being that thinks would
be a necessary being. *Prima facie*, there is a fallacy here, the
error consisting in an inference from (1) "It is necessary
that if *p*, then *q*" to the proposition (2) "If *p*, then it is
necessary that *q*"—*p* in this case standing for "Something
thinks" and *q* for "It exists." We cannot pass from "It is
necessary that anything that thinks exists" to "If a thing
thinks, it is necessary that it exists" or ". . . it exists necessarily" without committing a logical fallacy—a fallacy that
Kant may have committed in other places (for example, in
my opinion, in the Second Analogy). But I do not think
he commits it here. For a necessary being is a being whose
definition, taken in the sense of a simple description, implies
its existence. And, if the proposition "Everything that thinks
exists" is indeed a necessary proposition and, moreover,
"thought" or "thinking" is the description of a possible being,
then we can conceive of a being whose definition would imply existence—that is, a necessary being.

This amounts to saying that "Everything that thinks exists"
does not express a relation between two properties, as does,
for example, "Everything that eats breathes." And for just
this reason we may wonder whether the proposition is not
formulated in such a way as to lend itself to confusion.

Shall we say then with Kant that the proposition "I think"
"contains within itself" the proposition "I exist"? We should

---

[9] *Critique of Pure Reason*, B 422 n.: Paralogisms.

have to know what this means. Kant seems to have had in mind a thought expressed earlier by Spinoza:

> *Cogito ergo sum* est propositio, quae huic, *ego sum cogi-tans*, aequivalet.[10]

This would suggest that in the *cogito*—even if there is not, for Kant as for Spinoza, an inference in a strict sense—there may be an inference of a sort from *Ego sum cogitans* to *Ego sum* analogous to an inference that might be drawn from *Ego sum ambulans* to *Ego sum*—or, in English, from "I am walking" to "I am." In a sense, such inferences are possible; but the question to be raised is, by virtue of what principle? One thing is certain: we cannot infer *Ego sum* from *Ego sum ambulans* by virtue of a principle relating the whole to its parts, as we might infer "*p*" from "*p* and *q*."

That this procedure was, again, not the one proposed by Descartes in the *cogito* seems to emerge clearly from what Mme. Rodis-Lewis writes on the point:

> The Cartesian procedure is more complex: from an ini-tial intuition, *cogito* (sive *sum cogitans*), where the *sum* has only a predicative function, Descartes moves to an existential statement *ergo sum: sive existo;* he then makes explicit the reality so apprehended in *sum res cogitans*.[11]

There is, according to this account, a movement taking us from a predicative proposition to an existential proposi-tion, and it is based on a very general principle relating the two kinds of propositions. A great deal has been written about the exact nature of the relation in question, and I cannot enter into a thorough examination of the problem here. With regard to the point that interests us, it is enough to say that when we are concerned with a proposition of the form "f(a)," where f stands for the predicate and a for a proper name, a pronoun, or a definite description (leaving aside difficult cases), the proposition "f(a)" characteristically *presupposes*

---

[10] [" 'I think therefore I am' is a proposition equivalent to 'I am thinking.' "] *Renati Descartes Princ. Phil.*, I, Prolegomenon.
[11] *L'Individualité selon Descartes*, p. 96.

that there exists something corresponding to *a*. The relation
of presupposition appears to differ from that of implication
in this way: if *p* implies *q* and *q* is false, it follows that *p*
is also false, whereas if *p* presupposes *q* and *q* is false, then
p is neither true nor false.[12] Thus, if I say, "The man in the
garden is singing," and there is no one in the garden, what I
have said is neither true nor false—there is no subject of
which the proposition can be right or wrong. If we are prepared to accept a relation of presupposition of this nature,
it provides us with a kind of principle of inference; namely, if
p presupposes *q* and *p* is true, *q* must also be true. For since
"*p* presupposes *q*" means "*q* must be true for *p* to be either
true or false," it follows *a fortiori* that *q* must be true for *p*
to be true; in other words, if *p* is true, *q* is also true. And
this I take to be the principle of the *cogito*.

A possible objection to this line of reasoning is that even
if we admit that there is a logical relation of presupposition
between "f(a)," on the one hand, and "There exists something designated by 'a',", on the other, it does not follow
that we can extract from this relation anything of the nature
of a principle of *inference*. For it might be said that a principle of inference is a principle authorizing us to infer one
thing from another—say, "*q*" from "*p*." But to infer "*q*" from
"*p*" is to *come to know* "*q*" on the basis of "*p*"; and, in the
case that interests us, this is inconceivable. Anyone who
knows that "f(a)" is true (for example, who knows that the
man in the garden is singing) must already know that "a"
designates something (that is, that there is a man in the
garden); hence, it is impossible for me to *come to know* that
something is designated by "a" on the basis of the fact that
I know that "f(a)" is true. It follows from this that I cannot
infer the first proposition from the second, and so the relation of presupposition existing between these two propositions is not the basis of a principle of inference.

This objection points up a real difficulty—a difficulty of
which Descartes seems to have been aware in the case of the
cogito. I do not believe, however, that the objection is valid,

[12] P. T. Geach, "Russell's Theory of Descriptions," *Analysis*,
1949, and P. F. Strawson, "On Referring," *Mind*, 1950.

for it seems to confound psychological, or at any rate epistemological, and logical considerations. It is extremely useful
in logic to be able to say, for instance, that there is a principle allowing us to infer "*p*" from "*p* and *q*" even on the assumption that it is in fact impossible to know the truth of
"*p* and *q*" without first knowing the truth of "*p*." I do not
see why we should not also be justified in considering the
relation of presupposition between "I think" and "I exist"
as the basis of a principle of inference and hence of the *cogito*
itself in so far as it is an inference—not, of course, in the
sense of a syllogism with a suppressed major premise. If this
is correct, there appears to be a close relation between Descartes's "eternal truth" or "maxim" and a rule of language.
And language—we should not forget—has at no time been
eliminated by doubt: "Descartes, and even more his reader,
begins to meditate in a universe of existing discourse."[13]

So far we have at most established that it is not incorrect
to regard the *cogito* as an inference with an identifiable underlying principle. I shall return to this point later. But we are
now in a position to begin to probe more deeply into the
certainty of the *cogito* by examining its premise.

The first thing to be noted is that there is something particularly revealing, and very well suited to Descartes's purpose, in the use that he makes of the first person. "I" is
clearly a referring term. If I say, "You, I, he—we are all dark"
—which is to say "I, you, he—each of us is dark"—I have
clearly referred to three different persons. I have, as it were,
pointed them out one by one. What differentiates "I" from
"you" and from third-person pronouns is that, unlike the others, it appears to be incapable of failing in its mission of referring. I can say, "He is dark," and discover that there is no
one about and hence no one of whom I could say that he is
dark. I may say, "You . . ." and realize that I am talking to
a void. But "I" always points in the right direction and never
misses its mark. So long as it introduces an intelligible expression, the "I" used grammatically in uttering the expression invariably points to the speaker. The objection might be

---

[13] Merleau-Ponty, *Phénoménologie de la Perception*, p. 459.

raised that this rule admits of several exceptions. If, for example, a wall little by little exhibited cracks that might be taken to be the shape of the words "I am dying," we might read the series of marks as words forming an intelligible sentence and yet not on that account suppose that the "I" refers to a person. In parks in Great Britain and especially in the United States, I know there are baskets bearing the inscription "I am for your litter," an expression doubly impossible to translate into French because of the ambiguity of "I am for" and the use of the first person. We might try to render it, "Donnez-moi vos détritus; je suis là pour cela," thus retaining what is artificial and objectionable in the procedure of making a dustbin talk in order to give us a lesson in tidiness. But enough of this example, for we obviously know perfectly well what "I" stands for in this case. The example of the wall is more persuasive and more difficult. Everything depends on how we regard the marks on the wall. Certainly, we may see them simply as cracks that resemble writing and not take them to have meaning or to refer to anyone. Or we may, on the contrary, read a message in them, and this would mean that we think the wall is speaking or that a spirit is using the wall in an attempt to communicate something to us. Between these two extremes, we may find a place for the state of mind of someone who in fact reads the marks as words and sees an actual sentence there but none the less does not invoke spirits or believe in talking walls. We may, if we like, compare this state of mind with our attitude toward a *quotation* written on a blackboard. We may wonder how the sentence quoted might be used but not how, at this instant on the blackboard, it is being used. To summarize this point, we may say that "I" has this peculiar feature: if we consider a sentence containing it as an actual *assertion*, we cannot doubt that "I" refers to someone.

It seems to follow that if Descartes in his quest for certainty had uttered *any sentence whatever* containing the term "I" used correctly, he could equally well have concluded that he existed and "I think" in no way constitutes a privileged case. I am not of course the first to have raised this objection. To someone who objected, "Why not 'I breathe'?" Descartes's reply is very interesting:

> When someone says, "I breathe therefore I am," and purports to demonstrate his existence from the fact that breathing could not exist without it, he demonstrates nothing at all, for he would first have had to prove that it is true that he breathes, and this is impossible without also having proved that he exists. But, if he intends to demonstrate his existence from the feeling or opinion he has of breathing, in the sense that he judges it to be impossible that, even if this opinion should be false, he should have had it if he did not exist, his conclusion is sound. For then the thought of breathing occurs in the mind before the thought of his existing, and he cannot doubt that he has it while he has it. To say in this sense, "I breathe therefore I am," is nothing other than "I think therefore I am." And, if we examine other propositions from which we can in like manner prove our existence, we shall see that all of them come to the same thing.[14]

I believe that what Descartes is trying to point out in this passage is not what we might at first think. He seems to be saying this: it is possible to doubt that I breathe but not possible to doubt that I think. But what I am looking for in doubting is something that I cannot doubt is true, and this is that I think. It is from the certainty attained here that I infer that I exist. But, if this is what he is saying, we might object that it is of little importance whether "I breathe" is true or false; for, according to the principle of presupposition, the moment that "I breathe" is capable of being true or false, Descartes has the right to infer that he exists. What is important is that he should be able to assert that he breathes and not that it should be true that he breathes. But is this not just what Descartes wants to bring out? To be sure that he breathes, he would first have to identify himself with a body and assume certain things that doubt will not permit. The important point is that he is able to assert that he breathes, and it is his reflection on this assertion that brings

[14] Letter of March 1638, p. 1003. Cf. Replies to the Fifth Set of Objections (to Gassendi), p. 478.

him to his conclusion. But reflection on his assertion is nothing other than the recognition of *the fact that he thinks.* There is no need for the assertion to be made overtly—for it to stir the air or leave marks on paper—for doubt would attach to the marks and to the sounds. It is from considerations like these that Descartes reaches the conclusion that what is of consequence in any proposition in the first person and enables him to succeed in proving his existence is the fact that he is able to assert it, in the restricted sense of assertion involved in the very act of thinking it. And this leads him to say that any proposition that I may try to put in the place of *cogito* will, if it is to perform the same function, bring me back to *cogito.*

It is evidently necessary that the assertion "I think" turn out to be indubitable. For if it could be doubted that I was, in the limited sense of assertion, asserting something about myself, the principle of presupposition, together with the infallible power of "I" to refer, would not be enough to establish with certainty that I existed. But it is just this proposition that is indubitable. As I said earlier, the proposition that I am asserting something, in the sense of uttering sounds, is still vulnerable to doubt, at least by Cartesian criteria; but, in the sense that I am thinking something, it is not. This is because the proposition "I think" contains within it the very conditions of its truth. As Professor Ayer has said, "If anyone does claim to know that he exists or that he is conscious, his claim must be valid, simply because its being valid is a condition of its being made."[15] "I think" is, in a sense, the limiting case of a phenomenon that we find in propositions like "I am now speaking," "I am now taking notes," "I am now making a statement," etc. The first proposition is true if we are speaking. It is not true when written. Conversely, with the second. The third is true in all circumstances except those in which I merely entertain the proposition or say it to myself. And so on to "I think," which is true whether I entertain it, say it, take note of it in writing, or in general no matter what I do so long as I think of it.

---

[15] *The Problem of Knowledge,* p. 53, or p. 86 here.

For the mere fact that I consider any proposition at all is a sufficient condition of the truth of the statement that I think. But these are exactly the same conditions that, according to the principles I formulated, establish that "I" refers to someone.

None of this of course amounts to saying that "I think" or "I exist" is a logical truth or a tautology. It is, in a sense, perfectly clear that these propositions belong to a class of propositions that are true if they are asserted, conceived, etc., and not to the class of propositions that are true no matter what the facts may be. Unlike tautologies, they are not compatible with every state of affairs. It is not easy, however, to state this point precisely without falling into confusion. Someone might, for instance, raise the objection that in certain circumstances "I exist" or "I am thinking" might not be true, and it would be tempting to reply: "Yes, this would admittedly be so in circumstances in which we did not exist or we were not thinking." But are we concerned here with the same proposition? I was speaking before of "I"—not of "we" or of "you." The reply contains an apparent sophism, but it is not easy to say exactly what it is. This is a question that Professor Ayer discussed in a study of the *cogito* earlier than the one I quoted before:

> What makes this proposition ["I am not thinking"] appear self-contradictory is the use of the personal pronoun, as can be easily seen if one replaces the pronoun by a name or a description. If Descartes asserts that Descartes is not thinking, what he asserts is here again made false by his asserting it, but there is no temptation to suppose that the proposition "Descartes is not thinking" is self-contradictory. On the contrary, there is every reason to believe that it is at this moment true.[16]

This argument appears to rest on the following principle: if a sentence of the form "f(a)" is a contradiction in terms, and if "b" is an expression referring to the same thing as "a," it follows that "f(b)" is necessarily contradictory. But this principle is not acceptable. Consider the sentence "Descartes

[16] "Cogito, ergo Sum," *Analysis*, 1953.

was not Descartes." We may assume that it contains an internal contradiction. But now take any expression, such as "the tutor of Queen Christina," that also refers to Descartes, and substitute it for the second "Descartes" in the preceding proposition. We obtain the sentence "Descartes was not the tutor of Queen Christina," which may indeed be historically false but is nevertheless not contradictory. We have here an example of what Professor Quine very aptly called "referential opacity."[17] According to Leibniz's principle, I can, in any sentence of the form "f(a)," substitute "b" for "a" if "b" refers to the same thing as "a" without changing the truth value of the whole sentence—provided that the sentence occurs in its usual context. But I cannot perform this substitution if "f(a)" occurs in a context in which the sentence is—directly or indirectly—in quotation marks; for example, in "'f(a)' is a tautology." In this way Professor Ayer's argument fails, if I have interpreted what he says correctly.

But there are other ways to show that "I think" is not a tautology. We might adopt the definition of an analytic proposition that Waissman gives when he says it is a proposition that "can, by means of mere definitions, be turned into a truth of logic,"[18] and try to see whether, proceeding in this way, we are able to reduce "I think" to a formal logical truth. We find that it is impossible. For even if we were to stretch Descartes's conceptions to the point of having him say that "I" is defined as "a thinking thing" and if we then write "A thinking thing thinks" for "I think," the sentence would be a logical truth only if we take it in the sense of "Any thinking thing thinks." But clearly this would eliminate the very essence of what Descartes or anyone thinks he achieves with the "I" in writing "I think," namely, an implication of existence.

It does not seem, then, that the *cogito* is a tautology. It appears, rather, to be a kind of inference from one proposition that is certain to another and to be based not only on the

[17] W. V. Quine, "Reference and Modality," in *From a Logical Point of View* (Harvard University Press, 1954). Cf. G. Frege, "On Sense and Reference."
[18] "Analytic-Synthetic," *Analysis,* 1949 *et seq.*

principle of presupposition and the unique properties of the word "I" but also on the autonomy of "I think." Can we go further? Would it not be appropriate at this point to speak of the indefinable but persistent feeling that we experience before the absolute character of a certainty that encounters a sheer void and of our uneasiness before the idea that the exact point at which doubt is turned back is the point at which language itself is emptied of all content? It is very difficult to conceive what this "I" is that Descartes has proved to exist or what constitutes its existence. At this point Descartes addresses himself to the question and answers it. But can he turn to it only at this point? Should he not have answered it before? As he says elsewhere: "According to the laws of true logic, we should never ask of something *whether it is* unless we already know *what it is*. . . ."[19] If so, should we not conclude *a fortiori* that we ought not to assert of something that it is if we do not already know what it is?

We could not pretend to discuss the difficult problems at issue here without venturing into the philosophy of mind and an examination of methodic doubt. I shall instead make some concluding remarks—which will perhaps appear disconnected —about the problem of the content of the *cogito*.

I should first point out the ambiguity surrounding the word "I" when we read Descartes, which we also find in philosophers who raise questions of the sort "What do I know?" The "I" in sentences of this kind appears to be almost a stylistic sleight-of-hand. It tends to be used in a general and impersonal sense, and it is not of himself that a philosopher is for the most part thinking. It is the continuous use of this "I," however, that gives the world he describes its infrangible appearance. M. Merleau-Ponty has emphasized this aspect in Descartes:

> It is indeed a question of the I, but of an ideal I that is not properly mine nor Descartes's but the I of any thinking person.[20]

[19] Replies to the First Set of Objections, p. 348.
[20] *Op. cit.,* p. 459.

I am pleased to be able to note in passing a point of convergence between France and Great Britain, for the same aspect, with regard to its consequences for the interpretation of skeptical theses, has recently been pointed out by two of our philosophers.[21]

Leaving this aspect aside, however, consider simply Descartes's meditations and the point in these meditations at which we could say that the "I" in fact signified Descartes personally. We certainly could say that it did, but is this not because we know that it is Descartes in question and hence a philosopher answering to certain descriptions? But Descartes himself has eliminated these descriptions in his thinking in the course of his meditation on methodic doubt. What remained for him to think of himself? Was anything left? Here, we might be tempted to return to the "principle of presupposition." This principle, as you will recall, is that a proposition of the form "f(a)" "presupposes that there exists something designated by 'a'." The last part of the statement of the principle calls for more detailed examination at this point, for it does not specify the way in which the existential proposition comprised in the presupposition is to be formed. When the expression "a" is a descriptive expression, there is no problem, for we can form the existential proposition directly from "a." Thus, in the case of "The man in the garden is singing," the existential presupposition is "There is a man in the garden." But if the expression "a" is a proper name or a pronoun, we have a more complicated case. The existential presupposition of "Charles is in the garden" cannot be "There is (a) Charles," for this has no meaning. Similarly, in the case of "He is in the garden." In both cases we require an existential presupposition in which a description answering to the thing in question is substituted for the name or for the pronoun. This description, or an analogous paraphrase, constitutes an answer to the question "Who is (a)?" in the case of a person or "What is (a)?" in the case of a thing. If someone says to us, "Charles is in the garden," and then

---

[21] J. F. Thomson, "The Argument from Analogy," *Mind*, 1950, and S. N. Hampshire, "The Analogy of Feeling," *Mind*, 1951.

has no answer when we ask him, "Who is Charles?," we do not understand. In similar fashion, "he" calls for the question, "Who is he?" or more simply, "Who?" This question is answered by a description, like "the man over there," that can in turn be used in the statement of the existential presupposition.

If this is acceptable, the objection may be raised that in the *cogito* we have exactly the type of sentence in which the principle of presupposition cannot operate. For in itself the assertion "I exist" appears—if indeed it is only an appearance —to have no content unless we can fill the gap with a descriptive proposition as a substitute for "I." But Descartes in doubting has eliminated the possibility of giving any description at all of this kind. We may for this reason contend that the *cogito* presents an illegitimate application of the principle of presupposition, since the principle applies only if we can furnish a descriptive expression to "explain" a noun or pronoun and fill the gap in the existential proposition. And this condition is not satisfied in the present case.

It is not altogether clear, however, that this criticism applies to the use of the word "I" in the *cogito*. For, as Professor Ayer has pointed out, we can imagine cases in which "I am conscious" would have an intelligible sense even if the subject himself were unable to attach any descriptive expression to the "I"—cases of amnesia or of coming out of a coma, for example.[22] Also, "I" is admittedly less closely tied in a certain sense to descriptive expressions than "you" or third-person pronouns. And the reason for this is clear. "I," unlike other pronouns, *cannot fail to refer to a certain person*, as we have already seen. But the descriptive proposition, which indicates exactly the thing that the speaker means, is needed just to eliminate any possibility of confusion among a number of things that he may have in mind when he uses a pronoun. Since in the case of "I" there can be no possible equivocation and since the word cannot fail to refer, the need of a description is therefore less great.

But even if we were disposed to accept "I think" in the

[22] *The Problem of Knowledge,* pp. 50–51, or pp. 84–85 here.

case in which no satisfactory explanation of what "I" stands for is possible, we might still be in doubt about "I exist" or "I am" in the sense of "I exist." For if the meaning of "exist" is to be clear, we must be able to replace it with "There exists a . . ." which in turn has meaning only if it is followed by a descriptive expression. This might lead us to think that there is always something paradoxical in saying "I exist," and the paradoxical character will perhaps appear more clearly if we again invoke the principle of presupposition. If the use of referring words like "I" presupposes the existence of what is designated, the presupposition at work in the case of "I" in "I exist" is such that the proposition will presuppose itself. A condition of its being true will be that it was already true— a condition that seems to create a certain uneasiness from a logical point of view. It would be an exaggeration to say that we can never attach the least meaning to "I exist." I indeed can if I already know in addition a certain number of descriptive propositions about myself, and it is to these propositions that I appeal in giving content to what I say when I say, "I exist."

Nevertheless, it must be said—at least I shall for my part say it—that all these reasons taken together do not succeed in persuading me that Descartes's conclusion is lacking in sense, nor even that in its logical form it is, strictly speaking, incorrect. We should, rather, apply ourselves to attaining a deeper understanding of the way in which the *cogito* does violence to the principle of presupposition in the use of "I." As we have seen, "I" has the characteristic of referring infallibly to the person who uses it in speaking; but "I" fulfills this unique function only by isolating the speaker and detaching him from others and from the world. In a solipsistic universe, in which nothing and no one exists except in me and "for me," what function can it fulfill? None, for the "I" is ubiquitous. There is nothing, nor can there be anything, from which it is to be distinguished. Yet it is in this way that the world appears to Descartes at the crucial point at which the *cogito* is situated.

It is in this direction, I believe, that we must look for a

deeper examination of the *cogito*. I must content myself here with indicating the general course of such an investigation. To undertake it would lead me far beyond the limits of this discussion.

COGITO, ERGO SUM:
INFERENCE OR PERFORMANCE?

JAAKKO HINTIKKA

1. *Cogito, ergo sum as a problem.* The fame (some would say the notoriety) of the adage *cogito, ergo sum* makes one expect that scholarly industry has long since exhausted whatever interest it may have historically or topically. A perusal of the relevant literature, however, fails to satisfy this expectation. After hundreds of discussions of Descartes's famed principle we still do not seem to have any way of expressing his alleged insight in terms which would be general and precise enough to enable us to judge its validity or its relevance to the consequences he claimed to draw from it. Thirty years ago Heinrich Scholz wrote that there not only remain many important questions concerning the Cartesian dictum unanswered but that there also remain important questions unasked.[1] Several illuminating papers later, the situation still seems essentially the same today.

2. *Some historical aspects of the problem.* This uncertainty of the topical significance of Descartes's dictum cannot but reflect on the discussions of its historical status. The contemporaries were not slow to point out that Descartes's prin-

The Philosophical Review, Vol. LXXI, No. 1, Jan. 1962, pp. 3–32. Reprinted with the permission of the author and *The Philosophical Review*. The paper is as revised and reprinted in *Meta*-Meditations: *Studies in Descartes*, Alexander Sesonske and Noel Fleming, eds. (Belmont, California: Wadsworth Publishing Company, Inc., 1965) pp. 50–76.

[1] Heinrich Scholz, "Über das Cogito, ergo sum," *Kant-Studien*, XXXVI (1931), 126–147.

ciple had been strikingly anticipated by St. Augustine. Although later studies have unearthed other anticipations,[2] notably in Campanella and in the Schoolmen, scholars still seem to be especially impressed by Descartes's affinity with St. Augustine, in spite of his unmistakable attempts to minimize the significance of Augustine's anticipation. It cannot be denied, of course, that the similarities are striking. One may wonder, however, whether they are all there is to the matter. Perhaps there are also dissimilarities between Descartes and Augustine important enough to justify or at least to explain the one's reluctance to acknowledge the extent of the other's anticipation. But we cannot tell whether there is more to Descartes's *cogito, ergo sum* than there is to St. Augustine's similar argument before we can tell exactly what there is to the *cogito* argument.

If there are important differences between Descartes and his predecessors, the question will also arise whether some of the anticipations are closer than others. For instance, Descartes could have found the principle in St. Thomas Aquinas as well as in St. Augustine. Which of the two saints comes closer to the *cogito, ergo sum?*

3. *What is the relation of* cogito *to* sum? What kind of topical questions does *cogito, ergo sum* give rise to? One of the most important questions is undoubtedly that of the logical form of Descartes's inference. Is it a formally valid inference? If not, what is logically wrong about it?

But there is an even more fundamental question than these. Does Descartes's dictum really express an inference? That it does is suggested by the particle *ergo*. According to Descartes, however, by saying *cogito, ergo sum* he does not logically (syllogistically) deduce *sum* from *cogito* but rather perceives intuitively ("by a simple act of mental vision") the

---

[2] See e.g. L. Blanchet, *Les antécédents du "Je pense, donc je suis"* (Paris, 1920); Étienne Gilson, *Études sur le rôle de la pensée médiévale dans la formation du système cartésien (Études de philosophie médiévale, XIII)* (Paris, 1930), 2d pt., ch. ii, and the first appendix; Heinrich Scholz, "Augustinus und Descartes," *Blätter für deutsche Philosophie*, V (1932), 406–423.

self-evidence of *sum*.[3] Similarly, Descartes occasionally says that one's own existence is intuitively obvious without bringing in *cogito* as a premise.[4] Sometimes he intimates that his "first principle" is really the existence of his mind—and not the principle *cogito, ergo sum*, by means of which this existence is apparently deduced.[5] Once he formulates the *cogito* principle as *ego cogitans existo* without using the word *ergo* at all.[6]

But if it is true that the Cartesian dictum does not express an inference, equally perplexing questions are bound to arise. Not only is the particle *ergo* then misplaced; the word *cogito* is likewise out of place in a sentence which only serves to call attention to the self-evidence of *sum*.

But is the word *cogito* perhaps calculated to express the fact that thought is needed for grasping that *sum* is intuitively evident? Was it perhaps an indication of the fact that intuition was not for Descartes an irrational event but an act of the thinking mind, an "intellectual intuition," as it has been aptly expressed?[7] Even if this is part of the meaning of the word, the question will remain why Descartes wanted to stress the fact in connection with this particular insight. The same point would equally well apply to most of the other propositions of the Cartesian system; and yet Descartes does not say, for example, *cogito, ergo Deus est* in the way he says *cogito, ergo sum*.

Clearly the word *cogito* must have some further function in Descartes's sentence. Even if the sentence did not express a syllogistic inference, it expressed something sufficiently like

[3] *Œuvres de Descartes*, published by C. Adam and P. Tannery (Paris, 1897–1913), VII, 140; *The Philosophical Works of Descartes*, trans. by E. S. Haldane and G. R. T. Ross (London, 1931), II, 38. In the sequel, these editions will be referred to as AT and HR, respectively, with Roman numerals referring to volumes. Normally I shall not follow Haldane and Ross's translation, however; I shall make use of the existing translations (notably of those by N. Kemp Smith and by Anscombe and Geach) rather eclectically.

[4] AT X, 368; HR I, 7.

[5] AT IV, 444; AT VII, 12; HR I, 140.

[6] AT VII, 481; HR II, 282.

[7] L. J. Beck, *The Method of Descartes* (Oxford, 1952), ch. iv.

an inference to make Descartes call his sentence a reasoning (*ratiocinium*),[8] refer to expressing it as inferring (*inferre*),[9] and call *sum* a conclusion (*conclusio*).[10] As Martial Gueroult has trenchantly summed up the problem: "1° Descartes se refuse à considérer le *Cogito* comme un raisonnement. . . . 2° Pourquoi s'obstine-t-il alors au moins à trois reprises (*Inquisitio veritatis, Discours, Principes*) à présenter le *Cogito* sous la forme qu'il lui dénie?"[11]

Since the word *cogito* is not dispensable and since it is not just a premise from which the conclusion *sum* is deduced, the relation of the two becomes a problem. One of the main objectives of this essay is to clear up their relation.

4. Cogito, ergo sum *as a logical inference.* But can we be sure that Descartes's dictum does not express a logical inference? In many respects it seems plausible to think that it does. Its logical form seems quite easy to define. In the sentence "I think" an individual receives an attribute; for a modern logician it is therefore of the form "$B(a)$." In the sentence "I am," or "I exist," this same individual is said to exist. How can one represent such a sentence formally? If Quine is right in claiming that "to be is to be a value of a bound variable," the formula "$(Ex)\ (x = a)$" serves the purpose. And even if he is not right in general, in this particular case his claim is obviously justified: "a exists" and "there exists at least one individual identical with a" are clearly synonymous. Descartes's dictum therefore seems to be concerned with an implication of the form

$$(1) \qquad B(a) \supset (Ex)\ (x = a).$$

[8] AT X, 523; HR I, 324.

[9] AT VII, 352; HR II, 207; cf. AT III, 248.

[10] *Principia philosophiae* I, 9; AT VIII, 7; HR I, 222; cf. AT II, 37, and AT V, 147.

[11] Martial Gueroult, "Le *Cogito* et la notion 'pour penser il faut être,'" *Travaux du IXᵉ Congrès International de philosophie (Congrès Descartes)* (Paris, 1937; reprinted as the first appendix to Gueroult's *Descartes selon l'ordre des raisons*, Paris, 1953, II, 307–312). See p. 308.

Descartes perceives that he thinks; hence he obtains the premise $B(a)$. If (1) is true, he can use *modus ponens* to conclude that he exists. Those who want to interpret the *Cogito* as a logical inference may now claim that (1) is in fact true, and even logically provable; for is not

$$B(a) \supset (Ex) (x = a \,\&\, B(x))$$

a provable formula of our lower functional calculi? And does not this formula entail (1) in virtue of completely unproblematic principles? It may seem that an affirmative answer must be given to these questions, and that Descartes's argument is thus easily construed as a valid logical inference.

Views of this general type have a long ancestry. Gassendi already claimed that *ambulo, ergo sum*, "I walk, therefore I am," is as good an inference as *cogito, ergo sum*.[12] It is obvious that on the interpretation just suggested, Gassendi will be right. The alleged provability of (1) does not depend on the attribute "*B*" at all. The gist of Descartes's argument is on the present view expressible by saying that one cannot think without existing; and if (1) is an adequate representation of the logical form of this principle, one can indeed equally well say that one cannot walk without existing.

This already makes the interpretation (1) suspect. In this reply to Gassendi, Descartes denies that *ambulo, ergo sum* is comparable with *cogito, ergo sum*.[13] The reasons he gave are not very clear, however. A part of the burden of his remarks is perhaps that although the inferences *ambulo, ergo sum* and *cogito, ergo sum* are parallel—as being both of the form (1)—their premises are essentially different. *Ambulo* is not an indubitable premise in the way *cogito* may be claimed to be.

But even if we make this allowance, there remain plenty of difficulties. As we saw, Descartes sometimes denies that in the *cogito* argument *sum* is deduced from *cogito*. But on the view we are criticizing the argument is a deduction. The view is therefore unsatisfactory.

12 In his objections to the *Second Meditation* (AT VII, 258–259; HR II, 137).
13 AT VII, 352; HR II, 207.

It is also unsatisfactory because it does not help us to understand the role of the *cogito* argument in the Cartesian system. In so far as I can see, it does not, for example, help us to appreciate the consequences Descartes wanted to draw from his first and foremost insight.

The gravest objection, however, still remains to be made. It may be shown that the provability of (1) in the usual systems of functional calculus (quantification theory) has nothing to do with the question whether thinking entails existence. An attempt to interpret Descartes's argument in terms of the provability of (1) is therefore bound to remain fruitless.

By this I mean the following: if we have a closer look at the systems of logic in which (1) can be proved, we soon discover that they are based on important *existential presuppositions*, as I have elsewhere called them.[14] They make more or less tacit use of the assumption that all the singular terms with which we have to deal really refer to (designate) some actually existing individual.[15] In our example this amounts to assuming that the term which replaces *a* in (1) must not be empty. But since the term in question is "I," this is just another way of saying that I exist. It turns out, therefore, that we in fact decided that the sentence "I exist" is true when we decided that the sentence "I think" is of the form $B(a)$ (for the purposes of the usual systems of functional logic).[16] That we were then able to infer (Ex) $(x = a)$ from $B(a)$ is undoubtedly true, but completely beside the point.

It is possible to develop a system of logic which dispenses

[14] In "Existential Presuppositions and Existential Commitments," *Journal of Philosophy*, LVI (1959), 125–137.

[15] All the singular terms (e.g. names or pronouns) which in an application may be substituted for a free individual variable are assumed to do so; and as a consequence all the free individual variables have to behave like singular terms which really possess a reference (or "bearer," vulgarly "referent").

[16] Cf. Leibniz' incisive remark: "And to say *I think, therefore I am,* is not properly to prove existence by thought, since to think and to be thinking is the same thing; and to say, I am thinking, is already to say, *I am*" (*Nouveaux Essais,* tr. by A. G. Langley (La Salle, Ill., 1949), IV, 7, sec. 7).

with the existential presuppositions.[17] If in such a system we could infer "I exist" from "I think"—i.e. (Ex) $(x = a)$ from $B(a)$—it would be highly relevant to the question whether thinking implies existence in Descartes's sense. But this we cannot do. The truth of a sentence of the form (1) turns entirely on existential presuppositions. If they are given up, the provability of (1) goes by the board.

My point may perhaps be illustrated by means of an example constructed for us by Shakespeare. Hamlet did think a great many things; does it follow that he existed?

5. *Descartes's temptation.* In spite of all this, there are passages in Descartes which seem to support the interpretation under criticism. I do not want to deny that it expresses *one* of the things Descartes had more or less confusedly in mind when he formulated his famous dictum. But it is important to realize that this interpretation is defective in important respects. It does not help to elucidate in any way some of Descartes's most explicit and most careful formulations. It is at best a partial interpretation.

One can see why some interpretation like the one we have been criticizing attracted Descartes. It gave him what must have seemed a very useful way of defending his own doctrines and of silencing criticism. He could always ask: How can it possibly be true of someone that he thinks unless he exists? And if you challenge the premise that he is thinking (why cannot the all-powerful *malin génie* make it appear to him that he is thinking?), Descartes could have replied that in a sense the premise is redundant. He could have resorted to some such argument as the following: If I am right in thinking that I exist, then of course I exist. If I err in thinking that I exist or if I as much as doubt whether I exist, then I must likewise exist, for no one can err or doubt without existing. In any case I must therefore exist: *ergo sum.*

This neat argument is a *petitio principii,* however, as you may perhaps see by comparing it with the following similar argument: Homer was either a Greek or a barbarian. If he was a Greek, he must have existed; for how could one be a Greek without existing? But if he was a barbarian, he likewise must have existed. Hence he must have existed in any case.

The latter argument is obviously fallacious; the celebrated Homeric question cannot be solved on paper. By the same token, the former argument is also fallacious.[18]

Did Descartes realize that it is misguided to represent his insight in the way we have been discussing? It is very difficult to tell. Certainly he never realized it fully. He seems to have realized, however, that on this interpretation the validity of his argument depends essentially on existential presuppositions. For when he tried to present his fundamental doctrines in a deductive or "geometrical" form, he tried to formulate these presuppositions in so many words by saying that "we can conceive nothing except as existent (*nisi sub ratione existentis*)" (AT VII, 166; HR II, 57). This statement is all the more remarkable since it prima facie contradicts what Descartes says in the *Third Meditation* about "ideas . . . considered only in themselves, and not as referred to some other thing," namely that "they cannot, strictly speaking, be false." It also contradicts the plain fact that we can think of (mentally consider) unicorns, or Prince Hamlet, without thereby committing ourselves to maintaining that they exist.

The fact also remains that Descartes resorted to the interpretation we have been criticizing mainly in his more popular writings. As Gueroult noticed, he does not resort to it in the *Meditationes*. His most explicit use of it occurs in *Recherche de la vérité*, in a dialogue whose didactic character has been particularly emphasized by Ernest Cassirer.[19] Des-

[18] But maybe you are not convinced; maybe you feel that the question of Descartes's own existence is essentially different from the question of Homer's existence. If so, you are right. I have not wanted to deny that there is a difference, and an important one. All I am saying is that the reconstruction we are considering does not bring out this difference.

[19] *Descartes: Lehre, Persönlichkeit, Wirkung* (Stockholm, 1939), p. 126.

cartes's most careful formulations of the *cogito* argument, notably those in the *Meditationes de prima philosophia*, seem to presuppose a different interpretation of the argument.

    6. *Existential inconsistency.* In order to understand this second interpretation of the *Cogito* we have to have a closer look at the logic of Descartes's famed argument. Descartes's formulations in the *Meditationes* and elsewhere suggest that his result may be expressed by saying that it was impossible for him to deny his existence. One way in which Descartes could have tried to (but did not) deny this would have been to say, "Descartes does not exist." As a preliminary to our study of Descartes's first-person sentence *cogito, ergo sum* we shall inquire into the character of this third-person sentence. The reasons why Descartes could not have maintained the latter will turn out to be closely related to the reasons why he asserted the former, if I am right.

    What, then, are these reasons? What general characteristic of the sentence "De Gaulle does not exist" makes it awkward for De Gaulle to assert it?[20] I shall try to formulate this general characteristic by saying that it is *existentially inconsistent* for De Gaulle to assert (to utter) this sentence. The notion of existential inconsistency may be defined as follows; let p be a sentence and a a singular term (e.g. a name, a pronoun, or a definite description). We shall say that p is *existentially inconsistent for the person referred to by a to utter* if and only if the longer sentence

(2)   "*p*; and *a* exists"

is inconsistent (in the ordinary sense of the word). In order to avoid our own objections we must of course require that the notion of ordinary inconsistency which is used in the definition involves no existential presuppositions. Provided that this is the case, we may write (2) more formally as

(2)′   "$p \,\&\, (Ex)\,(x=a).$"

[20] My example is inspired by his predilection for referring to himself in the third person.

(As the informed reader has no doubt already noticed, we should really use quasi quotes instead of double quotes in (2) and (2)'.)

A trivial reformulation of the definition shows that the notion of existential inconsistency really formulates a general reason why certain statements are impossible to defend although the sentences by means of which they are made may be consistent and intelligible. Instead of saying that (2) is inconsistent, we could have said that p entails "a does not exist" (without the use of any existential presuppositions but otherwise in the ordinary sense of entailment). Uttering such a sentence, p, will be very awkward for the bearer of a: it means making a statement which, if true, entails that its maker does not exist.

It is important to realize that the ills of such *statements* cannot be blamed on the *sentences* by means of which they are made.[21] In fact, the notion of existential inconsistency cannot be applied at all to sentences. As we defined the notion, it is a relation between a sentence and a singular term rather than a property of sentences. The notion of existential inconsistency, however, can often be applied to statements in a fairly natural sense. In order to specify a statement we have to specify (*inter alia*) the sentence uttered (say, q) and its utterer. If the latter refers to himself by means of the singular term b when he makes his statement,

[21] It may be worth while to recall here the distinction between a sentence, an utterance, and a statement. A sentence is of course a grammatical entity that involves no reference to any particular utterer or any particular time of utterance. An utterance is an event (a speech-act) that may be specified by specifying the uttered sentence, the speaker, and the occasion on which he makes his utterance.

Utterances of declarative sentences (with prima-facie fact-stating intent) are typical examples of *statements*. (The term does not seem especially happy, but I shall retain it because it appears to be rather widespread.) A statement is an event (an act) occurring in some particular context. Usually it is a speech-act of a certain kind, but we shall not insist on that. For our purposes a statement may equally well be made, e.g. by writing a sentence. *Any* act will do which is prima facie designed to serve the same purposes as the act of uttering a declarative sentence with the intention of conveying bona fide information.

we may say that the notion applies to the statement if and
only if it applies to q in relation to b.

A simple example will make the situation clear. The *sentences* "De Gaulle does not exist" and "Descartes does not
exist" are not inconsistent or otherwise objectionable any
more than the moot sentence "Homer does not exist." None
of them is false for logical reasons alone. What would be (existentially) inconsistent would be the attempt of a certain
man (De Gaulle, Descartes, or Homer, respectively) to use
one of these sentences to make a statement. Uttered by somebody else, the sentences in question need not have anything
wrong or even strange about them.

It lies close at hand to express this important feature of
the notion of existential inconsistency by means of a term
which has recently enjoyed wide currency. The inconsistency
(absurdity) of an existentially inconsistent statement can in
a sense be said to be of *performatory* (performative) character. It depends on an act or "performance," namely on a
certain person's act of uttering a sentence (or of otherwise
making a statement); it does not depend solely on the means
used for the purpose, that is, on the sentence which is being
uttered. The sentence is perfectly correct as a sentence, but
the attempt of a certain man to utter it assertively is curiously
pointless. If one of these days I should read in the morning
paper, "There is no De Gaulle any more," I could understand what is being said. But no one who knows Charles de
Gaulle could help being puzzled by these words if they were
uttered by De Gaulle himself; the only way of making sense
of them would be to give them a nonliteral meaning.

We can here see how the existential inconsistency of De
Gaulle's fictional utterance (as well as the inconsistency of
other existentially inconsistent statements) manifests itself.
Normally a speaker wants his hearer to believe what he says.
The whole "language-game" of fact-stating discourse is based
on the assumption that this is normally the case. But nobody
can make his hearer believe that he does not exist by telling
him so; such an attempt is likely to have the opposite result.
The pointlessness of existentially inconsistent statements is
therefore due to the fact that they automatically destroy one

of the major purposes which the act of uttering a declarative sentence normally has. ("Automatically" means here something like "for merely logical reasons.") This destructive effect is of course conditional on the fact that the hearer knows who the maker of the statement is, that is, that he identifies the speaker as the same man the uttered sentence is about.

In a special case a self-defeating attempt of this kind can be made without saying or writing anything or doing anything comparable. In trying to make *others* believe something I must normally do something which can be heard or seen or felt. But in trying to make *myself* believe something there is no need to say anything aloud or to write anything on paper. The performance through which existential inconsistency arises can in this case be merely an attempt to think—more accurately, an attempt to make oneself believe—that one does not exist.[22]

This transition from "public" speech-acts to "private" thought-acts, however, does not affect the essential features of their logic. The reason why Descartes's attempt to *think* that he does not exist necessarily fails is for a logician exactly the same as the reason why his attempt to tell one of his contemporaries that Descartes did not exist would have been bound to fail as soon as the hearer realized who the speaker was.

7. *Existentially inconsistent sentences.* It can be seen that we are approaching Descartes's famous dictum. In order to reach it we have to take one more step. We have found that the notion of existential inconsistency is primarily applicable to statements (e.g. declarative utterances) rather than to sen-

---

[22] This means, in effect, that Descartes arrives at his first and foremost insight by playing for a moment a double role: he appears as his own audience. It is interesting and significant that Balz, who for his own purposes represents Descartes's quest as a dialogue between "Cartesius, who voices Reason itself," and "René Descartes the Everyman," finds that they both "conspire in effecting this renowned utterance," the *cogito ergo sum*, wherefore "in some sense, its meaning is referable both to Cartesius and René Descartes." See Albert G. A. Balz, *Descartes and the Modern Mind* (New Haven, 1952), pp. 89–90.

tences. In a sense, it may of course be defined for sentences, too, namely by making it relative to a term (name, pronoun, or definite description) occurring therein. This is in fact what we did when we first introduced the notion; we said *inter alia* that the *sentence* "De Gaulle does not exist" is existentially inconsistent for De Gaulle (i.e. for the person referred to by "De Gaulle") to utter. Sometimes it may even be possible to omit the specification "for . . . to utter," namely when the intended speaker can be gathered from the context.

In a frequently occurring special case such an omission is not only natural but almost inevitable. It is the case in which the speaker refers to himself by means of the first-person singular pronoun "I." This pronoun inevitably refers to whoever happens to be speaking. The specification "inconsistent for . . . to utter" therefore reduces to the tautology "inconsistent for whoever happens to be speaking to utter," and may therefore be omitted almost always. In a special case, the notion of existential inconsistency may therefore be defined for sentences *simpliciter* and not only for sentences thought of as being uttered by some particular speaker. These are the sentences which contain a first-person singular pronoun. The existential inconsistency of such a sentence will mean that its utterer cannot add "and I exist" without contradicting himself implicitly or explicitly.

There are purposes, however, for which it may be misleading to forget the specification. Forgetting it may be dangerous since it leads one to overlook the important similarities which obtain between existentially inconsistent *sentences* and existentially inconsistent *statements*. In a perfectly good sense, existentially inconsistent sentences are all right as sentences. They may be said to be consistent and sometimes even significant (e.g. when they occur as parts of more complicated sentences). According to their very definition, existentially inconsistent sentences are not so much inconsistent as such as absurd for anyone to utter. Their (existential) inconsistency is therefore of performatory character exactly in the same sense as that of the existentially inconsistent statements. The only difference between the two lies in the fact that the latter are inconsistent for some particular man to make while the former are inconsistent for anyone to utter. The inconsistency of existentially inconsistent sentences means that whoever tries to make somebody (anybody) believe them, by so doing, helps to defeat his own purpose.[23] Such an attempt may take the form of uttering the sentence assertively; or it may take the form of trying to persuade oneself of the truth of the sentence in question.

In the same way as existentially inconsistent sentences defeat themselves when they are uttered or thought of, their negations verify themselves when they are expressly uttered or otherwise professed. Such sentences may therefore be called existentially self-verifying. The simplest example of a sentence of this kind is "I am," in Descartes's Latin *ego sum, ego existo.*

8. *Descartes's insight.* Now we have reached a point where we can express precisely the import of Descartes's insight (or at least one of its most important aspects). It seems to me that the most interesting interpretation one can give to it is to say that Descartes realized, however dimly, the existential inconsistency of the sentence "I don't exist" and therefore the existential self-verifiability of "I exist." *Cogito, ergo sum* is only one possible way of expressing this insight. Another way actually employed by Descartes is to say that the sentence *ego sum* is intuitively self-evident.

We can now understand the relation of the two parts of the *cogito, ergo sum* and appreciate the reasons why it cannot be a logical inference in the ordinary sense of the word. What is at stake in Descartes's dictum is the status (the indubitability) of the sentence "I am." (This is shown particularly clearly by the formulations of the *Second Meditation.*) Contrary appearances notwithstanding, Descartes does not demonstrate this indubitability by deducing *sum* from *cogito.* On the other hand the sentence "I am" ("I exist") is not by itself logically true, either. Descartes realizes that its indubitability results from an act of thinking, namely from an at-

[23] For this reason it might be more appropriate to call them (existentially) *self-defeating* than (existentially) *inconsistent.*

tempt to think the contrary. The function of the word *cogito*
in Descartes's dictum is to refer to the thought-act through
which the existential self-verifiability of "I exist" manifests
itself. Hence the indubitability of this sentence is not strictly
speaking perceived *by means of* thinking (in the way the indubitability of a demonstrable truth may be said to be);
rather, it is indubitable *because* and *in so far as* it is actively
thought of. In Descartes's argument the relation of *cogito* to
sum is not that of a premise to a conclusion. Their relation
is rather comparable with that of a *process* to its *product*.
The indubitability of my own existence results from my
thinking of it almost as the sound of music results from playing it or (to use Descartes's own metaphor[24]) light in the
sense of illumination (*lux*) results from the presence of a
source of light (*lumen*).

The relation which the particle *ergo* serves to express in
Descartes's sentence is therefore rather peculiar.[25] Perhaps
it would have been less misleading for Descartes to say, "I am
in that I think," or "By thinking I perceive my existence,"
than to say, "I think, therefore I am." It may be worth noting
that one of our formulations was closely anticipated by St.
Thomas Aquinas when he wrote: "Nullus potest cogitare se
non esse cum assensu: in hoc enim quod cogitat aliquid, per-
cipit se esse" (*De veritate*, X, 12, *ad* 7). The peculiarity of
this relation explains Descartes's vacillation in expressing it
in that he sometimes speaks of the *Cogito* as an inference
and sometimes as a realization of the intuitive self-evidence
of its latter half.

[24] See his letter to Morin, dated July 13, 1638 (AT II, 209).
[25] Martial Gueroult has again neatly located the source of trouble
by calling our attention to the peculiarities of this relation. He has
realized that Descartes's dictum does not (merely) express a logical
relation between thinking and existing but that it is concerned with
an additional "fact" or "act" ("le fait ou l'acte," "le fait brut de
l'existence donnée") which is just what is needed to show the certainty of my existence. However, his explanations leave the status of
this fact or act (which cannot be an ordinary fact given to us by our
senses or by introspection) rather vague. Nor does Gueroult realize
that the logical aspect of Descartes's insight is in principle completely
dispensable. See Gueroult's *Descartes*, II, 310.

Similarly we may now appreciate the function of the word *cogito* in Descartes's sentence as well as his motives in employing it. It serves to express the performatory character of Descartes's insight; it refers to the "performance" (to the act of thinking) through which the sentence "I exist" may be said to verify itself. For this reason, it has a most important function in Descartes's sentence. It cannot be replaced by any arbitrary verb. The performance (act) through which the existential self-verifiability is manifested cannot be any arbitrary human activity, contrary to what Gassendi claimed. It cannot be an act of walking or an act of seeing. It cannot even be an instance of arbitrary mental activity, say of willing or of feeling. It must be just what we said it is: an attempt to think in the sense of making myself believe (an attempt to think *cum assensu*, as Aquinas put it) that I do not exist. Hence Descartes's choice of the word *cogito*. This particular word is not absolutely indispensable, however, for the act of thinking to which it refers could also be called an act of doubting; and Descartes does admit that his insight is also expressible by *dubito, ergo sum* (in *Recherche de la vérité*, AT X, 523; HR I, 324; cf. also *Principia philosophiae*, I, 7).

But did I not say that the performance through which an existentially self-verifying sentence verifies itself may also be an act uttering it? Is this not incompatible with Descartes's use of the word *cogito*? There is no incompatibility, for Descartes says exactly the same. In his second meditation on first philosophy he says in so many words that the sentence "I exist" is necessarily true "whenever I utter it or conceive it in my mind"—"quoties a me profertur, vel mente concipitur" (AT VII, 25; HR I, 150).[26]

[26] What we have said shows that Descartes's verbs *cogitare* and *dubitare* are not, in the last analysis, the most accurate ones for describing the act through which the sentence "I don't exist" defeats itself. It is not strictly true to say that an inconsistency arises from Descartes's attempt to *think* that he does not exist or to *doubt* that he does. Somebody else may think so; why not Descartes himself? He can certainly think so in the sense of contemplating a "mere possibility." What he cannot do is to *persuade* anybody (including himself) that he does not exist; wherefore he cannot try to *profess* (to others or to himself) that he does not exist without defeating

The performatory character of Descartes's insight presupposes a characteristic feature of his famous method of doubt which has frequently been commented on in other contexts. Descartes's doubt does not consist in the giving up of all opinions, as a skeptic's doubt might. Nor is it an attempt to remove certain specific sources of mistakes from our thinking, like Francis Bacon's. It amounts to an active attempt to think the contrary of what we usually believe. For this reason Descartes could claim that in an important point this rather doctrinaire doubt of his defeats itself. A skeptic's passive doubt could never do so.

The performatory character of Descartes's insight is in fact part and parcel of the general strategy of his *reductio ad absurdum* (or perhaps rather *projectio ad absurdum*) of skepticism. This strategy is brought out very well by Richard Popkin in his important work *The History of Skepticism from Erasmus to Descartes.*[27] As Popkin writes, "Only by forcing oneself to doubt and negate to the greatest possible degree, can one appreciate the indubitable character of the cogito."

9. *The* Cogito *and introspection.* The attempt to see the *Cogito* as a logical inference is not the only one-sided interpretation of Descartes's insight. Sometimes it has been understood, on the contrary, as a more or less purely factual statement, as a mere *Tatsachenwahrheit.*[28] This interpreta-

---

his own attempt. In fact, Descartes himself resorts to explanations of this kind when he gives his most explicit explanation of the moves which made him recognize the self-evidence of his own existence. In the passage just quoted he uses the Latin verb *proferre* and a little earlier the verb *persuadere* for the purpose. A literal-minded Cartesian might thus want to conclude as his basic truth, *ego sum professor* rather than *sum res cogitans.*

[27] *The History of Skepticism from Erasmus to Descartes* (Wijsgerige Teksten en Studies IV, Van Gorcum & Co., Assen, 1960) ch. ix, especially pp. 185–187. See also Henri Gouhier, "Doute méthodique ou négation méthodique?" *Études Philosophiques,* IX (1954), 135–162.

[28] For the history of this view as well as for an interesting argument for its importance, see P. Schrecker, "La méthode cartésienne et la logique," *Revue philosophique,* CXXIII (1937), 336–367, especially pp. 353–354.

tion is often combined with a definite view as to how this particular truth is ascertained, namely by introspection. The function of the *Cogito*, on this view, is to call our attention to something every one of us can ascertain when he "gazes within himself."

It is very misleading, however, to appeal to introspection in explaining the meaning of the *Cogito*, although there is likely to be a connection between the notion of introspection and the peculiarities of the Cartesian argument. We have seen that an existentially inconsistent sentence may also defeat itself through an "external" speech-act. The reason why Descartes could not doubt his own existence is in principle exactly the same as the reason why he could not hope to mislead anybody by saying "I don't exist." The one does not presuppose introspection any more than the other. What the philosophers who have spoken of introspection here are likely to have had in mind is often performatoriness rather than introspectiveness.

The independence of Descartes's insight of introspection is illustrated by the fact that there is a peculiarity about certain sentences in the *second* person which is closely related to the peculiarities of Descartes's *ego sum, ego existo*. In the same way as it is self-defeating to say "I don't exist," it is usually absurd to say "You don't exist." If the latter sentence is true, it is *ipso facto* empty in that there is no one to whom it could conceivably be addressed.

What makes us connect the *Cogito* with introspection is the "spiritualization" which takes place when an "external" speech-act is replaced by a thought-act and on which we commented above. In the *Cogito* it is presupposed that a man not only can converse with his fellow men but is also able to "discourse with himself without spoken sound" in a way closely reminiscent of Plato's famous definition of thinking "as a discourse that the mind carries on with itself" (and also reminiscent of Peirce's pertinent remarks on the dialogical character of thought[29]).

[29] *Collected Papers* (Cambridge, Mass., 1931–1958), VI, sec. 338; V, sec. 421.

Another reason why it is natural to connect the *Cogito* with one's self-knowledge is implicit in what was said above. In order to ascertain that a statement like "De Gaulle does not exist" (supposing that it is made by De Gaulle himself) is existentially inconsistent, I have to know the speaker; I have to identify him as the selfsame man whom his statement is about. In the same way, appreciating the existential inconsistency of an utterance of the form "I don't exist" presupposes realizing that the man whom it is about is necessarily the speaker himself. Descartes's *cogito* insight therefore depends on "knowing oneself" in the same literal sense in which the insight into the self-defeating character of the statement "De Gaulle does not exist" depends on knowing De Gaulle. Expressed in less paradoxical terms, appreciating the *cogito* argument presupposes an ability to appreciate the logic of the first-person pronoun "I." And although mastering the latter is not the same thing as the capacity for introspection, the two are likely to be connected with each other conceptually (logically). The *cogito* insight is essentially connected with one's own case in the same way introspection is, we might say.

10. *The singularity of the* Cogito. Descartes realized that his *cogito* argument deals with a particular case, namely with his own. This is in fact typical of his whole procedure; it is typical of a man who asked "What can *I* know?" rather than "What can men know?" Descartes denied that his argument is an enthymeme whose suppressed major premise is "Everybody who thinks, exists." He seems to have thought, nevertheless, that this general sentence is a genuine generalization of the insight expressed by his singular sentence.[30]

The general sentence cannot be such a generalization of the *Cogito*, however; it cannot serve as a general truth from which the sentence *cogito, ergo sum* could be inferred, as Descartes seems to have thought. This is perhaps seen most readily by making explicit the existential presuppositions which are implicit in the general sentence. If they are re-

[30] See AT IX, 205–206; HR II, 127; cf. AT VII, 140–141; HR II, 38.

moved, the sentence takes the form "Every actually existing individual that thinks, exists" and becomes a tautology. This tautology is useless for the purpose Descartes had in mind; it can entail "I think, therefore I exist" only in conjunction with the further premise "I exist." This further premise, however, is exactly the conclusion that Descartes ultimately wanted to draw by means of the *cogito* argument. Hence the alleged deduction becomes a *petitio principii*.

Alternatively we might try to interpret the word "everybody" which occurs in the general sentence as somehow ranging over all *thinkable* individuals rather than all *actually existing* individuals. I am sure that such a procedure is illicit unless further explanations are given. But even if it were legitimate, it would not help us to formulate a true generalization of the Cartesian sentence. For then our generalization would take the form "Every thinkable individual that thinks, exists" and become false, as witnessed by Shakespeare's meditative Prince of Denmark.

In a sense, therefore, Descartes's insight is not generalizable. This is of course due to its performatory character. Each of us can formulate "for himself" a sentence in the first person singular that is true and indubitable, namely the Cartesian sentence *ego sum, ego existo*. But since its indubitability is due to a thought-act which each man has to perform himself, there cannot be any general sentence which would be indubitable in the same way without being trivial. The *cogito* insight of each of us is tied to his own case even more closely than Descartes realized.[31]

11. *The role of the* Cogito *in Descartes's system.* Our interpretation is supported by the fact that it enables us to appreciate the role of Descartes's first and foremost insight in his system, that is, to understand the conclusions he thought he could draw from the *Cogito*. For one thing, we can now see the reason why Descartes's insight emerges from his own descriptions as a curiously *momentary* affair. It is a conse-

---

[31] As Popkin aptly observes (*op. cit.*, p. 187), "the method of doubt is the *cause* rather than the *occasion* of the acquisition of new knowledge" (my italics).

quence of the performatoriness of his insight. Since the certainty of my existence results from my thinking of it in a sense not unlike that in which light results from the presence of a source of light, it is natural to assume (rightly or wrongly) that I can be really sure of my existence only as long as I actively contemplate it. A property which a proposition has *because* and *in so far as* it is actually thought of easily becomes a property which belongs to it only *as long as* it is thought of. In any case, this is what Descartes says of the certainty of his own existence. I can be sure of my existence, he says, "while" or "at the same time as" I think of it or "whenever" or "as often as" I do so.[32] "Whereas I had only to cease to think for an instant," he says, "and I should then (even although all the other things I had imagined still remained true) have no grounds for believing that I can have existed in that instant" (*Discours*, Part IV; AT VI, 32–33; HR I, 101).

This shows, incidentally, that the sole function of the word *cogito* in Descartes's dictum cannot be to call attention to the fact that his insight is obtained *by means of* thinking. For of an ordinary insight of this kind (e.g. of a demonstrative truth) we may of course continue to be sure once we have gained it.

In the same way we can perhaps see why Descartes's insight *cogito, ergo sum* suggested to him a definite view of the nature of this existing *ego*, namely that its nature consists entirely of thinking. We have seen that Descartes's insight is not comparable with one's becoming aware of the sound of music by pausing to listen to it but rather with making sure that music is to be heard by playing it oneself. Ceasing to play would not only stop one's hearing the music, in the way ceasing to listen could; it would put an end to the music itself. In the same way, it must have seemed to Descartes, his ceasing to think would not only mean ceasing to be aware of his own existence; it would put an end to the particular way in which his existence was found to manifest itself. To change the metaphor, ceasing to think would not be like

[32] See, e.g. *Principia philosophiae* I, 7; I, 8; I, 49.

closing one's eyes but like putting out the lamp. For this reason, thinking was for Descartes something that could not be disentangled from his existence; it was the very essence of his nature. We may thus surmise that the original reason why Descartes made the (illicit but natural) transition from *cogito, ergo sum* to *sum res cogitans* was exactly the same as the reason for the curious momentariness of the former which we noted above, namely the performativeness of the *cogito* insight. In any case, the two ideas were introduced by Descartes in one and the same breath. The passage we just quoted from the *Discours* continues as follows: "From this I knew that I was a substance whose whole essence or nature consists entirely in thinking." In the *Meditationes* Descartes is more reserved. He has already become aware of the difficulty of converting his intuitive idea of the dependence of his existence on his thinking into a genuine proof. The way in which the idea of the dependence is introduced is, nevertheless, exactly the same: "*Ego sum, ego existo.* This is certain. How long? As long as I think. For it might indeed be that if I entirely ceased to think, I should thereupon altogether cease to exist. I am not at present admitting anything which is not necessarily true; and, accurately speaking, I am therefore only a thinking thing" (AT VII, 27; HR I, 151–152).

The transition from *cogito, ergo sum* directly to *sum res cogitans* remains inexplicable as long as we interpret the *Cogito* in terms of the logical truth of (1). For then the blunt objections of Hobbes carry weight: Even if it were true that we can validly infer *ambulo ergo sum* or *video ergo sum,* there would not be the slightest temptation to take this to suggest that one's nature consists entirely of walking or of seeing in the way Descartes thought he could move from *cogito, ergo sum* to *sum res cogitans.* (Cf. AT VII, 172; HR II, 61.)

12. *Descartes and his predecessors.* It seems to me that Descartes is distinguished from most of his predecessors by his awareness of the performatory character of his first and

foremost insight.[33] In spite of all the similarities that there
obtain between Descartes and St. Augustine, there are also
clear-cut differences. In so far as I know, there is no indication that Augustine was ever alive to the possibility of interpreting his version of the *Cogito* as a performance rather
than as an inference or as a factual observation.[34] As far as
Augustine is concerned, it would be quite difficult to dis-
prove a "logical" interpretation such as Gassendi and others
have given of the Cartesian *cogito* argument. What he dwells
on is merely the "impossibility of thinking without existing."
I do not see any way in which Augustine could have denied
that *ambulo, ergo sum* or *video, ergo sum* are as good inferences as *cogito, ergo sum* and that the sole difference between them lies in the different degree of certainty of their
premises.

In this respect, there is an essentially new element present,
however implicitly, in Descartes's formulations. This difference also shows in the conclusions which Descartes and
Augustine drew from their respective insights. For instance,
Augustine used his principle as a part of an argument which
was designed to show that the human soul is tripartite, consisting of being, knowing, and willing. We have already seen
that Descartes's insight was for him intimately connected
with the notion of thinking (rather than, say, of willing or
feeling): the performance through which an existentially inconsistent sentence defeats itself can be an act of thinking
of it, but it cannot possibly be an act of willing or of feeling.
Hence Descartes could use the performatorily interpreted
cogito insight to argue that the human soul is a *res cogitans*,
but not to argue that it is essentially a willing or feeling
being. In view of such differences, is it at all surprising that
Descartes should have emphasized his independence of
Augustine?

If there is a predecessor who comes close to Descartes,

[33] The difference is marked even though Descartes himself was
not fully aware in all respects of the nature of his insight.

[34] To some extent this may be merely an indication that the
cogito insight was in Augustine less fully developed than it is in
Descartes.

he is likelier to be St. Thomas than St. Augustine. We have already quoted a passage in Aquinas which shows much more appreciation of the performatory aspect of the *Cogito* than anything in Augustine. The agreement is not fortuitous; Aquinas' ability to appreciate the performatoriness of the *Cogito* was part and parcel of his more general view that "the intellect knows itself not by its essence but by its act."[35] The significance of this crucial similarity between Aquinas and Descartes is not diminished by the interesting dissimilarities which also obtain between them. For instance, it is not diminished by the fact that for Aquinas the relevant acts of intellect needed an object other than the intellect itself, whereas Descartes denies "that a thinking being needs any object other than itself in order to exercise its activity" (AT IX, 206; HR II, 128). This dissimilarity is smaller than it first appears to be. Descartes did not hold that the thinking mind could apprehend itself directly, but only by means of its activities (see his reply to Hobbes's second objection; also AT VII, 422; HR II, 241; HR II, 343), exactly as Aquinas did. I should go as far as to wonder whether there is more than a coincidence to the fact that Descartes was particularly close to Aquinas (as far as the *cogito* insight is concerned) in that work of his, in the *Meditationes,* in which the Thomistic influence on him is in many other respects most conspicuous.

13. *Summing up.* Some of the main points of our analysis of the *Cogito* may be summed up as follows: Whatever he may have thought himself, Descartes's insight is *clear* but not *distinct,*[36] to use his own terminology. That is to say, there are several different arguments compressed into the apparently simple formulation *cogito, ergo sum* which he does not clearly distinguish from each other.

(i) Sometimes Descartes dealt with the *Cogito* as if it were an expression of the logical truth of sentences of the

[35] *Summa theologica,* I, Q.87, art. 1.
[36] For the relation of the two notions in Descartes, see N. Kemp Smith, *New Studies in the Philosophy of Descartes* (London, 1952), pp. 52 ff.

form (1) or at least of the indubitable truth of a particular
sentence of this form. On this interpretation the argument
cogito, ergo sum is on the same footing with such arguments
as *volo, ergo sum*. Arguments like *video, ergo sum* or *ambulo,
ergo sum* can be said to be less convincing than the *Cogito*
merely because their premises are not as indubitable as that
of Descartes's argument. The word *cogito* may thus be replaced by any other word which refers to one of my acts of
consciousness.

(ii) Descartes realized, however, that there is more to the
Cogito than interpretation (*i*). He realized, albeit dimly, that
it can also serve to express the existential self-verifiability of
the sentence "I exist" (or the existential inconsistency of
"I don't exist"). On this interpretation the peculiarity of the
sentence *ego sum* is of performatory character. The verb
cogitare now has to be interpreted rather narrowly. The word
cogito may still be replaced by such "verbs of intellection" as
dubito (or *profero*) but not any longer by verbs referring to
arbitrary mental acts, such as *volo* or *sentio*. This interpretation, and only this one, makes it possible to understand Descartes's rash transition from *cogito, ergo sum* to *sum res
cogitans*.

By comparing the two interpretations we can further elucidate certain peculiarities of Descartes's thought. We shall
mainly be concerned with the following two points:

(A) Descartes does not distinguish the two interpretations
very clearly. We cannot always expect a clear answer to the
question whether a particular instance of the *cogito* argument
is for him an inference or a performance. The two types of
interpretation merge into each other in his writings in a
confusing manner.

(B) Nevertheless, the relation of these two possible interpretations of the Cartesian *Cogito* throws light on the
meaning of the critical verb *cogitare* in the different parts of
Descartes's philosophy.

14. *The ambiguity of the Cartesian* Cogito. (A) Interpretation (*ii*) easily gives rise to an expectation that is going to be
partly disappointed. It easily leads us to expect a definite

answer to the question: What was Descartes thinking *of* in that thought-act which to him revealed the indubitability of his own existence? Interpretation (*ii*) suggests that Descartes should have been thinking of *his own existence*. This agrees very well with some of Descartes's most explicit pronouncements. One of them was already quoted above (in the penultimate paragraph of section 8). In the same connection Descartes writes: "Let him [viz. Descartes's *malin génie*] deceive me as much as he will, he can never cause me to be nothing so long as I shall be thinking that I am something." The same point is repeated in the *Third Meditation* (AT VII, 36; HR I, 158–159).

Elsewhere, however, Descartes often uses formulations which clearly presuppose that his crucial thought-act pertains to something different from his mere existence. These formulations can be understood, it seems to me, as hybrids between the two arguments (*i*) and (*ii*). This hybridization was undoubtedly encouraged by the following (correct) observation: If the sentence "I don't exist" is existentially self-defeating, then so are a fortiori such sentences as "I think, but I don't exist" or "I doubt, but I don't exist." In other words, there are no objections in principle to saying that what is at stake in the *Cogito* is the status of these latter sentences rather than that of the sentence "I don't exist."

On this intermediate interpretation the word *cogito* has a curious double role in Descartes's dictum. On one hand, it is a part of the proposition whose status (indubitability) is at stake. On the other hand, it refers to the performance through which the indubitability of this proposition is revealed. If we are on the right track, we may expect that this duality of functions will sometimes be betrayed by Descartes's formulations, that is, that he will sometimes use two "verbs of intellection" (such as *think, doubt, conceive,* and the like) where on interpretation (*i*) there should be only one. This expectation turns out to be justified: ". . . from this very circumstance that I *thought* to *doubt* [*je pensais à douter*] the truth of those other things, it very evidently and very certainly followed that I was . . ." (*Discours,* Part IV; my italics); ". . . but we cannot in the same way *conceive* that we who *doubt* these things are not . . ." (*Principia philoso-phiae* I, 7; my italics).

This duplication of verbs of intellection[37] shows that we still have to do with a performatory insight. Where Augustine would have said that nobody can doubt anything without ex-isting, Descartes in effect says that one cannot think that one doubts anything without thereby demonstrating to oneself that one exists. But he does not clearly distinguish the two arguments from each other. He thinks that interpretation (*ii*), thus expanded, is tantamount to interpretation (*i*). For instance, the passage which we just quoted from the *Principia* continues as follows: ". . . for there is a contradiction in conceiving that what thinks does not, at the same time as it thinks, exist." The change may seem small, but it makes all the difference. In the first passage Descartes is saying that it is impossible for him to think that *he himself* should not exist while he doubts something. In the second passage he says that it is impossible for him to think that *anybody else* should not exist while he (the other man) doubts something. The former passage expresses a performatory insight, whereas the latter cannot do so. We have moved from the ambit of interpretation (*ii*) to that of interpretation (*i*).[38]

15. *The ambiguity of the Cartesian* cogitatio. (B) To tell what Descartes meant by the verb *cogitare* is largely tanta-mount to telling what is meant by his dictum: *sum res cogitans*. We saw that this dictum originally was for Des-cartes a consequence (a fallacious, albeit natural one) of the

[37] That a verb of intellection should in Descartes serve to describe the object of another thought-act is all the more remarkable as it is virtually inconsistent with his explicit doctrines. For Descartes held that "one thought [conscious act, *cogitationem*] cannot be the ob-ject of another" (Reply to Hobbes's second objection; cf. AT VII, 422; HR II, 241).

[38] This is not strictly true, for the second passage is concerned with the alleged inconsistency of sentences of the form "*b* thinks that *a* does not exist while *a* doubts something," whereas interpreta-tion (*i*) was concerned with the alleged inconsistency of sentences of the form "*a* does not exist while he doubts something." The dif-ference is immaterial for our purposes, however, and was obviously neglected by Descartes.

principle *cogito, ergo sum*, which for this purpose had to be given interpretation (*ii*). From this it follows that the word *cogitans* has to be interpreted as referring to thinking in the ordinary sense of the word. It is not surprising, however, that Descartes should have included more in his alleged conclusion *sum res cogitans* than it would have contained on the basis of the way in which he arrived at it even if this way had amounted to a demonstration.

Descartes had to reconcile his "conclusion" that the essence of a human being consists entirely of thinking (in the ordinary sense of the word) and the obvious fact that there are genuine acts of consciousness other than those of thinking, for example those of willing, sensing, feeling, and the like. This he sought to accomplish by extending the meaning of the verb *cogitare*. He tried to interpret all the other acts of consciousness as so many modes of thinking.[39] In this attempt he was helped by the following two facts:

(a) The meaning of the verb *cogitare* was traditionally very wide. According to Alexandre Koyré, "it embraced not only 'thought' as it is now understood, but all mental acts and data: will, feeling, judgment, perception, and so on."[40] Because of this traditionally wide range of senses of the word Descartes was able to smuggle more content into his "result" *sum res cogitans* than the way in which he reached it would, in any case, have justified.

It is significant that nonintellectual acts of consciousness enter into the argument of the *Meditationes* at the moment when Descartes pauses to ask what a *res cogitans* really is, that is, what is meant by the *cogitatio* of a *res cogitans*:

> What then am I? A thinking thing [*res cogitans*.] What is a thinking thing? It is a thing that doubts, understands, asserts, denies, wills, abstains from willing, that also has sense and imagination. These are a good many properties—if only they all belong to me. But how could they fail to? [AT VII, 28; HR I, 153]

[39] Cf. N. Kemp Smith, *op. cit.*, pp. 324–331.
[40] See his introduction to *Descartes, Philosophical Writings*, ed. and trans. by E. Anscombe and P. Geach (Edinburgh, 1954), p. xxxvii.

Descartes is not here simply stating what is meant by a *res cogitans*. He is not merely formulating the conclusion of an argument; he is proceeding to interpret it.[41] This is shown by the last two quoted sentences. For if willing and sensation were included in Descartes's thinking *ego* already in virtue of the argument which led him to conclude *sum res cogitans*, there would not be any point in asking whether they really belong to his nature.

(b) However, the wide range of senses of the verb *cogitare* in Descartes is not all due to external influence. There are factors in his own thinking which tend in the same direction. Among other things, the confusion between the two interpretations is operative here. Descartes can hope (as we saw) to be able to jump from *cogito, ergo sum* to *sum res cogitans* only if interpretation (*ii*) is presupposed. This interpretation in turn presupposes a narrowly "intellectual" meaning of the verb *cogitare* in that it cannot be replaced by any arbitrary verb which refers to some act of one's immediate consciousness. In contrast, on interpretation (*i*) the verb *cogitare* could be understood in this wide sense. The confusion between the two interpretations made it possible for Descartes to deal with the "conclusion" *sum res cogitans* as if it were based on a *cogito* argument in which *cogitatio* covers all one's acts of consciousness—as he strictly speaking is not justified in doing.

This explains Descartes's apparent inconsistency in using the verb *cogitare*. It is interesting to note that some of the critics (e.g. Anscombe and Geach; see *op. cit.*, p. xlvii) who have most strongly stressed the wide extent of this verb in Descartes have nevertheless been forced to say that in the *cogito* argument the verb is used in a rather narrow sense to refer to what we nowadays call thinking. This may seem paradoxical in view of the fact that the broad interpretation is applied in the first place to the sentence *sum res cogitans* to which Descartes moved directly from the *cogito* argument. In our view, this prima-facie paradox disappears if we realize the ambiguity of the *cogito* argument.

[41] A little earlier Descartes had written: "I am, then, a real thing. . . . What thing? I have said it, a thinking thing. And *what more* am I?" (my italics; AT VII, 27; HR I, 152).

The close connection between this argument and the notion of *cogitatio* in Descartes is amply demonstrated by his formulations. In our last quotation Descartes was left asking whether doubt, understanding, will, sense, imagination, and the like belong to his nature. He reformulates this question successively as follows: ". . . how can any of these things be less true than my existence? Is any of these something distinct from my thinking [*cogitatione*]? Can any of them be called a separate thing from myself?" Only such things could belong to Descartes's nature as were as certain as his existence. Why? The reason is seen from the context of the quotation. Descartes had already pronounced his *Cogito*; he had already ascertained the indubitability of his existence. He held that nothing he did not have to know in order to ascertain this could, in the objective order of things, constitute a necessary condition of his existence.[42] Such things could not belong to his essence, for "nothing without which a thing can still exist is comprised in its essence."[43] Hence nothing could belong to his essence or nature that he could not be sure of already at the present stage of his argument, that is, nothing that he could not ascertain in the same way and at the same time as he ascertained his own existence. For this reason, nothing that belonged to his nature could be "less true than his existence."

What this requirement amounts to is that everything that Descartes was willing to accept as a part of his nature (even in the sense of being a mere mode of his basic nature of thinking) had to be shown to belong to him by means of the *cogito* argument in the same way in which he "demonstrated" that thinking belonged to him by "deducing" *sum res cogitans* from *cogito, ergo sum*. A mental activity was for Descartes a part of his nature if and only if the corresponding verb could function as the premise of a variant of the *cogito* argument. For instance, the sense in which apparent sensation can be

[42] This part of his doctrine was criticized by Arnauld and others. In the preface to the *Meditationes* and in his replies to objections Descartes sought to defend himself. The question whether he succeeded is not relevant here.

[43] AT VII, 219; HR II, 97.

said to belong to his nature (as a mode of thinking) is for Descartes exactly the same as the sense in which he could infer *sentio, ergo sum*. The former is explained by Descartes as follows:

> Finally, it is I who have sensations, or who perceive corporeal objects as it were by the senses. Thus, I am now seeing light, hearing a noise, feeling heat. These things are false [it may be said], for I am asleep; but at least I seem to see, to hear, to be warmed. This cannot be false; and this is what is properly called my sensation; further, sensation, precisely so regarded, is nothing but thinking [*cogitare*]. [AT VII, 29; HR I, 153]

The latter is explained in a strikingly similar way:

> Suppose I say *I see* or *I am walking, therefore I exist.* If I take this to refer to vision or walking as corporeal action, the conclusion is not absolutely certain; for, as often happens during sleep, I may think I am seeing though I do not open my eyes, or think that I am walking although I do not change my place; and it may even be that I have no body. But if I take it to refer to the actual sensation or awareness [*sensu sive conscientia*] of seeing or walking, then it is quite certain; for in that case it has regard to the mind, and it is the mind alone that has sense or thought [*sentit sive cogitat*] of itself seeing or walking. [*Principia* I, 9; cf. Descartes's similar reply to Gassendi's objections to the *Cogito*.]

In short, the reason why sensation belonged to Descartes's nature was for him exactly the same as the reason why he could argue *sentio, ergo sum*. For him, doubting, willing, and seeing were modes of his basic nature of thinking exactly in the same sense in which the arguments *dubito ergo sum, volo ergo sum*, and *video ergo sum* were variants or "modes" of the argument *cogito ergo sum*.

Why, then, is one of these arguments a privileged one? If Descartes could argue *volo, ergo sum* and *sentio, ergo sum* as well as *cogito, ergo sum*, why did he refuse to infer that his nature consists of "Wille und Vorstellung," claiming as he did that it consists entirely of thinking? The answer is again implicit in the ambiguity of the *cogito* argument. Such parallel arguments as *volo, ergo sum* presuppose interpretation (*i*). Now there was more to the Cartesian *Cogito* than this interpretation; Descartes was also aware of the "performatory" interpretation (*ii*). It is the latter interpretation that gives the verb *cogitare* a privileged position vis-à-vis such verbs as *velle* or *videre*. Descartes could replace the word *cogito* by other words in the *cogito, ergo sum*; but he could not replace the performance which for him revealed the indubitability of any such sentence. This performance could be described only by a "verb of intellection" like *cogitare*. For this reason, the verb *cogitare* was for Descartes a privileged one; for this reason nothing could for him belong to his nature that was "something distinct from his thinking."

This special role of the verb *cogitare* seems to me difficult to explain otherwise. If I am right, the conspicuous privileges of this verb in Descartes therefore constitute one more piece of evidence to show that he was aware of interpretation (*ii*).

There is a further point worth making here. We have already pointed out that the verb *cogitare* is not the most accurate one for the purpose of describing the performance which for Descartes revealed the certainty of his existence (see note 26). This inaccuracy led Descartes to assimilate the peculiarities of the existentially self-defeating sentence "I do not exist" to the peculiarities of such sentences as "I doubt everything" or "I am not thinking anything." There is an important difference here, however. The latter sentences are not instances of existential inconsistency. They are instances of certain related notions; they are literally impossible to believe or to think in a sense in which "I do not exist" is not. I have studied the peculiarities of some such sentences elsewhere (in *Knowledge and Belief, An Introduction to the Logic of the Two Notions.* Ithaca, N.Y.: Cornell University Press, 1962). In many respects, their properties are analogous to those of existentially self-defeating sentences.[44]

[44] I am indebted to Professors Norman Malcolm and G. H. von Wright for several useful suggestions in connection with the present essay.

DESCARTES'S *MEDITATIONS*

H. A. PRICHARD

III

Descartes considers that by the process he has described in the first two Meditations he has become certain of and so knows his own existence, though doubtful of the existence of everything else.

He then in effect asks himself: 'As I have attained this one certainty, is it not now open to me to attain others and so come to have other knowledge?' His reader naturally expects him to answer 'no'; for he has expressly said that he has found the existence of everything else doubtful, and that seems to finish the matter. Indeed, the plan on which he proceeds in the first two Meditations really requires him to stop—as having finished the task he has set himself.

Descartes, however, inconsistently, thinks otherwise. His idea (a fallacious idea) is that by analysing the process by which he has become certain of his own existence, he can discover the general nature of the process of becoming certain of something, and that once we know its general nature, we can use this knowledge to attain other certainties, and indeed all such certainties as we are capable of attaining.

Descartes at once proceeds to carry out this analysis. In fact, however, he gives a different account from that implied in the second Meditation, and we should first consider the latter.

The key to the earlier account is to be found in Descartes's saying in effect: 'The mere fact that I was persuaded of some-

From H. A. Prichard, *Knowledge and Perception* (1950), pp. 80–104, by permission of the Clarendon Press, Oxford.

thing, whether truly or falsely, e.g. that there was no such thing as a world, involves my existence'. This statement implies that if he had been asked, when writing the second Meditation, what rendered him certain of his own existence, he would have had to say that it was his *certainty* that he had had a certain persuasion, together with the certainty that any persuasion involves the existence of a self which is persuaded, distinct from the persuasion. And we could say that according to this account we become certain of some fact in nature by consideration of certain other facts in nature.

The account of the Third Meditation is, however, different. Unfortunately it is obscure. What he says[1] is:

> In this first knowledge, doubtless, there is nothing which makes me certain of its truth except the clear and distinct perception of what I say, which would not indeed suffice to make me certain that that which I say is true, if it could ever happen that a thing which I conceived thus clearly and distinctly should prove false; and accordingly it seems to me that already I can establish as a general rule that all the things which we conceive[2] very clearly and very distinctly are true.

Here, if we put in what is necessary to complete the sense, what Descartes appears to be saying is this:

> In this knowledge that I exist, what renders me certain that the thought that I exist is true, is my *certainty* that this thought is an act of perceiving clearly and distinctly that I exist; but this certainty would not be sufficient to do this, unless I was also certain, that any state of perceiving clearly and distinctly is necessarily true.

And he should have added not—as he does—'hence it now *seems* to me that any such state must be true', but 'hence I now know that I have already been certain, and so already know that any such state must be true'. Also, he should have

[1] Pp. 115–116. [Prichard cites the Veitch translation. In Haldane and Ross, the reference is I, 158; and, in Adam and Tannery, VII, 35.]
[2] The Latin version uses *percipere*.

added that this knowledge that I exist requires an additional certainty, viz. that where a thought is necessarily true, the fact must correspond.

This account is obviously different in two ways. For (1) it introduces a new note—that of perceiving something clearly and distinctly, and (2) according to this account we become certain of a fact in nature only indirectly, by considering a certain state of our own mind. We first come to perceive clearly and distinctly that we exist, presumably by perceiving clearly and distinctly that some persuasion of ours implies our existence—this perceiving not being the being certain; then by reflecting on this state we become certain that it is one of clear and distinct perception, and so necessarily true, and thence become certain that we exist.

Further (2), it should be noticed, if 'perceiving clearly' had to be introduced into the *earlier* account, it could be done only by assuming that Descartes considered that what he calls perceiving clearly is the same thing as the 'being certain' of this earlier account.

One implication of the new account is obvious. This is that there is at least one certainty which we must have before we can be certain even of our own existence, viz. the certainty that any state which is one of clear perceiving is necessarily true—so that in this respect, too, the second account is inconsistent with the first.

The differences between the two accounts can be put generally thus:

Suppose I am to become certain that an A is B, e.g. that a three-sided figure has also three angles. According to the first account, I must first, by considering the nature of an A and of B-ness, become certain that something in the nature of an A and of B-ness necessitates that an A is B—this being certain being what Descartes calls perceiving clearly and distinctly. According to the second account, I must first, by considering the nature of an A and B-ness, come to perceive clearly that an A is B, this perceiving clearly *not* being the same as being certain; then secondly, by considering the nature of my state of mind become certain that it is one of perceiving clearly; and then thirdly, become certain that this fact necessitates that *A* is *B*. The difference is fundamental, because while according to the first account we attain knowledge by consideration of the facts, according to the second we do so by a consideration of the state of mind which we reach by considering the facts. Thus, suppose we had tried to discover the product of 7 and 9 and were doubtful about our conclusion, according to the first account the proper procedure would be to do the sum again, while according to the second account we should consider once more the state of mind we had previously reached in doing the sum.

Strangely enough Descartes does not notice that the two accounts are different. What we find is the two accounts left side by side undistinguished. For later on he often treats perceiving clearly as if it were the same as being certain, thereby reverting to the first account.

Descartes, having formulated this second account, then finds himself harassed by two reasons for doubting whether a state of clear perceiving *is* necessarily true. And he naturally goes on to consider whether they are good reasons, since as according to this account all our other certainties are based on the certainty that such a state is necessarily true, then if such a state is not necessarily true, in being certain of something we may be mistaken, and so even in being certain of something we do not *know*, since no state in which we may be mistaken can possibly be one of knowledge.

And it may be noticed that on his other version of the process of becoming certain, he would equally have to consider these reasons. For on this version, perceiving clearly is the same thing as being certain, and therefore on this version also, if perceiving clearly is a state in which we are liable to error, in being certain of something we are not knowing.

Moreover the reasons are important for *us* to consider, because we, too, when we reflect begin to doubt whether we know even when we are certain, and if we do not, knowledge seems unattainable—since no better state seems possible than that of being certain.

Descartes's general contention in favour of this doubt is that we often have perceived things very clearly and yet afterwards been convinced that we have or at least may have been

mistaken. In favour of this contention Descartes puts forward
two types of case.

1. He says he has received the existence of the various objects of the senses, i.e. the earth, the sky, the stars, &c., as
very certain and manifest; i.e. he has very clearly and distinctly perceived their existence, and yet afterwards has found
their existence doubtful.

This particular source of doubt, he thinks, however, can
be easily disposed of. What, he asks, did I distinctly perceive
about these objects? Simply that ideas of them were present
to my mind, and this, he says, I do not even now think doubtful. But besides distinctly perceiving this, I did something
else; I thought I perceived clearly that realities independent
of me existed from which these ideas proceeded, and it was
in having this thought that I was or at least may have been
mistaken.

This reply enables Descartes to save the view that where
our state *is* one of clear perceiving it is necessarily true.

He fails, however, to notice that in taking this step he has
only gone from Scylla to Charybdis. For he has only saved
his view (that a state of clear perceiving is necessarily true)
at the cost of admitting that we may always be mistaken in
being certain that a state in which we are is one of clear
perceiving; and if this be so, since the certainty of anything
else will imply such a certainty, then in being certain of anything we shall not be knowing it.

2. The second type of case is one which Descartes thinks
much more difficult to dispose of. It is that of our state of
mind when considering some easy proposition in arithmetic
or geometry. If we read what Descartes says here in the third
Meditation with the passage from Meditation V, we can say
that what Descartes is saying to himself is this:

While I am actually following the argument put forward
in support of any simple proposition such as 'The angles of a
triangle are equal to two right angles', it does most clearly
appear to me that the angles are equal to two right angles.
In this case, unlike the preceding type of case, there is no
doubt about it. Here I do perceive clearly. So much is this so
that, when in this condition, I find it impossible to believe

otherwise; i.e. I am certain. Indeed if at such a time I ask myself whether even an omnipotent deity can have been deceiving me here by giving me a nature which makes me mistaken in my present state, though certain, I answer 'No. Even such a being could not do this.' Yet afterwards I can doubt whether even when in this state I was not mistaken. For once I cease to follow the proof, then even though I remember I did follow it, I can think that in my past state an omnipotent deity may have been deceiving me.

Consequently, even in those cases where unquestionably my state is one of perceiving something clearly and distinctly, I may be mistaken, i.e. the state is not necessarily true, so that in being certain as I was that such a state, as being one of clear perceiving, is necessarily true I may have been mistaken, and consequently in being certain I am not knowing.

The conclusion which Descartes draws is that in order to know something it is necessary not only to have and to know that we have a clear and distinct perception of it; we must also come to know, and know by having some proof, that in such a state God cannot be deceiving us; and that therefore in order to know anything else whatever we must first come to know that there is a deity who does not deceive us when we are in such a state.

Naturally, therefore, his next step is to inquire whether there is a God and whether, if there is, he can be a deceiver.

Here we may notice two things by the way.

1. The existence of God is the third thing Descartes has come in the course of his thought to say we must know first, i.e. as a condition of knowing anything else, the other two being, of course, our existence, and the truth of a clear and distinct perception. Yet plainly Descartes can at best have only one thing as what we must know first.

2. Though Descartes says the ground of doubt is slight, it is not really so. The ground is serious. When, however, he adds that it is metaphysical, though he is saying what is important (viz. that it arises only when we come to consider whether we have the capacity to know, and not from doubts raised in ordinary life), to say this does not make the difficulty any less serious.

We are now in a position to consider the tenability of this view of Descartes. There is no need to wait until we are acquainted with the proof of God's existence which Descartes goes on to offer, because whatever the proof the general nature of the view will be the same.

The first thing to be noticed is that Descartes could, and indeed should, have stated the reason for doubt more generally, in a way which is independent of a theological setting. He could have said that we can only have come to perceive something clearly by using such a capacity of thought as we have, i.e. our intelligence—this being necessarily so however we have acquired this capacity, i.e. whether it be due to God or not; and that consequently the doubt arises whether this capacity is equal to the task of attaining a state in which we cannot be mistaken. Therefore, he could have said, before we know anything else we must come to know that our capacity of thought is such that the use of it will give us knowledge; or, to put it otherwise, before we can know that in any particular state we cannot be mistaken and so must know some particular thing, we must first come to know that the use of our intelligence is capable of giving us knowledge. This indeed is the more general form in which the doubt presents itself to us, and in fact it was the form in which Locke presented it to himself.

The next thing to be observed is that Descartes's idea of how the doubt has to be allayed, if at all, is obviously mistaken; and we can see that it is mistaken without even considering the actual way in which Descartes considers that he allays it, viz. by discovering what he considers a *proof* that there exists a deity who is no deceiver. For as Descartes is representing the matter, such a proof could only consist in perceiving clearly and distinctly that certain things which he perceives clearly involve a necessity that such a God exists; and as precisely what he is doubtful of is whether even when he perceives something clearly and distinctly he is not mistaken, he will become doubtful, when he reflects on his having this proof, whether here, too, he is not mistaken. In exactly the same way, if we were to come to perceive clearly that our capacity of thought is competent to yield knowledge, the mere reflection that this perception is the result of our capacity would produce the very doubt about the truth of this state, which we are trying to dissipate generally. In other words, any process by which we seek to dissipate the doubt by proving it to be mistaken will itself be exposed to the very doubt which we are anxious to dissipate.

Descartes, therefore, it is obvious, is setting himself an impossible task; and we can discover it to be impossible without considering his attempt to execute it. Admitting as he does the existence of the general doubt, he would have done better to admit that it was irremovable, and that therefore even when we are certain we do not know. But if he had, he would also have had to allow that our certainty of anything could only be momentary, since on becoming certain of something we should have only to reflect on our certainty to become certain that it is not knowledge, and so to become uncertain of the thing.

Yet, as it is easy to see, there must be something wrong about Descartes's doctrine, for as we see if we reflect, we can only be uncertain of one thing because we are certain of something else, and therefore to maintain, as the sceptic does, that we are uncertain of everything is impossible.

Still what we really want to discover is what precisely is wrong with Descartes's position and what is the proper way to deal with Descartes's doubt. And to do this is not easy.

To succeed, there are two things which we absolutely must do first.

1. We must first recognize the fundamental nature of the difference between knowing and believing.

2. We must recognize that whenever we know something we either do, or at least can, by reflecting, directly know that we are knowing it, and that whenever we believe something, we similarly either do or can directly know that we are believing it and not knowing it.

As regards (1), that there is such a fundamental difference is not something which everyone will readily admit, and some will go on to the end denying it. Nevertheless, I am confident that at least the more you consider the matter the more difficult you will find it to deny the existence of the difference.

For the sake of brevity and clearness I propose to try to state dogmatically the nature of the difference, and in doing so, I shall for the most part only be trying to state Cook Wilson's view.[3] In saying that I am going to speak dogmatically I mean two things. I mean first that I am not going to offer reasons for what I am going to assert. These for the most part would from the nature of the case have to take the form of trying to meet objections; and this I propose to try to do later. I mean secondly that the statements are meant to express what I know to be *knowledge* on my part and not *opinion*, and so what is beyond controversy.

But if 'controversial' stands for any doctrine which has been disputed, then my statements will express a doctrine which is controversial, and controversial in the highest degree. Thus any of you who have had the benefit of knowing or hearing Professor J. A. Smith or Professor Joachim will realize that they would deny the truth of every statement I am going to make. But, of course, it does not follow from the mere fact that a statement is controversial in this sense that it does not express knowledge on the part of the individual who states it, and that therefore, since everything is controversial in this sense, it is useless for you to try to attain knowledge about anything.

1. Knowing is absolutely different from what is called indifferently believing or being convinced or being persuaded or having an opinion or thinking, in the sense in which we oppose thinking to knowing, as when we say 'I think so but am not sure'. Knowing is not something which differs from being convinced by a difference of degree of something such as a feeling of confidence, as being more convinced differs from being less convinced, or as a fast movement differs from a slow movement. Knowing and believing differ in kind as do desiring and feeling, or as do a red colour and a blue colour. Their difference in kind is not that of species and genus, like that of a red colour and a colour. To know is not to have a belief of a special kind, differing from beliefs of other kinds;

[3] Cook Wilson, *Statement and Inference*, Part I, chap. 11; Part II, chaps. 1, 2, 3.

and no improvement in a belief and no increase in the feeling of conviction which it implies will convert it into knowledge. Nor is their difference that of being two species of a
common genus. It is not that there is a general kind of activity, for which the name would have to be thinking, which
admits of two kinds, the better of which is knowing and the
worse believing, nor is knowing something called thinking at
its best, thinking not at its best being believing. Their relat-
edness consists rather in the facts (*a*) that believing presupposes knowing, though, of course, knowing something other
than what we believe, and (*b*) that believing is a stage we
sometimes reach in the endeavour to attain knowledge.

To convince ourselves of the difference between knowing
and believing we need only notice that on the one hand we
should only say that we know something when we are certain
of it, and conversely, and that in the end we have to allow
that the meaning of the terms is identical; whereas, on the
other hand, when we believe something we are uncertain of
it.

Further there are certain things about knowing and believing which it is essential to recognize, i.e. know, when we are
considering Descartes.

(*a*) Though obviously knowledge is not false, and though
obviously, when we know, we are not mistaken, knowledge is
not *true*. It is neither true nor false, just as a colour is neither
heavy nor light. On the other hand, beliefs are either true or
false.

(*b*) Though some beliefs are true and others are false,
there is no special kind of belief distinguished from others by
some special characteristic such as that of being a condition of
perceiving something clearly and distinctly, which, as being
the kind it is, is necessarily true. Or, to put this otherwise,
there is no such thing as a kind of opinion called true opinion
—as Plato often implies that there is. In fact there is no sort
of condition of mind of which it can truly be said that it is
necessarily true; what seems nearest to this is the condition
of knowing, which is necessarily not false, but yet is not true.
And it may be noticed here that it is a tribute to Plato's philosophical insight, that though he considered there was a kind

of opinion called true opinion, a kind which if it existed
would be necessarily true, in the *Theaetetus*, where he tries to
answer the question 'What is knowledge?', he will have nothing to do with the view that it is true opinion.

2. Consider the second condition, which I said must be
satisfied before we can get the matter straight. We must recognize that when we know something we either do, or by
reflecting can, know that our condition is one of knowing that
thing, while when we believe something, we either do or can
know that our condition is one of believing and not of knowing: so that we cannot mistake belief for knowledge or vice
versa.

Consider instances: When knowing, for example, that the
noise we are hearing is loud, we do or can know that we are
knowing this and so cannot be mistaken, and when believing
that the noise is due to a car we know or can know that we are
believing and not knowing this. The knowledge, however, is
in both cases direct; we do not know, for example, that our
state is one of knowing that the noise we hear is loud indirectly, i.e. by knowing that it has some character, other
than that of knowing, which we know any state must have
if it is to be one of knowing—such as that of being an act of
clear and distinct perceiving; we know directly that it is of
the sort which knowing is; and so, too, with our knowledge
that our state is one of believing.

Further, it should be noticed that in knowing that some
state in which we are is one of knowing or of believing, as
the case may be, we are necessarily knowing the sort of thing
which knowing is and the sort of thing which believing is,
even though it is impossible for us or anyone else to define
either, i.e. to state its nature in terms of the nature of something else. This is obvious, because even in knowing in a given
case that my condition is one of believing and not of knowing,
I must be knowing the sort of thing that knowing is, since
otherwise I should not know that my condition is not one of
knowing, just as in knowing that some line is not straight, I
must—as Plato saw—be knowing what straightness is.

Now with these two considerations in mind return to Descartes's doubt whether he was not mistaken in some past state

in which he was following the proof that the angles of a tri-angle are equal to two right angles; and consider what we can say about it. The first thing to do is obviously to answer the question 'Was the condition of mind on which Descartes was reflecting one of knowing, or was it one of believing, or (as we say) of being convinced, as when we say we are con-vinced it was X who killed Y?' And, obviously, only one an-swer is possible. Descartes here was *knowing*; it was not a case of being *convinced*. This is something that we *know*, and to know this all we have to do is to follow the argument our-selves and then ask ourselves 'Is this condition in which, as Descartes would say, we perceive clearly for certain reasons that the angles are equal to two right angles one of *knowing*, or is it only one of being convinced?' We can only answer 'Whatever may be our state on other occasions, here we are knowing this'. And this statement is an expression of our *knowing* that we are knowing this; for we do not *believe* that we are knowing this, we know that we are.

But if that is the proper answer about Descartes's state of mind, then, of course, we know that in it he could not have been liable to deception; and therefore for ourselves we have cut off the doubt at its source. We do not require a proof of God's existence, because we know that Descartes could not have been deceived. In the same way, if his doubt had been the wider doubt whether he was not deceived because his state might have resulted from the use of an imperfect intelligence, that also is cut off for us for the same reason. For obviously a condition of knowing cannot be the result of the use of imperfect faculties.

Further, if someone were to object that after all Des-cartes's condition may have been liable to error, because for all we know we can later on discover some fact which is in-compatible with a triangle's having angles that are equal to two right angles, we can answer that we *know* that there can be no such fact, for in knowing that a triangle must have such angles we also know that nothing can exist which is in-compatible with this fact.

Further we can add: Descartes himself is just on the verge of discovering the truth when he says that *at the time*, i.e.

when following the argument, he finds it impossible to believe otherwise, and finds himself saying 'Here no one can be deceiving me', and that it is only afterwards he can think that he may have been wrong. Plainly, this is just on the verge of saying 'If I consider my state at the time, I *know* that it is one of knowing'. And plainly also he afterwards only comes in fact to doubt whether even in such a state he may not have been mistaken, because he has somehow in the interval come to misrepresent to himself the character of his past state. If he had not, he could no more have doubted the truth of his state then than, as he admits, he could doubt it at the time.

And an indication that there is misrepresentation is to be found in the fact that he has to give different accounts of his state while following the demonstration, according as he describes it as it presented itself to him at the time, and as he describes it as it presented itself to him afterwards. As it presented itself at the time, he describes it as one of perceiving clearly that the angles are equal to two right angles; as it presented itself afterwards, he describes it as one in which he only *thought* he perceived clearly; and although only one of these descriptions can be true he has to introduce the second, because otherwise he could not have represented himself as afterwards doubting the truth of that state.

On Descartes's own showing, therefore, he is thinking of the state differently at the time and afterwards.

We therefore can get Descartes out of the impasse, provided we allow, *as we can*, that the state to which he referred as one of perceiving clearly was in fact one of knowing, and one which he could have known at the time to be one of knowing. By doing this we stop the rot from starting. Descartes's trouble was that he let the rot begin, and once it is allowed to start, it cannot be prevented from going on indefinitely.

IV

We are now in a position to consider a question of interpretation which lies in the background, and to revert to Descartes's account in Meditation III of the process of becoming certain.

According to this account to become certain that an A is B, e.g. that a three-sided figure is three-angled, we have first to perceive clearly and distinctly that an A is B; we have then to become certain that our state is one of clearly and distinctly perceiving and also certain that any such state is necessarily true. Given these certainties we then become certain that an A is B.

Now unfortunately Descartes gives no elucidation of what he means by clearly and distinctly perceiving. Such elucidation as he offers is of clear and distinct *ideas*, and what he says about these gives us no help. But even if we waive this difficulty, once we have grasped the difference between knowing and believing, we find there is a question which we want Descartes to answer in order to understand what his doctrine is. We want to talk to Descartes thus:

> We won't worry you with the question what exactly you mean by perceiving clearly and distinctly. But, whatever you mean by it, obviously you think that the characteristic meant is one which necessarily belongs to a state of mind of a certain kind, and we must have from you *your* answer to the question. Is the state, which you are maintaining it to be a characteristic of, one of knowing, or is it one of believing truly? For the state of which you are maintaining this must be one or the other, and we must know which you consider it to be because your view will be quite different according to which you consider it is, and so if you don't say, we shall not know what your view is.

To appreciate the importance of getting an answer, we need only notice the difference it will make both to the view and to the difficulties to which it gives rise. Suppose Descartes

were to answer that he held that what he calls clearly perceiving was a characteristic of knowing. Then his view would
be this: In order to come to know that an A is B, we must
first know that an A is B, then, by reflecting on the general
characteristics of this state, come to know that it exhibits
a distinguishing characteristic of knowing, viz. perceiving
clearly, and thus come to know that an A is B by coming to
know that we *know* this.

If, however, Descartes were to give the other answer, his
view would be as follows: To come to know that an A is B,
we must first have a belief, of a sort which is necessarily true,
that an A is B, then by reflecting on this state come to know
that it exhibits a distinguishing characteristic of a belief that
is necessarily true, viz. that of being a condition of perceiving clearly, and then, by knowing that the belief is necessarily
true, for the first time come to *know* that an A is B.

The first view is obviously open to two fatal objections.

1. It is to involve oneself in sheer self-contradiction to
maintain that in order to come to know something, we must
go through a process which *ex hypothesi* starts from a condition in which we already know it. The view also leads to an
infinite process. For if, to know that an A is B, we must know
that we know it, then to know that we know it we must know
that we know that we know it and so on.

2. The view is obviously general, being the view that to
know anything whatever, we must first know it, and then
come to know that we know it, by applying to our first state
what we know to be a test of a state of knowing, i.e. a distinguishing characteristic of knowing, viz. that of being a
state of perceiving clearly, and thereby coming to know that
our first state possesses the characteristic forming the test.
But to be able to apply the test, we must already and without applying knowledge of the test know (a) that the characteristic forming the test is a test, i.e. that clear perceiving is a
distinguishing characteristic of knowing, and (b) that the
state to which we are to apply the test has the characteristic
which forms the test, that of being a state of clear perceiving.
Yet, if to know one thing we must apply what we know to be
a test, we must equally do so to know any other thing, in-

cluding the fact that the characteristic in question is a test. Hence no one can consistently maintain that to know something we must apply the knowledge of a test of knowledge. And, it may be noted, these criticisms are applicable to any suggested test, whether that of clear perceiving or not.

The alternative view also has two fatal defects.

1. Though some beliefs are true and others are false, there is in fact no special distinguishing characteristic of a belief which is true, whether that of clear perceiving or anything else; and so no sort of belief which is necessarily true. And in fact there is no way of discovering whether some belief is true except that of first obtaining *knowledge* of the fact to which the belief relates, that knowledge therefore necessarily not having been obtained by considering the truth of the belief. Consequently, it involves a mere inversion to hold that we can obtain knowledge of some fact by considering whether a belief about it is true.

2. Like the first view it cannot be maintained consistently. For it is that we can only come to know any particular thing whatever, say that I exist, by first acquiring the corresponding belief of a certain kind, viz. one in which we perceive clearly and distinctly, and then applying to this belief the knowledge of the test of a true belief, viz. clearness and distinctness of perception. But to maintain this is to imply inconsistently that we already know, without applying the test, (*a*) that the test is a test, (*b*) that the belief to which it is applied does exhibit the mark which forms the test.

This criticism, it may be remarked, can be extended to any suggested test or criterion of truth, i.e., really, of the truth of a belief. Thus what is called the coherence notion of truth is at bottom the doctrine that so far as knowledge is attainable, it is attainable only by applying to a belief the test of coherence or non-coherence with other beliefs. And obviously it implies that we know without applying any test (*a*) that the coherence of a belief with others is a distinguishing characteristic of a true belief, (*b*) that we have certain beliefs, and (*c*) that certain particular beliefs are, and that others are not, coherent with a given belief. Moreover this doctrine is exposed to two additional criticisms. The first is that, what-

ever precisely be meant by 'coherence with', the coherence of
a belief with all our other beliefs does not necessitate that it
is true, since, as we know, any number of coherent beliefs
may all be false. The second is that, as we know, the incoherence of a single belief with all our other beliefs does not
necessitate that it, rather than they, is false.

The broad fact is that there cannot be any such thing as a
test or criterion of truth. The phrase is used ambiguously
both for a distinguishing characteristic of a true belief, and,
under the mistaken idea that knowledge is true, for a distinguishing characteristic of knowledge, a characteristic other
than knowing which distinguishes a state of knowing from a
state of believing.

Of the two forms of the idea that knowledge can only be
reached by applying a test, the idea that what is required is a
test of *knowledge* is the more fundamental and the more
insidious. It, of course, arises from the idea that, though at a
given moment we *may* be knowing something, we neither
know at the time that we are *knowing*, nor can we, by reflecting on our activity, know directly that it is a state of knowing.
This, of course, gives rise to the idea that, though we *may* be
knowing something, our position is only as good as if we did
not, since what we want is not simply to know something but
to know that we are knowing. And then we think that the
remedy can only lie in finding out afterwards that there is
some characteristic specially characterizing a state which is
one of knowing, and then finding on reflection that our state
possessed this character. But though there may be only a few
things of which we can say we know that we know them,
one of them is that knowledge cannot be reached by applying
a test. And it is obvious that if there is to be such a thing as
knowing that we *know* something, that knowing can be attained only *directly*, we in knowing the thing knowing directly, either at the same time or on reflection, that we are
knowing it. Further, we have in fact only to take certain
instances to acquire such knowledge. I have, for example, in
fact only to do what is usually called thinking that a figure
having three sides must have three angles and to reflect on
my activity, to *know* that here I am *knowing* this, i.e. that

what is called thinking this is knowing it. Again if, speaking truthfully, I say 'I wonder whether you are agreeing with me', on reflection I know and know directly that I am *knowing* that I am wondering.

Notice, there is a parallel fact in the case of believing, viz. that we either do or can by reflecting know that we are believing and so *not knowing*.

We should now return to the interpretation of Descartes. The real difficulty which we find ourselves up against is this: Since we recognize that knowing and believing are different, so that the same state of mind cannot be both, we can only attribute a definite view to Descartes if we can express it in terms of the distinction, and yet the fact is that Descartes himself failed to recognize any such distinction.

It is not even as though Descartes had asked himself 'Do knowing and believing differ in kind?' and then made the mistake of answering that they do not. We could then have ascribed to Descartes a definite though mistaken view. Our real trouble is that Descartes had not even asked himself the question. If we speak quite strictly, we cannot say what Descartes's view was.

At best we can only consider what his statements suggest he would have said if he had asked himself the question. And here we get conflicting results. That he would have denied a difference in kind is suggested by his using, as he sometimes does, the phrases '*perfect* knowledge', 'a *perfect* and certain science', '*very* certain', '*very* clear and distinct', '*very* evident', and again by the mere phrase 'clear and distinct' perceiving or conceiving. On the other hand, the opposite conclusion is suggested by his references to a state in which doubt is *impossible* (not merely difficult or slight) and in which we are certain (N.B. not 'very certain').

The fact is that owing to Descartes's failure to notice the difference in kind between knowing and believing he alternately speaks of a state which is in fact one of knowing and which he describes as one of clear perceiving, both in terms which imply that it is one of knowing and not believing, and also in terms which imply that it is one of believing of a special kind. We thus, so far as Descartes's language goes, get two inconsistent doctrines set out side by side, without any consciousness on his part that they are different: (1) that a state of mind which is one of clear perceiving is necessarily one of knowing; (2) that such a state is a belief of a sort which is necessarily true. With the former doctrine is bound up the further doctrine, that to reach knowledge we must apply to knowledge a test of knowledge, and with the latter the further doctrine that to reach knowledge we must apply to a belief a test of the truth of a belief.

But further, there is this to be added: Descartes is getting very near the truth where he describes the process of becoming certain in mathematics while following the argument, and in doing so tacitly reverts to his first account of the process of becoming certain (that implied in the second Meditation). For here 'I perceive clearly and distinctly' can be understood as only a loose phrase for 'I know or am certain' and he seems only just to stop short of saying 'when, for example, I consider the nature of some triangle of the existence of which I am certain, I am certain that its character of having three sides necessitates that it has also the characteristic of having three angles, and thus I am certain that it has three angles, and in being certain of this, I am also certain that I am certain, i.e. know that I am knowing, and so know that I cannot here be deceived'.

V

In commenting on Descartes I have made many statements intended to state what the facts really are, and incidentally I have maintained that at times Descartes gets very near the truth himself.

But I do not expect to have convinced you of the truth of all I have said. In fact I should be rather sorry if I had. For the questions which Descartes raises are far too difficult for anyone to accept statements relating to them uncritically. Probably various objections will have occurred to you, and I now propose to try to anticipate what they are and to deal with them.

The doctrine I have been either stating or implying to be true can, I think, be summarized thus:

1. We are certain of certain things, e.g. that we are wondering what is going to happen next, that we did wonder a short time ago what was going to happen next (an act of memory), that a three-sided figure is three-angled and again that the three-sidedness of a three-sided figure necessitates that the number of its angles is three, that there cannot be a test of truth.

2. To be certain of something is to know it.

3. To know something is one thing and to believe something is another.

4. When we know something, we either do or can directly know that we are knowing it, and when we believe something we know or can know that we are believing and not knowing it, and in view of the former fact, we *know* that in certain instances of its use our intelligence is not defective, so that Descartes's difficulties fall to the ground.

Now I think you will find that the objections which you may feel will reduce to two. And these are best considered separately.

The first is really only a repetition of an objection which Descartes felt to the truth of his idea that a state in which we perceive something clearly is necessarily true. It will be urged that it is preposterous to maintain that, when we are certain, we know, since obviously we and others have often been certain, and yet afterwards found that we were mistaken. Men, for example, were at one time certain that the sun goes round the earth, or that local spirits interfered with the course of nature; again two men are frequently certain of contrary things, e.g. that motion is absolute and that it is relative, that space might have a fourth dimension and that it could not, that space is infinite and that it is not. But in such cases only one can be *right*, and as both are in the same kind of state, even the one who is right cannot *know*.

In considering this objection, we should first notice that there is a state of mind which we may fail to distinguish from one of certainty, and so regard as one of certainty when it is not. This is what we may describe as an unquestioning frame of mind—or as one in which it did not occur to us to doubt something, or—as Cook Wilson described it—one of 'being under the impression that'. I, for example, might be, as we say, thinking without question that the thing in front of me is a table, or that to-day is Tuesday, or that so and so came to see me last week. Cook Wilson said of this state that it simulates knowledge since, as is obvious, in this state there is no doubt or uncertainty. But it obviously is not the same as *being certain*. In such states we are, of course, constantly being mistaken, and unless we distinguish such states from being certain, we are apt to take instances of them as instances of our being certain and yet mistaken. And once we have noticed the distinction, we are forced to allow that we are certain of very much less than we should have said otherwise. Thus, we have to allow that we are not certain of the truth of any inductive generalization, e.g. that all men are mortal, or that sugar is sweet, for we are not *certain* that anything in the nature of a man requires that he shall at some time die; we are not even certain that the sun will rise to-morrow. And if you were asked in a law court, 'Are you certain of the truth of what you have just said?', you would probably answer, 'Well, if it comes to that there is precious little I am certain of'. It is no use to object, 'Well, if you are going to restrict what we know to what we are certain of, you are going to reduce what we know to very little'. For nothing is gained by trying to make out that we know when we do not, and the important thing is to be able to convince ourselves that there are at least some things that we know, whether the knowledge of them is important or not, especially as, if there were nothing which we knew, all our beliefs would be worthless, as having no basis in knowledge.

Next we should ask ourselves whether when we are prepared to say we know we are also prepared to say we are certain, or *vice versa*. Now, unquestionably, we should answer to the first question 'Yes'. For we should never think of ourselves as knowing something unless we thought of ourselves as certain. The converse, however, is not so obvious, viz. that where we should say we are certain, we should be prepared to say we know. But consider what is the alternative. If when

we are certain, for example, that the square of three must be
an odd number, we do not know, what *do* we do? The only
possible answer is, 'In such a state we *think* we know'. But
then consider what can be meant by a state of thinking we
know this. The answer must be, 'Only thinking this', i.e.
thinking that the square of three must be odd, as opposed to
knowing that it must. But if we consider our state of mind,
the retort is obvious—we do not *think* this, we *know* it. In
fact, in the end it seems impossible to distinguish the meaning of knowing and being certain; any reluctance to admit
this comes from a failure to distinguish being certain from
what we may call thinking without question.

Now if we bear these considerations in mind, we shall
come to allow that many asserted instances of mistaken certainties were not really instances of certainties. We should
say, for example, 'Though many have thought without question that the sun went round the earth, and many also have
been certain that they had certain perceptions, no one has
ever been *certain* that it was the sun which went round the
earth rather than that it was the earth which went round the
sun.' And we should add, as Descartes in effect did, that anyone who said that he was *certain* that the sun moved would,
when the difference between being certain and thinking without question had been pointed out to him, end by saying that
what really he was certain of was that he had had certain perceptions.

As regards the alleged certainties of opposite things, it will
on examination turn out that at best only one of the two people was certain. At least two kinds of cases of such alleged
certainties must be distinguished.

1. That in which one of the so-called certainties is really a
failure to be certain. A, for example, says he is certain of the
first law of motion, i.e. certain that a body's moving uni-
formly in a straight line requires it to go on moving with the
same speed and in the same direction unless it is interfered
with by another body. *B* says he is certain that it does not
require this. Here at best what can be true is only that *B*
fails to be certain that it does require this. Again, I am not
lying when I say I am certain (*a*) that space and time must be

infinite, and (*b*) that space must have as many as three dimensions and no more, so that to speak of a two- or a four-dimensional space is mere words. You might reply that you are certain space need not have more than two and might have, say, seven dimensions, though in fact the space with which we are acquainted seems to have only three. I should reply that at best all that is happening is that when you consider the matter, you are not certain that it must have three, and that at worst you are only uttering mere words which express no thought on your part.

2. That in which the so-called certainties of opposite things are really certainties about different things.

(1) I once made what I thought the unquestionable remark to a German mathematician who was also a physicist that only a body could move—so that, for example, the centre of gravity of a body or of a system of bodies, which is a geometrical point, could not move. He, as I rather expected, thought I was just mad. In this case I should certainly have said I was certain that a centre of gravity cannot move, and I think he would have said he was certain that it could. Here I personally should assert he could not possibly have been more than uncertain that it could not, and that, if he had thought a bit more, he would have become certain that it could not; you cannot make a man think, any more than you can make a horse drink.

But (2) I also made the same remark (viz. that only a body could move) to a mathematician here. What was in my mind was that it is mere inaccuracy to say that a wave could move, and that where people talked of a wave as moving, say with the velocity of a foot, or a mile, or 150,000 miles, a second, the real movement consisted of the oscillations of certain particles, each of which took place a little later than a neighbouring oscillation.

He scoffed for quite a different reason. He said that you could illustrate a movement by a noise—that, for example, if an explosion occured in the middle of Oxford the noise would spread outwards, being heard at different times by people at varying distances from the centre, so that at one moment the noise was at one place and that a little later it was somewhere else, and in the interval it had moved from one place to the other.

Now, of course, it was not in dispute that in the process imagined people in different places each heard a noise at a rather different time. The only question was, 'Was the succession of noises a movement?', and I think that on considering the matter you will have to allow that it was not, and that what happened was that he, being certain of the noises, and wanting to limit the term 'movement' to something he was certain of, used the term 'movement' to designate the succession of noises, implying that this was the real thing of which we were both talking. But if this is what happened, then he was using the term 'movement' in a sense of his own, and in saying that in the imagined case he was certain of a movement, he was being certain of something other than the opposite of what I was certain of.

Take some more instances in the same line of country.

Consider the controversy whether the motion of a body is absolute, or whether it is relative to some other body. Some would say they are certain that it is absolute. On the other hand, some disciples of Einstein at least would say that they are certain that it is relative, and that when we say, for example, that the earth is moving, what we mean is simply that it is moving relatively to some other body or bodies, e.g. the sun or the milky way.

Suppose someone inferred from certain observations that the sun and the earth were getting closer together at a steadily increasing rate. He might go on to think that the explanation lay either in the fact that the earth was at rest and the sun moving towards it with a constant acceleration, or *vice versa* (omitting, for simplicity, a combination of movements of both), and he might go on to inquire which was moving. In doing this he would of course be implying that motion was absolute, that it is just change of place, a change which one body could go through, without the existence of another body. What the relativist would maintain, however, is that these two alternative explanations are merely statements of one and the same fact, viz. that each body was moving towards the other with constant acceleration; and he would say he was certain of this. But it is clear that what he is thinking of and being certain about as being the same in both cases is the alteration of distance between the two, which, though it implies a movement of one or the other or both, is not identical with it. And if he insists that this alteration of distance is a movement, it can be retorted that he means by a 'movement' something different from what we do.

The second objection is one which it is specially important for us to consider because Descartes himself felt it acutely and also gets very near to answering it.

The certainties of which Descartes was thinking are all certainties attained by the operation or activity of thinking, in the sense in which we say that when we reason we *think*, a sense in which we speak of thinking as something opposed to perceiving and to being self-conscious and to remembering. As an indication of this, we should all be prepared to give a *reason* for the certainties of which Descartes was thinking, saying, for example, 'We are certain that we exist, *since* our persuasion that there is no world requires or necessitates the existence of ourselves as the subject of the persuasion, i.e. as that which is persuaded.' [Contrast an act of memory—'I am certain that I heard a sound a short time ago'. If someone asked me 'Why?', I should answer, 'I have no reason for being certain of this, I am simply certain of it'.]

Now the objection relates to our certainties reached by thinking—and it may be put thus:

The object of knowledge, i.e. what is known, if there be knowledge, is some part of an independent world of reality, i.e. some part of a reality which exists independently of the knower and whose character is independent of that of the knower. Now the only way in which the nature of anything in this independent world can come to be known is either by observing it, i.e. perceiving it, or, should the thing be a state of ourselves, by an act of reflection on our part which is analogous to perception. If we perceive something to have a certain characteristic, that is knowing it to have that characteristic, and that is all that need be said. And there is no other way of knowing it.

Now tne states of which Descartes is thinking are unquestionably states of certainty. Moreover, in them there is something which renders it inevitable or necessary that we are
certain of that of which we are certain—something which, as
we say, makes us certain. In being certain that a three-sided
figure is also three-angled, I am not simply certain of this,
there is something which necessitates that I am certain that
it is three-angled and not four-angled or five-angled, or in
some instances three-angled and in others, say, seven-angled.

But, though we know this to be so, yet if we ask, 'Must the
things about which we are certain correspond with our certainty by really having the property which we are certain they
have?', we have to answer 'No'. For even though there is something which renders it necessary that we are *certain* that the
thing has that property and not another, our being certain
that it has it does not require or necessitate that it *has it*.
For its possession or non-possession of the property depends
on its nature and not on the nature of any attitude of ours
towards its possession or non-possession of it. And even
though there is something which renders it inevitable that we
are certain that it has it, this something does not render it
inevitable that it has it. For this something can only be something in our own minds, and this cannot render anything in
the real world necessary or inevitable.

In fact, as Descartes put it in effect with reference to another instance, and using the language of thinking and conceiving clearly where he might have substituted 'being certain': 'Though I conceive, i.e. conceive clearly and distinctly,
that God exists, and though I cannot conceive God except as
existing, i.e. though there is something which makes it necessary that I conceive God as existing and not as not existing,
it does not follow that God exists: for my thought imposes no
necessity on things.' That is, my thought that, e.g. God exists,
even though there be something which renders it necessary
that I should think this, does not render it necessary that God
does exist. Consequently to be certain is *not* to know, for since
a thing is not required to have a property by our being certain
that it has it, even though something renders our certainty
inevitable, our certainty may be mistaken, and so cannot (not

'may not') be knowledge. And even if afterwards we observed some of the triangles we had been certain about to have three angles, this would not show that our certainty about them was knowledge.

The objection is of course serious, since it implies that general knowledge, i.e. knowledge that all things of a certain kind have a certain property, is obtainable only by observation of all the particular things, and that therefore to attempt to gain it, in advance of observations, by thinking is futile. And its seriousness is increased so far as knowledge of things in the physical world is concerned, as soon as we discover, as sooner or later we must, that we do not observe, i.e. perceive, physical things at all.

This being the difficulty, what are we to do about it?

The objection, of course, allows that in the certainties to which it applies there is something which makes us certain, i.e. renders it necessary or inevitable that we are certain. Now this something is what we should call our reason for being certain. And, as consideration of instances will show, we mean by our reason for being certain that an A is B, another certainty, and a certainty of something of a special kind, viz. our certainty that a certain characteristic of an A requires or necessitates that an A is B. Thus if we were asked what is our reason for being certain that a three-sided figure is three-angled, we should answer, 'Our certainty that the possession by a three-sided figure of the characteristic of being three-sided requires that the figure also has the characteristic of being three-angled.' And if we were to become certain by what we call a process of argument that a picture A on a wall was higher than a picture B, and if we were then asked, 'What made us certain', we might give some such answer as, 'Our certainty that A's being higher than X and B's being lower than X necessitated that of A and B, A was the higher'. To say this, is only to give our reason for being certain, in the same way that we might give our reason for thinking so and so, in the sense of believing so and so.

The objection therefore allows what is in fact true, that there is no such thing as our being barely or merely certain that an A is B, i.e. certain without having a reason; i.e. really, that our certainty that an A is B involves or implies our certainty that an A's possessing a certain characteristic requires it to have the characteristic of B-ness.

But once we realize this the objection assumes quite a different complexion. In fact the most direct answer to the question becomes paradoxically simple. For the objection is expressed in the statement, 'Though I am certain, for example, that a three-sided figure is three-angled, and though there is something which makes me certain of this, viz., my certainty that the three-sidedness of a three-sided figure requires it to be three-angled as well, yet a three-sided figure need not be three-angled.' And to this it can now be replied that the statement is really only mere words, and not an expression of an activity of our minds, whether one of being certain or one of having an opinion. For it means: 'Though I am certain that a certain definite character possessed by a three-sided figure in nature requires such a figure to have three angles, there is no definite character of such a thing in nature which requires this.' And obviously we do not actually think there is no such character, when *ex hypothesi* we are certain that there is such a character.

We ought, however, to go rather more below the surface. First we should ask, 'Can the certainty which is the reason for our certainty that an A is B be said to be knowledge; i.e. do we know, for example, that our certainty that the three-sidedness of a three-sided figure requires it to have three angles is knowledge?' Here, if we face the issue, the answer can only be 'Yes'. It may be objected that this state cannot really even be one of certainty, and so not one of knowledge, since it itself is something for which we have no reason. But to this the answer is, as we shall see if we think it out, that there cannot be such a thing as a reason for a reason, or more fully our having a reason for having a reason, and that the certainty that one thing necessitates another is in one respect analogous to such a certainty as that now our condition is one of perplexity, viz. in being simple, in the sense that our certainty does not depend on a reason.

Secondly, we should consider what has now become of the objection that our certainty that an A is B cannot be knowl-

edge because an A need not in the real world conform to our
certainty by being B. The fact is that it has simply vanished.
For now admittedly it is a condition of our being certain
that an A is B, that we know a certain fact in nature, viz. that
the possession by an A of a certain characteristic, *a*, necessitates its having the characteristic of being B, and knowing this
we cannot even raise the question, 'Need an A in nature have
the characteristic B?', because we know that a certain definite
characteristic which it has requires it to have that characteristic.

The only possible ground on which this might be disputed
would be the contention that what is called the necessitation
of B-ness in an A by an A's having a characteristic, *a*, is *not* a
fact in the real world. But this contention is merely the result
of the childlike and almost childish idea—though the idea
chiefly appears in grown-ups and especially in those whose interests are chiefly scientific—that only that is real which is
sensible, observable, or perceptible.

It is now possible to see—at any rate if you grant that what
I have been saying is true—how very nearly Descartes got to
the truth in trying to meet his own objection. For, speaking
of what he considers to be his inevitably conceiving that God
exists, he says, not that God's existence is brought about by
my thought, or that my thought imposes any necessity on
things, i.e. renders it necessary that the things about which I
think correspond to my thought, but on the contrary that the
necessity of the existence of God (i.e. really the fact that certain facts in nature necessitate that a God exists) determines
me to think in this way. Here Descartes seems just on the
verge of stating the truth, and if he had substituted for 'the
necessity' 'my thought of the necessity', or rather 'my knowledge of the necessity', he would have got it right, for he
would then have been saying what in principle can be stated
thus: what renders me certain that an A is B is my certainty
or knowledge of that which in nature necessitates that an A
is B; with the implication that just for that reason in being
certain that an A is B, I cannot possibly be mistaken.

THE BASIS OF KNOWLEDGE
IN DESCARTES

A. K. STOUT

In the Meditations, Descartes, pursuing the method of universal doubt, reaches three main grounds of certainty, the relation between which has been left obscure both by himself and by his critics and exponents. These are (1) the intuition of the necessity of his own existence, stated in the rather misleading form "*Cogito ergo sum*"; (2) the general rule that all that is clearly and distinctly perceived is true; and (3) the veracity of God. The purpose of this paper is to try to show how these three are related to each other, and to assign to each its relative importance.

The most straightforward account of the third Meditation so far as it bears on this question is as follows: "I find the existence of myself as a thinking being an indubitable fact. It is indubitable only because I clearly and distinctly perceive it; that is the ground of its certainty and must equally be a sufficient ground of the certainty of other judgments. I may therefore take it as a general rule that what is clearly and distinctly perceived is true.

"But here a speculative doubt occurs to me. There may be an all-powerful Being who has created me such that I am deceived even when my perception is clear and distinct. Until, therefore, I have proved that if God exists He is not a deceiver I am not justified in my certainty even when I am

Originally published in two parts in *Mind*, *N.S.*, Vol. XXXVIII, No. 151, July 1929, pp. 330–342, and No. 152, October 1929, pp. 458–472. Substantial sections of the second part have been omitted (as indicated), and minor revisions have been made. Reprinted by permission of the author and the editor of *Mind*.

in fact clearly and distinctly perceiving something (although *so long as I am doing so* I cannot help being certain and cannot entertain even the most speculative doubt) nor, *a fortiori*, am I justified in maintaining as a general rule that all that I clearly and distinctly perceive is true.

"But when I turn to consider the nature of an all-powerful and infinite Being, I clearly and distinctly perceive that He must exist and that He cannot deceive me. My doubt is thus wholly overcome."

It seems, then, that the general rule "all that is clearly and distinctly perceived is true," founded on the single instance of the *Cogito* and confirmed by the appeal to the veracity of God, can be applied as an infallible test of the truth of propositions whose clearness and distinctness has been independently discovered. It is as if each time we clearly and distinctly perceived something we could argue "All that I clearly and distinctly perceive is true; I am now clearly and distinctly perceiving A; therefore A is true."

The general rule, it appears, is reached from the examination of a single instance—namely, the self-evident truth that I am a thinking thing. The passage is very familiar and perhaps for that very reason its difficulties are usually overlooked. "I am certain," says Descartes,[1] "that I am a thinking thing; but do I not therefore likewise know what is required to render me certain of a truth? In this first knowledge there is nothing that gives me assurance of its truth except the clear and distinct perception of what I affirm, which would not indeed be sufficient to give me the assurance that what I say is true, if it could ever happen that anything I thus clearly and distinctly perceived should prove false; and accordingly it seems to me that I may now take it as a general rule that all that I very clearly and distinctly perceive is true."

Logically this argument involves a circle. Clearness and distinctness as a universal test of truth is derived from the *Cogito ergo sum*, and the truth of the *Cogito ergo sum* is derived from its clearness and distinctness. "I am certain of the truth of A because of certain marks BC (which I call

[1] Med. III. The translation is Veitch's.

clearness and distinctness). BC can only guarantee the truth of the judgment A if they guarantee the truth of the judgments in which they are present. But A is true. Therefore BC are universal signs of truth." Obviously you must prove BC to be a universal guarantee of truth before you know A to be true—that is if A really depends for its truth on BC. But this dependence is just what Descartes did not really mean and should not have implied. He is at fault because he suggests that the judgment "I think therefore I exist" taken as a whole, is inferred from another judgment "I clearly perceive that 'I think therefore I exist'"; or, in other words, that in apprehending the existence of the self as a thinking thing I am arguing "My perception of this is clear and distinct and therefore true."

It must be admitted that Descartes' words imply this; but it is not (I would urge) what he intended to say. The *Cogito ergo sum*, he tells us explicitly,[2] is itself an intuition, not an inference. It is "a simple act of mental vision," "known *per se*" and "not deduced by a syllogism"; the being, that is, is not inferred from the thinking. Nor did he mean to argue that intuitions are dependent for their truth on the validity of any general rule, even if the rule be itself intuited. In spite of his language in the passage quoted (which I think must be taken as in some measure tentative and provisional), he holds that what I perceive is self-evident and while I am perceiving it I cannot doubt its truth. I may expect to find the same general conditions present in all truths that appear to me self-evident, and, having found them, I may give them the names "clearness and distinctness"; and they may then serve me as a guide in trying to discover self-evident propositions. But these conditions can never be the guarantee of the truth of the self-evident propositions they condition. "To perceive clearly and distinctly" in the passage quoted simply means "to perceive in such a way that I cannot doubt the truth of my perception," and the general rule amounts to no more than "what I cannot doubt is true." But when I am attending to a

[2] Reply to Objections II., *Thirdly*. Adam and Tannery's edition of the complete works of Descartes [hereafter referred to as AT], vol. vii., p. 140.

proposition which I cannot doubt I do not argue to convince myself of its truth: "What I cannot doubt is true; I cannot doubt this, therefore it is true." Such a use of the general rule is futile because it is superfluous. We shall see later, however, that there is another and more legitimate use which can be made of it.

Passages in the fifth Meditation bear out the contention that Descartes does not maintain consistently that when I clearly and distinctly perceive something I argue from its clearness and distinctness to its truth. "And even if I had not demonstrated it [i.e. that all clear and distinct perceptions are true] the nature of my mind is certainly such that none the less I could not help assenting to them, at least as long as I am clearly perceiving them."[3] And again "But, indeed, whatever mode of proof I adopt in the end, it always comes to this, that only those things which I clearly and distinctly perceive entirely convince me."[4] The ultimate fact is, then, that there are certain truths which I grasp intuitively and cannot help believing; and their logical nature I call "clear and distinct." The passage in the third Meditation on this view expresses only a stage in Descartes' thought, a stage to be superseded by a more adequate explanation.

Why, then, does Descartes formulate the general rule at all? What is the use of it, since it cannot be the test of truth of those indubitable propositions from which apparently it is itself derived? The answer is that it must be established to overcome a doubt to which every clear and distinct perception is liable, not when we are attending to it, but when we reflect upon the general conditions of our knowledge. The doubt is that the world of which I am part may be caused by an infinitely powerful demon who is constantly endeavouring to deceive me; the one truth that cannot be doubted is that of my own existence, for even if I am deceived I must exist; indeed, the fact that I am deceived is itself proof of my existence.[5]

[3] Med. V., AT VII, 65, l. 6.
[4] *Loc. cit.*, 68, l. 21.
[5] Cf. Med. II., AT VII, 25, ll. 5–10; 28, l. 30–29, l. 3; Med. III., 36, ll. 12–17.

It is perhaps because the certainty of self-consciousness differs in this way from other intuitions that Descartes tries to derive the general rule from it alone. But although it is not itself affected by the hypothesis of a deceiver it affords no ground for defending other intuitions against that hypothesis. A general reason must be found for trusting the certainty which clear and distinct perception carries with it; in other words, it must be proved that "all that I clearly and distinctly perceive is true," and if the argument is not to be circular, either this proof must depend for its validity on something other than its own clearness and distinctness, or else its clearness and distinctness must differ from that of other perceptions in such a way that it logically justifies itself against all doubts. Evidently it is no use trying to infer the general rule from the particular instances of clear and distinct perception, still less from one of them alone—the *Cogito ergo sum*. Nor in fact does Descartes intend this, in spite of the passage at the beginning of Meditation III.

Descartes' argument is as follows.[6] Although I cannot help believing the truth of what I am actually perceiving clearly and distinctly, yet, unless I can prove that there does not exist an all-powerful Being who wills to deceive me, I am justified in doubting the truth of a conclusion which I remember to have drawn by a series of steps, each of which was clear and distinct, from clear and distinct premises, provided that I am no longer attending in detail to the steps of the argument. For instance, I am certain that the angles of a triangle are equal to two right angles, so long as I am attending to the geometrical proof; but when I have ceased to attend to it, however well I remember that I did perceive its truth most clearly, I may still be in doubt, unless I have the guarantee of God's veracity.[7] While I was attending to the proof I was incapable of doubting; now I can doubt, and my doubt cannot be overthrown unless I can prove that if there be an all-powerful Being He cannot deceive me. If I can go further and prove that there does exist an all-powerful Being who cannot deceive

[6] Med. V., AT VII, 69, l. 16—70, l. 9; and Reply to Obj. II., *Thirdly*, AT VII, 140.
[7] Med. V., AT VII, 69, l. 26—70, l. 4.

me, I can no longer have this or any other ground for doubting that what I clearly and distinctly perceive is true. It is from God's nature alone that the general rule can be derived.

It is not generally noticed that this argument admits of two interpretations. (1) It may be taken to mean that apart from the existence of a veracious God what I clearly and distinctly perceive may be false, even though I cannot help believing it to be true so long as I am perceiving it; it is only on reflexion that this doubt can occur to me, and it is only by proving the existence of a God who cannot deceive that I can dispel it once for all. On this view God is needed to guarantee the truth of the general principle that what I clearly and distinctly perceive is true; but the principle is for use only on reflexion, and might take the form "What I *have* clearly and distinctly perceived is true." (2) On the other view, Descartes is abandoning the position that the knowledge of God is necessary for assuring us that we were not mistaken in believing the truth of what we clearly and distinctly perceived to be true, and is maintaining that *if* I clearly and distinctly perceived something it was (and is) true—God or no God—nor can subsequent reflexion cast the shadow of a doubt on its truth. What part, then, does the knowledge of God play? It is needed to guarantee *the accuracy of my memory,* not the principle that what I have clearly and distinctly perceived is true. The doubt to be dispelled is not "Can I be deceived when I clearly and distinctly perceive something?" but "can I be deceived in my belief that the steps by which I reached a certain conclusion—a conclusion now before my mind, but divorced from the argument which led to it—were actually clear and distinct?" (It should be noted that the doubt in this form is better met by a direct appeal to God's veracity than by an appeal to a rule derived from God's veracity. The formula "God cannot deceive us in what appears most evident to us" can be extended to cover not only clear and distinct perception but some instances of memory also.)

It is hard to say whether Descartes ever explicitly distinguished these two views, but it is very important for an understanding of his position against his critics that they should be distinguished. The difference between them may most easily be shown in their bearing on the criticism that in appealing to the proof of God's existence Descartes was arguing in a circle. The first position, as we have stated it, seems clearly open to that criticism; the second can be defended against it, though Descartes does not formulate it with sufficient precision to meet the charge. His language suggests that when he is not interested in meeting this criticism he is assuming the first position, but in meeting it he has (perhaps without realising the change) passed over to the second. I take the second to be a refuge into which he is driven in his attempt to avoid an otherwise formidable criticism of the first. Let us take them in succession.

(1) I read the account in the Meditations as follows.[8] While I am actually perceiving something clearly and distinctly I cannot entertain even the most speculative doubt of its truth. But when I am not perceiving it I can find reason to believe that I may have been deceived when I was perceiving it, however strongly I remember myself to have been convinced at the time. This doubt cannot be overthrown unless I can prove that if an all-powerful Being exists He is not a deceiver. Thus, if I do not believe in a veracious God, I may doubt a conclusion which I remember to have drawn by a clear and distinct process of reasoning from premises whose truth I clearly and distinctly perceived, even though I do not doubt the accuracy of my memory. The same doubt applies to simple self-evident "truths" which do not involve a reasoning process; but though it is valid for these in general— in the form "I may be deceived in whatever I clearly and distinctly perceive"—the attempt to illustrate its validity by applying it to any one in particular defeats itself. For in

---

[8] The important passage for this doctrine is Med. V., AT VII, 69, l. 16–70, l. 9, which ends thus: "Possum enim mihi persuadere me talem a natura factum esse ut interdum in iis fallar quae me puto quam evidentissime percipere [N.B. not 'percepisse'] cum praesertim meminerim me saepe multa pro veris et certis habuisse, quae postmodum aliis rationibus adductus falsa esse judicavi," cf. Med. III., AT VII, 35, l. 30–36, l., 12, and Reply to Obj. VI., AT VII, 428, ll. 1–9. Obj. II., *Thirdly* (AT VII, 124) shows that some at least of Descartes' critics interpreted him as above.

remembering a self-evident "truth" I must re-think it; and while I am thinking it I cannot doubt it.[9] Consequently it is not possible to say (e.g.) "I remember that I clearly and distinctly perceived that I think, hence I am, but in so believing I may well have been deceived"; nor does Descartes attempt to do so,[10] but confines himself to the memory of conclusions whose proofs are no longer attended to in detail, but are remembered to have been clear and distinct.

Thus Descartes has in fact invoked God to prove the truth of the same general rule with which he started—that all that is clearly and distinctly perceived is true. But its use is now to guarantee that all that I have clearly and distinctly perceived was (and of course still is) true; it is to free me from my doubts when I am not clearly and distinctly perceiving, for when I am doing so I cannot doubt.

There is a point which Descartes does not settle. Granted that an all-powerful demon may deceive me, what precise form might the deception take? What sort of error does he lead me to make? It is perhaps worth while to put forward tentatively an answer suggested by some crucial passages in the Meditations. The judgments which appear to me most evident are mathematical judgments. While I am attending to the evidence I cannot doubt the truth of the judgment; in particular, I do not consider the question whether a corporeal world exists at all to which my judgments apply. Mathematics does not raise the question, but if a corporeal world did not exist mathematics would simply be an elaborate deception, because "corporeal nature serves as the object of mathematical demonstrations."[11] In the first Meditation Descartes distinguishes between physics, astronomy, medicine, etc., on the one hand, and arithmetic and geometry on the other; the

[9] Cf. Reply to Obj. II., AT VII, 145–146.

[10] It is true that in the first Meditation he asks: "How do I know that I am not also deceived each time I add together two and three, or number the sides of a square, or form some judgment still more simple, if more simple indeed can be imagined?" (AT VII, 21). But he takes care not to say "in judging that two and three are five" or "that a square has four sides." He refers to the judgments without actually making them.

[11] Med. V., French version, last sentence.

former are doubtful compared with the latter "because they depend on a consideration of composite objects," while the latter "treat of the most simple and most general things" and "are little concerned[12] whether they exist in nature or not." I take this to mean that Physics involves observation and experiment and is consequently dependent on sense-perception. In Physics we frequently seek to prove the existence of this or that particular piece of corporeal nature or to show whether matter exists or can exist in this or that form. Mathematics is satisfied if corporeal nature (which for Descartes is the same thing as space)[13] exists at all. That is why Mathematics as compared with Physics is said not to trouble itself much about existence. The geometrician does not ask whether extension exists, but the philosopher does; and on such a supposition as that of the all-powerful deceiver he may reasonably doubt its existence. Immediately after the assertion of the relative certainty of Mathematics Descartes puts forward this hypothesis to diminish that certainty. God may have "arranged that there should be neither earth nor sky nor any extended thing, nor figure, nor magnitude, nor place, providing at the same time, however, for the rise in me of the perception of all these objects and the persuasion that these do not exist otherwise than as I perceive them."[14] It is tempting to suppose that at the back of Descartes' mind was the thought that if I were deceived in judgments about extension it could only be because extension does not exist at all; and, speaking generally, that if I were deceived in judgments about what is clear and distinct it could only be because the content of my ideas had no basis in reality—they would be inapplicable, not confused. It might be objected that only the possible and not the actual existence of extension is necessary for Mathematics. (Certainly the possible existence of geometrical figures would be sufficient, but since these are modes of extension they depend on the actual or possible existence of extension.) This objection can be met as

[12] Latin: "parum curant"; French: "sans se mettre beaucoup en peine." Med. I., AT VII, 20, ll. 26–27 and IX, 16.

[13] Hence I use the word "extension" rather than "space."

[14] *Ibid.*, French version (quoted from Veitch's translation).

follows. What is clear and distinct *can* exist, but only if there is an all-powerful Being who can cause it to do so. Now, a deceiving demon cannot be all-powerful, for the same grounds which would prove him to be all-powerful would prove that he cannot be a deceiver.[15] Therefore until the existence of a veracious God is established we do not know even that extension *can* exist. The very possibility of the existence of material things "in so far as they constitute the object of pure mathematics" depends on the power of God.[16] If there were no God and Mathematics depended on the assumption that extension can exist, then Mathematics would be fallacious in virtue of that assumption. We should be deceived in believing that because the idea of extension is clear and distinct, therefore extension can exist; for God is needed to constitute even this possibility. Would the suggestion which we have made for judgments about extension apply also to judgments about number? Not necessarily, because number is independent of extension—ideas, for instance, can be numbered. But this is a question Descartes never discusses. He seems to class number, figure, and extension together, and might well have held that if there is no extension there can be no Arithmetic.

To return to our main argument. The important point to note in the position which we have now reached is that unless I can prove the existence of a God who is not a deceiver I may reasonably doubt the truth of what I have clearly and distinctly perceived; it is not merely that I may doubt whether I am now rightly remembering the conclusion I then reached; even if I assume that I am rightly remembering it, and that I did clearly and distinctly deduce it from clearly and distinctly perceived premises, yet I am justified in doubting its truth. Only when I have proved the existence of a veracious God shall I be able to say: "Whenever I clearly and distinctly perceive anything (or have clearly and distinctly perceived anything, or shall do so in the future) not only is it a fact that while so doing I am certain of the truth of what I am perceiv-

[15] Cf. Med. III., AT VII, 52, and Med. IV., 53.
[16] Med. VI. *ad init.*

ing, but also I am absolutely justified in my certainty, and no speculative doubt cast upon it afterwards can overthrow it."

The objection put to Descartes by his critics was that he was arguing in a circle.[17] Their formulation of it presupposes (*a*) that Descartes' argument in the third Meditation, involving the use of the general rule as a ground from which the truth of each separate perception is inferred, is his last word; and (*b*) that consequently the veracity of God is derived from the general rule, and is not a self-evident intuition from which the general rule may itself be derived.[18] Descartes is supposed to argue "I cannot know anything until I know that a veracious God exists. His existence I prove thus. From the clearly and distinctly perceived truth that 'I think hence I am' I draw the rule that all that I clearly and distinctly perceive is true; now, I clearly and distinctly perceive that God necessarily exists and that it belongs to his nature not to be a deceiver." To which the critic replies: "You say that you cannot know anything until you know that God exists; but as you had not proved His existence before you became certain of your own existence and of the truth of the general rule which follows from that certainty, that rule was not really certain, and the proof of God's existence, which depends on it, is not valid." The circularity involved in the argument so stated is too obvious to escape a mind of much less acuteness than Descartes'. We can partially acquit him by rejecting on his behalf the use of the general rule as a basis of inference. But even so the criticism will still hold, though not in exactly the same form. For after that rejection every clear and distinct perception has an equal claim to truth on its own behalf, and does not owe that claim to a rule drawn from the self-evident existence of the self. The "all-powerful deceiver" hypothesis casts doubt on all alike, and it is left to the clear and distinct perception of God, which the speculative doubt brings to the prominent position previously occupied by the perception of the self, to guarantee against that

[17] Obj. II., *Thirdly*, AT VII, 124–125.
[18] In Reply to Obj. I., AT VII, 115–116, Descartes explicitly refers to the rule as the major premise in the argument for God's existence.

hypothesis its own truth and so the truth of all the rest. It is
here that the imputation of circular reasoning comes in, and
we must formulate it in terms wide enough to apply to the
new position.

It is to guarantee the validity of all clear and distinct perception that the knowledge of the existence of God is invoked, yet this supposed knowledge itself depends for its
certainty only upon its clearness and distinctness; and so the
proof of God's existence already assumes the validity of that
principle which it is called upon to guarantee. To put it in
another way, the clear and distinct perception of the existence
of God is no more (and no less) certain than any other clear
and distinct perception, and whatever doubt affects them
must equally affect it. I cannot rid myself of my doubt, because that doubt infects the only means by which I could
dispel it.

(2) This criticism forced Descartes into a new position
(though perhaps he did not himself realise the change). He
could not (he assumed) meet it unless he ceased to maintain
that the hypothesis of an all-powerful deceiver could under-
mine the validity of clear and distinct perception. He had
now to hold not only that when we are clearly and distinctly
perceiving something we cannot doubt its truth, but that we
are justified in our certainty, and that no doubt can be validly
entertained against it even when we are no longer clearly and
distinctly perceiving it. What is clearly and distinctly perceived is true and is known to be true when so perceived and
does not become false when it has ceased to be so perceived.
I have now therefore to accept as true, even against the hypothesis of an all-powerful deceiver, and independently of the
knowledge of God, the general rule that what I have clearly
and distinctly perceived is true; this rule, however, is to be
used as a support only when I am not attending to the evidence for a conclusion; for when I am so attending no doubt
is possible against which it might be used.

It looks at first sight as if Descartes had been forced virtually to give up the view that all knowledge, except the *Cogito
ergo sum*, depends upon the knowledge of God. Here we have
an indefinite number of clearly and distinctly perceived

propositions which would be true and known to be true even if there were no God. But the independence of God is not so great as it at first appears. For even if we admit that clear and distinct perception maintains itself as true against the hypothesis of an all-powerful deceiver, we may still doubt all that depends on memory. God is needed to guarantee the truth of "such conclusions as can recur in memory when I do not further attend to the reasons for which I made the judgment."[19]

Suppose I remember that from certain grounds (which are not now before my mind in detail, but which I remember to have been clearly and distinctly perceived) I inferred by certain steps (which I remember in the same way) a conclusion A. My memory leads me to believe (*a*) that I did go through a certain inferential process, (*b*) that the grounds and the several steps were clearly and distinctly perceived, and (*c*) that A as I have it now before my mind was the conclusion which I then reached. On the supposition of an all-powerful deceiver any one of these three (and, if the first, all three) or the second and the third together may be false. Memory sometimes deceives, and I need God to guarantee the truth of a different rule—that under certain conditions I have the right to trust it.[20]

[19] Reply to Obj. II., *Thirdly*, AT VII, 140. Descartes is quoting Med. V., AT VII, 6, ll. 16 ff., and apparently believes that he is only reiterating what he said there. But the doctrine of the fifth Meditation suggests the interpretation which we have given in the preceding pages—namely, that the truth of the clearly and distinctly proved conclusions themselves, not merely the accuracy of our memory that they were reached by a valid argument from premises whose truth was clearly and distinctly perceived, may be called in question—whereas the argument here will not admit of such an interpretation; for so interpreted it is obviously no answer to the criticism which evoked it.

[20] Descartes does not explicitly formulate any such rule, and quite possibly would not have accepted this formulation. But any other would be equally unsatisfactory, for reasons which will appear shortly. We must note here that Descartes' language often suggests that he is appealing to God to ratify the truth of what is remembered rather than the accuracy of our memory. But the point is that it is only the latter which can be called in question, once the certainty of clear and

Now, if God is needed to guarantee the accuracy of our memory in this way, without Him we should have no Science, or system of knowledge, at all. We should have, indeed, the power of knowing one at a time a number of self-evident truths. We should also (Descartes seems to allow) be able to know the truth of the conclusion of certain arguments while attending to premises, proof and conclusion together; thus the atheist can "know clearly that the three angles of a triangle are equal to two right angles."[21]

But such isolated fragments of knowledge cannot be built into a Science or System of Knowledge without the constant aid of memory. And therefore "without God we can have Knowledge but not Science."[22]

· · ·

So far I have been concerned to show that the general rule "what is clearly and distinctly perceived is true," supposed to be inferred from the *Cogito* and confirmed by God's veracity, does not occupy the place in Descartes' epistemology which is commonly assigned to it. Each clear and distinct perception is self-evident, and needs no rule to guarantee it. The

---

distinct perception is admitted. This certainty being presupposed, we cannot doubt the truth of what we remember as clearly and distinctly perceived unless we doubt the accuracy of our memory.

[21] Reply to Obj. II., *Thirdly*, AT VII, 141. We must not be misled by the statement that "the atheist cannot be sure that he is not deceived in the things that seem most evident to him." The context (it follows immediately after the statement that the atheist can *know* clearly the equality of the angles of a triangle to two right angles) shows that the atheist is not supposed to be able to doubt the truth of a clear and distinct judgment while he is making it, but only the accuracy of his memory when he is no longer attending to the evidence on which he based it. This interpretation is corroborated by a remark in *Princ. Phil.* I., 13, where we are told that a mind sees reason to distrust the truth of its conclusions "where it has the remembrance of a conclusion without recollecting the order of its deduction, and is uncertain whether the author of its being has created it of a nature that is liable to be deceived even in what appears most evident." "What appears most evident" can here be nothing but the remembrance that the conclusion was clearly and distinctly proved.

[22] Reply to Obj. II., AT VII, 141, ll. 3 ff.

general rule plays a subordinate part, but one which is still essential to the ordered system of knowledge we call Science. It has to guarantee the truth of conclusions clearly and distinctly inferred when the course of proof is no longer attended to. But there are at least two ways, not distinguished by Descartes, in which it may do this. It may be taken either as guaranteeing the truth of what has been (without doubt) clearly and distinctly perceived, a truth indubitable so long as the sequence of clearly and distinctly perceived steps is the object of attention, but doubtful when, reflecting on the conditions of knowledge, we consider the conclusion alone; or its sole function may be to guarantee the accuracy of our memory of the conclusion and of the clearness and distinctness of the proof. The former interpretation involves a vicious circle, as Descartes' critics were not slow to point out, and though he did not admit the charge, he imperceptibly transferred the doubt from clearness and distinctness to memory. We have now to consider certain difficulties involved in this change of front, and if possible find ways of dealing with them not inconsistent with the general trend of Descartes' thought.

(1) Descartes seems to have been forced to cut the knot instead of untying it. He has not shown *why* the hypothesis of an all-powerful deceiver should not throw doubt on each clear and distinct perception. It is apparently only because he cannot otherwise escape the imputation of circular reasoning that he has had to concede autonomy to them.

(2) Descartes admits, without explicitly distinguishing, three orders of memory. (*a*) That which is so certain as not to depend on the authority of God—as, for instance, when he says that an atheist may know the equality of the angles of a triangle to two right angles (the proof of which involves memory in the sense of retentiveness).[23] (*b*) That which

[23] It might be argued that God would not deceive even an atheist, and that therefore the atheist's knowledge must depend on God. But the atheist could not himself use this argument to overthrow his doubts, among which is that presented by the hypothesis of an all-powerful deceiver. Any knowledge the atheist has cannot be liable to this particular doubt; therefore the knowledge of the equality of the

does not mislead, but without reference to God would be
open to speculative doubt. (*c*) That which is actually misleading and therefore cannot depend on God's veracity; a
frequent cause of error is that "We presume upon a past
knowledge of much to which we give our assent, as to something treasured up in the memory, and perfectly known to
us; whereas, in truth, we have no such knowledge."[24] The
question Descartes has to answer is why memory should
sometimes be challenged and sometimes not. Can we find a
basis for this distinction and a justification of it? In particular,
to which category belongs the memory involved in a single
scientific or philosophic train of thought? The urgency of
this question is obvious, since if the memory involved in the
proofs of the existence of God cannot be shown to be intrinsically certain, these are evidently still open to the charge
of circular reasoning.

· · ·

In the *Regulæ* Descartes already regarded arguments which
depend on memory as doubtful on that account, but held
that by the practice of constant repetition the movement of
thought can be so much speeded up that practically no
memory is involved. Speed by itself, however, is not enough.
The mind must be able to hold the different parts of the
argument together and take them in at a glance. To do this
it must both stand still and move—it must attend to each
part separately and at the same time pass freely on to others.
Let us illustrate from the process of understanding the proof
of a proposition in Euclid. To begin with, each step is understood separately, so that when we have reached the conclusion
we have not the whole argument before us, but only the final
step and the memory that we had reached it by a series of
clearly understood steps. The process at this stage is *Deduc-
tio,* and the memory involved is reminiscence, a reference to

---

angles of a triangle to two right angles, and consequently the work of
memory which is involved in holding together the different parts of
the proof, must be thought by Descartes not to require an appeal to
the veracity of God.
[24] *Princ. Phil.* XLIV., AT VIII, 21 (Veitch's trans.).

our own past experience. Then we go over the argument again and again, and after each repetition we are able to retain and carry forward more and more of the earlier stages of the proof so as to apprehend their connexion with the later. Finally we have the argument before us as a whole, the conclusion being seen to follow from the premises by a single inferential act. This act is either *Intuitus* or *Enumeratio* according to the complexity of the argument. Whichever it is, Descartes thinks that it is no longer made uncertain by its dependence on memory, because memory has all but disappeared. The truth is rather that memory in the sense of reminiscence has been replaced by memory in the sense of retentiveness. We no longer rely on our memory that we were certain of the previous steps. Instead, the steps themselves are retained, and we are not remembering as facts of our experience all or any one of the occasions on which we repeated the argument. There is now a present intuitive certainty as the result of repetition. Descartes is evidently puzzled to know whether memory is still present or not, but believes that at least it is not present in such a form as to throw doubt on the conclusion.

Suppose, however, that after an interval during which we have not thought of the proposition or its proof we have occasion to refer to the conclusion, e.g. that the angles of a triangle are equal to two right angles, we shall probably regard this judgment as a permanent part of our knowledge, and it will not occur to us as necessary to recall the proof. If the interval has been a long one, the effort might cost time and trouble. We remember that we were satisfied with the proof, and unless we are content not to question such memories, we can have no permanent possessions in the way of knowledge, and the growth of knowledge would be impossible, since we could have no foundations on which to build. But it is precisely this kind of memory which Descartes thinks liable to a speculative doubt that can only be vanquished by the appeal to a veracious God. The memory involved here is not retentiveness but reminiscence. We remember having had the experience of being convinced by the proof, and even if we cannot accurately determine the conditions of each or any

one occasion on which we had this experience, the reference
is none the less to facts in our past experience. Because
reminiscence rather than retentiveness is here involved
Descartes recognises the presence of memory in a form which
is open to speculative doubt; but because knowledge as an
ordered and growing system would be impossible if the doubt
held good, it can be overthrown by an appeal to the veracity
of God, who could not so completely deceive us.

We have suggested that retentiveness as it functions in
holding together the parts of a proof which we see as a single
whole is taken by Descartes to have the same certainty as
self-evident intuitions, and that the reminiscence involved in
remembering a certain conclusion to have been clearly and
distinctly proved by us may be guaranteed by an appeal to
the veracity of God. It remains to ask (1) if there is any
other work of the memory which is indubitable either with
or without an appeal to God, and (2) in what category we
must place the memory involved in the proofs of the existence of God.

(1) So far as reminiscence is concerned, Descartes evidently regards it, from the time of the Meditations, as inherently fallible, and there is no sign that he ever changed
this opinion. If there were any other instances in which
fallibility of memory would mean the collapse of Science,
then no doubt he would urge that in those instances (and
those only) its justification by the appeal to God is legitimate and convincing. But are there any such? I think not. If
no memory of past facts were assured, except the memory
that we had argued correctly to certain conclusions, Science
would still be possible, though History could not claim to be
scientific. Reminiscence, of course, remains practically useful,
and may lead to results the truth of which can be proved
without reliance on the reminiscence by which they were
reached. And for such purposes it may be helped out by
writing and other sensible aids, though these could not support it against speculative doubts.[25]

25 Cf. AT V, 148, where in reply to the objection that though
God may guarantee my *ingenium*, still my *memoria* may mislead me,
Descartes is reported by Burman as suggesting the use of writing and

As for retentiveness, it cannot itself mislead. It is the vehicle of evidence for judgments, but the evidence taken at its own face value is weighed at the time the judgment is made, and I am convinced or not by what is before me; there is no reference to or inference from the method by which it came before me. When I am relying on present insight into evidence which would not be before me if it were not for retentiveness, I am not relying on retentiveness; I am relying on the evidence itself in just the same way as I should rely on it if it were before me for the first time. So far as I take what is before me to be good evidence on the ground that I remember it, and not because I am now convinced by direct inspection of it, I am relying on reminiscence, not on retentiveness. Retentiveness certainly makes possible the growth of my knowledge and of my powers of dealing with evidence, but I do not argue from it as from evidence.

Following popular usage, Descartes confuses reminiscence and retentiveness under the one term "memory." Since reminiscence is fallible, retentiveness is for him tainted with the same suspicion, and escapes from it not because it is of a radically different nature from reminiscence, but because it seems to him to be reminiscence present in so slight a degree as not to carry any uncertainty with it.

(2) If either of the proofs of God's existence and veracity depended at any point on conclusions presented by retentiveness but believed true because we remember that the proof which led to them was clear and distinct, then it would be circular; for it is just that type of reminiscence which has to be guaranteed by God's veracity. The question is, are they so complex and involved that the mind cannot retain all the evidence required to draw the conclusion by a single intuitive

---

similar aids, if a man is doubtful about the goodness of his memory. He might have added that they cannot take the place of the appeal to God to support memory, because (*a*) they are sensible and therefore inherently misleading, and (*b*) the presence of the conclusion of a proof in writing, even if accompanied by the whole course of the argument, cannot prove that you are right in remembering the process to have been self-evident; unless you can rely on your memory you must attend to the whole argument again in detail.

act? It is true that the first or causal proof seems to occupy
the whole of the third Meditation, and the ontological argument the greater part of the fifth. But the "proofs" themselves are in each case brief and clear, if we separate them
from the preliminary matter which clears the ground for
them. Descartes himself remarks that once I have freed my
mind of prejudices and of the "images of sensible objects"
there is nothing I can know sooner or more easily than the
fact of God's existence.[26] He admits that those who do not
remember all that goes to the making of the proof will consider it sophistical,[27] but he evidently does not regard the
effort of retention as beyond the scope of an intelligent mind.
In fact, the essence of the "proof" is easily grasped. The
knowledge of our own existence as limited and imperfect
(and the knowledge is not upset by the possibility of a deceiver), is bound up with and inseparable from the knowledge of a perfect Being on whom we are dependent. Again,
the ontological argument merely gives a reason for the fact
that we can have no *mere* idea of the whole of Being.

It is time to sum up the conclusions we have so far reached.
The beginning of the third Meditation suggests that the
general rule "what is clearly and distinctly perceived is true,"
inferred from the *Cogito ergo sum* and guaranteed by the
veracity of God, is to be used as a basis of inference to prove
the truth of each clear and distinct perception. But (*a*) this
involves an obvious circular argument (independent of that
involved by the appeal to God's veracity) and (*b*) it is inconsistent with the general trend of Descartes' thought,
which, both in the *Regulæ* and in the Meditations treats
intuitions or clear and distinct perceptions as self-evident.
None the less the general rule is worth proving, because it is
needed to support the conclusions which I remember to have
reached by clear and distinct steps, when I am no longer
attending to those steps. Descartes confuses two possible
reasons for doubting these conclusions. (*a*) I may doubt
whether what was clearly and distinctly perceived was neces-

26 *Med.* V., AT VIII, 69, ll. 4–9. Cf. *Med.* III., AT VII, 47, l.
24–48, l. 2.
    27 Reply to Obj. II., AT VII, 120, ll. 3–9.

sarily true, without doubting that it was so perceived. (We suggested that the particular error I may commit in making mathematical judgments is the assumption that a material world exists to which the judgments apply.) (*b*) I may doubt simply whether I am rightly remembering the conclusion; or I may be mistaken in remembering the steps of the proof to have been clear and distinct. It is here the accuracy of memory, and not clear and distinct perception, which is doubtful. The general rule, no longer derived from the clear and distinct perceptions themselves but solely from the veracity of God, fails to overthrow the doubt in its first form, because a circular argument is still involved. The rule hardly applies to the doubt in its second form, unless we substitute "most evident" for "clear and distinct," as Descartes sometimes does; but he tends rather to substitute a direct appeal to the veracity of God for the appeal to a rule derived from that veracity. Descartes has been led by the fear of arguing in a circle to accept clearness and distinctness as ultimate and indubitable, but he still needs God to support memory. Unfortunately he does not make it clear how far this support is to extend, and he fails to distinguish between reminiscence and retentiveness. We suggested that he took retentiveness to be memory present in so slight a degree as not to mislead; that God is needed to support the memory that certain conclusions had the force of clearness and distinctness; and that all other memory is inherently fallible and open to speculative doubt. Since the proofs of God's existence need only retentiveness and not reminiscence they are not open to the imputation of circularity.

· · ·

If our attempt to give a coherent account of what underlies Descartes' general position has had any success, it will be evident that the *Cogito ergo sum* and the general rule supposed to be inferred from it must fall into the background. The *Cogito* proves nothing but itself—and even that is far less than Descartes supposed. It is not, as is still too often assumed, the first piece of firm ground appearing above the waters of universal doubt, on which the whole edifice of science can be erected. There is no Atlas in Descartes' philosophy to bear the world of human knowledge. The only point distinguishing the *Cogito* from other intuitions is this, that it alone stands firm against the hypothesis of an all-powerful deceiver. If the existence of a veracious God could not be proved, the existence of the self would alone be certain. But this is not enough to make it the basis of other certainties, unless the proofs of God's existence depend on it. Does any of them do so? Clearly the "ontological argument" does not. It involves only the existence of the idea of God; and if this idea involves a self to perceive it, then the argument may be said rather to prove the existence of the self than to depend on an independent proof of it. And Descartes himself says[28] that even if all the conclusions of the previous Meditations were false the existence of God would be at least as certain as any truth of Mathematics. In the "causal argument" the existence of an imperfect self and a perfect God are seen to involve one another, but the latter is certainly not inferred from the former. On the contrary, "in some way I possess the perception of the infinite before that of the finite, that is, the perception of God before that of myself."[29] The only argument for the proof of God's existence which seems to presuppose the existence of the self is that given at the end of the third Meditation in support of the "causal argument," to the effect that my existence cannot be explained except as derived from God; but even here what is proved is only that *if* I exist God must be the source of my existence and maintenance. Even if we admit that the *Cogito ergo sum* could be used here as a premise for the proof of God's existence, it is evident that (*a*) Descartes does not so use it and (*b*) the other two more important proofs are independent of it. The *Cogito*, then, is not essential to a coherent account of knowledge on Cartesian principles. As for the general rule, if it is merely a way of stating as a fact of experience that there are "perceptions" which are self-evident and that these have certain characteristics suitably described

[28] *Med.* V., AT VII, 65–66.
[29] *Med.* III., AT V, 45, ll. 26–29.

as "clearness" and "distinctness," then there is no harm in it; but it cannot be established from the *Cogito* and then used as a basis of proof for each clear and distinct perception. Descartes is fundamentally an intuitionist, who attempts to define the conditions of intuitive judgment. The appeal to the veracity of God—itself intuited—does not, as interpreted in this paper, mar the intuitional nature of knowledge. It is at bottom a claim that the world is rational and coherent and consequently capable of being known not in isolated fragments merely, but as a single ordered and continuous system.

THE CREATION OF THE ETERNAL TRUTHS
IN DESCARTES'S SYSTEM
ÉMILE BRÉHIER

I

The Cartesian theory of the creation of the eternal truths occupies, in the body of Descartes's writings, a rather curious position. As we see it in a letter to Mersenne of 1630, written while he is preparing "his Physics," the theory appears in the context of "metaphysical questions" that he will discuss there; for "it has nothing to do with matters depending on revelation or what I call 'Theology' proper, but is, rather, metaphysical and to be examined by human reason." After he has stated his answer, he adds, "I hope to write this down within two weeks in my Physics";[1] and he asks Mersenne to assemble objections that theologians might raise against it.[2] In his reply, Mersenne was obliged to point out that, as there was a close connection for theologians between this question and that of the production of the Word by the Father, Descartes's doctrine might meet with opposition from them. Descartes's reply to this, on May 6, 1630, is: "What you say about the

First published in *Revue Philosophique de la France et de l'Étranger* (Vol. CXIII, Nos. 5–6, 7–8, May–August 1937, pp. 15–29) and included in *La Philosophie et son passé*, pp. 103–124, by Émile Bréhier, in the series *Nouvelle Encyclopédie Philosophique* (Paris: Alcan, Presses Universitaires de France, 1940). The paper was translated by the editor, and the translation is published with the permission of Presses Universitaires de France.

[1] That is, the basis of the theory in the view that God's will is not subject to His understanding.

[2] Letter of April 15, 1630, Adam and Tannery edition, Vol. I, 143–146.

production of the Word is no objection. . . ." Nonetheless, he shows caution in claiming the right to treat the question as a philosopher: "But I do not wish to get involved with Theology; I am even afraid you may think my Philosophy goes too far in venturing an opinion regarding such exalted matters."

Though, in the spring of 1630, Descartes considered this doctrine of such paramount importance that he asked Mersenne to "proclaim it everywhere," not a word of it is breathed in the *Discourse,* nor in the *Meditations* and *Principles;* and not until eleven years later did it happen to reappear, thanks to an objection of Gassendi's (who certainly never dreamed of attributing such ideas to Descartes), in the Replies to the Fifth Set of Objections. There Descartes was prompted to say, very briefly, that the eternal truths, though immutable, are created. But this was enough to alert the theologian authors of the Sixth Set of Objections, who, in stating their eighth difficulty, indicated their surprise. They had been able to find nothing of the sort in the *Meditations.*

This silence, which is explained by Descartes's prudence, accounts for the doctrine's appearing as an excursion and is the reason that its place in the methodic development of Descartes's metaphysical ideas is not at first apparent. Yet such a place was assuredly given the doctrine by the first formulation in 1630. The questions I wish to consider here are: how this place is to be understood and what Descartes means in the theory by "creation"—a word which, applied to the eternal truths, has so strange a ring.[3]

II

In the statement of his doctrine in the letter to Mersenne, Descartes employs indifferently the Augustinian expression "eternal truths" and the Scholastic word "essence." "God," he

[3] For explication of the theory, see the notable thesis of Émile Boutroux, *De Veritatibus aeternis apud Cartesium,* translated into French by Canguilhem.

writes, "produces the eternal truths *ut efficiens et totalis causa*. For He is Author of the essence of created things as well as of their existence, and *the essence* [of created things] *is nothing other than these eternal truths*."[4] As an example of these truths, he cites, "Lines drawn from the center to the circumference are equal," which is in fact nothing other than the expression of the essence of the circle.

Scholastic theology had a precise doctrine about the relation of the essences of created things to God. I shall indicate what it was, and we shall see why Descartes could not accept it. Examining the question how God can possess knowledge of particular things, St. Thomas answers that, to have this knowledge, it is necessary

> that He is Himself the proper type of each. How this may be, we must investigate. . . . A certain philosopher, Clement by name, said that things of higher rank are the types of those of lesser rank. Now the divine essence contains in itself the excellences of all beings, not indeed by way of composition, but by way of perfection. . . . Wherefore God's understanding can comprehend within His essence what is proper to each thing, by understanding wherein each thing imitates His essence, and wherein it falls short of His perfection: for instance, by understanding His essence as imitable in respect of life and not of knowledge, it conceives the proper form of a plant. . . . But the types of things in the divine understanding are not multiple nor distinct, except in so far as God knows that things can be like Him in many and diverse ways.[5]

This is the familiar Neo-Platonic theme. In the One, essences are in no way distinguished, and the diversity of essences is nothing positive but rather marks a defect or fall from complete unity. There can be no question here of a creation of essences; rather, it is by a kind of attenuation of the divine unity that a multiplicity of essences is engendered. The only difference between St. Thomas and Plotinus on this question (and it is in itself a great one) is

[4] May 27, 1630, AT I, 152.
[5] *Contra Gentiles* I, Ch. 54.

this: to explain the multiplicity of essences, Plotinus invokes a natural necessity that makes the many flow from the One, whereas St. Thomas relies on the actual diversity of existing things created by God's power and relative to which alone this kind of multiplication of the divine essence is to be conceived. But this difference is of no consequence to the question at issue, and St. Thomas himself pointed out the alliance of his doctrine with Platonism: "Wherein the opinion of Plato is in a certain way preserved, in that he postulated ideas in accordance with which everything that exists in material things is formed."

In this doctrine, two points are of particular interest to us. The essences of created things are related to God's understanding to the exclusion of any other attribute, and the multiplicity of essences is not grounded in the absolute.

It is on the first of these points that the theologian Suárez insisted, seeking thereby to safeguard the truth of the eternal truths. According to Suárez, they are not true because they are known by God, but they are known by God because they are true. Otherwise, God would not know of necessity that they are true. If, that is, their truth derived from Him, this could only be through the intermediary of His will, which is free; and then there would be no more necessity in their truth than in any product of the divine will. Suárez insisted that their truth is the object of the divine understanding alone and that, in accordance with the nature of understanding *qua* contemplative, it must be given and not made. From this, he concludes: *Habent perpetuam veritatem, non solum ut sunt in divino intellectu, sed etiam secundum se ac praescindendo ab illo.*[6]

Thus the first aspect of the doctrine, considered in isolation, ends in a kind of theological Platonism: an eternal reality contemplated by God and distinct from God. Would there then be something eternal other than God? This consequence, which would be inadmissible, is immediately corrected and delimited by the second aspect of the thesis, which

[6] *Disputat. metaphys.*, Disp. XXXI, Sec. 12, No. 40, cited by Garin, *Thèses cartésiennes et thèses thomistes.*

sees these essences or multiple truths as facets or—better—
attenuations of the essence of the divine understanding—
with the consequence that God, in contemplating tnem, does
nothing but contemplate Himself. In this we again find a
Neo-Platonic theme. Contemplation of self is at the same
time the contemplation of the whole of intelligible reality
and the Platonism of the *Timaeus* is thus reabsorbed in Neo-
Platonism.

It should be added that tne union of these two aspects is a
rather embarrassing state of affairs. In the first aspect, we
speak as Augustinians of discrete eternal truths, such as
mathematical truths—each, considerea in itself, having its
own evidence and being, so to speak, self-sufficient. And we
see here the human intelligence at work with its concrete
and discrete apprehensions. In the second aspect, we speak
as Neo-Platonists of essences forming a world by virtue of
their mutual interpenetration. In the Neo-Platonism of
Plotinus (and in that of the Middle Ages), no truth can be
separated from the others. To think is of necessity to think of
the whole; and, under these conditions, not even *cogito ergo
sum* could be self-evident. For the *cogito* supposes the vantage point of thought; and, according to Plotinus, the vantage
point of thought is that of the whole of intelligible being. For
Augustine, on the other hand, *cogito ergo sum* is one of those
eternal truths or discrete insights that are added together
without forming a whole—one of those insights that, as Descartes says, "there is no need to enumerate."

This opposition between the eternal truths and the Neo-
Platonic intelligible had the gravest consequences for the
idea that we might have of the value and certainty of our
knowledge of created things. According to the Thomistic
theory, as we have seen, essences are distinguished from one
another only in relation to the things of which they are the
essences, and so knowledge by nature proceeds from the existing created thing to its essence. The created thing known as
existing is, then, the only means of disclosing the essence.
Moreover, supposing that knowledge of the essence is attained, it is quite deficient. For the essence has its full signifi-

cance only as reunited with other essences, and reabsorbed with them, in the unity of the essence of the divine understanding. There is a feeble reflection of this unity in the hierarchy of genera and species determining each of the inferior notions within the compass of the unity of a genus; and St. Thomas, borrowing the idea from Aristotle, compares each of these notions to a number in the series of numbers. So it seemed quite impossible to accept both the discrete character of the eternal truths, each possessing its own evidence, and also the radical unity of the eternal truths.

III

We see which side Descartes was on in the dispute. His real problem—how to compass truths that are certain—is insoluble within Scholastic philosophy, and indeed the very expressions Descartes uses in affirming the distinction of essences make us think of this. *Non plures vel distinctae,* St. Thomas says in speaking of essences; to which Descartes replies, "I call . . . that [perception] 'distinct' which is so precise and different from all others that it contains within itself only what is perfectly clear to the person who duly considers it."[7] And we recall examples from the *Rules:* "Thus anyone can see by intuition that he exists, that he thinks, that a triangle is bounded by just three lines. . . ."[8] These discrete insights and separately perceived essences cannot be ordered in a hierarchy of genera and species, which, for Descartes, is a mere human artifice of classification and not a means of disclosing essences.[9] "There are," he says, "notions so clear that we obscure them in trying to define them in the manner of the School, and they are not acquired by study but are born with us."[10] Of such a nature are the notions

[7] *Principles of Philosophy* I, 45.
[8] Rule III, AT X, 368.
[9] Cf. his reply to Gassendi: "What you then advance against the universals of the dialecticians does not affect me, since I do not conceive of them in the same way as they do."
[10] *Principles* I, 10.

of motion, of thought, extension, existence, and certainty.[11]

But the more Descartes insisted on the integral and discrete awareness that the human mind can have of essences, the more he precluded the possibility of the kind of correction of Augustinianism by Neo-Platonism which, in theology, could leave room for a thesis like Suárez's. Nor could he readily regard essences that are accessible and familiar to the human mind as containing some vestige, however remote, of the infinite divine understanding.

It should also be noted that if we wish to assign these essences to the divine understanding, we must draw the consequence that Suárez drew. Not only would these truths pertain to the divine understanding; but, given the nature of the understanding, they would have to be true in their own right and independently of the divine understanding, for—as the theologian partisans of Suárez observe in the Sixth Set of Objections—"it seems impossible that God could have brought it about that any of these essences or truths should not have been from all eternity." And then, to the Suárezian thesis, Descartes could oppose views accepted by the theologians themselves: "If men properly understood the sense of their words, they could never say without blasphemy that the truth of something precedes God's knowledge of it, for in God willing and knowing are the same."[12] He would side with the followers of Suárez, however, when Gassendi raised a difficulty about setting up "some immutable and eternal nature other than that of a sovereign God." For Descartes, like them, postulates these truths as distinct from God. But he decides against the theologians when they assign to these truths immutability of the same kind as God's.

[11] We also take it to be the case that this discrete character of evidence, which for Descartes is the condition of certainty, is an essential feature of his thought.

[12] Letter of May 6, 1630, AT I, 149.

IV

No compromise was possible between the discrete character of essences, the condition of self-evidence, and their radical union in the divine understanding. To retain the former, it was necessary to make the essences depend on the will and power of God—to make them created things, and this is what Descartes did. But has the notion of creation that Descartes had to employ here anything in common with the accepted notion of creation? In the ordinary notion, creation is positing of existence; here, it is positing of essence. Ordinarily creation is of a temporal existent; here, it is of an eternal essence. In the ordinary notion, a created thing is a being whose contingency is intelligible as such; that is, it can be conceived as not existing. But here "it is useless to ask how God could have brought it about from all eternity that two times four should not have been eight, etc., for I admit that this is something we cannot understand."[13]

Creation of this sort has nothing in common with the creation of theologians, and in particular it cannot be assimilated to Duns Scotus' theory of the primacy of the will. The God of Duns Scotus does not create possibilities, and His will finds its limit in the contradictory. No doubt certain statements of Descartes's in the Replies are Scotist in appearance: "The reason for their goodness [created things] derives from His having willed to make them so." Similarly, for Duns Scotus, "no rule is right except in so far as it is accepted by the divine will." But what Scotus says of a moral precept, which we can without logical contradiction imagine replaced by another, Descartes extends to truths the denial of which is a contradiction *in terminis* and unthinkable.

This is because his intention is quite different. For Descartes, theology comes in only in as much as it furnishes the bases of certainty. This certainty is itself assured only through methodic doubt, and doubt is methodic only if it is pushed to

[13] Replies to the Sixth Set of Objections.

the extreme—that is, if we have examined all the reasons, possible reasons included, that we may have for doubting. But in
the *Meditations* we find that the theory of the creation of
the eternal truths, though nowhere explicitly formulated, is
presupposed in two essential steps of Descartes's thinking;
viz., where we are able to carry doubt much further than it
has ever gone before and where we are able to free ourselves
of doubt with much greater assurance than ever before.

Hyperbolic doubt, at the outset, shows reasons for doubting truths that seem the clearest and most apparent, as in
adding two and three, counting the number of sides of a
square, or "something even simpler, if anything simpler than
that can be imagined." For doubt to be possible here, we must
imagine "a God who can do everything" or, if not God "who
is the source of truth," "some evil genius, as artful and deceitful as he is powerful, [who] has employed all his efforts in
deceiving me." But we must also imagine the stratagems of
this evil genius, and on this point Descartes is hardly explicit. They cannot consist in bringing about that I do not in
fact see what I seem to see; for instance, in bringing about
that I do not see that a square has four sides. For if this
were so, there would be no way of emerging from doubt, and
intuition would go no further than the *cogito*. The stratagem
of the evil genius can consist only in changing the truths
that we take to be eternal truths in such a way that we have
no assurance that if we look again, we shall again find the
sum of three plus two equal to five or a mountain with a
valley. Hence, to play his part, the evil genius—that imaginary being on whom Descartes has conferred the omnipotence of God without His goodness—must be a creator of essences, a creator who is completely arbitrary and continually
changing.

Thanks to the fiction of the evil genius, we discover one of
the positive conditions of certainty; namely, the permanence
of the essences that we intuit. Freedom from doubt will be
attained only if their permanence is assured; but one of the
conditions of this permanence is the same as that of hyperbolic doubt; namely, the creation of essences. If we proceed to
enrich the fiction of an omnipotent genius by adding that he

is entirely good and does not wish to deceive us, we shall be assured, on this second hypothesis, of the certainty of our intuition. If we then demonstrate that the hypothesis is true—that is, that a being possessing power alone without goodness is a fiction and, instead, that an infinitely perfect being possessing both is real—we are assured, beyond all hypothesis, of the validity of our intuition. From this we see how wrong it would be to say that, according to Descartes, the divine guarantee is necessary only for reasoning that cannot be grasped in its entirety by intuition. On the contrary, the guarantee bears on actual intuition, though it is also related to time and memory. By the very nature of human reason, it would be useless at the moment of intuition: for "as soon as I understand something very clearly and very distinctly, I cannot prevent myself from believing it to be true." The only problem is to know how I can foresee with certainty that, my intuition being, as it were, detached, what is intuited will continue to be true. This problem has significance only if the essences that I intuit are created beings capable of disappearing and being replaced by others: and the only answer to the problem, if we are to have genuine knowledge, is the creation of essences by an immutable and good God. It is not a matter of "guaranteeing memory" in the sense that God might provide us with a guarantee that we are not mistaken when we claim to be sure of having grasped something clearly and distinctly. Rather, what God guarantees is that, provided our memory of having grasped something clearly and distinctly is accurate, we are as assured of its truth as if we were now intuiting it.

We now see that the celebrated *loci classici* of hyperbolic doubt and the divine guarantee in the *Meditations* cannot be explained unambiguously without the theory of the creation of the eternal truths—a theory that Descartes wanted to make public as early as 1630, yet of which he said not a word in his books.

In this theory, the eternal truths, assigned the status of created things, can be grasped wholly and without remainder. But, for this very reason, they do not have the kind of certainty that they have in Plotinus—that is, the certainty of a

soul the superior part of which intuits an intelligible world.
Here we are concerned not with a pre-existing body of knowledge but with the starting points of a science to be achieved.
Father Mersenne, as a theologian, saw an affinity between the
production of essences and the prolation of the Word, and
Descartes has occasion to refer to this comparison when he
writes: "I do not conceive [of them] emanating from God,
like rays from the sun." Descartes's treatment of essences is
exactly analogous in import to the treatment of Christ by the
Socinians of his epoch. He humanizes essences, as they hu-
manized Christ; and he thereby makes it possible for there
to be human knowledge perfect of its kind, as they make
possible Christian perfection and the imitation of Christ:
"To imitate Christ, our lives do not have to express absolutely
His most perfect holiness and justness, but we must be holy
and just in the way in which He was." Just as the problem of
virtue is no longer to attain some transcendent Good of which
human virtue is but a pale reflection, so man is not reduced
to knowledge that is a distant shadow of God's: he can, *qua*
man, have knowledge complete in itself. Christianity and
science are, both of them, cut off from theology.

V

With one exception, theologians unanimously rejected the
thesis of the creation of essences. Leibniz did not forget that
exception: "We need not," he writes, "suppose with certain
persons that the eternal truths, being dependent on God, are
arbitrary and depend on His will, as Descartes, and afterward M. Poiret, seem to have held."[14] Poiret, before devoting
himself to mystical writings and to editing the works of
Antoinette Bourignon, had published in 1677 his *Cogitationes
rationales de Deo, Anima et Malo,* in which we find, according to the subtitle, "true metaphysics"—that is, the metaphysics that Descartes substituted for the *scientia hor-
ribilis* of the Scholastics. According to Poiret, that prickly

[14] *Monadology,* Sec. 46.

science begins with speculation on the transcendental terms Being, True, and Good as a preliminary to knowledge of God. Poiret takes it to follow that the Scholastics consider these terms anterior to God and independent of Him. Since the terms are applied to all reality, it follows that they "intermix creator and created thing as if they had being and truth in common—as if the sense of these terms was univocal. Or, if they do admit equivocation, they fall into perfectly inept definitions of the word 'equivocal,' since they have in fact rejected equivocation."[15]

This critique of Scholastic ontology is connected, in Poiret's mind, with the thesis of the creation of the eternal truths, which alone enables us to recognize the radical transcendence of a God whose essence is incommunicable to created things. If, according to Poiret, we make essences an object of the divine understanding, we reduce God to the level of created minds by teaching that He conceives of necessity the ideas, essences, and truths of things, "as if they flowed, immediately and without the intervention of a decree, from the very essence of God." We also contravene His unity, conferring on Truth, distinguished in this way from Him, an eternity that belongs only to Him. The good and the true that God creates by a free decree is, for God, mere fancy and fiction. "It is not at all necessary that God, to make use of His intelligence, consider anything other than Himself, although, if it happens to please Him that something external be true and He wills to imagine it, He knows that this is true and is known and seen by Him."[16]

This theory furnishes Poiret with a justification of the negative theology that the Neo-Platonists had introduced:

In the presence of His supreme essence, all essence, form, nature, truth, goodness of things vanish absolutely in sheer nothingness. And this is perhaps what certain early theologians had in mind when they said that the essence of God is above all essence, that His goodness is super-

[15] *Cogitationes,* p. 121.
[16] *Ibid.,* Ch. VII, Sec. 4.

essentially good, and that He is super-essentially one and true—that is, more than one and more than true.[17]

Thus, in a striking way, the ideas of the mystic complement those of the philosopher, Poiret emphasizing an aspect of the theory complementing the one pointed out by Descartes. By such a profound separation of God from created things, we put essences on a level with human intelligence, but at the same time we place God beyond our grasp. The notion of the divine Word or intermediary—instead of being, as for Malebranche, a philosophic notion—is a sheer given of revelation, and the fusion of revelation and philosophy appears clearly impossible.

VI

The great Cartesians of the seventeenth century—Spinoza, Malebranche, and Leibniz—did not retain the theory of the creation of the eternal truths and in fact took it to task more or less violently. In Descartes we have seen the essential connection of the theory with methodic doubt, which it makes possible. For these philosophers methodic doubt does not play the same propaedeutic role as it does for Descartes, and the theory was discarded along with it. By the same token, however, they returned to the Neo-Platonic metaphysics of essences and intelligible reality, though they had to emend it at some point to allow for the use of clear and distinct ideas.

On this question, Spinoza finds himself closer to Descartes than to the Scholastics:

I admit that this opinion [Descartes's], which subjects everything to an indifferent will of God's and affirms that everything depends on His favor, is less distant from the truth than the opinion of those who hold that God does everything for the sake of the good; for . . . that amounts to subjecting God to fate [this is Descartes's own criticism], and nothing more absurd can be asserted of God,

17 *Cogitationes*, p. 133.

whom we have shown to be the first cause and sole free cause of the essence of things as well as of their existence.[18]

When Spinoza affirms that "God is the efficient cause not only of the existence of things but also of their essence," he agrees with Descartes on a basic point. Both are of the opinion that the divine causation productive of essence is of the same type as that productive of existence. For the Scholastics, on the contrary, they are of different types: eternal and necessary emanation for essences, creative and free causation for existences. Spinoza's divergence from Descartes comes out in their determination of this single type of causation. For Spinoza, it is akin to the mathematical causation of a definition, while, for Descartes, it is free and creative. Despite this difference, however, the unity of causation in God is a basis of agreement, as Leibniz noted with hostile intent.[19] This unity, in Descartes as in Spinoza, effaces all analogy between divine causation and that of the human will, which acts *sub ratione boni* inasmuch as it is subject to essences provided externally by the understanding. For both, no reflection of human nature comes to intervene between mind and reality; and the nature of the real is such that rational knowledge is possible, whether the object of this knowledge has been created by God (Cartesian essences) or whether it is God Himself.

But Spinoza, where he does not follow Descartes, runs afoul of the contradictory implication of Neo-Platonism, which places rational knowledge infinitely above the reach of the human mind. He avoids this consequence only by certain artifices. The first is the distinction of divine attributes. To introduce the Cartesian physics of clear ideas, he must in some way isolate essences in God. (Descartes would have us isolate them from God as created things.) Spinoza is in a position to do this because he substitutes attributes for God in the thought that the mind has of God and includes

[18] *Ethics* I, Prop. XXXIII, Scholium 2, end.
[19] *Discourse on Metaphysics*, Sec. II: "This opinion verges closely on that of the recent innovators."

among these attributes extension, which is the object of a clear and distinct idea. Second, there is a difference of kinds of knowledge. While knowledge of the third kind is directed toward the singular in so far as it has its intelligible foundation in God, knowledge of the second kind has for its object notions that are both common and adequate, or the "true universals" that also form the basis of Cartesian science. Thus the theory of attributes and that of knowledge of the second kind appear to have the same role for Spinoza that the creation of essences has for Descartes. They isolate within the intelligible immensity perspectives by means of which it becomes accessible to the mind and, so to speak, on a level with it. This isolation of essences, whereby they are objects of adequate knowledge, is the condition of certainty that Descartes attains by transforming essences into created things; and Spinoza, with his theory of divine attributes, attains the equivalent of the infinite distance of creation between God and essences. In both cases—extension as created essence or as attribute of God—we have the object of a physics that is perfect in itself and does not aspire, like the Neo-Platonic intelligible, to self-completion.[20]

Malebranche also rejects, more energetically than Spinoza, the thesis of the creation of the eternal truths. As a Catholic theologian, he brings the mediocrity of Descartes's arguments into relief. Descartes maintained that essences, though created, are immutable because God is immutable in His decrees. To this, Malebranche replies that divine immutability entails neither permanence in the things created nor absence of change. Granting this, the inevitable consequence of the thesis is the most complete Pyrrhonism—that of hyperbolic doubt, since we escape this consequence only by assuming that the entailment holds.[21] But what especially predisposes Malebranche against the Cartesian thesis is that it in effect separates man from God with respect to knowledge, as Socinianism separated him from God in religion. Male-

---

[20] Leibniz returns to Neo-Platonism when he demonstrates the deficiency and obscurity of the notion of extension conceived independently (*Discourse on Metaphysics*).

[21] *Éclaircissement* X, p. 382.

branche's position is that universal reason, which is the light of the human mind, is also the Word: it is "the wisdom of the Father, wisdom eternal, immutable, and necessary, which informs creatures and Creator as well, though in a very different way."[22] And he suggests that the separation of man from God may be the real impetus behind such a theory as the creation of the eternal verities, for it caters to man's pride by placing his confidence in created things and offering him an alternative to having to consult God.[23]

This return to Platonism ran the risk of bringing about just what Descartes had wanted to obviate; namely, making human knowledge appear to be a feeble vestige of divine knowledge and precluding the possibility of a physics relying on the complete intelligibility of an idea considered in itself and apart from others. Malebranche is well aware that the fate of science rests with the "diversity" of intelligible ideas.[24] But how is he to reconcile vision in God—which, since God is simple, is defective if it is not total—with awareness of separate and distinct essences? This is what Arnauld asks him, and Malebranche replies:

> In a sense what we immediately perceive is God. But . . . we see Him only insofar as His substance is related to created things. For, although whatever is in God is God, we do not, strictly speaking, see God when we see Him by way of the idea He has of His works, or in the respect in which created things may participate in Him.[25]

Thus the multiplicity of essences is introduced, as in St. Thomas, by reference to the multiplicity of things that God

[22] *Méditations Chrétiennes*, beginning.

[23] Cf. *Éclaircissement X* of *Recherche de la Vérité*, pp. 371–382 (Garnier), where Descartes is named only at the end, p. 379, with reference to the text of the Replies to the Sixth Set of Objections. On the fundamental atheism of this thesis, cf. p. 375: "They protest in vain . . ."; and p. 377: ". . . despite the aversion of certain learned men . . ."

[24] *Éclaircissement X*, p. 380 (Garnier).

[25] *Réponse au livre des vraies et des fausses idées*, Ch. IX, Sec. 14.

has the intention of creating. There is this difference, however: Malebranche treats these essences (which are reduced to one; viz., the model of the material world or intelligible extension) as if their separation, far from being an imperfection, gave them a positive and autonomous reality. An artifice of this sort is necessary if he is to succeed in uniting Cartesian science with Neo-Platonism.

Finally, Leibniz attacks the Cartesian thesis by showing that the creation of essences is far from being an extension of the Christian dogma of creation and, on the contrary, robs it of all intelligibility. What he does is to assimilate Descartes's God—bare absolute power that does not act for the sake of the good—to Spinoza's God. To Leibniz it seems that "to say that such a God made things comes to the same as saying that they have been produced by a blind necessity." Thus, by a complete reversal of reasons pro and con, this, so to speak, hyperbolic creation of the eternal truths makes creation in the ordinary sense incomprehensible, and creation is a sheer dogma of revelation relating to piety and not to philosophy. As for the creation of the eternal truths, it is the reverse side of the autonomy of reason, seeking not to rise toward a divine model of which it would be a trace but to progress toward new truths.

DESCARTES' VALIDATION OF REASON

HARRY G. FRANKFURT

In the First Meditation, Descartes raises the possibility that there is a demon of unlimited power bent on deceiving those who reason. Later on in the *Meditations* he attempts to eliminate the doubts nourished by consideration of this possibility by developing proofs for the existence of God and by arguing that the benevolence of God guarantees the reliability of reason. To many critics, Descartes' procedure in this matter has seemed defective. They point out that his arguments rely upon the very rational faculty whose reliability is presumably at stake, and they insist that the attempt to validate reason is therefore vitiated by circularity.[1]

In my opinion, those who have discussed this matter have often failed to understand Descartes' argument correctly. My purpose in this essay is to make clear just what question about reason Descartes found it necessary to ask in the *Meditations* and how he thought it possible to give a reasonable answer to it. When I have done so, I believe, it will be easier to judge fairly whether or not his reasoning is free of vicious circularity and other defects.

American Philosophical Quarterly, Vol. II, No. 2, April 1965, pp. 149–156. Reprinted with the permission of the author and the *American Philosophical Quarterly*.

[1] It is evident that Descartes is not guilty of circularity in the sense of offering an argument whose conclusion appears among its premisses. If his reasoning is circular at all, the circularity is, I take it, of a less formal variety. I shall not undertake to define this variety of circularity but shall assume that, in an intuitive way at least, its nature is sufficiently clear for the purposes of my essay.

I

1. It may seem difficult to understand how anything can rationally be said in behalf of reason without transparently begging the question of whether reason is worthy of trust. Some commentators have consequently been attracted to the alternative that Descartes is not actually concerned with validating reason (the faculty by means of which, when we use it rightly, we perceive things clearly and distinctly) at all, but with establishing the trustworthiness of memory.[2] Their position is that he makes no attempt to determine whether what is clearly and distinctly perceived (intuited) is properly to be regarded as true, but that he tries rather to provide grounds for trusting recollections of intuitions.[3] Descartes is alleged by them to be preoccupied with the possibility that an omnipotent demon victimizes us by causing us to *think* we remember perceiving clearly and distinctly what we have never in fact intuited at all.

So far as I can see, this interpretation of the metaphysical doubt is inconsistent with Descartes' account of his doctrines and, in any case, it does not satisfactorily allow him to escape the charge of circularity.[4] Descartes does indeed sometimes describe the problem with which he is concerned as one which may be encountered in contexts where something is remembered. But even in such contexts his problem is not to establish the reliability of memory. It is to validate propositions which are correctly remembered to have been intuited.

Suppose that two weeks ago, in the course of studying a geometry text, a person clearly and distinctly perceived that *p*.

---

[2] For an important defense of this alternative, cf. Willis Doney, "The Cartesian Circle," *Journal of the History of Ideas*, vol. 16 (1955), 324–338.

[3] The terms "to intuit" and "to perceive clearly and distinctly," and their corresponding derivates, will be used interchangeably throughout this essay.

[4] I have argued in support of these claims in "Memory and the Cartesian Circle," *Philosophical Review*, vol. 71 (1962), 504–511.

Suppose this person now correctly recalls having intuited on that earlier occasion that *p*. Given such a situation, Descartes wants to know whether the person is justified in accepting *p* as certainly true—whether, that is, the fact that he once intuited that *p* is now acceptable as conclusive evidence for *p*'s truth. His answer is that the person is justified if he knows that God exists, but not otherwise.[5]

2. Before proceeding, it will be helpful to remove an obstacle which may otherwise stand in the way of a sound understanding of Descartes' problem. This obstacle is the erroneous notion that whenever Descartes says that something is indubitable, that is tantamount to his saying that it is true. Despite the fact that his metaphysical labors are largely devoted to exploring the relations between what is indubitable and what is true, it is not at all uncommon to find able writers on Descartes apparently overlooking the distinction between them.

For example, in the course of discussing the account given of mathematical propositions in the First Meditation, Leonard Miller remarks: "Descartes is puzzled by the nature of these propositions whose truth appears to be self-evident, for he is inclined to say both that we cannot possibly be mistaken about them provided that we apprehend them clearly and distinctly and that we can be deceived by the demon no matter how clearly and distinctly we perceive them."[6] But what is the evidence that Descartes inclines to the view that even if there is a demon we cannot be mistaken about what we intuit? The only evidence cited by Miller is to the effect

[5] "It is enough for us to remember that we have perceived something clearly, in order to be assured that it is true; but this would not suffice if we did not know that God exists and that He cannot be a deceiver." Charles Adam and Paul Tannery, eds., *Oeuvres de Descartes* (Paris, 1957), vol. VII, 246 (Latin); vol. IX, 190 (French); hereafter cited as "AT." Elizabeth Haldane and G. R. T. Ross, eds., *The Philosophical Works of Descartes* (New York, 1955), vol. II, p. 115; hereafter cited as "HR." I shall at times depart from the text of HR in order to avoid inaccurate or clumsy translations.

[6] "Descartes, Mathematics, and God," *Philosophical Review*, vol. 66 (1957), 452.

that what is intuited is not dubitable.[7] As if in saying (as he wishes to do) that we cannot doubt what we are intuiting, Descartes is also saying (as he does not wish to do) that we cannot be in error about what we are intuiting but know it to be true whether or not we know that God exists.

Another capable critic, Willis Doney, ascribes to Descartes the settled opinion that even without knowing God's existence a person can know that what he at present clearly and distinctly perceives is true. In elucidating this interpretation, Doney goes on to say: "Present clear and distinct perceptions were never subject to doubt. Anything so perceived did not depend on God as guarantor of its truth."[8] Notice how readily Doney moves from speaking of something clearly and distinctly perceived as being not subject to doubt to speaking of it as being known to be true. Evidently he assumes that if something intuited is not subject to doubt, that is the same as its being known to be true. This explains why he is inclined to suppose that the second of the two statements just quoted from his essay is established when the first is shown to be true.

3. In fact, however, Descartes' metaphysical doubt is precisely a doubt whether being false is compatible with being indubitable. His position is that as long as the demon remains a possibility, we must acknowledge that what we intuit may be false. But he also holds that we cannot doubt the truth of what we intuit while we are perceiving it clearly and distinctly. "Our mind is of such a nature," he affirms, "that it cannot refuse to assent to what it apprehends clearly."[9]

[7] Cf. *ibid.*, 451–452. I shall not consider whether more appropriate evidence is available for Miller's statement. My only point is that to show that Descartes believes it is impossible, demon or no demon, to *err* about what is intuited, it is not appropriate merely to offer evidence that he thinks it impossible, demon or no demon, to *doubt* what is intuited.

[8] *Op. cit.*, 325–326. As with the passage quoted from Miller, my point here is not that either of Doney's statements is false, but that the relation between them is not what Doney seems to suppose.

[9] Letter to Regius (24 May 1640), AT III, 64. Descartes enunciates this doctrine on a number of occasions. Thus, in the Third Meditation, he says: "I cannot doubt that which the natural light causes me to believe to be true." AT VII, 38 (Latin); AT IX, 30

While the intuition lasts, the inclination to believe what is being intuited is irresistible, and no doubt is then possible. But doubt may well arise at other times, if God's existence is unknown. "Before a man knows that God exists," Descartes declares, "he has an opportunity of doubting everything (viz., everything of which he does not have a clear perception present in his mind, as I have a number of times set forth)."[10]

Now at a time when we are intuiting nothing, we may recall having once perceived something clearly and distinctly. Descartes maintains that if we know that God exists, we are entitled to accept the fact that something was once intuited as conclusively establishing its truth; hence, the recollection then suffices to establish the truth of what we remember intuiting. But if God's existence is not known, he claims, we must acknowledge that what we remember intuiting may be false even though we once clearly and distinctly perceived it and were at that time incapable of doubting it.

For without the knowledge of God, "I can persuade myself of having been so constituted by nature that I can easily deceive myself even in those matters which I believe myself to apprehend with the greatest evidence and certainty."[11] Thus, our finding something to be indubitable—our apprehending it "with the greatest evidence and certainty"—cannot be regarded as itself a sufficient sign of truth. On the contrary, as long as we are ignorant of God's existence we must

---

(French); HR I, 160. Again, in *Principles of Philosophy*, I, 43, he says: "We are by nature so disposed to give our assent to things that we clearly perceive, that we cannot possibly doubt of their truth." It is essential that the questions raised by this doctrine be answered if Descartes' theory of knowledge is to be understood. For instance, what are his grounds for saying that it is impossible to doubt what is being intuited? Is his claim a contingent one, leaving the indubitability in question "merely psychological" and "subjective"? Or is there more to the claim than the assertion that as a matter of fact it happens that no one—no matter what he does—can experience any doubt about what he is intuiting? My own opinion is that there *is* more to it, but this is not the place to go as deeply into the matter as would be necessary to make it clear that this opinion is correct.

[10] AT VII, 546; HR II, 333.

[11] AT VII, 70 (Latin); AT IX, 55 (French); HR I, 184.

fear that it may be due to the malice of a demon who delights
in making us find error irresistible.[12]

It is important to avoid the mistake of taking this to commit Descartes to the view that before God's existence is
known any proposition can be doubted. As is suggested by
the reservation introduced within parentheses in the passage
cited above in footnote 10, Descartes carefully leaves open
the possibility that there are propositions so simple that they
cannot be thought of at all without being intuited. Such a
proposition could never be doubted by anyone, with or without a knowledge of God's existence. For no one could doubt
it without thinking of it, and anyone who thought of it would
intuit it, and hence be unable to doubt it.[13]

[12] In the passage just quoted, Descartes speaks of matters which
he *believes* himself to apprehend with great evidence and certainty,
and not simply of matters which he apprehends thusly; and in passages quoted below, he speaks of things which *seem* to him most
manifest, or matters which he *regards* himself as intuiting, and of
things which he *believes* himself to be apprehending clearly. But this
hardly jeopardizes the point that Descartes does not assume that
whatever is indubitable is true. For if he did assume it, then whenever he believed himself to have intuited something it would be
reasonable for him to believe that what he believed himself to have
intuited is true. However, he says repeatedly that even when he does
think that something has been intuited he must nonetheless acknowledge that it may be false (assuming that he does not know of God's
existence). In any case, whatever doubts there may be about how to
construe these passages are resolved by considering the latter part of
the text cited in footnote 14, and the passages cited in footnotes 15
and 16.

[13] Indeed, Descartes maintains explicitly that there are such propositions, and he regards the *cogito* as one of them (AT VII, 145–
146; AT IX, 114; HR II, 42). Now Descartes repeatedly asserts (e.g.,
in the passages I cite in footnotes 11 and 14), without any qualification or limitation whatever, that as long as he is ignorant of God's existence he must fear that a proposition may be false even though he
intuits it in the most perfect way. He does not exempt the *cogito*
from his general concern that unless God exists even what is intuited
may be false. To be sure, the *cogito* is his paradigm of certainty,
from which he derives the rule that whatever is intuited is true. But
until this rule is vindicated the relation between the indubitability of
the *cogito* and its truth is problematic. The *cogito* is so simple that it
cannot be thought of without being intuited and found irresistible.
But the fact that it can never be doubted is not identical with its

4. To provide further clarification and support for my interpretation, let me discuss two important passages in which Descartes tries to explain the problem he claims is solved by his demonstration of God's existence and veracity.

Toward the beginning of the Third Meditation, in the course of making clear why it is essential for him to inquire into the existence and nature of God, Descartes explains the metaphysical doubt to which he is still subject. He says that this doubt is aroused by considering the possibility that "perhaps some God might have endowed me with a nature such that I may be deceived even in respect of the things which seem to me the most manifest of all. . . . It is easy for Him, if He so wishes, to cause me to err even in those matters which I regard myself as intuiting . . . in the most evident manner."[14] This seems to be a clear enough statement that Descartes is concerned with the possibility that even what is intuited may be false.

Some readers may nonetheless find it difficult to accept this understanding of Descartes' problem because of what he says immediately following the statement which has been quoted:

> When I direct my attention to the things which I believe myself to be apprehending quite clearly, I am so persuaded of their truth that I cannot but break out into protestations such as these: Let me be deceived by whoever can do so, he will never be able to bring it about that . . . 2 and 3 could make more or less than 5; or that any other such things which I clearly see, can be other than I apprehend them as being.[15]

But there is surely no difficulty whatever in reconciling this statement with the view that Descartes is concerned with the possibility that even what is being intuited may be false. For Descartes clearly does not assert that no one could bring it about that he is deceived about the sum of 2 and 3 or about other things which he apprehends clearly. He only says that

---

being true or with its being known to be true. Descartes can still wonder whether its indubitability, however inescapable, is sufficient to establish its truth.

[14] AT VII, 36 (Latin); AT IX, 28 (French); HR I, 158–159.
[15] *Ibid.*

while apprehending them clearly, he is "so persuaded of their truth" that he cannot help protesting that he cannot be deceived about them.

Now the fact that he is persuaded of their truth to this extent is not the same as their being true; nor is his inability at the time to conceive that he could be mistaken the same as his being in fact free of error. In this passage, Descartes describes the convictions he is irresistibly inclined to hold under certain circumstances, and he reports the assertions he feels urgently moved under these circumstances to make. But he does not say either that the convictions are reasonable or that the assertions are true.

The second passage I wish to discuss is from Descartes' "Reply" to the second set of "Objections" against the *Meditations*:[16]

> There are other things which our understanding also perceives very clearly, when we pay close attention to the reasons on which our knowledge of them depends; and while we are doing so we cannot doubt them. But since we can forget those reasons and yet remember the conclusions which were drawn from them, the question arises if we can have a firm and immutable conviction concerning these conclusions during the time we recollect that they were deduced from principles which were most evident; for this recollection must be supposed in order that they may be called conclusions. My answer is that such conviction can be had by those who, in virtue of their knowledge of God, are aware that the faculty of understanding given by Him must tend toward truth; but others cannot have it.

Here Descartes is supposing that someone once deduced a conclusion from premises which he was at the time intuiting, but that he no longer remembers these premises. Thus, the person does not now perceive clearly and distinctly that the conclusion follows from premises which he is intuiting. He only remembers that the premises were evident to him at one time—i.e., that he once perceived them clearly and distinctly—and that he deduced the conclusion from them—i.e., once intuited that from them the conclusion follows.

While he was intuiting the premises, Descartes maintains, he was not able to doubt them; nor was he able to doubt that the conclusion follows from the premises while he was intuiting its relation to them. But now he is free to doubt these things, and his problem is to decide whether doubt is justified or whether what he remembers suffices to establish the soundness of the argument being considered. The question is this: given that a proposition has been intuited to follow from premises which were themselves intuited, is it possible that the proposition should be false? Is it possible, in other words, that a proposition should be perceived clearly and distinctly to follow from a set of premises—i.e., be deduced from the set—without actually following from it? And is it possible that premises should be evident—i.e., be perceived so clearly and distinctly as to be subject at the time to no doubt at all—without being true?

5. The metaphysical doubt arises for Descartes when he remembers some intuition, but it is not a doubt about the reliability of memory. Indeed, it should now be apparent that there is no reason why metaphysical doubt may not arise even in situations in which there is no recollection of anything being intuited. For what is required as a context for metaphysical doubt is not necessarily a situation in which a person recollects having intuited something. A suitable context is provided by any set of circumstances in which a person can consider the validity of an intuition.

Thus, suppose that at a certain time one man A perceives something clearly and distinctly, and that another man B knows right then and there that A is doing so. Suppose further that B is uncertain whether the occurrence of A's clear and distinct perception is sufficient to establish the truth of what is being intuited by A. Then B is engaging in metaphysical doubt about what A is intuiting, and it is quite evident that B need not be remembering anything at all while doing so.

Descartes' failure to make this altogether clear is rather easily explained. When he discusses these matters in the

Meditations, the development of his metaphysics is at a stage
in which he does not know that anyone exists but himself. He
does not, accordingly, consider any intuitions but his own.
Since he cannot doubt the validity of his own intuitions
while they are occurring, he can engage in metaphysical doubt
about them only after they have occurred and while he recollects their occurrence. Thus, metaphysical doubt arises *for
Descartes* only when he recollects having perceived something
clearly and distinctly. But this is due to the order in which
matters are taken up in the *Meditations* and not to the nature
of the doubt itself.

II

6. Assuming that the preceding interpretation of Descartes
is correct and that he is trying to validate reason (intuition)
by coping with metaphysical doubts concerning the truth of
what is intuited, can his procedure in the *Meditations* escape
the common charge of circularity?

One of the first to be struck by the apparent circularity of
Descartes' reasoning was Arnauld, who made the point as
follows:

> The only secure reason we have for believing that what
> we clearly and distinctly perceive is true, is the fact that
> God exists. But we can be sure that God exists only be-
> cause we clearly and evidently perceive it. Therefore,
> prior to being certain that God exists, we should be cer-
> tain that whatever we clearly and evidently perceive is
> true.[17]

Now if to be sure of something were to be unable to doubt it,
then Arnauld would be mistaken in supposing that, according
to Descartes, we can be sure of God's existence only if we already know that whatever is intuited is true. For if we intuit
that God's existence follows from premises which are at the
same time also intuited, then while these intuitions occur we
shall be unable to doubt that God exists even if we do not

[17] AT VII, 214 (Latin); AT IX, 166 (French); HR II, 92.

know that whatever is clearly and distinctly perceived is true. We shall be sure of God's existence during that time because we shall actually be intuiting that God exists and hence we shall be, as we are whenever we are intuiting something, irresistibly impelled to believe it.

As a matter of fact, Descartes does believe that all the steps in the proof of God's existence can be intuited simultaneously.[18] It is not implausible (and I shall suppose) that he also thinks it possible to intuit simultaneously not only these steps but also the further steps involved in arguing that the truth of whatever is intuited is guaranteed by the existence of God. Thus, without begging any questions or in any way committing the fallacy of circularity, Descartes allows the possibility of our being sure that whatever is intuited is true. For our belief in this principle may be rooted in present intuitions so that we are incapable of doubting it no matter what else we know or believe.

7. Of course, this hardly settles whether or not Descartes argues in a circle. What it shows is merely that without relying upon a circular argument it is possible, in terms of Descartes' position, to *be sure* that whatever is intuited is true. To eliminate doubt and attain assurance of this one need only run through the argument that God exists and validates reason, keeping all relevant intuitions in mind at once. But being sure of the principle that what is intuited is true is not the same as knowing it to be true, and it would certainly seem that—like other objects of intuition—this principle can well be doubted when one is not intuiting it but is, say, only remembering that it has been intuited.

The remarkable thing, however, is that Descartes denies this. Indeed, he maintains quite straightforwardly that after it has once been demonstrated that what is intuited is true, one need not run through all the intuitions comprising this demonstration each time it is necessary to invoke the divine guarantee of the truth of what is clearly and distinctly perceived. What he says is this:

[18] AT V, 148–149; Charles Adam, ed., *Entretien avec Burman* (Paris, 1937), pp. 9–13.

> After I have recognised that there is a God . . . and
> have inferred that what I perceive clearly and distinctly
> cannot fail to be true, although I no longer pay attention
> to the reasons for which I judged this to be true, provided
> that I recollect having clearly and distinctly perceived it,
> no contrary reason can be brought forward which could
> ever cause me to doubt its truth; and thus I have a true
> and certain knowledge of it.[19]

When one wishes to invoke the principle that what is intuited is true, Descartes assures us, it is sufficient to remember
having demonstrated it. It is not necessary to repeat the intuitions comprising its demonstration.

But why not? Why should this principle be established
by the recollection that it was once demonstrated when, in
general, recalling that something has been intuited is not
sufficient to establish it? Does it not surely seem that Descartes is guilty here of the egregious blunder with which he
has so often been charged? For does he not sanction accepting
as evidence for the principle that intuitions are true the fact
that this principle was once intuited? And would not anyone
who accepted such evidence for the principle be begging the
entire question—the question, precisely, of whether such evidence is acceptable?

8. Before taking answers to these questions for granted, let
us examine carefully the last quoted passage, in which Descartes explains how things stand, in his view, when the existence of God has once been demonstrated and when it has
once been seen clearly and distinctly that from this it follows
that what is intuited is true.

Notice what Descartes claims to be the case when he recollects having intuited that God guarantees the truth of what
is clearly and distinctly perceived. He claims that then "no
contrary reason can be brought forward which could ever
cause me to doubt its truth." He does not assert that when he
recollects having intuited that the principle in question is
true he cannot then *experience* doubts as to its truth. Nor
does he deny what is in any case surely not deniable—that he
can always *state* that he doubts it. But he indicates that any

19 AT VII, 70 (Latin); AT IX, 55–56 (French); HR I, 184.

such statement, at least from the logical point of view, will be capricious. For he cannot, Descartes claims, *have a reason* for doubting it.

Now the possibility that there is not a veracious God is, of course, accepted by Descartes as a reason for doubting that whatever is intuited is true. So his claim involves the view that when one remembers both that God's existence was once intuited and that it was also intuited at one time that what is intuited is true, it is not then reasonable to entertain the possibility that a veracious God does not exist. But why is it unreasonable? We may doubt other things which we recall having intuited. Why can we not with equal reason doubt the existence of a veracious God when we remember intuiting it?

Consider just what it is that is being recalled in the case at issue—namely, that exercising reason in the most rigorous way (i.e., accepting only what is clearly and distinctly perceived) results in the intuition that a veracious God exists. That this is what results when reason is used in the most impeccable manner means that the soundest use of reason leads to the exclusion of the possibility that there is an omnipotent demon and, indeed, to the exclusion of the possibility that man's being derives from any source lacking in power or in perfection. Descartes has undertaken to show that intuition provides no basis for supposing that what is intuited may be false, and it is the establishment of this conclusion that is recalled.

Far from leading to the discovery of reasons for mistrusting reason, Descartes attempts to show, the most conscientious use of reason leads to the discovery that such mistrust has no rational ground. Hence, when someone remembers having perceived clearly and distinctly that intuition is guaranteed by God, what he remembers is that there is no good reason for doubting the trustworthiness of intuition. In other words, he remembers something which makes it plain that the metaphysical doubt is utterly capricious.[20]

[20] That Descartes regards this (rightly or wrongly) as sufficient to establish the truth of what is intuited is readily apparent in the latter part of the passage cited in footnote 18, and in such passages as this one from his "Reply" to the second set of "Objections": "After

9. How Descartes' reasoning is to be understood and eval-
uated will become more apparent if the focus of this discussion is broadened to include the general nature of the enterprise he undertakes in the *Meditations.* As everyone knows,
Descartes is largely concerned in the *Meditations* with the
problem of scepticism. Now so far as scepticism with regard
to reason is concerned, the classical gambit of the sceptic is
to show that the use of reason leads ineluctably to the conclusion that reason is unreliable. Indeed, this is the sceptic's
only available gambit, if he is to argue at all. All he can do
is attempt to provide arguments which demonstrate the untrustworthiness of reason.

Naturally, his attempt will only succeed if his arguments
are good ones—i.e., if he can give good reasons for regarding
with suspicion the significance of good reasons. The sceptic
must show that reason can be turned against itself, by showing that there are reasons of the very strongest sort for
doubting the reliability of reason. We may say, then, that
the sceptic's arguments are designed to provide a *reductio ad
absurdum* of the assumption that reason is reliable.

In order to dispose of scepticism with regard to reason,
therefore, Descartes believes he need only show that the
sceptic's attempt to overthrow reason is a failure. And he
regards this as having been accomplished as soon as he shows
that the most rigorous use of reason does not lead to a mistrust of reason but, rather, to conclusions which exclude all
basis for such mistrust. What Descartes takes to be his task,
in other words, is to show that the sceptic's *reductio* argument
cannot be generated.

He attempts to do this by offering a proof that there is an
omnipotent deity who is not a deceiver and whose existence,

becoming aware that God exists, it is necessary to imagine that He
might be a deceiver if we wish to cast doubt on what we perceive
clearly and distinctly; *and since we cannot even imagine that He is a
deceiver, we must admit these things as most true and most certain."*
AT IX, 113; HR II, 41. The emphasis has been added by me to call
attention to the "negative" character of Descartes' procedure: he
establishes truths by removing the grounds for doubting them rather
than by proving them more directly to be true.

accordingly, entails that reason is reliable. The value of this proof depends on its success in showing where the right use of reason in fact leads: neither to the conclusion that there is an omnipotent demon devoted to deception, nor to any other conclusion involving the untrustworthiness of reason. The proof purportedly makes it clear that when reason is put properly to use it produces reasons of the very best sort (i.e., clear and distinct ideas) for trusting reason. It produces no such reasons for mistrusting reason, and so the sceptic's attempt to reduce reliance on reason to absurdity is seen to fail.

Descartes' argument is thus to be understood as an attempt to show that there are no good reasons for believing that reason is unreliable. Its purpose is to reveal that the hypothesis which provides a basis for mistrusting reason is not one which reason supports, and that the mistrust of reason must accordingly be regarded as irrational. If reason is properly employed—that is, if we give assent only to what is intuited —we are not led to doubt that reason is reliable. On the contrary, we are led to assent to the propositions that God exists and that He guarantees the reliability of reason.

As long as the existence of an omnipotent demon had to be acknowledged by reason to be a possibility, it had to be acknowledged that the use of reason might lead to the conclusion that the demon does exist and that therefore reason is not reliable. Hence, what is essential in Descartes' argument is not so much the discovery of the existence of a benign deity, but the discovery that reason leads to the conclusion that such a deity exists.[21]

[21] Alan Gewirth makes a similar point in his excellent essay, "The Cartesian Circle," *Philosophical Review*, vol. 50 (1941), 389–390: "The ground upon which the clear and distinct perception of God's existence and veracity is regarded by Descartes as overthrowing the metaphysical doubt, then, is that the rationality of the former reveals the 'reasons' of the latter to be irrational." Gewirth's work on Descartes, to which I am very greatly indebted, deserves more attention. In my opinion, his three essays on Descartes' theory of knowledge are by far the best things of their kind in English. The other two essays are "Experience and the Non-Mathematical in the Cartesian Method," *Journal of the History of Ideas*, vol. 2 (1941), 185 ff;

10. Suppose someone recalls having perceived something clearly and distinctly and wonders if he is entitled to regard what he intuited as certainly true. If he does not know whether or not the sceptic can succeed in the attempt to provide a *reductio ad absurdum* of the trustworthiness of intuition, then he must properly be uncertain whether whatever is intuited is true. For all he knows, it may be possible to find impeccable grounds for regarding reason as unreliable —for example, by showing clearly and distinctly that there is an omnipotent demon bent on spoiling the work of reason.

But such doubts are legitimately dispelled, Descartes maintains, if the person can recall that the existence of a veracious God has been demonstrated, for he then recalls that reason does not fall victim to the sceptic's *reductio* but instead decisively escapes it. That the existence of a veracious God has been clearly and distinctly perceived answers the question concerning the possible success of the sceptic's line of argument. It means that the sceptic's line of argument fails. This question being answered, there remain no reasonable grounds upon which to base metaphysical doubts.

It is evident that Descartes' argument does not suffer from the circularity with which it is commonly charged.[22] Meta-

---

and "Clearness and Distinctness in Descartes," *Philosophy*, vol. 18 (1942), 17 ff [reprinted here pp. 250–277].

[22] But Descartes' reasoning may well be defective, and it may even be circular. Indeed, the following serious question must be raised about it. Given that reason leads to the conclusion that reason is reliable because a veracious God exists, may it not also lead to the conclusion that there is an omnipotent demon whose existence renders reason unreliable? Of course, these conclusions are incompatible, and if the proper use of reason established both of them it would mean that reason is unreliable. But surely Descartes cannot take for granted that this is not the case. His procedure does, therefore, seem to beg the question, though in a rather different way than has generally been thought.

To put the same point differently: what Descartes attempts to do is to provide a proof of the consistency of reason; but this proof is decisive only if we suppose (thereby begging the question?) that reason is consistent, since otherwise it might still be possible to construct an equally cogent proof of the inconsistency of reason. Descartes seems to have been unaware that his procedure is open to this line of

physical doubt concerns the truth of what is intuited, and
the removal of this doubt is effected without assuming that
what is intuited is true. It is removed simply by the knowledge that a certain demonstration has been successfully accomplished. This knowledge is, of course, the knowledge that
certain things have been clearly and distinctly perceived. But
it is not required that the *truth* of these things be supposed,
and so the question is not begged. All that is relevant to the
removal of metaphysical doubt is that the sceptic's *reductio*
be discovered not to materialize, and this discovery can be
made and recalled without anything intuited being supposed
to be true.

11. If I am correct in what I have ascribed to Descartes,
his reasoning in the *Meditations* is designed not so much to
prove that what is intuited is true as to show that there are
no reasonable grounds for doubting this. Now it may be objected that in that case he leaves the main question still open,
since it may be that what we intuit is sometimes false even
if we can have no reasonable grounds for supposing so. Whatever may be the weight of this objection, it bears against
Descartes' doctrines and not against the authenticity of my
interpretation of them. Indeed, some confirmation for my
interpretation is to be seen in the fact that Descartes
acknowledges that an objection of this sort may be raised
against his position.

Thus, he begins a summary statement of his position by
making it clear that in his view "if . . . we can never have
any reason to doubt that of the truth of which we have
persuaded ourselves, there is nothing more to inquire about;
we have all the certainty that can reasonably be desired."[23]

Immediately thereafter, he anticipates the objection that
certainty based upon the unavailability of reasonable grounds
for doubt is compatible with the falsity of that of which

---

criticism, and I do not propose to enter here into the difficult investigation that would be necessary in order to arrive at a just evaluation of its significance.

[23] Both this passage and the one quoted next are from Descartes'
"Reply" to the second set of "Objections," AT VII, 145 (Latin); AT
IX, 113–114 (French); HR II, 41.

there is certainty. It is particularly interesting to consider his manner of formulating this objection and of responding to it. Concerning something of which we have "all the certainty that can reasonably be desired," he says:

> What is it to us if someone should feign that the very thing of whose truth we are so firmly persuaded appears false to the eyes of God or of the Angels and that hence, speaking absolutely, it is false? Why should we concern ourselves with this absolute falsity, since we by no means believe in it or even have the least suspicion of it? For we are supposing a belief or a conviction so strong that nothing can remove it, and this conviction is in every respect the same as perfect certitude.

Evidently Descartes recognizes his position to entail that from the fact that we know something with perfect certitude, it does not follow that it is, "absolutely speaking," true. He concedes, that is, that he has not proven that whatever is intuited is absolutely true.

If what is perfectly certain may be absolutely false, Descartes suggests, the notions of absolute truth and absolute falsity are irrelevant to the purposes of inquiry. Presumably he would wish them to be replaced with other notions of truth and falsity. But what are these notions and how are they related to those which Descartes rejects? This line of reflection leads rapidly to a large number of questions: concerning Descartes' conceptions of certainty, of knowledge, and of the relation between knowledge and reality. To explore these matters is likely not only to enhance the understanding of his position, but to be of considerable philosophical interest as well.[24]

[24] For helpful comments on an earlier version of this paper, I wish to express my appreciation to Carlos Blanco, Bruce Lercher, Maurice Mandelbaum, C. Wade Savage, Sydney Shoemaker, and Richard Sorabji.

DESCARTES ON IDEAS

ANTHONY KENNY

I

Once Descartes has established his own existence as a conscious being, he goes on to consider the existence of God and of the external world. He proves the existence of everything except himself by examining the properties of ideas which he finds within himself. Before considering his proofs, therefore, it is worth examining what he meant by "idea."

The word "idea" is now at home in ordinary language; but it is a word, like "quality" and "intention," which was once primarily a philosophical technicality. Its modern use derives, through Locke, from Descartes; and Descartes was consciously giving it a new sense. Before him, philosophers used it to refer to archetypes in the divine intellect: it was a new departure to use it systematically for the contents of a human mind. Descartes several times explained the sense he meant to give the word; but it is not easy to make all his explanations cohere.

One of the clearest points he made about ideas is this: "I cannot express anything in words, provided that I understand what I say, without its thereby being certain that there is within me the idea of that which is signified by the words in question" (AT VII, 160; HR 2, 52). This may suggest that there is an idea corresponding to every significant word, and that it is a sufficient condition for a man's having an idea of X that he should know how to use a word for X intel-

ligently. Other passages give a similar impression. When an
objector complained that he could not understand what was
meant in the *Meditations* by the ideas of God and the soul,
Descartes wrote to Mersenne that if the objector conceived
anything at all when he used the words "God" and "soul"
then he knew what the ideas of these things were (AT III,
393).

It seems, however, that there is no simple one-to-one correspondence between words and ideas. We are told that,
strictly speaking, no idea corresponds to the word "nothing"
(AT V, 153, to Burman) and we learn that two ideas correspond to the word "sun" (AT VII, 39; HR 1, 161). All
ideas, it seems, purport to be of things (*nullae ideae nisi
tanquam rerum esse possunt*) (AT VII, 44; HR 1, 164).
Certainly there are ideas of things of many different kinds:
we hear of the ideas of God, of angels, of animals, of men,
of sun, of wax, of heat and cold, of colors, sounds, and shapes,
of length and motion and time, of thought and of existence.
But the idea of existence is displayed not only when I use
the word "existence" but also when I say "I exist." Some
ideas seem to correspond not to particular words, but to
whole sentences. Thus, Descartes speaks of ideas of "common
notions"; and he gives as an example of a common notion
"That which can effect what is greater or more difficult, can
also accomplish what is less" (AT VII, 166; HR 2, 56). But
when we speak of such ideas, Descartes told Burman, we
are using "idea" in a broad sense (AT V, 153). When
Mersenne asked whether ideas were expressed by simple
terms, Descartes replied, "I do not understand the question
you ask; for words are human inventions, and we can use
one or more of them to express the same thing" (AT III,
417).

The circumstances which Descartes is prepared to describe
as constituting the presence of an idea vary considerably from
case to case. Thus, when he says that a man has an idea of
God, he may mean no more than that the man has the ability
to come to know God (e.g. AT IV, 187). When he speaks
of having an idea of truth, he may mean understanding what
truth is (e.g. AT VII, 438; HR 1, 160). When he speaks of

having an idea of a Syren, he may be referring to imaginative creation (*ibid.*). And when he speaks of having an idea of heat, he may be thinking of a case where someone is actually feeling the heat of a particular fire (*ibid.*). When Descartes announces the presence of an idea, therefore, he may be intending to signal anything from a remote capacity to a particular actual experience. Sometimes, he speaks of ideas in general in terms which are appropriate to the description of capacities, as when he connects them with the ability to use words. At other times he speaks of them in terms appropriate to episodes, as when he says that ideas are "operations of the intellect" (AT VII, 232; HR 2, 105).

Even when the context makes clear that what is in question is an episode and not a capacity, Descartes seems inconsistent in the manner in which he speaks of ideas. Sometimes, as in the passage just cited, an idea is an operation or act of the mind; at other times it is not so much an act of the mind as the *object* or content of such an act. This ambiguity was signaled by Descartes himself in the Preface to the *Meditations*. "In this term *idea* there is an equivocation: it may either be taken materially, as an act of my understanding . . . or objectively, as what is represented by this act" (AT VII, 8; HR 1, 138; cf. L. J. Beck, *The Metaphysics of Descartes*, p. 152).

But the distinction between act and object does not solve all the difficulties latent in Descartes's terminology. There are many different relationships between acts and their objects. Some acts are identical with their objects: when I score a goal, the goal is nothing more nor less than my scoring it. Some objects are produced by acts, as a poem is produced by my act when I write it. Some objects are modified by acts, as a chair is altered in color when I paint it. Other objects are objects of intentional acts, in which case the object modifies the agent instead of the agent modifying the object: when I notice a spider, that is a change in me, not in the spider.

A man's relation to his ideas is described by Descartes in verbs appropriate to acts of all these different kinds. Thus I "form" ideas (AT VII, 57; HR 1, 174) or "construct" them

(AT VII, 75; HR 1, 188); I also "grasp" them (AT VII, 57; HR 1, 175), "find" them in myself (AT VII, 63), "bring them out of" my consciousness, "as if out of a treasury" (AT VII, 64; HR 1, 180); they "present themselves" to me (AT VII, 54, 75; HR 1, 172) and I "notice" them (*ibid.*, 54, 75), "perceive" them (*ibid.*, 56), and my mind "looks at them" (*ibid.*, 73). It is difficult to decide, in any particular case, whether these locutions are just natural metaphors for such events as coming to understand a word, or calling to mind a familiar face; or whether, on the other hand, they embody a particular explanatory theory of such events. When two formulations clash, have we to deal with alternative metaphors, or an inconsistent theory?

The difficulties are illustrated, and in part elucidated, by two passages in letters. Both passages deal with the question whether every man has an idea of God. "I do not doubt that all have within themselves at least an implicit idea of God, that is to say, an aptitude to perceive it explicitly; but I am not surprised that they do not feel themselves to have it, or do not notice that they have it, and perhaps will not notice it even after the thousandth reading of my meditations" (*To Hyperaspistes*, AT III, 430). "The idea of God is so imprinted on the human mind that there is no one who does not have in himself the faculty of knowing him; but this does not prevent many people from being able to pass their whole lives without ever distinctly representing this idea to themselves" (AT IV, 187). In both passages an idea can be a capacity (an "aptitude" or "faculty"): such an idea is called, in the first passage, an "implicit idea." But the idea of God is also something which can be "perceived" or "represented to oneself." That makes it sound like something which is the object, or the product, of a particular mental action. But it is not clear whether the mental action in question is coming to know what the word "God" really means, or thinking a thought about God.

The ambiguities must be borne in mind in considering Descartes's famous doctrine of innate ideas. In the *Meditations*, he says "Of my ideas, some seem to be innate, some acquired, and some devised by myself" (AT VII, 38; HR 1,

160). This suggests a classification of ideas into three kinds according to a difference of origin. But when he goes on to give examples, it seems that the ideas of the different classes are entities of different kinds quite apart from the differences in their origins. The innate ideas listed are capacities: namely, the concepts of *thing, truth,* and *consciousness.* The acquired ideas are particular sensations: hearing a noise, seeing the sun, feeling the fire. When Descartes says that the idea of truth is innate, he does not mean that one is born thinking of the truth; and on the other hand, in saying that the idea of heat comes from the fire, he does not mean that the *concept* of heat is acquired by sensation.

The classification in the *Third Meditation* is in any case provisional and is elsewhere improved upon. To Mersenne, Descartes wrote in 1641: "Some ideas are adventitious, such as the idea we commonly have of the sun; others are factitious, in which class we can put the idea which the astronomers construct of the sun by their reasoning; and others are innate, such as the idea of God, Mind, Body, triangle, and in general all those which represent true, immutable, and eternal essences" (AT III, 303). Later in the same year he wrote that an infant in its mother's womb "has in itself the ideas of God, itself, and all truths which are said to be self-evident; it has these ideas no less than adults have when they are not paying attention to them, and it does not acquire them afterwards when it grows up" (AT III, 424).

From this it appears that though an unborn baby does not actually think of God, it understands very well what God is, and when it is later taught the word "God" it merely learns to give an expression to a concept which it has always possessed. This, however, seems to be contradicted by what Descartes wrote in 1647 in his *Notes Against a Programme.* "I have never written, nor been of opinion, that the mind needs innate ideas in the sense of something different from its faculty of thinking." Ideas were innate, he explained, only in "the sense of the word that we say generosity is innate in certain families; or again that in others certain diseases, e.g. gout and the stone, are innate; not that infants of these families suffer from these diseases in their mother's womb, but because they are born with a certain disposition or liability to contract them" (AT VIII, 357; HR 1, 442). But if an unborn baby has the idea of God in the same way as an adult who just happens not to be thinking of God, then the baby has something more than a mere "faculty of thinking." And what corresponds, in the case of ideas, to the "disposition or liability" to contract gout? Is it the ability to *learn* what God is? If so, then an innate idea is nothing distinct from the thinking faculty; but it is not comparable to the concept of God held by a man who has already learnt what the word "God" means. Or is it the ability to *exercise* the knowledge of what God is? If so, then the unborn baby is in the same position as the instructed adult; but it cannot be said that his innate idea is nothing more than his faculty of thinking.

In a well-known passage of the *De Anima*, Aristotle observed that "when a man possesses knowledge as an unexercised disposition, he is still in a state of potentiality, though not in the same way as before he learnt what he knows" (*De Anima* III, 4, 429 b6–10). For instance, a man may (a) not know French at all, (b) know French but not be using his knowledge or (c) be actually speaking French. In the first and second cases he is in "a state of potentiality" in two different ways.

Descartes, with his contempt for the Aristotelian notion of potentiality, was unable to distinguish between the unrealized capacity to acquire knowledge and the nonexercise of knowledge already acquired. There is no room in his system for the concept of *learning*.

Even adventitious ideas are in a sense innate, Descartes explained in the *Notes Against a Programme*.

> In our ideas there is nothing which was not innate in the mind, or faculty of thinking, except only those circumstances which concern experience—the fact, for instance, that we judge this or that idea, which we now have present to our thought, is to be referred to certain extraneous things, not that these extraneous things transmitted the ideas themselves to our minds through the organs of sense, but because they transmitted something

which gave the mind occasion to form these ideas, by means of an innate faculty, at this time rather than at another. For nothing reaches our mind from external objects through the organs of sense beyond certain corporeal movements . . . but even these movements, and the figures which arise from them, are not conceived by us in the shape they assume in the organs of sense. . . . Hence it follows that the ideas of the movements and figures are themselves innate in us. So much the more must the ideas of pain, color, sound and the like be innate, that our mind may, on occasion of certain corporeal movements, present those ideas to itself, for they have no likeness to the corporeal movements. [AT VIII, 358; HR 1, 443]

And to Mersenne he wrote: "I hold that all those ideas which involve no affirmation or negation are innate: for the organs of our senses do not bring us anything which is like the idea which arises in us on the occasions they provide, and so that idea must have been in us beforehand" [AT III, 418].

These passages make clear in what sense it is true for Descartes that all ideas are innate. No matter what X may be, the idea of X is innate in the sense that the capacity to think of X, imagine X, feel X, experience X is inborn in us and is not given us by the stimulus which on a particular occasion makes us think of or experience X. But if the idea of X is in my mind—if the innate capacity to think of or experience X is exercised—in such a way that I accompany the idea with a judgment ("affirmation or negation") that its occurrence is due to extra-mental reality, then this occurrence of the idea, this exercise of the capacity, is an *adventitious* idea. So the distinction between innate and adventitious ideas is not that there are some ideas (such as that of God) which are innate, and others (such as those of heat) which are adventitious, but that one and the same idea (e.g. that of heat) is *qua* capacity innate and *qua* episode accompanied with extra-mental judgment, adventitious. (The judgment about the extra-mental reality may be that the occurrence of the idea is due to something in the world *like* the idea; in which case the adventitious idea will be confused; or it may be that the idea is caused by something of a different form in the world; in which case the adventitious idea will be distinct [AT VIII, 33; HR 1, 248].)

Descartes's argument for the innateness of all ideas is based on the premise that no idea is *like* the sensory stimulus which brings it to mind. He seems to envisage only two possibilities: that ideas are innate or that they are likenesses copied from elements of the external world. "Some of my thoughts," he said in the *Third Meditation*, "are as it were pictures of objects, and these alone are properly called ideas." The comparison between ideas and pictures seems likely to mislead in the context of a discussion of innate ideas. Ideas *qua* capacities may plausibly be held to be innate; but capacities are not like pictures. Ideas *qua* episodes may plausibly be compared to pictures before the mind; but ideas *qua* episodes are not innate. How far was Descartes misled by the comparison between ideas and pictures?

On the same page on which he asserted that ideas were likenesses of things, Descartes condemned as a disastrous error the belief that ideas in the mind were similar to things outside (AT VII, 37; HR 1, 160). And in controversy with Hobbes and Gassendi he insisted that by an idea he did not mean an image. Hobbes, for instance, denied that we had any real idea of an angel. "When I think of an angel, what comes into my mind is the image sometimes of a flame, sometimes of a fair winged child; and I feel certain that this has no likeness to an angel, and is thus not the idea of an angel." Descartes replied: "Here he will have the term *idea* to mean only the images of material things, pictured in the corporeal fancy" (AT VII, 179–181; HR 2, 67). Hobbes went on: "We have no idea at all of the soul. We infer by reasoning that there is something within the human body that gives it animal motion and by means of which it feels and moves; we call this, whatever it is, the *soul*, without having an idea of it." Descartes retorted: "This comes to the same as saying that there is no image of the soul formed in our fancy, but that there is what I call an idea" (AT VII, 133; HR 2, 70). He wrote later in similar terms to Gassendi (AT VII, 366; HR 2, 217).

This, however, does not settle the matter. In denying that ideas are images, Descartes uses "image" very literally: he is denying not so much that ideas are mental images as that they are cerebral images. In the definition in the *Second Objections* he wrote: "It is not only images pictured in the fancy that I call ideas; nay, to such images I here decidedly refuse the title of ideas, in so far as they are pictures in the corporeal fancy, i.e., in some part of the brain. They are ideas only in so far as they inhere in the mind itself when it is directed towards that part of the brain" (AT VII, 161; HR 2, 52).[1]

Descartes believed, then, that the exercise of the imagination or fancy—I use this term to correspond to his technical term *phantasia*—consisted in looking at pictures in the brain. In consequence, when he denies that ideas are images, we cannot be quite sure that he is denying that ideas are mental images in the sense of pictures in the mind's eye. For mental images are not material pictures in the brain. Mental images are indeed in one sense material. There can be mental pictures only of things of which there can be real pictures: primarily, of material objects and things perceptible by sight. There can, of course, be mental pictures of justice or eternity, just as there can be painted pictures of these things; but any mental picture of an abstract entity must represent it by representing first of all something perceptible, like a pair of scales or a white circle. Again, mental images, like material pictures, last for periods of time and have spatial parts such as a top and a bottom and a left-hand and right-hand side. But mental images are immaterial in another sense. They are not made out of any stuff, however tenuous. Unlike material pictures, they do not exist unless before the mind, nor can they have properties which pass unperceived. Having mental images is no doubt connected with events in the brain— according to certain philosophers it is identical with such events—but nonetheless is not the perception of any cerebral entity. What Descartes said of his ideas is true also of mental images, that they are not "composed of any matter" (AT VII, 232; HR 2, 105).

[1] In the *Regulae* cerebral images are called "ideas" (AT X, 443).

It is customary nowadays to distinguish between mental images and concepts. To have a concept of X is to know what X is: knowledge which is expressed, for instance, in the ability to distinguish between what is X and what is not X, or in the ability to use a word for X in some language. One and the same concept, in this sense, may be exercised when different images are in the mind; and the same image may be the vehicle for several concepts. When Descartes insists against his critics on the distinction between images and ideas it looks *prima facie* as if he is marking off mental images from concepts. In part, no doubt, he is: that is to say, some of the criteria by which he is drawing his distinction are the same as the criteria by which we make our distinction. But in fact, his ideas have some of the properties of material pictures, some of the properties of mental images, and some of the properties of concepts. Like material and mental pictures, they are representations which exhibit things. Like mental pictures, and unlike cerebral pictures, they are not made out of any matter. More, they can represent immaterial things (e.g. God) without doing so by representing something material (e.g. a bearded sage). Like material pictures, but unlike mental images, they exist even when not before the mind, and when before the mind they can contain details which the mind has not noticed.

In all these respects Descartes's ideas are unlike concepts. The acquisition and use of a concept cannot be described as if it were like the acquisition or inspection of a representation. The ability to recognize a man which is part of the possession of the concept of *man* cannot be explained by postulating the presence of a representation of a man against which any alleged man can be checked for correspondence. For the representation would itself have to be correctly recognized each time it presented itself to consciousness. If a further representation is needed to explain this ability, we are started on a vicious regress; if not, then no representation need have been postulated in the first place.

If we are to evaluate Descartes's claim that the intelligent use of words presupposes the presence of innate ideas, we must make several distinctions. That the intelligent use of words presupposes the possession of concepts is correct; that it presupposes the presence of something like a picture is incorrect. The quasi-pictures which Descartes postulates are neither necessary nor sufficient to explain the intelligent use of words; moreover, they are intrinsically incoherent entities, combining as they do the properties of material and immaterial images. That the concepts which are exercised in the intelligent use of words are not acquired on the occasions of their use is correct; that they are inborn is incorrect. In general, the concepts expressed in words are acquired when language is learnt: what is inborn is not the concepts themselves but the ability to acquire them, the faculty of linguistic intelligence in which men surpass other animals.

In any argument in which Descartes employs the term "idea" we have to ask ourselves whether he means a capacity or an episode, whether he means an act or its object, and whether he means a mental image, the exercise of a concept or the occurrence of an experience. Having done so, we have to check whether the premises of his arguments are true and whether his conclusion follows if the interpretation of "idea" is held constant throughout. Such a procedure often throws light not only on Descartes's own theses about ideas but on the arguments brought against them by later critics such as the British Empiricists.

II

We must now turn to the relation between the notion of "idea" and some of the other technical terms of Descartes's philosophy. What is the relation, for instance, between ideas and thoughts? *Cogitatio* shares some of the ambiguities of *idea*. To Hobbes, Descartes wrote: "Thought is taken sometimes for an act, sometimes for a faculty, sometimes for the subject possessing the faculty" (AT VII, 174; HR 2, 62). When he discusses the relationships between ideas and thoughts, however, commonly he seems to be taking both words in their episodic senses as conscious events.

Occasionally the words "idea" and "thought" are used as

synonyms (e.g. AT VI, 559; HR 1, 102; to Clerselier, AT 5, 354); elsewhere, ideas are described as "*modi cogitandi,*" modes of thought or ways of thinking (e.g. AT VII, 40, 44; HR 1, 161). In Descartes's fullest definition of "idea," an idea is said to be the form of a *thought*. "By the word 'idea' I mean the form of any *thought*, that form by the immediate awareness of which I am conscious of that said *thought*" (AT VII, 160; HR 2, 52). The word "form" is a piece of scholastic jargon, but no scholastic theory seems to be involved. By calling ideas "forms" Descartes seems to mean simply that they are nonmaterial representations of things (AT VII, 232; HR 2, 105). In the *Third Meditation*, when Descartes has said that only those of his *thoughts* which are like pictures really deserve the name of "idea," he goes on to say: "Other thoughts have other forms in addition (*aliae vero alias quasdam praeterea formas habent*): when, I will, am afraid, assert or deny, there is always something which I take as the topic of my thought; but my thought comprises more than the likeness of the thing in question; of these experiences, some are termed volitions or emotions, others are termed judgements" (AT VII, 37; HR 1, 159). This passage gives the impression that the pure thought of X, the desire for X, and the fear of X, all involve the idea of X; but the first consists of this idea alone, while the second and third consist of the same idea plus something extra.

Now is this something extra itself an idea? The natural way of reading the passage suggests that it is not: what makes the difference between the thought of X and the fear of X is not itself an idea, though it is like an idea in being a "form." However, this would make it difficult to understand the definition of "idea" quoted above from the *Second Objections*. For there it is said that it is by the awareness of the idea that I am conscious of a thought; but awareness merely of the idea of X will not suffice to make me conscious that I fear X.

This difficulty puzzled Hobbes, who wrote:

> When anybody wills or is afraid, he has an image of the thing he fears or the action he wills; what more is com-

prised in the thought of one who wills or is afraid is not explained. Fear is a thought, but so far as I can see it can only be the thought of the thing a man fears. What is fear of an onrushing lion but the idea of an onrushing lion together with the effect that this idea produces in the heart, which leads the one who fears to make the animal motion called running away? Now the motion of running away is not a thought. [AT VII, 182; HR 2, 68]

Descartes replied brusquely: "It is obvious that seeing a lion and at the same time fearing it is different from just seeing"; but in an earlier reply to Hobbes he had given a more instructive answer. "I take the term 'idea' to stand for whatever the mind is directly aware of (*a mente percipitur*). For instance, when I wish or am afraid, I am at the same time aware of (*percipio*) wishing or being afraid; thus I count *volition* and *fear* among ideas" (AT VII, 181; HR 2, 68).

This is still not decisive. Does he mean by the last sentence that there are, among ideas, ideas *of* volition and ideas *of* fear: so that when I fear a lion there are simultaneously present in my mind the idea of a lion and the idea of fear? Or does he mean that volition and fear are themselves ideas, so that the fear of a lion is just a special kind of idea of a lion— as it were, a picture of a lion in a particular color appropriate to fear? The former account seems to fit better the description of fear in *The Passions of the Soul* (AT XI, 359; HR 1, 350), though there the terminology of ideas is not used. But the latter seems to square better with some remarks on volition in a letter of 1641: "I claim that we have ideas not only of everything which is in our intellect, but also of everything which is in the will. For we cannot will anything without knowing that we will it, nor know it, except by an idea; but I do not claim that this idea is different from the action itself" (AT III, 295).

Perhaps it is possible to reconcile these contrasting statements in the following way. Whenever I am conscious of X, or think of X, then I have an idea of X. If X is something other than my own mental activity—say, the heat of the fire, or God—then this idea is something distinct from X which represents X. If X is one of my own mental activities—say, willing, or fearing—then I am directly aware of X; that is to say, the idea of X is not a representation of X, but is X itself. If I think of a lion, my thought simply is the occurrence of the idea of a lion in my mind; and I am aware of my thinking simply by perceiving that idea. (Thinking being a mental activity, I need no further representation—no idea of the idea of a lion—to perceive the thinking.) On the other hand, if I am afraid of a lion, there occurs in my mind not only the idea of the lion, but also the fear. There is, in one sense, no idea of the fear: that is to say, there is no representation of the fear, distinct from the fear itself, present in the mind. But as the fear is itself directly perceptible, on Descartes's theory, and as an idea is that by which something is made conscious, the fear itself can be called an idea. Thus, that which differentiates being afraid of the lion from merely thinking of the lion, in one sense is, and in another sense is not, an idea. Here we meet again the ambiguity of "idea" as between act and object; it is the idea of a lion *qua* act of the mind, and not *qua* object of such an act, which can be said to be identical with my thinking of a lion.

It is time to investigate further this notion of "object."

So far we have been considering ideas as properties or events in the mind which has them. It is also possible to look at them from a reverse point of view. When I see the sun, the sun is seen by me. If I begin to think of the sun, then at the same time the sun begins to have a new property, namely the property of being thought of by me. The sun, we might quite naturally say, comes into my mind. This, we may feel, is not a very important property of the sun, nor one very intimately connected with it; but still, it is a genuine property of the real sun: a relationship between it and my mind. Scholastics contemporary with Descartes spoke of this property as that of "being 'objectively' in the understanding" —"objectively" meaning "as an object of thought." So that they would say that when I have an idea of the sun, the sun is "objectively" in my understanding.

Descartes adopted this mode of speaking.[2] A marginal note to the Latin *Discourse of Method* reads: "The noun 'Idea' is generally used for every thing which is thought of (*res cogitata*), in so far as it has only a certain objective existence in the intellect" (AT VI, 559). But for Descartes, the *res cogitata* which exists in my mind when I think of the sun is not the sun itself, but some proxy for the sun. The scholastic Caterus, objecting to Descartes's manner of investigating the causes of ideas, wrote: "What is an idea? It is the thing thought of itself in so far as that is objectively in the understanding. But what is 'existing objectively in the understanding'? As I was taught, it is simply being the object of an act of thought, which is merely an external attribute of the thing and adds no reality to it" (AT VII, 92; HR 2, 2). The sun's being seen, or coming into my mind, is no real change in the sun.

Descartes's reply is very illuminating.

He refers to the thing itself, which is as it were placed outside the understanding, and respecting which it is certainly an extrinsic attribute to be objectively in the understanding, and what I speak of is the idea, which at no time exists outside the mind, and in the case of which "objective existence" means precisely being in the understanding in the way in which objects are wont to be there. Thus, for example, if someone asks what happens to the sun when it exists objectively in my understanding, it is correct to reply that it acquires nothing but a merely extrinsic attribute, that of providing the object with which my thought is concerned. But if the question be, what the idea of the sun is, and the answer be given that it is the thing thought of (*res cogitata*) in so far as it exists objectively in the understanding, then no one will think that it is the sun itself with its merely external attribute. And in this case "objective existence in the understanding" will not mean merely providing the object with which my thought is concerned, but existing in the understanding in the way in which its objects are wont to exist there. Hence the idea of the sun will be the sun it-

[2] So far as concerned clear and distinct ideas: cf. AT VII, 233; HR 2, 106.

self existing in the understanding, not indeed formally,
as it exists in the sky, but objectively, i.e. in the way in
which objects are wont to exist in the mind. [AT VII,
102; HR 2, 3]

In this passage we can see clearly a certain reduplication
taking place. "To think of the sun" can be rephrased, if you
like, as "to have an idea of the sun." But to think of the sun
is not the same as to think of an idea of the sun; and so "to
think of an idea of the sun" is not the same as "to have an
idea of the sun." If I think of the sun, then the sun is thought
of by me; and "the sun is thought of by me" can be rephrased,
if you like, as "the sun has objective existence in me." Putting
our two rephrasings together, we can say that whenever I
have an idea of the sun, then the sun has objective existence
in me; we can even say that my having an idea of the sun
and the sun's having objective existence in me are one and
the same thing. But that is not the same as saying, as Descartes does, that when I have an idea of the sun, an idea of
the sun has objective existence in me. For if we decode this, it
means that when I think of the sun, I think of an idea of
the sun. And this has not been proved, and is indeed false.
An extra entity has been spirited into existence. And this
comes out in the way Descartes actually contradicts himself,
saying first of all that what exists in the mind in the way in
which objects exist in the mind is not the sun, but the idea
of the sun, and then going on to say that the idea of the sun
is the sun itself existing in the mind in the way in which
objects are wont to exist in the mind.

III

Ideas, according to Descartes, may have various properties.
Of these, two types are most important. First, an idea may
be true or false, and secondly, it may be either clear and distinct, or obscure and confused.

Descartes quite often speaks of ideas as being true or false;
but in the *Third Meditation* he says:

Ideas considered in themselves, and not referred to
something else, cannot strictly speaking be false; whether
I imagine a she-goat or a chimera, it is not less true that
I imagine one than the other. Again, falsehood is not to
be feared in the will or the emotions; I may desire what
is evil, or what does not exist anywhere, but it is none
the less true that I desire it. Only judgments remain: it
is here that I must take precaution against falsehood.
[AT VII, 37; HR 1, 159]

This seems an odd piece of reasoning. Could one not as
well argue that judgments in themselves could not be false,
on the grounds that whether I judge the sun to be larger than
the earth, or judge it to be smaller than the earth, it is none
the less true that I judge? A false judgment is a real judgment; so you cannot prove that the imagination of a chimera
is not a false imagination by showing that it is a real imagination. However, it is true that the imagination of a chimera is
not made a false imagination by the fact that there is no such
thing as a chimera, and that the wish for a chimera is not
made a false wish by the same fact: whereas the chimera's
nonexistence does make a judgment that here is a chimera
false. Moreover, the idea of a chimera is no less the idea *of a
chimera* than the idea of a goat is the idea of a goat. Again,
the desire for Utopia is a desire for nothing less than Utopia
itself, even though there is no such place as Utopia. Perhaps
this is the point Descartes wished to make. But would he
have said that a judgment about God, if there is no God, is
not really a judgment about God?

However this may be, with regard to truth and falsity, ideas
can be defective in two ways. First an idea may not be a real
idea (*vera idea: idée veritable*). We have no real idea of
immobility, or darkness, or nothingness; we conceive these
things by negation only (AT VII, 45; HR 1, 166). Secondly,
an idea can be materially false: it can, he says "represent
what is not a thing as if it were a thing." Suppose, for instance, that cold is merely the absence of heat, and I take it
for a reality in its own right. In that case I have a "materially
false" idea of cold. Descartes explained to Burman:

There can be matter for error, even if I do not refer my
ideas to anything outside me, since I can be mistaken
about their nature. For instance, if I considered the idea
of color and said that it was a thing, a quality—or rather
that color itself, which is represented by that idea, is
something of the kind; for instance, if I said that whiteness is a quality, even if I did not refer this idea to anything outside me, even if I said or supposed that there
was not a single white object, none the less I might make
a mistake in abstract, about whiteness itself and its nature or idea. [AT V, 152]

(Color, for Descartes, was not a real quality: the sensation of
color being caused by the action of subtle matter on the optic nerve).

This notion of "materially false" ideas puzzled Arnauld. If
cold is just an absence, he said, then there can be no positive
idea of it, and hence no false idea of it. "What does that
idea of cold, which you say is false materially, display to your
mind? Absence? In that case, it is a true idea. A positive
reality? Then it is not the idea of cold" (AT VII, 206; HR 2,
87). Descartes insisted in reply that the idea of cold "furnishes me with material for error, if in fact cold is an absence
and does not possess so much reality as heat, because in considering either of the ideas of heat and cold just as I received
them both from the senses, I am unable to perceive that more
reality is represented to me by one than by the other."
The ideas of heat and cold "are referred to something other
than that of which they are in truth the ideas." Thus, if cold
is the mere absence of heat, "the idea of cold is not cold itself
existing objectively in the understanding, but some other
thing which is wrongly taken for that absence, namely, some
sensation which has no existence outside the mind" (AT
VII, 232; HR 2, 106).

Several things are confusing in Descartes's account of false
ideas. First of all, the same word *vera* is used to mark the
distinction between genuine ideas and negations and the distinction between true and false ideas. The two distinctions
are not the same: the idea of cold is a genuine idea, but a
materially false one. All genuine ideas are "as it were of

things" (*tanquam rerum*); true ideas really are ideas of things (*rerum quarundam ideae*), false ideas are ideas of nonthings (*non rerum*) (AT VII, 43; HR 1, 164). Perhaps Descartes means the order of words to be significant: *vera idea* will mean "genuine idea," and *idea vera* will mean true idea. (Contrast AT VII, 45, l. 24; with AT VII, 46, ll. 5 ff.)

Secondly, what does Descartes think that the idea of cold is really an idea *of?* He says that it is "referred to something other than that of which it is in truth the idea." "To refer an idea to something" means, in Descartes's terminology, "to judge that some extra-mental existent is similar to the idea." Such a judgment, in the case of cold, Descartes believed to be false: there is no extra-mental existent similar to the idea of cold. The correct judgment would be that the idea is a sensation which has no existence outside the mind. In that case, it seems, the idea cannot be the idea *of* anything but itself.

Throughout the exchange with Arnauld, Descartes appears to be confused about the criterion for the object of an idea. What is it that makes a particular idea the idea *of cold?* Is it the idea's resembling cold? Or is it the idea's being meant by its possessor to resemble cold?

The question recalls Descartes's comparison between ideas and pictures. It corresponds to the question: what makes a particular picture a picture *of Napoleon?* Is it the picture's resembling Napoleon? Or is it the picture's being meant by the painter to resemble Napoleon—e.g. having "Napoleon" as its caption? In this case the answer seems clear. A picture is a picture of Napoleon if it is meant to resemble Napoleon; and if it does not in fact resemble Napoleon, then it is a bad likeness. Clearly, Arnauld would be foolish to argue that there could not be a poor portrait of Napoleon on the ground that any portrait was either like Napoleon or if unlike Napoleon not a portrait of Napoleon at all.

Descartes, it seems, cannot give a consistent answer to the question about the criterion for the object of an idea. The idea of cold does not resemble cold. None the less it really is the idea of cold. The criterion which settles this, then, cannot be its resembling cold, but must be its being believed by its possessor to resemble cold, i.e. its being "referred to cold."

On the other hand, if an idea is the idea *of* whatever it is "referred" to, then it cannot be the case that the idea of cold is referred to something other than that of which it is in truth the idea. Once again, the comparison between ideas and pictures has led Descartes into incoherence.

The most important properties which Descartes attributes to ideas are those of clarity (*versus* obscurity) and distinctness (*versus* confusedness). To conclude this treatment of ideas in Descartes, I wish to consider the exact nature of these properties as applied to simple ideas such as sensations, without for the moment considering the epistemological use which Descartes makes of the principle that whatever is clearly and distinctly perceived is true.

The fullest account of clarity and distinctness is given in the *Principles*.

> The knowledge upon which a certain and incontrovertible judgement can be formed, should not alone be clear but also distinct. I term that clear which is present and apparent to an attentive mind, in the same way as we assert that we see objects clearly when, being present to the regarding eye, they operate upon it with sufficient strength. But the distinct is that which is so precise and different from all other objects that it contains within itself nothing but what is clear. When, for instance, a severe pain is felt, the perception of this pain may be very clear, and yet for all that not distinct, because it is usually confused by the sufferers with the obscure judgment that they form upon its nature, assuming as they do that something exists in the part affected, similar to the sensation of pain of which they are alone clearly conscious. [AT VIII, 21; HR 1, 237]

We are told, however, that we may have a clear knowledge of our sensations if we take care to include in the judgments we form of them that only which we know to be precisely contained in our perception of them, and of which we are intimately conscious. Thus, "there is no reason that we should be obliged to believe that the pain, for example, which we feel in our foot, is anything beyond our mind which exists in our foot." We can avoid error if we judge that there is something, of whose nature we are ignorant, which causes the sensation of pain in our minds (AT VIII, 32; HR 1, 247).

Now there seem here to be three separate elements in Descartes's account: namely, the pain, the perception of the pain, and the judgment about the pain. The perception of the pain seems to be something distinct from the pain, for there are properties such as clarity and distinctness which belong to the perception but not to the pain. The perception seems to be something distinct from the judgment; judgment is an act of the will which it is in our power to make or withhold, and we are enjoined to restrict our judgment to what we clearly and distinctly perceive. But it is not at all easy to work out what Descartes considers to be the relationships between these three.

In so far as pain is a *cogitatio*, it would seem that pain cannot occur without being perceived. Can it, however, occur without being perceived clearly? Descartes seems to give two different answers to this. On the one hand, he says that "when a man feels great pain, he has a very clear perception of pain"; on the other hand, he says that to have a clear perception of our sensations only if we carefully restrict our judgment about them, and "this is a condition most difficult to observe." If we ask, however, whether a pain may be perceived clearly without being perceived distinctly, the answer is plain. "A perception may be clear without being distinct, though not distinct without being clear" (AT III, 22; HR 1, 237). Again, Descartes seems explicit enough on the relationship between perception and judgment. Judgment differs from perception in being an act of the will, in being concerned with extramental reality, and in being liable to error. The faculty of perceiving is infallible, that of assenting can err (AT VIII, 21; HR 1, 236). Judgment may occur without perception; that is precisely the cause of error: ". . . people form judgments about what they do not perceive and thus fall into error" (AT VIII, 21; HR 1, 236). What of the converse case: can clear and distinct perception occur without judgment? Here there are some puzzles. On the one hand, we learn that "we are by nature so disposed to give our assent to things that we clearly perceive, that we cannot possibly doubt of their truth"

(AT VIII, 21; HR 1, 236). Yet on the other hand, does not the whole procedure of methodic doubt suppose that one can withhold one's judgment even about what seems most clear?

When we examine Descartes's doctrines closely, the reason for the inconsistencies seems to be this. The clear and distinct perception of pain is not in fact identifiable separately from the occurrence of pain and the judgment about the origin of the pain.

First, to perceive a pain clearly simply is to have a severe pain. Descartes says: "I call clear that which is present and manifest to an attentive mind; just as we are said to see clearly objects when they are present and operate strongly, and when our eyes are in the right disposition to survey them" (AT VIII, 22). Here there seem to be two elements in clarity: that the object of perception be manifest, and that the perceiving faculty be attentive. In the case of sight, such a distinction is possible; in the case of pain it is illusory. Descartes nowhere suggests what would be the difference between the unclear perception of a manifest pain, and the clear perception of an obscure pain. Yet it must be possible to make out such a difference if the distinction between the occurrence of a pain and the perception of a pain is to be a genuine one.

Secondly, to perceive a pain distinctly is simply to make the correct judgment about one's pain. It is to make the correct, cautious, judgment that "what I feel is caused by I know not what," rather than the incorrect judgment that "what I feel is something in my foot." The difference between a distinct and a confused perception is explained precisely in terms of the nature of the accompanying judgment. When the perception of pain is not distinct—that is because it is "confused by the sufferers with the obscure judgment that they form upon its nature" (AT III, 21).

The perception of pain, then, is not a genuine intermediary between the occurrence of pain and the judgment on pain. Of the two properties of the perception, one, clarity, is really a property of the pain which occurs, and the other, distinctness, is really a property of the judgment made about it.

This incoherence which we have noted in the *Principles*

is to be found also in the *Third Meditation.* Sometimes, there, clarity and distinctness are properties of our perception of ideas and thoughts (AT VII, 34, 35; HR 1, 158), a perception which is described as "looking with the eyes of the mind" (AT VII, 35, 36); sometimes they are properties of what is looked at, the idea itself (AT VII, 31, 43; HR 1, 164). In particular the idea of God is itself clear and distinct (AT VII, 15, 46; HR 1, 166); its elements are clearly and distinctly *perceived* (AT VII, 17, 46; HR 1, 166). This reduplication is the fruit of the ambiguity of "idea" which means sometimes an act and sometimes its object. That ambiguity, as we have said, was pointed out by Descartes himself; but he did not realize that it had fatal consequences for his epistemology.

CLEARNESS AND DISTINCTNESS
IN DESCARTES

ALAN GEWIRTH

1. Descartes's general rule that "whatever is clearly and distinctly perceived is true" has traditionally been criticized on two closely related grounds. As Leibniz, for example, puts it, clearness and distinctness are of no value as criteria of truth unless we have criteria of clearness and distinctness; but Descartes gives none. And consequently, the standards of judgment which the rule in fact evokes are purely subjective and psychological. There must hence be set up analytic, logical "marks" by means of which it can infallibly and without arbitrariness be recognized whether any ideas or propositions are or are not clear and distinct.[1]

In a general sense, these criticisms had been laid before Descartes himself. In the *Fifth Objections* Gassendi writes: "Why are there so many and so varied opinions among men? Each one thinks that he perceives clearly and distinctly the opinion which he defends. And lest you say that many are either being partisan or pretending, I want you to notice that there are those who even face death for the sake of the

Philosophy, Vol. XVIII, No. 69, April 1943, pp. 17–36. Reprinted with the permission of the author and the editor of *Philosophy*. This is the third in a series of articles on some basic problems in the philosophy of Descartes. The first two are "Experience and the Non-Mathematical in the Cartesian Method," *Journal of the History of Ideas*, Vol. II, No. 2, April 1941, pp. 183–210, and "The Cartesian Circle," *The Philosophical Review*, Vol. L, No. 4, July 1941, pp. 368–395.

[1] Cf. L. Couturat, *La Logique de Leibniz* (Paris, 1901), pp. 196, 202–3, with texts there cited. For a more recent version of this criticism, cf. C. S. Peirce, *Collected Papers*, 5. 391.

opinions which they hold, even though they see others facing it for the sake of the opposite opinions." Hence, Gassendi concludes, Descartes's main concern should have been to "propound a method which should direct us and teach us when we are deceived and when not deceived in thinking that we clearly and distinctly perceive something."[2] In the face of this objection, Descartes's reply is significant. The instance of men who face death on behalf of their opinions, he writes, "proves nothing . . . because it can never be *proved* that they clearly and distinctly perceive that which they pertinaciously affirm. And as for what you then add, that the concern must be not so much with the truth of the rule as with a method to discern whether or not we are deceived when we think that we clearly perceive something, I do not deny this; but I contend that this very thing has been accurately set forth by me in its place, where first I discarded all prejudices, and then enumerated all the principal ideas and distinguished those which were clear from the obscure or confused."[3]

Descartes is here referring, of course, to the procedure followed in the first three *Meditations*. But before examining the relevant details of that procedure, it should be noted what he considers to be the general character of the "proof" of clearness and distinctness such as he mentioned to Gassendi. Whereas Leibniz demands that the criterion be "palpable," "mechanical," and lacking in "even the least difficulty," and declares that "there is no need for prolix discussions concern-

---

[2] *Vae Obj.*, VII, 278–9. Cf. *ibid.*, 318. References are to the volume and page of *Œuvres de Descartes*, ed. Adam-Tannery.

[3] *Vae Resp.*, VII, 361–2. (Italics here and in all other quotations are mine.) An anonymous exponent of Gassendi took up the debate at this point, "denying" that Descartes had set forth a method for distinguishing the really from the apparently clear and distinct (*X*** to Descartes*, July 1641; III, 402). Unfortunately, however, his examples of men firmly convinced of the clearness and distinctness of their perceptions, and nevertheless in contradiction to one another, were all taken from theological controversy, so that Descartes was able to say in rebuttal merely that "reply to them would be very easy for one who distinguishes the light of faith from the natural light, and sets the former before the latter" (*to X****, Aug. 1641; III, 426).

ing our prejudices,"[4] Descartes states already in the *Discourse* that "there is some difficulty in noting well what are the things which we conceive distinctly,"[5] and tells Gassendi that "I do not believe that those who are so little concerned with the uprooting of prejudices that they complain that I have not spoken of them 'simply and in few words,' will readily perceive the method whereby we can distinguish that which is really perceived clearly from that which is only thought to be clearly perceived."[6] The setting forth of criteria of clearness and distinctness, then, will for Descartes necessarily involve a psychological discipline. Among his basic comments concerning formal logic and the "synthetic" method of demonstration, both of which he opposed to his own method, were that the former permits the mind to "go on a holiday from the evident and attentive consideration of the inference itself,"[7] and the latter "wrests assent from the reader, no matter how unwilling and pertinacious he may be."[8] Both of these methods, in their formal character, thus realize Leibniz's ideal, but only, Descartes holds, at the expense of losing all heuristic value. His own method, on the other hand, is dedicated not to exhibiting the formal interrelations of ideas and propositions but to research into subject-matters the truth concerning which is not yet known to the mind, so that the necessity which it achieves cannot be a merely formal one but must derive from the impact of the subject-matter itself upon the mind. Hence, even when the results of the method are set down in writing, but exhibiting the same procedures as were followed in the original investigation, the method "has nothing whereby it may impel an inattentive or unwilling reader to believe: for if the least bit of what it propounds be not attended to, the necessity of its conclusions is not apparent."[9] When this consideration is put within the framework of a theory of representative perception, where

[4] Couturat, *op. cit.*, p. 100, nn. 2 and 3; p. 203, n. 2.
[5] *Disc.* IV, VI, 33.
[6] *Vae Resp.*, VII, 379.
[7] *Reg.* X, X, 405–6.
[8] *IIae Resp.*, VII, 156.
[9] *Ibid.*, VII, 155–6.

only ideas can be directly perceived by the mind, the reason for the psychological orientation of Descartes's method becomes evident.

Yet if Descartes's criteria of clearness and distinctness will not be logical in the formal, "mechanical" sense demanded by Leibniz, neither will they be so radically psychological as to be divorced from all logical considerations. At least there is a difference, Descartes insists, between the evidentness of clear and distinct perception and the "precipitation," "pertinacity," and "persuasion" of minds which cannot prove what they assert, or whose assertions vary according to arbitrary whim.[10] And the accomplishment of the difference comes through a certain prudence acquired by habituation: "only the prudent correctly distinguish between that which is clearly and distinctly perceived, and that which only seems or appears so";[11] for "there are few who are accustomed to clear and distinct perceptions."[12] This difference is accentuated from the side of the subject-matter itself; for if Descartes insists upon the ease and infallibility of the deduction prescribed by his method,[13] he also warns that the deduction must first be "prepared for" and "discovered," and the order of the deduction "excogitated,"[14] so that the clearness and distinctness exhibited by the process will have had to meet the tests presented by these preliminary operations upon the specific problem in hand.

2. But let us now examine the basis and development of these considerations, following the Cartesian order from the simple to the complex. The direct object of the mind's act of perception is for Descartes always an idea.[15] Ideas, however,

---

[10] Cf. *Disc. II, VI,* 18. *IIIae, IIae Resp.,* VII, 146, 192. *Reg. II,* X, 363. *To Regius,* 24 May, 1640; III, 65. *To X***,* Aug. 1641; III, 430–1. *Princ. I,* 50, 68. *Notae in Prog.,* VIII (2), 352.

[11] *VIIae Resp.,* VII, 461–2.

[12] *Ibid.,* 511.

[13] *Reg. II, III, IV, XII,* X, 365, 369, 372, 429.

[14] *Ibid., IV, XII, XIV,* X, 372, 428, 439–40, 451.

[15] ". . . ostendo me nomen ideae sumere pro omni eo quod immediate a mente percipitur." *IIIae Resp.,* VII, 181.

have a double status: on the one hand, they are themselves existents, "formal essences," modes of thought; on the other hand, they are significances, "objective essences," representative of things other than themselves.[16] In order that ideas be susceptible of truth, they must be viewed not in the first way, or "materially," but in the second way, or "formally."[17] The total cognitive situation for Descartes thus contains three factors: perceptive act, idea (the direct object or content perceived), and thing purportedly represented by the idea. From this characterization, it is at once apparent that the clearness and distinctness of an idea cannot directly consist in the relation of "correspondence" or "conformity" between the idea and the thing. For since "we can have no knowledge of things otherwise than through the ideas which we conceive of them,"[18] it follows that if clearness and distinctness were qualities consisting in some direct relation between the idea and the thing it purports to represent, the mind, not knowing the thing without the idea, could never know whether it had attained these qualities, so that the first precept of Descartes's method, to accept as true only what is clearly and distinctly perceived, could lead only to obscurity and indecision. Clearness and distinctness, then, cannot in their essential nature be the same as truth; it remains that they are qualities internal to ideas and perceptive acts.

And yet the significatory character of ideas plays an important part in their being clear and distinct. It is precisely from the relation between these two aspects of ideas, the internal and the representative, that the difficulties which have traditionally been found in Descartes's doctrine arise. To understand the nature of those difficulties, we must first consider Descartes's general description of clearness and distinctness:

A clear perception I call that which is present and open to the attending mind; just as we say that those

16 *Med.* III, VII, 40 ff. Cf. *ibid.*, 37: "Quaedam ex his (cogitationibus) tanquam rerum imagines sunt, quibus solis proprie convenit ideae nomen."

17 *IVae Resp.*, VII 232.

18 *To Gibieuf*, 19 Jan. 1642; III, 476.

things are clearly seen by us which, being present to the regarding eye, move it sufficiently strongly and openly. But that perception is distinct which is not only clear but is so precise and separated from all others that it plainly contains in itself nothing other than what is clear.[19]

It will be noted that the word which Descartes here uses is "perception," not "idea." But that he means by it the perceived rather than the perceiver, the object rather than the act, is apparent from the analogy which he draws with sight: "perception" is given the same relative status as "things seen by us." Since, however, idea and perceptive act are correlative, the requirements indicated for either will to a certain extent belong to the other as well.

In order to be clear, then, an idea must be (1) "present" to the mind, (2) "open" to the mind, and (3) the mind in turn must be "attending" to the idea. Some of the problems of Descartes's doctrine are already apparent in this formulation. It might seem that the first and third requirements are really the same, that an idea cannot be "present" to the mind at all unless the mind is "attending" to it, for "there can be no thought in us of which we are not conscious at that same moment at which it is in us."[20] Moreover, it might be held that there cannot even *be* an idea unless these two requirements are fulfilled, since an idea is "all that which is immediately perceived by the mind." In these respects, difficulty might be found with Descartes's analogy of vision. For an object can be locally "present" to the eye without the eye's "regarding" the object; moreover, the objects of vision can presumably exist even while they are not being seen; but an idea is constituted both as to its very existence by the mind's act of perception, and as to its significance or representative character by precisely that about which the mind is thinking. The case is the same with Descartes's other requirement, that the idea be "open" to the mind. The analogous phrase on the side of vision is that things "move the eye sufficiently strongly and openly." The "sufficiency" to which Descartes is here referring obviously is the ability of the mind to recognize

[19] *Princ. I*, 45.
[20] *IVae Resp.*, VII, 246.

the object which is seen. But here again, does not the mind recognize *any* idea, since an idea is precisely that, and all that, of which the mind is at any moment thinking? At least, such would seem to be the tenor of definitions like these: "I call generally, by the name 'idea,' all that which is in our mind when we conceive a thing, in whatever manner we conceive it";[21] and "by the name 'idea' I understand that form of any thought, through the immediate perception of which I am conscious of that same thought."[22] In the *Nouveaux Essais*, Leibniz protests against just this definition of an idea when, to Philalethes' question, "Is it not true that the idea is the object of thought?" he has Theophilus reply, "I grant it, provided you add that it is an immediate internal object, and that this object is an expression of the nature or qualities of things. *If the idea were the form of thought, it would arise or cease with the actual thoughts which correspond to it; but since it is their object, it can be anterior or posterior to the thoughts.*"[23]

Now for Descartes it is also correct to say that ideas, at least those which are clear and distinct, represent the essences of things. But apart from the difference in the interpretation of this statement owing to fundamental metaphysical dissimilarities from Leibniz, the statement itself cannot be used by Descartes in a methodological context; i.e. he cannot consult the essences of things in order to specify the clearness of an idea, because things themselves cannot be directly perceived. It is only after the nature of clearness and distinctness has been determined, and the veracity of God demonstrated, that Descartes is able to assert that clear and distinct ideas are true. And this difference in the initial interpretation of the status of ideas also prevents a solution of our general problem along the lines given by Leibniz. The problem to which the above considerations have pointed is, of course, how can any idea whatsoever fail to be clear and distinct, i.e. how can clearness and distinctness in any way constitute

[21] *To Mersenne*, July 1641; III, 392–3.
[22] *IIae Resp., Def. II*, VII, 160.
[23] *Nouv. Ess.*, II, i, 1.

a normative requirement for ideas when, on Descartes's formulation, every idea seems *ipso facto* clear and distinct? For if what has been said about ideas makes all ideas clear, then it also makes them distinct, since the mind perceives only that which it is in fact perceiving, and nothing "other" than that. In the later discussion of the same problem by Locke and Leibniz,[24] the solution of the former, based upon the relation of ideas to their names, was amended by the latter to rest upon the relation of the idea to the thing it purports to represent: an idea is not clear if it does not permit recognition of its object. But in the Cartesian context whereby things in any case can be perceived only through ideas, this solution cannot be accepted, at least without serious qualification.

3. The difficulties which we have been canvassing arise out of the need to find in Descartes's doctrine distinctions, analogous to Locke's between idea and name, and Leibniz's between idea and thing, which will explain how clearness and distinctness can be normative qualities and yet capable of ascertainment in a methodological context, within the sphere of ideas and perceptive acts. The Cartesian distinctions are forthcoming when it is seen that the idea and the perceptive act are less simple than our above interpretations have indicated. Let us examine some instances where Descartes calls ideas obscure and confused; for the considerations on which he bases this characterization should help to reveal the nature of the opposite qualities as well. Sense perceptions are the best-known class of Descartes's obscure and confused ideas. Yet this is not the only characterization which he applies to them. They are called clear and distinct in two different contexts: (1) "when they are viewed only as sensations or thoughts,"[25] and (2) when they are used as "signifying to the mind what is helpful or harmful to the composite of

[24] *Essay concerning Human Understanding*, II, xxix, 5–6. *Nouv. Ess.*, *ad loc.* For Kant's echo of the same difficulty, cf. *Krit. d. r. V.*, *Paralog.*, B 414–15 Anm.

[25] *Princ. I*, 68. Cf. *Med. III, VII*, 35. *Reg. XII, X*, 423.

which it is a part."[26] They are called obscure and confused, however, when viewed as representing the essence of material things outside the mind.[27]

From this example we may infer that the clearness and distinctness, or obscurity and confusion, of an idea are neither intrinsic to the idea nor explicable in terms of a simple relation between idea and perceptive act; for the same ideas of sensation may be both clear and obscure, distinct and confused. It seems hardly possible to say that the ideas involved in these different instances are in no way the same; at least Descartes applies to all of them the common name "sense perceptions." There must, then, be some additional factor whose combination with the two already indicated gives to the idea or perceptive act one or another of these qualifications. This third factor is revealed in Descartes's significant expression that the sensations are "viewed as" (*spectantur ut*). For the situation in which there enter clearness and distinctness involves not merely the passive apprehension of a directly perceived content, but also some interpretation with regard to that content. In each of the three instances given above of the perception of ideas of sensation, the same content was directly perceived; but in the first case the ideas (e.g. colours) were "viewed" or interpreted simply as sensations, in the second case as having some biologically symbolic function, and in the third as being "similar" or cognitively adequate to external material things. It would hence seem that it is in the relation of direct and interpretive contents or perceptions that the clearness and distinctness, or obscurity and confusion, of an idea are to be found.

The same conclusion emerges from consideration of other ideas which do not involve the sharp distinction between essential and non-essential representation found in Descartes's account of sense perception. Thus the ideas of the modes thought and extension, Descartes writes, "can be clearly and distinctly understood if they be *viewed not as*

26 *Med.* VI, VII, 83.
27 *Princ.* I, 66–70. *Med.* VI, VII, 83.

substances, or things separated from other things, but only as modes of things. . . . But if, on the other hand, we were to consider them without the substances in which they are, by that very fact we would *view them as* subsisting things, and so we would *confuse* the ideas of a mode and of a substance."[28] Here again the same content is directly perceived, and it is from the relation of that content to the way in which it is "viewed" or interpreted that clearness and distinctness, or confusion, result.

Descartes's doctrine admits, however, of greater generality than is envisaged in these two examples. For in each of these examples, the direct content (sense qualities, or "the modes thought and extension") is held constant, while the interpretive content varies. But Descartes also discusses clearness and distinctness in situations where the direct content varies while the interpretive content remains fixed. For example, not every idea which is interpreted to be representative of God is clear and distinct. The idea will have these qualities only if "we do not put anything fictitious into it, but note those things alone which are really contained in it, and which we evidently perceive to pertain to the nature of the most perfect being."[29] Among these "real" attributes Descartes lists "eternal, omniscient, omnipotent, source of all goodness and truth, creator of all things, and in sum having in himself all those things in which we can clearly note some perfection which is infinite, or terminated by no imperfection."[30] On the other hand, the idolaters' "idea of God," which in its direct content representatively includes, together with perfection, such attributes as vindictiveness and corporeality, is obscure and confused.[31]

We can now see the sense in which Descartes's description of clear and distinct perception in the *Principles* is a normative characterization, and not one belonging to any idea whatsoever. For in every perceptual situation there is *some* content "which is present and open to the attending mind" (e.g.

---

[28] *Princ. I, 64.*
[29] *Ibid., 54.*
[30] *Princ. I, 22.*
[31] *IIae, IVae Resp.,* VII, 138–9, 233–4.

sense qualities, or "vindictive corporeal being") but this content "need not be an integral and complete perception of the
thing,"[32] i.e. what is directly perceived may be other, or less,
than what the mind interprets (or wishes to interpret)[33] itself to be perceiving (e.g. "matter," or "God"). Thus the
direct content which, in Descartes's statement, is required
to be "present and open to the attending mind" is not any
content whatsoever (since every perceptual situation fulfills
this condition), but rather that content which shall be
"integral and complete" in relation to the mind's interpretation of it. When the interpretive content is taken as basic,
then, an idea is clear if its direct content (e.g. "incorporeal,"
"good") includes all that which is included in the interpretation ("God"), and distinct if the direct content includes
nothing other than this. And similarly, when the direct content is taken as the point of reference, an idea is clear if its
interpretive content (e.g. "having biological utility") includes
all that which is included in its direct content (sense qualities), and distinct if the interpretation includes nothing
else.[34] In most general terms, then, the clearness and distinctness of an idea may be said to consist in the
"equality"[35] of its direct and interpretive contents.

[32] *Princ. I, 34.*

[33] Thus Descartes writes that "the ideas which I have of heat and
cold are so little clear and distinct that I cannot learn from them
whether cold is only a privation of heat, or heat a privation of cold,
or each is a real quality, or neither" (*Med. III,* VII, 44). It is hence
in relation to such contemplated interpretation of their direct content, in which one wishes to "learn from them" the nature of the
qualities they represent, that these ideas are lacking in clearness and
distinctness. On the other hand, an interpretation of them in terms
of biological utility finds the same ideas, i.e. the same direct contents,
clear and distinct.

[34] From this it can readily be seen that when the direct content is
the basis of evaluation (as in Descartes's example of the clear but
confused perception of pain in *Princ. I,* 46), ideas are usually clear,
but their distinctness may come into question; on the other hand,
when the interpretive content is made the basis, ideas may often be
lacking in clearness, but if they are clear, they will usually be distinct
as well.

[35] Cf. *Reg. XIV,* X, 439–40.

This equality is, of course, a logical rather than a narrowly quantitative relation. In the context of science, where the concern is with the essences of things, the connection between the two contents must be necessary. The minimum requirement for an idea to be clear, then, is that whichever content be taken as basic, the other include what in the *Replies* is called the "formal nature" (*ratio formalis*)[36] of its object, and what in the *Principles* is called the object's "leading property, which constitutes its nature and essence."[37] Thus the equality between the square of the base and the square of the other two sides of a triangle "is not clearly understood unless in a right triangle";[38] i.e. the idea which is interpreted to be representative of that equality is not clear unless what is essential to such a proportion, its inherence in a right triangle, be included in the idea's direct content. Similarly, the minimum requirement for an idea to be distinct is that nothing contradictory to the essence of its object be included in it; it is in this sense that Descartes defines a distinct idea as one which "contains nothing *other* than what is clear." Thus a right triangle "cannot be distinctly understood if the proportion of equality between the squares of its sides and of its base be denied,"[39] for then the contradictory of that proportion, an essential property of the triangle, would be contained in the idea of the triangle. Similarly, "an atom can never be conceived distinctly, since the very signification of the word implies contradiction, viz. to be body and to be indivisible";[40] and "as for a true part of matter, the determinate quantity of space which it occupies is necessarily included in the distinct thought which one can have of it";[41] i.e. if the idea in which a direct content is interpreted to represent a part of matter is to be clear

---

[36] *Iae, IIae, IIIae, Vae Resp.*, VII, 113, 147, 175, 368.
[37] *Princ. I*, 53.
[38] *IVae Resp.*, VII, 225.
[39] *Ibid.*
[40] *To Mersenne*, 30 Sept. 1640; III, 191. Cf. *IIae Resp.*, VII, 152. *Conversation*, V, 160.
[41] *Ibid., loc. cit.*

and distinct, that direct content must representatively include the occupancy of a determinate quantity of space.

4. But has not our discussion been confusing idea with judgment? It is perhaps a sign of the correctness of the above formulation that this same objection was made to Descartes himself by Arnauld.[42] For although Descartes insists that neither ideas nor perceptive acts, but only judgments, may incur error,[43] he holds that there is a "material falsity in ideas, when they *represent as* real what is not real."[44] It will be noted that just as perceptive acts "view as," so ideas "represent as": in each case the orientation is interpretive rather than consisting in simple apprehension. Now if ideas be viewed normatively, from the standpoint solely of what they "really" represent, it is nonsense to speak of ideas not "representing" their objects "as" those objects are. Thus Descartes tells Gassendi that "the idea represents the essence of the thing, and if something be added to or subtracted from it, it forthwith becomes the idea of a different thing."[45] And from precisely the same standpoint Arnauld objects to Descartes: "that idea of cold, which you call materially false, what does it exhibit to your mind? A privation? Then it is a true idea. A positive being? Then it is not the idea of cold."[46] Descartes's reply stresses that the issue involves not merely a normative conception of ideas, but a mixture of direct content with interpretation: "I cannot *decide* whether what it exhibits to me is something positive outside my sense, or not."[47]

Such interpretation does not, of course, make the idea or perceptive act judgmental; for judgment involves an act of will in addition to perception. Hence, any object of the understanding, no matter how complex, is an idea so long as there enters no volitional act. Now a proposition or inference

[42] *IVae Obj.*, VII, 206.
[43] *Med.* III, IV, VII, 37, 56–8.
[44] *Ibid.*, III, VII, 43.
[45] *Vae Resp.*, VII, 371.
[46] *IVae Obj.*, VII, 207.
[47] *IVae Resp.*, VII, 234.

is not of itself volitional; it may, and in this context it indeed must, be an object of perception in the same sense as the simplest idea. For if it is simply by the act of willing an idea or perception that the judgment comes into being, must not the idea or perception have previously been a proposition or group of propositions? If the idea were logically equivalent only to a term, the addition thereto of the act of will could in no way result in a judgment. What one affirms or denies is not a term but a proposition which, having previously been simply a perceptual interpretation of a significant content, is transformed into a judgment by the volitional act of affirmation or denial.

That the interpretive perception is not a judgment is, indeed, indicated explicitly by Descartes in one of his letters:[48] "What men judge frequently disagrees with what they understand. . . . Thus, when they judge that space, which they call empty, is nothing, they none the less *understand it as* a positive thing. Thus, too, when they think that accidents are real, they *represent* them to themselves *as* substances, although they do not judge them to be substances." To "represent as" or to "understand as" is hence different from judging; and the idea which results from such an interpretive operation takes the logical form of a proposition or inference.[49]

The non-formal orientation of Descartes's method bears out these considerations. For even the "simple natures" are described as "propositions,"[50] and of course intuition, which is the elementary act of perception, is stated to have as its

[48] *To X****, Aug. 1641; III, 430.

[49] For a statement of indifference as to whether ideas are expressed as terms or as propositions, cf. *to Mersenne,* July 1641; III, 395: "Car, qu'elles (les idées) s'expriment par des noms ou par des propositions, ce n'est pas cela qui fait qu'elles appartiennent à l'esprit ou à l'imagination; *les unes et les autres se peuvent s'exprimer de ces deux manières. . . .*" In another letter to Mersenne (22 July 1641; III, 417), Descartes writes: "Je n'entends pas bien la question que vous me faites, savoir si nos idées s'expriment par un simple terme; car les paroles étant de l'invention des hommes, on peut toujours se servir d'une ou de plusieurs, pour expliquer une même chose. . . ."

[50] *Reg.* V, VI, XI, XII, X, 379, 383, 409, 410, 428.

object now propositions, now the simple natures and their necessary connections, now consequences or series of propositions. Both the simple natures and the act of intuition are by Descartes opposed primarily to judgments, in virtue of the volitional character of the latter, which may result in "formal" falsity. But since ideas may be propositions, there is no absurdity in calling them "materially" false.

5. Once an idea has what we have seen to be the minimum of clearness and distinctness, it can become clearer if, while it is still interpreted to be representative of the same object, its direct content comes to include additional attributes necessarily connected with the interpretive content. "The more attributes we apprehend in the same thing or substance, the more clearly do we know it."[51] And by the same token, the idea will become more distinct, for the richer its content, the more is it distinguished from what is other than it: "A concept is not made more distinct by the fact that we comprehend fewer things in it, but only by the fact that those things which we do comprehend in it we accurately distinguish from all others."[52]

This variation in degree reveals another distinction, in addition to that between direct and interpretive contents, required to give clearness and distinctness a normative basis. This other distinction is between the explicit and implicit contents of an idea. We have seen that although a clear and distinct perception is "integral and complete," it nevertheless can become more clear, i.e. even more "complete." The limit of such increase is an "adequate" idea, in which are representatively "contained absolutely all the properties which are in the thing known."[53] Only God can have such adequate knowledge; the human mind is incapable of it, although it may have "complete" knowledge. Thus man may have a complete and hence a clear and distinct idea of God although this idea is by no means adequate to God's infinite perfec-

---

[51] *Princ. I*, 11. Cf. *Med. II*, VII, 33.
[52] *Ibid.*, 63.
[53] *IVae Resp.*, VII, 220. Cf. *IIae Resp.*, VII, 140, 152.

tion, just as "we do not doubt that one unlearned in geometry has the idea of a whole triangle, when he understands it to be a figure comprehended by three lines, although many other things can by geometers be known about that triangle, and be noted in the idea of it, of which he is ignorant."[54] For a direct content not to "contain absolutely all the properties which are in the thing known" is possible only because of the logical orientation of Descartes's view of ideas. Metaphysically, of course, an idea refers beyond itself to a thing which the mind can never perceive directly; but in denying adequacy to human cognition Descartes is not relying exclusively, or even primarily, upon this basic fact; rather, he is referring to what can be ascertained in ideas themselves. Now for a strictly psychological position, an idea is precisely and exhaustively that content of which the mind is at any time aware, so that (putting Descartes's definition of adequate knowledge in terms of ideas and perceptive acts) to speak of a perception which is not aware of everything contained in an idea is a contradiction in terms. For Descartes, on the other hand, a distinction is possible between those ideas which are "fictitious," i.e. arbitrarily compounded by the mind itself, and those which the mind merely discovers without adding to their "objective reality." It still remains true that every idea not only depends upon the mind for its existence, but consists in that very content of which the mind is directly aware. But once thus constituted as a direct object of perception, an idea of the latter sort is, with regard to its further significance, an independent logical entity containing within itself a system of implications, of simple natures and their relations, which deduction may gradually reveal, and which indeed it is the task of science progressively to discover. Thus, to take again Descartes's favourite example of the idea of a triangle,

when I imagine a triangle, although perhaps such a figure exists nowhere in the world outside my thought, and never has existed, yet it has forthwith a determinate nature, or essence, or form, immutable and eternal, which

[54] *Vae Resp.*, VII, 368.

has not been made up (*efficta*) by me, and does not depend upon my mind; as is shown by the fact that various properties can be demonstrated of this triangle, viz. that its three angles are equal to two right angles, that its greatest side is subtended by the greatest angle, and the like, which willy-nilly I now clearly perceive, even if I have in no way thought of them previously when I imagined a triangle, so that they have not been made up by me.[55]

Hence, even though the properties revealed by such deductive development have not previously been suspected by the mind, these operations do not basically "augment" the idea, but merely "render it more distinct and explicit, because all these properties must have been contained in that idea which was had at first."[56]

It is important to note, however, that this variation in the degree of clearness and distinctness is possible only because an idea for Descartes involves an interpretive as well as a direct content. The "idea" which remains fixed and unchanged throughout the process in which properties previously unknown are discovered in "it" is not merely the initial direct content, since this undergoes obvious increase; it is rather the interpretive content which, equated at the outset with the direct content, is found to be necessarily connected with the "new" properties, since these are found to be necessarily connected with the initial direct content, so that the mind interprets each succeeding property to be representative of the same object. It can readily be seen how this interpretive perception is the initial methodological basis of Descartes's doctrine of substance and essence.[57]

6. Thus far we have been discussing the clearness and distinctness of ideas simply in terms of the characteristics

[55] *Med.* V, VII, 64. Cf. *Reg.* XII, X, 422. *Conversation*, V, 151–2.

[56] *Vae Resp.*, VII, 371. Cf. *ibid.*, 368.

[57] Cf. *IIae Resp., Def. II*, VII, 161, and especially *IVae Resp.*, VII, 222, where Descartes shows that substance is that which is interpreted to be the subject of directly perceived ideas.

which the ideas themselves must possess. But we must now turn to consider just how these characteristics of ideas are to be ascertained, i.e. what is that "method" of which Descartes spoke to Gassendi, whereby that which is really clear and distinct can be distinguished from that which is only thought to be so. In terms of the preceding discussion, this question has a special urgency. For on the one hand, Descartes has said that things can be known only through the ideas of them; on the other hand, in calling sense perceptions, or the idea of corporeality, obscure and confused when they are viewed as representing, respectively, the essence of material things, and God, he seems to have assumed that the mind has some independent insight, apart from ideas purporting to represent them, into the "real" essence of things. The question of how the clearness and distinctness of ideas are to be ascertained is thus basically the same as the question of how the mind, within the methodological context of ideas and perceptive acts, can ascertain that its definitions of objects, which it employs as a basis for evaluating the clearness and distinctness of the equating of direct and interpretive contents, are real and not merely nominal or arbitrary. This problem, it must be emphasized, is different from the ultimate metaphysical question of whether clear and distinct ideas are true. The divine guarantee enters only to give final sanction to the decisions already arrived at by methodological means.

These means are set forth in the *Rules* and in the second part of the *Discourse*. It will be recalled that in telling Gassendi of his "method," Descartes emphasized first the removal of "prejudices." Now a prejudice is a judgment made prior to clear and distinct perception of the content which is judged.[58] Does this mean that clearness and distinctness must be employed to attain these very qualities? The answer is given by the distinction between the perceptive act and the idea or content perceived. For it is possible that direct and interpretive contents be "equal" or necessarily connected, while the full perception of the grounds for this be lacking.

[58] Cf. *Princ.* I, 47.

This would be the case if the idea were not "open" to the mind, i.e. if its elements and the relations between them were not revealed to the extent required to justify, or to permit the deduction of, this necessary connection. In this perceptual, as against the preceding logical, sense, an idea is obscure and confused not because of an actual inequality between its direct and interpretive contents, but "only because there is contained in it something which is unknown."[59] Indeed, it is from this latter obscurity and confusion that ideas become contradictory, i.e. confused in the logical sense.[60] To make an idea "open" to the mind, to render known its elements and to see how the necessary connection of its direct and interpretive contents follows from them, is thus the purpose of Descartes's basic methodological precept whereby "we reduce involved and obscure propositions step by step to simpler ones," until we come to an "intuition of the simplest ones of all."[61]

The ultimate conceptual elements of ideas are called by Descartes "simple natures." They include, on the side of material things, such concepts as "figure," "extension," "motion," and on the side of mental phenomena, "cognition," "doubt," "ignorance," "volition." Unlike composite ideas, in which it is possible to discriminate from one another not only direct and interpretive contents, but also various parts of the direct content, the necessity of whose connection with one another in the idea is not self-evident, the simple natures cannot be misinterpreted, for it is impossible to discriminate in them a direct and an interpretive content. To think of these simples at all is to think of them completely, and hence clearly; similarly, their very simplicity makes it difficult for the mind to confuse them with, i.e. interpret them as, anything "other" than themselves, so that they are perceived distinctly

[59] *IIae Resp.*, VII, 147.
[60] *Ibid.*, 152.
[61] Reg. V, X, 379. The *de omnibus dubitandum* of the *First Meditation* is just such a systematic reduction of ideas received "from the senses or through the senses," to the thoughts which are their elements.

as well.[62] Since all composite ideas involve these simples, it follows that to attain a clear and distinct perception of any composite idea requires the reduction of the idea to these self-evident elements and then the perception of the precise way in which they are combined in a necessary nexus to form the idea originally in question.

This reduction does not, of course, result in an "adequate" idea. For in order to be clear and distinct, the idea must in its direct content represent only the "formal nature" of the object which it is interpreted as representing, but not the object or "matter" itself—the idea of infinity, for example, must not itself be infinite, just as the idea of obscurity need not be obscure[63]—so that the reduction will attain not the total system of implications in which an idea is involved, but those elements which are "sufficient"[64] to establish (or refute) the necessary connection of the idea's direct and interpretive contents. The various "relations or proportions" in which the proposition was initially involved will hence have been so "reduced" that the equality between its direct and interpretive contents will itself be "clearly seen."[65] The reduction attains this perceptual clearness and distinctness because it enables the mind, within the methodological context of ideas and perceptive acts, to "distinguish that which pertains to the true and immutable essence of a thing, from that which is attributed to it only through a fiction of the understanding."[66]

The contents of a fictitious idea, such as that of a winged horse or of a triangle inscribed in a square, can be clearly and distinctly conceived in separation from one another, i.e. even if one part be explicitly denied of the other, each can still

---

[62] *Reg. XII*, X, 418–20, 422. The further refinements which Descartes makes on this doctrine of the simple or primitive "notions" (*Princ.* I, 47 ff., and *to Elizabeth*, 21 May 1643; III, 663), since they involve essentially the same principle as the discussion of the *Regulae*, although in a broader context, are here passed over.

[63] *Iae, IIae, Resp.*, VII, 113, 147–8.

[64] Cf. *IIae, IVae Resp.*, VII, 140, 152, 221.

[65] *Reg. XIV*, X, 440.

[66] *Iae Resp.*, VII, 116.

be fully conceived without in any way contradicting the significance which it presents to the mind. An idea will be representative of a true and immutable nature, then, if the connection of its contents is necessary, not contingent, so that they cannot be sundered by way of a "real" distinction: "although one can think of the one without paying any attention to the other, one cannot, however, deny it of that other when one thinks of both."[67] "Those ideas which do not contain true and immutable natures, but only fictitious ones compounded by the understanding, can be divided by that same understanding not only by abstraction, but *by a clear and distinct operation*, so that those which the understanding cannot thus divide have undoubtedly not been compounded by itself."[68] If, then, the mind finds that it cannot deny the parts of ideas of one another and still be true to the meaning which each part directly presented to it, such ideas are representative of objects which are essential natures independent of the mind for their being what they are. The direct contents of these ideas are seen, as a result of this "method of difference," to represent the essence, or at least part of the essence, of the objects which they are interpreted as representing, so that the direct and interpretive contents are equal to one another.

It will have been noted, however, that the criterion of "immutability" stated in the second quotation given above was the inability of ideas to be divided "by a clear and distinct operation," which Descartes goes on to specify as meaning "rightly understanding what I say." Here again, as previously in the discussion of the discarding of "prejudices," the logical sense of clearness and distinctness, as characteristics of ideas, is stated to be ascertained by clearness and distinctness as characteristics of the perceptive act which, resulting from the reductive process, finds necessity of connection within the ideas. An excellent example of this process is the famous operation upon the wax in the *Second Meditation*. It is required to ascertain the essential nature of matter.

[67] *To Gibieuf*, 19 Jan. 1642; III, 474. Cf. **VI***ae Resp.* VII, 443.
[68] ***I***ae *Resp.*, VII, 117.

A direct content which is interpreted to be representative of matter is chosen, consisting in the various sense qualities which the wax initially presented. Then these qualities are put through a series of reductions to see whether they and the interpretive content "so depend upon one another, that one can in no way be changed while the other remains unchanged."[69] It is found that the sense qualities are changed, although the wax still "remains the same." Hence, those qualities are essentially "other" than the wax, and the interpretive perception of them as representing the essence of the wax was not distinct. This "identity" of the wax throughout the changing of the direct content, which is greatly emphasized by Descartes,[70] can be understood only through the interpretive aspect of his doctrine of ideas. It is because the interpretive perception is held constant that the reductive process can be viewed, in the methodological context, as going from accidental to essential attributes of the *same* object, and not from one set of ideas to another set wholly unrelated thereto. The process consists, then, in gradually divesting the direct content interpreted as representing a certain object of the "forms external" to that object, i.e. of those qualities with whose denial the object can still be conceived, so that there is no necessary connection between the object and those qualities. The end of the process comes when a direct content is attained which survives every reductive device, remaining so long as the object can be conceived, and without which the object can no longer be conceived. This direct content is hence necessarily connected with the interpretive content whereby the mind thinks of the object in question, and constitutes the essential definition of that object. And only in virtue of such a reductive process is the resultant perceptive act clear (as attaining the essence of the object, in that the direct content which is actually representative of the es-

[69] *Reg. XII*, X, 429.

[70] "Remanet adhuc eadem cera? Remanere fatendum est; nemo negat, nemo aliter putat. Quid erat igitur in ea quod distincte comprehendebatur? Certe nihil eorum quae sensibus attingebam; nam . . . mutata jam sunt: remanet cera." *Med. II*, VII, 30. Cf. *Princ. II*, 4.

sence of the object which it is interpreted as representing has been made "present and open to the attending mind") and distinct (as excluding everything "other than" what is essential). The wax is thus ascertained to consist essentially of extension and mobility, not of any peculiar colours, sounds, and tastes; hence, at the conclusion of the reductive process whereby the sense qualities are removed, Descartes writes that the perception of the wax "can be either imperfect and confused, as it was before, or clear and distinct, as it now is, in so far as I attend less or more to the things of which it consists."[71]

The physical manipulation which the procedure of the wax involves is the most graphic but not the only form which the reductive operation leading to this perceptual clearness and distinctness may take. The culmination of the process, Descartes points out, consists in an "inspection of the mind alone." The same operation in principle occurs when infinite perfection is found to be essential to God: ultimately it is the impossibility which the mind finds in conceiving the latter without the former that methodologically shows the idea equating them to be a real definition, representative of a "true and immutable nature."[72] These essential definitions consist, of course, not in genus and differentia but in various combinations of simple natures.[73] Once attained, they can

----

[71] *Med. II*, VII.

[72] *Med. V*, VII, 67, ll. 21–4. It is because Descartes holds that he has shown in this way that the idea of God as an infinitely perfect being represents a true or real essence, and is not merely a nominal definition, that he maintains that his ontological argument, unlike that of St. Anselm as reported by Thomas Aquinas, is neither verbal nor fallacious. Cf. *Iae Resp.*, VII, 115–19. *To Mersenne*, 15 June 1641; III, 383.

[73] Definitions by genus and differentia, as viewed in the Aristotelian tradition, presuppose essentially different kinds of things, so that to define any given species requires showing the genus to which the species belongs, and then the form which differentiates it from other species of the genus and constitutes it what it is. Such definitions are hence basically additive: the differentia adds a characteristic which is essentially other than that of any other species. The Cartesian definition by simple natures, on the other hand, adds no "new" characteristic, but consists in a different arrangement or "mixture" of the

then be used to test the clearness and distinctness of all other ideas which are interpreted to be representative of the objects defined. It is thus that the idolaters' "idea of God," where the direct content includes "vindictiveness" and "corporeality," is shown to be confused; for both these qualities imply imperfection, the former because it is a tendency away from goodness, and hence toward non-being, the latter because whatever is corporeal is divisible, and "it is a greater perfection not to be divided than to be divided," so that "if you mean (by 'God') only what is most perfect in the nature of body, this is not God."[74] The procedure is now deductive, and consists in "comparison" of the essential definition with other ideas, through as many intermediate steps as are necessary.[75] It is in this sense that Descartes mentioned to Gassendi, as the second part of his method of ascertaining what is really perceived clearly and distinctly, after the removal of prejudices by the process of reduction, that he "enumerated all the principal ideas and distinguished those which were clear from those which were obscure or confused"; i.e. he set forth which ideas constituted the real definitions of God, the mind, material objects, and which not, so that deductive comparison could then ascertain what further ideas interpreted as representative of these objects would be clear and distinct.

---

same basic elements possessed by all other things; such definitions are hence "mechanistic" (cf. the example of a right triangle to exhibit what is meant by "species," *Princ. I*, 59). The only point at which the Aristotelian differentia would enter into the Cartesian scheme is in the initial separation of the "material" from the "intellectual" natures. There is, however, a certain analogy between the two methods; just as for Aristotle if the definition of a species states the genus alone it has not differentiated the species in question from other species, i.e. the definition is not "distinct," but if it states the differentia it also includes the genus (cf. *Met. VII*, 12, 1037b, 29 ff.); so for Descartes if a definitory idea contains that mixture of simple natures which represents the "formal nature" of its object, but other ingredients not necessarily connected therewith, the idea is clear but not distinct, but if it is distinct it is also clear (cf. *Princ. I*, 46).

[74] *IIae Resp.*, VII, 138. Cf. *Med. V*, VII, 67–8. *Conversation*, V, 161.

[75] Cf. *Reg. XIV*, X, 439.

The discovery of what ideas represent the essences of things is thus effected by operations internal to ideas and perceptive acts. It is precisely because ideas are viewed by Descartes as being representative of things which are not themselves perceived directly, that clearness and distinctness, characteristics emerging within these operations, are not in their immediate nature the same as the transcendental relation of conformity between ideas and things which Descartes calls "truth,"[76] so that the methodological orientation must be supplemented by a metaphysical one culminating in the divine guarantee. This addition, which later rationalists, like Spinoza, were to find superfluous, indicates from the side of things the circumspection which similarly controls Descartes's internal approach to clearness and distinctness themselves. It is by subjecting the mind to the coerciveness exercised by the internal meanings of ideas, rather than by subjecting those ideas to the whims of a dogmatic mind, that these qualities are ascertained. That this is Descartes's real emphasis has been overlooked by the traditional interpretation of his method because of the opposition, insisted upon in that interpretation, between the rationalistic and the experimental approaches to science. Yet both the formulae themselves of clearness and distinctness and Descartes's actual application of them show that these qualities pertain as much to the experimental methods of agreement and difference which he employed in his physical operations as to the operations dealing with the "intellectual" natures in which sense experience plays no part.

The purpose of physical science for Descartes is to explain the phenomena of material nature by a deductive system of ideas whose principles are the simple concepts of extension, figure, and motion, which represent the essence of all bodies. The clearness and distinctness of the ideas or propositions of physics will require necessity of connection, then, not only within the deductive system itself but also between each explanatory proposition and the class of phe-

[76] *To Mersenne*, 16 Oct. 1639; II, 597.

nomena which it is designed to explain: the phenomena, or effects, or direct contents, and the explanations, or causes, or interpretive contents, will similarly have to be "proved so to depend upon one another that the one can in no way be changed while the other remains unchanged." The ascertainment of this mutual dependence, in turn, involves recourse to "crucial" experiments whereby it is determined which of various possible explanations, each a certain "composition" or "mixture" of the material simple natures logically compatible with the prior propositions of the system, is in fact necessarily connected with the phenomenon in question: "in order to be able to ascertain which of these causes is the true one, it is necessary to consider experiments which cannot agree both with the one and with the other";[77] or, in another statement, "to seek out some experiments which will be such that their outcome will not be the same if it is in one of these ways that the effect is to be explained, as if it is in another."[78] A clear and distinct idea in physics, then, especially when detailed problems are being dealt with, must be an experimentally verified idea: a proposition purporting to be explanatory of a given phenomenon must be "equal" to that phenomenon and not "other" than it, but the ascertainment of this requires recourse to experiment, because science must be of the actually existing world, whose objects, as existing, the senses alone reveal determinately to the mind, whereas the pure understanding would be unable to differentiate which of its ideas represented actually existing material things and which only possible ones. Nor is this appeal to phenomena and experiment a departure from the intraideational orientation of Descartes's method. For the phenomena, as dealt with in the method, are themselves "ideas" directly perceived through the senses, and representative, although confusedly, of the existing material things which the scientific ideas represent clearly and distinctly. A scientific idea, then, finds its place as clear and distinct within

[77] *Description du Corps Humain*, XVIII, XI, 242.
[78] *Disc.* VI, VI, 65.

the system of physics in virtue of a triple necessary connection: (1) with the basic principles of extension, motion, and figure which, as the example of the wax showed, represent the essence of material things; (2) with the ideas preceding it in the deductive system; and (3) with the particular phenomena physically caused by and hence representative of the particular material existents which are to be explained.[79]

The basic emphasis of the method of clearness and distinctness is thus upon the testing and confirmation of scientific ideas: the principle is that "for right philosophizing . . . the greatest care must be taken not to admit anything as true which we cannot prove to be true."[80] And the factor determining which ideas are representative of the essences of various objects, and hence clear and distinct, consists in that which the ideas themselves compel the mind to perceive after it has reduced them to their elements and tried to separate and combine them in various ways. There is, indeed, a psychological aspect of the method also, as is shown, for example, in Descartes's description of intuition as "a pure and attentive mind's conception, so facile and distinct that there remains no doubt concerning that which we understand."[81] But this facility and indubitableness are regarded by him as effects rather than as causes of clearness and distinctness in the logical and perceptual senses, as culminating the process whereby the mind recognizes the contents of ideas to be of such sort that it is unable to perceive them in any way other than the connection before it. It is in this sense, not in a narrowly psychological one, that Descartes can say, as Burman reports, that "whether or not perceptions are clear we shall know best from our own consciousness, and for this it is of the greatest help to know all those elucidations of things which the author set forth in the first book of the *Principles*."[82] The method of clearness and distinctness as

---

[79] Cf. *IIae Resp.*, VII, 135.
[80] *Vae Resp.*, VII, 354.
[81] *Reg. III*, X, 368.
[82] *Conversation*, V, 160. Cf. *Princ. I*, 47 ff.

Descartes develops it hence exhibits no merely psychological or subjective criteria, but rather logical and perceptual ones which the mind is to use in order to ascertain the conformity of its thought with a world external to it.

THE ONTOLOGICAL ARGUMENT
REVISITED

WILLIAM P. ALSTON

The ontological argument has often been criticized on the grounds that it mistakenly supposes "exists" to be a predicate. I am going to argue (1) that the way in which this criticism is usually presented is faulty, (2) that these faults result from overlooking certain basic features of the concept of existence, and (3) that when these features are fully taken into account, new and sounder reasons can be given for denying that "exists" is a predicate and for rejecting the ontological argument. In the first section I shall present the traditional kind of criticism in what I take to be its strongest form; in the second, I shall try to show that it does not hold up; in the third I shall attempt to enrich it so as to avoid those defects.[1]

The Philosophical Review, Vol. LXIX, No. 4, October 1960, pp. 452–474. Reprinted with the permission of the author and the editors of *The Philosophical Review*.

[1] It may be helpful to relate this essay to Professor Norman Malcolm's very interesting article, "Anselm's Ontological Arguments," which recently appeared in the *Review* (LXIX, 1960, 41–62). There Malcolm distinguishes two different arguments in Anselm's *Proslogion*. My treatment of Anselm is restricted to what Malcolm calls the first argument, and is concerned with the sort of considerations which are commonly used in rejecting it. About what Malcolm calls the second argument, I have nothing to say in this essay. My opinion is that the second argument is ultimately dependent on the first, but that is a long story.

I

Undoubtedly the ontological argument does depend on using "exists" as a predicate.

> . . . each time I happen to think of a first and sovereign being, and to draw, so to speak, the idea of him from the store house of the mind, I am necessitated to *attribute* to him all kinds of perfections, though I may not then enumerate them all, nor think of each of them in particular. And this necessity is sufficient, as soon as I discover that *existence is a perfection,* to cause me to infer the existence of this first and sovereign being: just as it is not necessary that I should ever imagine any triangle, but whenever I am desirous of considering a rectilineal figure composed of only three angles, it is absolutely necessary to *attribute* those *properties* to it from which it is correctly inferred that its three angles are not greater than two right angles . . .[2]

It is clear that Descartes is assuming a logical parallel between "A triangle has angles equal to two right angles" and "A perfect being exists."[3] There is no conceivable alternative to the former, because having its angles equal to two right angles is part of what we mean by a triangle, or at least follows from part of what we mean by a triangle. Likewise there is no conceivable alternative to predicating "exists" of a perfect being, since existing is part of what we mean by a perfect being (existence is a perfection). In both cases we simply attribute to the entity one of the properties which serve as a necessary condition of its being the thing it is. Without this logical parallel the principle from which Des-

[2] R. Descartes, *Meditation* V, trans. J. Veitch (La Salle, Illinois, 1937), pp. 79–80. Italics mine.

[3] Of course it may be doubted that the former is logically necessary, or at least that "the predicate is contained in the subject." But since we are not at present concerned with mathematics, we can ignore this. It is enough that Descartes treats this statement as if the predicate were contained in the subject.

cartes starts—". . . because I can draw from my thought the idea of an object, it follows that all I clearly and distinctly apprehend to pertain to this object, does in truth belong to it"[4]—would have no application to the existence of God.

What reasons are there to deny that "exists" is a predicate? Where the support for this denial goes beyond pious asseveration, which is less often than one would like to think, it usually takes the form of pointing out logical differences between admitted subject-predicate statements and statements which differ from these only in the substitution of "exists" for the predicate.[5] But it is never shown that these differences are such as to prevent "exists" from being a predicate, rather than making it a very special sort of predicate, as a stubborn Cartesian might insist. After all, there are very great logical differences between admitted subject-predicate statements, too. To remedy this deficiency, it is necessary to exhibit the nature of predication. Until we have made explicit what it is to predicate, we are not likely to determine conclusively whether or not a given term is capable of being predicated. Now without going beyond the orbit of the traditional critique, I want to try to give it a stronger and more fundamental formulation than it usually receives. Only when the traditional criticism is stated in the strongest possible form will its basic defects be seen clearly.

I am incapable of giving, nor is it necessary for my purpose to give, an exhaustive analysis of predication. It will suffice to bring out one of its essential features. Before we can attach any predicate to anything ("round," "heavy," "in my pocket," "belongs to Jones," "difficult to understand"), we must presuppose that it exists. If we were not making that assumption we could not even raise the question whether a given predicate attaches to it. To predicate sweetness of the pie in the oven without presupposing that there is a pie in the oven would be as self-defeating as asking you to take the pie out

[4] R. Descartes, *Meditation V*, p. 77.

[5] For a good example of this, see G. E. Moore, "Is Existence a Predicate?," *Proceedings of the Aristotelian Society*, supp. vol. XV (1936). Reprinted in A. Flew (ed.), *Logic and Language* (Second Series; Oxford, 1953).

of the oven, or asking you whether the pie in the oven is done, without that supposition. But we must put this point carefully. I can *deceitfully* say that the pie in the oven is sweet, knowing all along that there is no pie in the oven, just as I can deceitfully ask you to take it out, knowing there is none. Still, there is an important sense in which I am, even here, presupposing that there is a pie in the oven. This sense can be brought out as follows: one (logically) could not openly admit that *a* does not exist (or doubt, wonder, or express ignorance about whether *a* exists) and still predicate *P* of *a*. This would be logically impossible simply because in the face of this admission we would not (could not) interpret what the speaker says as predicating *P* of *a*. "There is no pie in the oven, and the pie in the oven is sweet" cannot be used to make a predication, though it might be used to propound a riddle, be ironical, or test one's voice.

On this basis it is easy to show that "exists" cannot be a predicate. If the existence of the subject must be presupposed before we can set about attaching (withholding, wondering whether to attach) any predicate to (from) it, we will always be too late either to apply or to withhold a predicate of existence. The application of such a predicate would simply repeat the preliminary conditions for any predication. (Compare "I am speaking," "You are being spoken to.") And the denial of such a predicate would contradict the essential conditions of any predication. (Compare "I am not speaking," "You are not being spoken to.") In other words, on the predicative interpretation, any positive existential statement, for example, "A perfect tennis player exists," would be trivial. Since I must already have settled (or pretend to have settled) the existence of a perfect tennis player before I can say anything about him, going on to say that he exists would just be going over something which had already been completed behind the scenes. But obviously such an assertion is not trivial; it constitutes a substantive claim, whereas any negative existential ("A perfect tennis player does not exist") on the predicative interpretation would be self-defeating. If I first presuppose that a perfect tennis player exists and then

go ahead to deny existence, I am taking away with one hand
what was offered with the other. I am destroying an essential
condition of what I set out to say. And equally obviously,
not all negative existentials are self-defeating. We do sometimes succeed in denying the existence of something.[6]

The application of all this to the ontological argument is
obvious. Descartes can get from the principle "Perfection implies existence" or "Existence is a perfection" to the conclusion he wants, "A perfect being exists," only by using that
principle to show that existence must be predicated of a perfect being. But we can predicate, or refuse to predicate, anything of a perfect being, only if we purport to have already
settled that there is a perfect being. However true it may be
that being unmarried is contained in the notion of bachelor-
hood, I cannot conclude that it is necessarily true that the
bachelor next door is unmarried, unless I have been assured
that there is a bachelor next door.

II

It is my contention that this line of criticism is vitiated by
the neglect of important distinctions. The heart of the argument, let us remember, was the claim that any attempted
predication of existence where positive would be trivial, and
where negative would be self-defeating. I now wish to show
that this is not always so. But first a note on procedure. It
should be clear from the above that I side with Strawson
against Russell in denying that "The P is Q" can be accurately translated by "There is one and only one x which is
P, and anything which is P is Q"; the reason being that the
former presupposes the first conjunct of the latter rather than

---

[6] This argument has been presented by several recent writers, but
without clearly exhibiting its dependence on the nature of predica-
tion. See C. D. Broad, *Religion, Philosophy, and Psychical Research*
(London, 1953), pp. 182–183; John Wisdom, *Interpretation and
Analysis* (London, 1931), p. 62; A. J. Ayer, *Language, Truth, and
Logic* (2nd ed.; London, 1947), p. 43.

explicitly asserts it. Nevertheless the triviality of (1A) "The P exists" can be most clearly exhibited by making the presupposition explicit and showing the redundancy of (2A) "There is one and only one P and it exists." And it would be true to say that the triviality of (1A) rests on the redundancy of (2A). In the same way the self-defeating character of (1B) "The P does not exist" could be said to rest on the contradictoriness of (2B) "There is one and only one P, and it does not exist." Since these more explicit models reveal more sharply the logical features in which we are interested, it will be more convenient, and perfectly harmless, to work with them, even if they are not strict synonyms of the ones in which we are ultimately interested.

A. My contention is that 2A-form statements are not always redundant, and that 2B-form statements are not always self-contradictory. To an ear dulled by the habitual blurring of distinctions in philosophical discourse, this may seem outrageous. But in fact plainly substantive statements of this form occur fairly often.

(A) There are centaurs in Greek mythology, but no such creatures exist.
(B) In many old legends there is a British king named Arthur who leads the British against the Saxons, and, according to some scholars, he really existed.

Lest it should be supposed that such statements depend on a difference in meaning between "there is" and "exists," consider other examples which do not exhibit this terminological shift.

(C) That ghost exists only in your imagination. (It does not really exist.)
(D) Perfectly unselfish people exist only in literature. (No such people really exist.)[7]

[7] In treating these sentences as of the same form as 2A and 2B, I am taking "there is" and "exists" to be roughly synonymous, wherever grammar allows the use of either. And the "one and only one" qualifier is not important for the present problem. Hence all the

In citing these sentences as counter-instances, I am so construing them that the phrases "in Greek mythology," "in literature," "in your imagination," and so forth, modify "there is" and "exists," thereby specifying what sort of existence is being asserted. On this interpretation, in uttering one of these sentences, one would be asserting that something has one mode of existence, and then denying that the same thing has another mode of existence. But this interpretation may be questioned. Why not read (A) like "There are kangaroos in Australia, but kangaroos do not exist in South America." No one would claim the latter to be of the 2B form. The prepositional phrases plainly belong with the specification of what is said to exist. It is kangaroos in Australia which we are saying there are, kangaroos in South America which we are saying there are not. Kangaroos *überhaupt* are not in the picture at all. If we adopt this sort of interpretation for our examples, they do no damage to the standard argument. Once we fully specify what is claimed to exist in each clause, it is plain that we are not really asserting and denying existence of the same thing.

But this alternative interpretation will not hold water. On this interpretation there is one and only one mode of existence, which things can be said to have in various places—Australia, Tahiti, or the Milky Way. But once we stretch the notion of place to include fiction, mythology, imagination, and the real world, it becomes very unclear what could be meant by the existence which could indifferently be exercised in these locales. We can understand one sort of existence being possessed either in Australia or Greenland, but that is because we are holding it constant to, say, real as opposed to fictional existence. Vary that, too, and with what are we left? I can say "There (really) is a key to this box"

---

following sorts of statements can be counted as of the same form as 2B (and parallels could easily be constructed for 2A):

There are *P*'s . . . . ,	but they do not exist. . . . . .
P's exist . . . . ,	but they do not exist. . . . . .
A *P* exists . . . . ,	but it does not exist. . . . . . .
There is an *x* named "*P*" . . . ,	but it does not exist. . . . . . .
That *P* exists. . . . . ,	but it does not exist. . . . . . .

without saying where the key is, and I have told you something, though perhaps you would like to have fuller information. But if I say "Sea serpents exist," and leave it open whether I mean in mythology, in literature, in reality, or in my imagination, what have I told you? Have I excluded anything? Can I conceive of anything which would not exist in at least one of these "places"? It seems that I must, implicitly or explicitly, add one of these qualifications in order to get any assertion at all. This means that "in literature," "in reality," and so forth, are not independent of "exists" in the way "in my pocket" and "in Labrador" are. (This is the justification for denying that existence is a genus. To assign something to a genus without giving its species is to give real, though relatively abstract, information. The generic term stands on its own feet predicatively, whereas, as we have just seen, we must have in mind some specific mode of existence in order to get an assertion.) The supposition that "There are centaurs in Greek mythology, but they do not exist in reality" is properly analyzed as "$(\exists x)$ (x is a centaur in Greek mythology) and $\sim$ $(\exists x)$ (x is a centaur in reality)," breaks down through inability to give any interpretation to "$\exists$" which is common to both these occurrences.

Hence the standard argument against treating "exists" as a predicate collapses. If I can say, without redundancy, "There is in many old legends a British King named Arthur who fought against the Saxons, and the evidence is that he really existed," it would seem that I can just as well set up a subject on the presupposition of the first conjunct, and then, without triviality, predicate real existence of this subject. And if I can, without contradiction, say "There are centaurs in Greek mythology, but centaurs do not really exist," it would seem that I can presuppose the first conjunct in setting up legendary centaurs as subjects of predication, and then, without self-stultification, deny that the predicate of real existence attaches to these subjects. The way is then open to regarding "King Arthur really existed" and "Centaurs do not really exist" as subject-predicate statements. We can use one mode of existence to set up the subject, and another mode of existence as the predicate. At least, once we recognize diverse modes of existence, the standard arguments are powerless to prevent this.

And this means that the ontological argument has not finally been disposed of. Granted different modes of existence, we can restate the argument in a form which is not open to the standard objections. We can get our subject of predication by presupposing the existence of a perfect being in some nonreal mode, where the existence is obvious. Then we can argue that an analysis of this being shows that it possesses the characteristic of real existence.

It is interesting that St. Anselm's version of the ontological argument (in his *Proslogium*) is explicitly in this form. The difference between Anselm and Descartes in this regard has been too little remarked. Instead of saying, with Descartes, that existence is contained in the idea of a perfect being, Anselm speaks of a being than which nothing greater can be conceived, which he initially supposes to have a certain kind of existence—existence in the understanding. He takes considerable pains to justify this presupposition.

> . . . the fool hath said in his heart, there is no God (Psalms xiv. 1). But, at any rate, this very fool, when he hears of this being of which I speak—a being than which nothing greater can be conceived—understands what he hears, and what he understands is in his understanding; . . . . Hence even the fool is convinced that something exists in the understanding, at least, than which nothing greater can be conceived. For, when he hears of this, he understands it. And whatever is understood, exists in the understanding.

He can then raise the question of what can (or must) be attributed to this being; the argument is, of course, that real existence must, on pain of contradiction, be attributed to it.

> And assuredly that, than which nothing greater can be conceived, cannot exist in the understanding alone. For, suppose it exists in the understanding alone: then it can be conceived to exist in reality; which is greater.
> Therefore, if that, than which nothing greater can be conceived, exists in the understanding alone, the very

being, than which nothing greater can be conceived, is one, than which a greater can be conceived. But obviously this is impossible.[8]

In this form the argument has recognized the principle that all predication presupposes the existence of a subject, and so is not subject to any attack based on this principle.

And yet we know something must be wrong. Else the perfect island, et al., return to haunt (or enchant) us.

B. Before giving my diagnosis I must take notice of a protest which, if heeded, would obviate the need for one. It may take many forms: "Being in literature is not existing in any sense." " 'Existing in legend' is just a way of talking about what people say when they repeat legends." "Since 'existing in the understanding' is just a misleading reformulation of 'have an idea of,' Anselm is not really different from Descartes."

So far as these protests simply amount to an *exclusion* of such phrases as "exists in your imagination" (perhaps on the grounds that only real existence is *real* existence), they can be safely ignored. But a more serious thesis may be concealed therein. It may be claimed that all other types of existence can be reduced to real existence, that we could say everything we ever want to say without employing such phrases. For example, instead of saying "There are centaurs in Greek mythology," we could do the same job by saying "In the recitation of their myths the ancient Greeks used a word or phrase synonymous with 'centaur.' " Similarly, "There were three flying saucers in my dream" can be replaced by "I dreamed about three flying saucers," or "In my dream it was as if I were seeing three flying saucers"; and "That ghost exists only in your imagination" becomes "You are just imagining a ghost." Similarly, "The perfect being exists in the understanding" will, when fumigated, become "We can form a concept of a perfect being," which may in turn be transformed into "We can learn how to use the phrase 'perfect

---

[8] St. Anselm, *Proslogium,* trans. by S. N. Deane (Chicago, 1939), ch. 11.

being.'" In these replacements the only sort of existence which is asserted or presupposed is real existence.

Doubts could be expressed as to the feasibility of such a general reduction. For example, in "You are just imagining a ghost," is "a ghost" a referring phrase? And if it is, are we presupposing a nonreal mode of existence for a ghost? But even granted that it could be carried through, what bearing would it have on our present problem? Well, in a language which is stripped down in this way, the standard argument against the possibility of predicating existence would hold good, and for that reason the ontological argument could not be given a valid formulation in such a language. But that falls short of showing that in language as we have it the argument collapses. I am sure Anselm would be willing to settle for the validity of his argument in ordinary medieval Latin. But, says the reconstructionist, the languages are different only in form, not in content. This follows from the premise that everything sayable in the one is equally sayable in the other. Hence the fact that existence cannot be a predicate in the revised language shows that, despite appearances, it cannot be a predicate in ordinary language either. But there are two difficulties with this. (1) How do we know which way to read the equivalence? What if Anselm said, "The fact that existence can be used as a predicate in ordinary language shows that, despite appearances, it can be so used in the revised language"? (2) We have not explored all the complications involved in the claim that in each of the above pairs the one sentence can be used to say just what is said by the other. Once Anselm saw that in the second language he could not say that the most perfect being necessarily exists, he would have second thoughts about his admission that the two are equally rich. More generally, whenever any translation gets rid of some supposed metaphysical presupposition or implication, but otherwise preserves the meaning of the original, those who want to preserve this metaphysical concomitant, once they see what is going on, will refuse to admit the accuracy of the translation. But it is just such folk for whom the translation is designed. (Compare translating "Courage is a virtue" into "Anyone who is courageous is virtuous," in order to get rid of universals; or "The fact that he took bribes is well known" into "Many people knew that he took bribes," in order to get rid of facts.)

These are special cases of ills which are endemic to reductionism. The apparent use of "exists" as a predicate, and its most famous offspring, the ontological argument, arose in language as we actually have it. It is in the course of using that language that we have fallen under the spell of this argument. The spell will not be broken by showing that the incantations could not be intoned in another language, however akin it may be in other respects. So long as we are under the spell, the fact that it gives no place to those incantations shows that it is not close enough. What we must do is to discover what, if anything, there is in language as we use it that prevents the use of "exists" as a predicate (and spikes the ontological argument). If that cannot be done, then the proposed revision is invalid as well as inept. If using "exists" as a predicate is possible in ordinary language, then any language in which this is not possible is not equivalent.[9]

III

What is wrong with predicating real existence of a perfect being which exists in the understanding? There are many predications which are plainly all right here. We can say of this being that it is infinite, wise, just, merciful, all-knowing, and so forth. But when we add "and really exists," something jars us; we are seized with logical vertigo. This, we want to say, is different. But can this feeling be justified? What is so different about it? Well, in all the other cases, we remained

[9] If it could be shown that the rules of ordinary language are inconsistent on this point, that would alter the situation. In that case these rules would have to be altered in some way. But no one has shown that a reduction of fictional to real existence is needed to avoid inconsistency, or even unintelligibility. No one has shown that employing "exists" as we ordinarily do leads us into contradictions. The virtues which could be plausibly claimed for the reduction would be, rather, economy and the avoidance of possible confusions.

within the sphere of ideas or concepts, but when real existence is asserted we step outside that sphere, and this cannot
be done solely from an examination of its contents. We must
look outside and see what is there. Dissection of what is in
the understanding can never tell us what is in the real
world, any more than analysis of my dreams will ever tell me
which of their contents, if any, faithfully represent real objects (at least not without some dream theory which is itself
partly based on evidence concerning real things), or any more
than any literary analysis of the character of Achilles in the
Iliad can determine whether this is a historical figure. To do
this would mean lifting ourselves by our bootstraps, or un-
locking a door by staring at the lock.

But, comes the inevitable rejoinder, this case is different.
In general it is true that one cannot show that *x* really exists
simply by analyzing its existence in the understanding. But
here is the one case where this is possible. Here the nature
of the being in the understanding is of such ontological richness as to burst its bonds; its inherent expansive power impels
it across the boundary into real existence.

These metaphors get us nowhere. We cannot cross the
border without a passport which has been approved on the
other side, but a rocket can, with luck, burst into outer space
on the strength of energy developed within the earth's at-
mosphere. And so it goes. Which of these metaphors is the
more illuminating? Is deciding whether an envisaged being
really exists more like applying for a passport or rocketing into
space? Evidently we need a more literal characterization of
the situation. Here is such a characterization.

A.   Earlier we saw that an existential statement has the
function of setting up a subject for predication. Now that we
have recognized different modes of existence we can add a
further stipulation: the kind of existence which is being
stated will place limits on the sorts of predication that can
be made with respect to that subject, that is, on the logical
status of statements which can be made about it. A few examples should make this clear.

1. As I come into the house, I hear my wife who, unbe-

knownst to me, is reading a story to some children, say, "The cookies in the pantry are delicious." Being hungry, I go to the pantry, but am disappointed to find the cookies there stale and tasteless, whereupon I upbraid my wife for deception.

2. In a discussion of Dostoevski's *The Brothers Karamazov* in which undue emphasis was being given to Dmitri and Alyosha, someone might say, "After all, old man Karamazov had three sons." An unlettered youth who had just come into the group might ask, "Are any of them still living?"

3. A physics student tells me that the electrons of which my desk is composed are moving around with great speed. When I ask him how powerful a microscope would be needed to see them, he replies that they cannot be seen through any existing microscope, nor would he expect to see them through any microscope, no matter how powerful, whereupon I accuse him of talking nonsense.

In these cases a subject-predicate statement was misunderstood because of a misapprehension as to the kind of existence being presupposed. Under this misapprehension the hearers took the statements to have a kind of logical status they lacked. In particular, the statements were misinterpreted as to their implications, theoretical or practical. The statements were mistakenly supposed to have the following implications:

1. A hungry man who wants good cookies would be well advised to go into the pantry.
2. Either the sons of Karamazov are still living, or they have died since the time under discussion.
3. If one could achieve sufficient power of magnification, he could see the ultimate particles of which this desk is composed.

A mistake was also made concerning the considerations and procedures relevant to supporting or attacking the statements:

1. Examination of the contents of the pantry.
2. Questioning of elderly citizens in the neighborhood or friends of the family. Consultation of official records.
3. Scanning the desk through the highest-power microscope available.

Generalizing from these cases, we can say that the kind of considerations which are relevantly adduced in defending or attacking a subject-predicate statement, and the sorts of implications which can be drawn from it, are a function (in part) of the kind of existence presupposed. Presuppose that there were three flying saucers in my dream, and nothing tells for or against any statement about these three objects except my (sincere) report. But presuppose that there really were three flying saucers over the Grand Canyon yesterday, and now the testimony of others, consideration of laws of aerodynamics, and so forth, become relevant to the evaluation of statements about them. Presuppose that there was a King of the Round Table in legend, and all sorts of statements about him can be conclusively established by an examination of documents like *Morte d'Arthur*, without looking into their historical accuracy. But presuppose that there was a real historical king who had such a court, and much more is needed. Whether or not the statement "That ghost is in the house again" implies that abnormal phenomena are to be expected in the house in the immediate future depends on whether the assumption on which that statement rests is that a certain ghost exists in your imagination, or that a certain ghost really exists. "The men from Mars are approaching Plainfield, New Jersey" implies that Plainfield, New Jersey is in imminent danger only if real existence has been presupposed for men from Mars.

Note that in general it is the logical status of the predication which is delimited, not the possible predicates themselves. In general anything that can be said of a real man can be said of a legendary, fictional, or imaginary man. It is what gets said in applying any predicate which will differ in the way specified above.

Thus an existential statement determines a logical framework within which predications can be made of what has been said to exist. It can be construed as a license to make certain sorts of subject-predicate statements, and not others. In fact we might take the determination of such logical frameworks as a principle of differentiation for modes of existence. If the same logical status is conferred, then there is only one mode of existence in question. It is on this kind of ground that we might refuse to distinguish between existing in the understanding and existing in the mind, or between the mode of existence involved in existing in Australia and existing in South America, while insisting on a distinction between either of the first pair and either of the second.

One more step is needed before we can return, sufficiently girded, to the ontological argument. An existential statement has the same sorts of implications as the subject-predicate statements it licenses and to that extent falls within the logical framework it determines. This principle might be defended by saying that a licensing bureau cannot authorize anyone to do anything it does not have the authority to do, but this would be riding the metaphor too hard, or else regressing to the scholastic principle "The cause must contain at least as much perfection as the effect." A more sober defense would run like this. It seems that an existential statement not only permits a certain kind of subject-predicate statement but also guarantees that there will be true statements of that kind. To say that there really are sea serpents is to imply that there are true statements of the form "Sea serpents are . . ." which have the logical status of statements about physical objects. To say that there are P's is to imply that something can be truly said about them. This entailment can be brought out by considering the logical oddity of the following dialogue.

A. There are a lot of bones six feet under my back yard.
B. Well, what about them?
A. Nothing. They are just there, that's all.
B. You mean you haven't looked at any of them yet?
A. No. It's not that I haven't found out anything about them yet. There is nothing to find out, except that they are there.

Why is this? Why do we refuse to admit the possibility that there are things about which nothing can be truly (synthetically) predicated? Perhaps it is because a referring expression is used to direct attention to something which goes beyond the characteristics connoted by the expression. If nothing could be said of the bones under my back yard other than that they are bones under my back yard, there would be no distinctive use for a referring expression here or for the subject-predicate form within which it gets its use. There would be no point in distinguishing between "the bones under my back yard" and "bone under my back yard." The point in talking about *things which are* bones under my back yard is that each of those things possesses characteristics other than those connoted by the descriptive phrase used to refer to it. The very concept of a thing (and of its linguistic correlates, the referring expression and the subject-predicate sentence) requires such an overplus.

B. Now we can return to the ontological argument in its Anselmian form. Anselm escapes the standard criticism by presupposing existence in the understanding so as to get a subject of which he can show real existence to be necessarily predicated. But an equally unhappy fate awaits him. The statement which he is claiming to be necessarily true is a statement about a being in the understanding, and as such exhibits the logical features of statements based on a presupposition of mental existence. Among these features are: (1) It can be conclusively tested, if at all, by reflection. The person in whose understanding a certain being exists has only to reflect, to ask himself what he means by a certain term, in order to determine whether or not any statement about that being is true. A simple and instantaneous self-question is all that is needed to enable me to state with complete assurance that the girl of my dreams has eyes of blue. Nothing could possibly shake that assurance. (2) Existence in the understanding shares with other nonreal modes of existence the following features. For each existent in some nonreal mode, we can specify two sorts of real existents. First, there is some real existent of a given sort, which is always of the same sort for a given nonreal mode, the existence of which is entailed by the nonreal existence of the thing in question. Whenever something exists in my dreams, there must be a real conscious dream state; whenever something exists in legend or myth, there are real activities of repeating, hearing, thinking about the legends and myths in question; whenever something exists in my understanding, there are real thoughts, ideas, images, and so forth, in my mind which would ordinarily be said to be about this thing, perhaps real dispositions to behave in certain ways toward things of this kind, and so forth. It is this entailment which lends plausibility to the project of reducing all other modes of existence to real existence. Let us call such a real existent the *real correlate* of a nonreal existent. Second, we can specify something which really exists and has all the characteristics (excluding existence, if that exclusion is necessary) of the nonreal existent. Let us call this the *real archetype* of the nonreal existent. Thus the real archetype of a mountain in my dream would be a real mountain of the same size, shape, and so forth; the real archetype of Ivanhoe would be a Saxon nobleman of the twelfth century who did (some of) the things with which this character in Scott's novel was credited.

Now it seems to be a defining feature of all nonreal modes of existence that any statement about something which exists in such a mode will have no implications with respect to real things, except for its real correlate and any implications that might have. In particular it has no implications concerning the real archetype. This latter is an essential feature of the concept of different modes of existence. If the existence of something in one mode should imply its existence in another mode, the distinction between these two modes would crumble. To say that (the legendary) King Arthur won twelve battles implies nothing about the political or military fortunes of the past, or about historical records of the present and future, except that certain unspecified individuals have said and heard such things in legend-reciting contexts. To say that the mountains in my dream had very sharp peaks has no geographical implications; it is of significance not to the map-maker but to the psychoanalyst. Likewise any statement which attaches a predicate to something which exists in my understanding can have no implications for the real world except for the fact that I have, or have had, certain thoughts.

This means that if "The being than which nothing greater can be conceived exists in reality" is to be interpreted as the attribution of a predicate to a being in the understanding, it can have no implications with respect to the real world other than the fact that Anselm, or whoever else forms this concept, had a certain idea in his mind. But it is plain that as this sentence would ordinarily be understood, it implies much more than this about the real world. In accordance with the principle enunciated above, this existential statement implies that there are some true statements about a really existing perfect being, having the sorts of implications that such statements typically have; and in addition it specifically implies the truth of any statement of the form "The perfect being is *P*," where *P* is analytically contained in perfection, together with whatever implications such statements as these have. And it is equally plain that Anselm understands it, and purports to have established it, in this sense. The ensuing sections of the *Proslogium* make it plain that he supposed his thesis to entail the following propositions (by way of the fact that perfection analytically entails omnipotence and perfect goodness): (1) everything in the world is arranged for the best; (2) the righteous will ultimately be rewarded and the guilty will be punished, at least those who are not pardoned by divine mercy; (3) the world causally depends for its existence on a perfect spiritual being; (4) every man is under an obligation to worship and seek a real contact with this being. Obviously none of this follows from the fact that Anselm or anyone else has certain thoughts.

Thus Anselm, though more subtle than Descartes, is finally brought to the same pass. "The perfect being exists in reality" can only be claimed to be necessarily true, at least on the grounds adduced by Anselm, provided we construe "exists in reality" as a predicate of the perfect being, the existence of which in the understanding has been presupposed. But this gives us a statement the logical status of which sharply distinguishes it from an ordinary statement of real existence and prevents it from having the sort of religious significance for the sake of which the conclusion was sought. If, per contra, we make a statement of real existence in the ordinary sense, which has the sort of implications we want, this prevents it from being construed as the attribution of a property to a being which exists in the understanding, and neither Anselm nor anyone else has given any reasons for considering the statement to be necessary.

At this point we might get the old refrain, "But this case is different. It is generally true that statements about nonreal existents can have no implications for reality outside their real correlates. But this principle gained its plausibility from a survey of cases which omitted the one in hand. Here is the one case to which they do not apply. In this one case a statement about a mental being has implications for the real world outside our ideas and thoughts, for this case is unique in that the predicate involved is real existence. And this claim cannot be overthrown by the use of principles built on other cases, from which this one differs in crucial respects."

But it is too late in the day for this maneuver. The claim to be examining this case in itself will not hold up. Such an examination, however narrowly concentrated, must make use of general terms like "predicate," "exists in reality," and the like, and its (apparent) force depends on (apparently) using these terms in their ordinary senses. If Anselm did not suppose "The perfect being exists in reality" to be a predication in the ordinary sense of "predication," his argument that this statement is necessary could never get off the ground. If he were not using "exists in the understanding" in its customary sense, his existential presupposition would have no force; if he were not using "exists in reality" in its ordinary sense, his conclusion would not have the religious relevance for the sake of which it was sought. It is essential for his argument that this case *not* be different in the sense given these terms. But my argument depended solely on an elucidation of the ordinary senses of these terms. It is impossible that there should be exceptions to the principles I have been invoking, so long as we are using "predicate," "really exists," and so forth, in the usual way. Thus Anselm is barred from claiming idiosyncrasy for his case in any way which would confer exemption from these principles.

C. It might look as if this revised critique of the ontological argument has been developed without relying on the denial that "exists" is a predicate; indeed, without having refurbished that denial after it had collapsed in the face of a plurality of modes of existence. But this would be a superficial view. The above considerations have only to be generalized to provide a revised proof that "exists" is not a predicate.

The standard argument was seen to be faulty in failing to rule out the possibility that statements of real existence, for example, could be construed as attributions of real existence to a subject which had been assumed to exist in some other mode. But now a closer look at the distinctions between the various modes of existence has shown them to be unfitted for this role. We have seen that no statement which attributes something to a nonreal being can have the logical status (implications, and so forth) of a statement of real existence. Hence this attempt to interpret real existence as a predicate collapses. This argument can then be further generalized to show that no mode of existence can be construed as an attribute. For the mode of existence presupposed by the subject term (which has to be different from the mode of existence predicated, or the traditional argument comes back into force) will give the statement a logical status which will inevitably fail to coincide with the status it must have if it is to be a statement of existence of the sort embodied in the (supposed) predicate. Thus if we try to construe "King Arthur exists in legend" as the attribution of legendary existence to a subject presupposed to exist in the imagination, we run into the difficulty that no statement about what exists in the imagination can have the sort of implications about what goes on in legend-narrating activities that a statement of legendary existence must have. And if we try to construe "There were two of the Karamazov brothers in my dream" as attributing dream-existence to two men who are presupposed as having fictional existence, we run afoul of the fact that my statement has implications as to what was going on in my consciousness during the night which no statement about fictional characters can have.

I am not saying, of course, that we cannot make a transition from one mode of existence to another. We can consider a mythological figure, a character in fiction, a scene in a dream, or a theoretically envisaged entity like a cosmic designer or a solar vortex, and ask whether it also really exists. We very often do this, and sometimes the answer is in the affirmative. I can say that the legendary figure, King Arthur, was a really existing British monarch, that in California last summer I came upon the very mountains I have been dreaming of so persistently for years and so discovered that they really existed after all. But in doing so am I not predicating real existence of that which I have already presupposed to exist in my dreams? It might look that way, but there are less obvious features of these statements which save us from the dire consequences of that interpretation. Note that they can all be restated as a simple conjunction of two independent statements each of which is on the same level, neither presupposing the other. "King Arthur exists in legend, and King Arthur really existed in the sixth century." "Mountains of such-and-such a description exist in my dreams, and mountains of that description really exist in California." And this sort of statement gives a more faithful reflection of our intent. What we want to say is that Arthur exists both in legend and in reality, that is, we want to treat both modes of existence on a par, as having the same connection to Arthur. But on a subject-predicate interpretation this would not be the case. Real existence would be predicated of the legendary figure, but legendary existence would not be predicated of the real figure. They can be treated alike only if what we say amounts to a simple conjunction of two logically independent existential statements, whereas an admitted subject-predicate statement like "King Arthur won twelve victories" cannot be so translated. Undoubtedly there are two statements involved here, namely, "There is in legend a figure called King Arthur," and "He won twelve victories," but they are not independent. The second cannot be stated without a backward reference to the first (for the antecedent of "he"). It is this asymmetry that is the mark of the subject-predicate form. A subject-predicate statement is one with respect to which two questions must be raised. One question concerns the existence of something, and the other, concerning the applicability of an attribute to that something, cannot be raised until the first question has been answered in the affirmative. By this criterion "The legendary figure, King Arthur, really existed" is not a subject-predicate statement. We need not treat it in any such two-layered fashion.

One source of the tendency to treat "King Arthur really existed in the sixth century" as a subject-predicate statement is the strong inclination to allow such a question as "Who is it that is being said to have really existed in the sixth century?" Discussing the matter in those terms will lead us straight to the subject-predicate framework; indeed that question springs from that framework. It is the part of wisdom to recognize that the above discussion, in showing the fundamental differences between that sentence and any sentence in the subject-predicate mold, has demonstrated that the question is badly put. And having recognized that, and having seen that we can say everything we want to say without it, we must avoid it like the plague.

Thus, even admitting various modes of existence, it is impossible to construe existential statements as predicative. And yet in this more adequate perspective, the denial cannot be so clear-cut. On the standard approach (recognizing only one mode of existence) "exists" could in no way function as a predicate. But if we recognize a plurality of modes, it must be admitted that there are (rather infrequent) statements which involve something like a predicate of existence. For example, a novelist can present a character as a real man, as a character in a story, or as contained in a dream. Thus in *The Brothers Karamazov*, Ivan is a really existing man, but the Grand Inquisitor is only a figure in a dream of Ivan's. In *Tom Jones* Parson Thwackum is a real person, but Sir George Gresham only appears in a story narrated by the Man of the Hill. That is, a fictional character can, within the novel, have real, fictional, or dream existence. Again, I can dream about real people or fictional people. (By this I do not mean that the people about whom I dream can really be either real or fictional, but rather that they can be presented in the dream as either real or fictional.) Or I can dream of thinking about

Eisenhower, in which case in my dream Eisenhower has existence in the understanding. In other words, among other ways of distinguishing between the characters in a novel or in a dream, we can consider the modes of existence attached to them. This gives us fictional or dream duplications of real existence, dream existence, fictional existence, and so forth. The various modes of existence, like the whole apparatus of qualities, substances, relations, and the like, are carried over bodily into fiction and dreams and exist there with all their interconnections intact. And we can put this, if we like, by saying that real existence, fictional existence, and so forth, can be predicated of a fictional or of a dream character.

But of course the possibility of this sort of predication gives no support to the thesis that existence is an attribute. These very special sorts of statements are clearly distinguishable from ordinary statements of existence. No one would confuse our initial example about Alyosha and the Grand Inquisitor with an assertion that Alyosha really exists whereas the Grand Inquisitor does not. The heart of the denial that "exists" is a predicate is the claim that statements of existence are not predicative; this remains unshaken by the sort of predication we have just considered.

D. I have done nothing to show that "A perfect being exists" is not, or cannot be shown to be, a necessary statement; still less have I shown that there are, or can be, no necessary existential statements. Such claims are often made with great confidence, but I have never seen any conclusive arguments in their support, nor have I been able to find any. Certainly the demonstration that "exists" is not a predicate does nothing to show that no existential statements are necessary. For there are many necessary statements which turn on the logical properties of terms other than predicates, for example, the statement that if I am writing with either pen or pencil, then it is not the case that I am writing with neither pen nor pencil. The most that can be done, it seems to me, is to examine and evaluate each claim that is made for the necessity of an existential statement. This essay is designed to make a contribution to that enterprise. In it I have attempted to reveal more clearly the deficiencies in the ontological argument, and in the course of so doing to show more conclusively that "exists" is not a predicate.

ALSTON ON THE ONTOLOGICAL ARGUMENT

ALVIN PLANTINGA

After rejecting traditional explanations and arguments for the dictum that existence is not a predicate, Professor Alston suggests a more adequate reading of it in which, he thinks, it really does refute Anselm's argument. I shall consider in detail both Alston's objection to Anselm's argument and the relevant portions of the more general doctrine of predication contained in his article. . . .

Alston's criticism of Anselm's argument can be encapsulated as follows:

(a) Anselm's argument is successful only if its conclusion predicates real existence of a being assumed to have existence in the understanding.

and

(b) No statement about a being presupposed to have existence in the understanding entails that it really exists.

Suppose we begin with (b). Presumably it is to follow from

(b1) If real existence were predicated of a being assumed to have mental existence, the resulting proposition

From a forthcoming book on the philosophy of religion, to be published by the Cornell University Press, the Contemporary Philosophy Series, edited by Max Black. Published with the permission of the author and of Professor Black.

would lack the entailments that make the proposition *God exists* religiously interesting.

But (b1) is not entirely clear. The idea, presumably, is that there is no difficulty in attributing real existence to a being B assumed to exist in the understanding. The result of doing this, however, is not equivalent to the proposition B *exists in reality*; the former lacks the latter's entailments "for the real world." We can predicate either mythical or real existence of a being existing in the understanding. The chimera, for example, exists in the understanding, and presumably mythical existence ought to be predicated of it. But exactly how does one predicate real existence of a being—e.g. God—presupposed to have existence in the understanding? What is the resulting proposition—i.e. the proposition that God, presupposed to exist in the understanding, exists in reality? Alston seems to suggest that there *is* such a statement. What statement is it? Is there a clue in the fact that "the various modes of existence . . . are carried over bodily into fiction and dreams and exist there with all their interconnections intact" (p. 301)? Within the realm of fiction there are beings presented as having real existence, and also beings presented as having dream existence (such as the Grand Inquisitor, who is a figure in a dream of Ivan's in *The Brothers Karamazov*). The Red Queen was a character in Alice's dream; Alice herself has real existence in the story. Similarly someone might write a novel in which the main character writes novels about what is presented in the novel as a fictional character named Deadeye Dick. (In this case Deadeye Dick might be said to have fictional existence to the second power.)

Can we find an analogous situation in the case of existence in the understanding? Can we see what it would be, for example, to predicate dream existence of something presupposed to exist in the mind? Suppose I imagine a certain egregious animal that is a cross between a kangaroo and a dragonfly. Suppose I name it Ferdinand. Then Ferdinand has existence in the mind. Suppose further I report a dream I had about Ferdinand. Is this a case where I am (in the rele-

vant way) predicating dream existence of a being presupposed to exist in the understanding? No. For the statement
that I dreamt about the being Ferdinand that I imagined
yesterday has the implication that *any* similar dream statement has—it entails that I really did have a dream. But to be
parallel to the fiction case, it can have no such implication.
So how *can* I predicate dream existence of a being presupposed to exist in the mind?

The crucial case, however, is that of predicating real existence of a being *B* presupposed to exist in the understanding.
Now the result of the predication is not, according to Alston,
to entail that *B* really exists. Must we say that *B*, which
exists in the understanding, is *thought of* as existing in
reality?

On this interpretation Anselm's conclusion would be equivalent to the proposition that

   (c) God exists in the understanding and is thought of as
       existing in reality.

Now Alston concedes that the conclusion of Anselm's argument, if he is predicating real existence of a being existing in
the understanding, is necessarily true. And of course (c) is
not necessarily true; it entails that someone believes that God
exists in reality, which is certainly contingent. So apparently
the statement Anselm makes when he predicates real existence of a being that exists in the understanding—the statement "the logical status of which sharply distinguishes it from
an ordinary statement of real existence and prevents it from
having the sort of religious significance for the sake of which
the conclusion was sought"—is not (c). But what statement is
it? What statement is it that results when Anselm predicates
real existence of a being he presupposes to exist in the
understanding?

Perhaps, then, we should understand Alston as holding that
one *cannot* predicate real existence of a being presupposed to
exist in the understanding. At any rate he certainly means to
hold that one cannot *assert a proposition entailing that such
a being really exists* by predicating real existence of it. Why
not? "It seems," Alston says, "to be a defining feature of all

nonreal modes of existence that any statement about something which exists in such a mode will have no implications with respect to real things, except for its real correlate and any implications that might have." How are we to take "implication" here? In explaining the notion of "real correlates," Alston points out that any statement about some being that exists in a nonreal mode *entails* the real existence of the real correlate of that thing. So presumably we can read "implications" in the quoted statement above as "entailments." So taken, the principle needs more careful statement. For presumably I am no part of the real correlate of Cerberus; but the proposition *Cerberus is my favorite beast of fable* is about Cerberus and entails that I exist. Similarly for such a statement as *More books have been written about Hamlet than about Lyndon Johnson*; this is about Hamlet and entails something about Lyndon Johnson. Further, a man may mistakenly *believe* that Cerberus really exists; in that case, no doubt, he might assert that Boston was once really visited by the chimera. Boston is certainly not the real correlate of Cerberus.

We might note with respect to the first difficulty that the counter-examples are about me and Lyndon Johnson as well as the chimera and Hamlet; they are not *merely about* beings existing in some nonreal mode. And the second difficulty can be met as follows: what is important here is not whether the being in question *exists* in some nonreal mode, but whether the statement in question (or the maker of that statement) *presupposes* that it does. Hence Alston's principle can be restated:

> (d1) If p is any statement merely about some being presupposed to have existence in some nonreal mode, then any statement about real things entailed by p will be about the real correlate of p's subject.

There is another perplexing matter here, however. Why is it that a statement cannot presuppose both existence in reality *and* existence in the understanding for its subject? It is clear, I think, that many beings exist both in the understanding (as Alston understands that phrase) and in reality. For

Alston apparently means to use that phrase in pretty much the way Anselm does; but in the latter's use, from the fact that someone hears and understands the name "the Taj Mahal," it follows that the Taj Mahal exists in the understanding. But of course it also exists in reality; so many things exist both in reality and in the understanding. Anselm's proof is designed to show that God has just this status. But if beings often exist both in the understanding and in reality, there seems to be no reason why a statement might not presuppose such dual existence for its subject: a statement like *The Taj Mahal is generally but mistakenly believed to be pink* is a good candidate for this status. Such a statement, of course, is about a being presupposed to have existence in the understanding; nevertheless it entails that the Taj Mahal really is not pink. But no doubt (d) can easily be restated so as to accommodate this matter:

> (d2) If *p* is a statement merely about some being presupposed to have some nonreal mode of existence, but not presupposed to have existence in reality, then any statement about real things entailed by *p* will be about the real correlate of *p*'s subject.

Is (d2) true? There is a question about entailment that must be resolved before we can tell. If we take it that *p* entails *q* if the conjunction of *p* with the denial of *q* is necessarily false, then any necessary statement is entailed by any statement whatever. Now Alston does not believe that what he says constitutes an argument against the existence of necessary existential statements. But if we construe entailment as above, a consequence of (d2) is that there are no necessary existential statements, i.e. necessary statements attributing real existence to something. For any necessary existential statement (e.g. *There is a least prime number*) would then be entailed by any statement at all and hence by any statement merely about a being for which some nonreal mode of existence was presupposed. It follows from (d2) that any statement about the real world entailed by such a statement would be about the real correlate of the statement's subject; the least prime is not, presumably, the real correlate of any such statement; hence *There is a least prime*—which is certainly a necessary existential statement if there are any at all —could not be both necessary and existential. . . .[1]

If we characterize entailment as I have been suggesting, (d2) has the consequence that there are no necessary propositions asserting real existence. But perhaps we can take advantage of the difference between entailment and formal entailment to restate (d2) as (d3):

> (d3) If *p* is any statement merely about a being presupposed to have existence in some nonreal mode (but not presupposed to have existence in reality as well), then any statement about real things *formally* entailed by *p* will be about the real correlate of *p*'s subject.[2]

It does not follow from (d3) that there are no necessary existential propositions. This is small consolation, however, for Anselm can accept this version of (d) with utter equanimity. He maintains not that *God exists in reality* formally follows from *God exists in the understanding alone*, but that it follows from the latter statement together with the principle that existence in reality is greater than existence in the understanding alone. And this principle, while no doubt necessarily true according to Anselm, need not be supposed to be a truth of logic. Accordingly, Anselm is not refuted by the observation that *God exists in reality* is not formally entailed by *God exists in the understanding*. And of course it is obvious that we cannot strengthen (d3) by replacing its consequent with "then any statement about real things formally entailed by the conjunction of *p* with any necessary statement will be about the real correlate of *p*'s subject." For then once more the principle will entail that there are no necessary

---

1 [In the section omitted, the author supports the view that a necessary statement *is* entailed by any statement.]

2 ["Formal entailment" is used in such a way that *p* formally entails *q* if, and only if, a contradiction can be deduced from *p* and *not-q* by means of the laws of logic alone.]

existential statements; so revised the principle is equivalent to (d2). . . .

The project of finding a satisfactory statement of (d)—i.e. one that will defeat Anselm's argument but not entail that there are no necessary existential statements—is beginning to look pretty implausible. But suppose we did have an adequate statement of it. Why should we accept it? What are the reasons in its favor? Alston does not explicitly argue for (d); his procedure is to give some examples (pp. 290–291) that illustrate it. Presumably he hopes that in reflecting upon these examples we will be led to see that the principle holds quite generally. And, indeed, the examples do illustrate the principle; restricted to cases of the sort the examples typify, the principle would be sound. But as a perfectly general principle, it seems to be without support and without a great deal of initial plausibility; it is hard to see that Anselm, for example, ought to feel even the smallest obligation to accept it.

Alston's objection to Anselm's argument could be encapsulated, I said, in the following two premises:

(a) Anselm's argument is successful only if it treats existence as a predicate by predicating real existence of a being assumed to have existence in the understanding,

and

(b) No statement about a being presupposed to have existence in the understanding entails that it really exists.

We have found reason to mistrust (b); (a), it seems to me, is also dubious. For Anselm proposes to show that the proposition *God exists in reality* is true by showing that *God exists in the understanding but does not in reality* is necessarily false. And if Anselm is treating real existence as a predicate *merely* by arguing that *God exists in the understanding but not in reality* is necessarily false, then anyone, in arguing that any proposition of the form *x exists in the understanding but not in reality* is necessarily false, is guilty of the same indiscretion. Now Alston is not prepared to argue that there are no necessary existential statements. But if he did think that one can argue for the necessary falsity of a proposition of the above form only by treating real existence as a predicate, then he *would* have an argument for the conclusion that there are no necessary existential propositions (or at least that no one can soundly argue for the necessary truth of any existential statement). For suppose a given proposition *p* is a necessary existential proposition; then the proposition that the subject of *p* exists in the understanding but not in reality will be necessarily false. Hence any argument for the necessary truth of an existential proposition will yield an argument for the necessary falsity of a proposition of the form *x exists in the understanding but not in reality*. And so it is not easy to see why Alston believes that Anselm's procedure involves treating existence in reality as a predicate. Whether or not it is a predicate, there will be necessarily false statements of the form *x exists in the understanding but not in reality*. But if so, a man is not treating existence in reality as a predicate simply in arguing that *God exists in the understanding but not in reality* is necessarily false.

Finally, Anselm's argument can easily be restated so that the notion of existence in the understanding plays no part in it, in which case it cannot be thought to involve predicating real existence of a being presupposed to exist in the understanding:

(1) Suppose that the being than which it is not possible that there be a greater does not exist (assumption for *reductio*).

(2) Any existent being is greater than any non-existent being.

(3) The Taj Mahal exists.

(4) Hence the Taj Mahal is greater than the being than which it is not possible that there be a greater (1, 2, 3).

(4) is necessarily false; hence the conjunction of (1), (2) and (3) is necessarily false. (2) is necessarily true. Therefore, the conjunction of (1) and (3) is necessarily false; and so *The Taj Mahal exists* entails *The being than which none*

greater can be conceived exists. But the former proposition is obviously true; hence the latter is, too.

We have no reason to believe, therefore, either that existence in reality cannot be predicated of a being presupposed to exist in the understanding, or that Anselm's argument necessarily involves predicating real existence of such a being. I think the conclusion to be drawn is that we do not yet have a general refutation of Anselm's ontological argument.

DESCARTES'S PROOF
THAT HIS ESSENCE IS THINKING

NORMAN MALCOLM

1. *Sum res cogitans.* It is not difficult to understand Descartes's conviction that by means of his "first principle," *cogito ergo sum,* he had proved his own existence with certainty. It is more difficult to understand how he moves from the thesis that since he thinks therefore his existence is certain, to the thesis that his nature is nothing but thinking and he is entirely distinct from body.[1] His critic, Hobbes, regarded the transition from *cogito ergo sum* to *sum res cogitans* as obviously fallacious: it was like saying "I am walking, *hence* I am the walking."[2] Another contemporary, Arnauld, was unable to find in the *Meditations* anything like a sound proof of the doctrine *sum res cogitans.*[3] Locke addressed himself to the Cartesian view that "actual thinking is as inseparable from the soul as actual extension is from the body."[4] He saw no support for it save an arbitrary stipulation: "it is but defining the soul to be 'a substance that always thinks,' and the

The Philosophical Review, Vol. LXXIV, No. 3, July 1965, pp. 315–338. Reprinted with the permission of the author and *The Philosophical Review.*

[1] C. Adam and P. Tannery (eds.), *Œuvres de Descartes* (Paris, 1897–1913), VII, 78; E. Haldane and G. Ross (eds.), *The Philosophical Works of Descartes* (Cambridge, 1931), I, 190. The edition of Adam and Tannery is hereafter cited as AT, and that of Haldane and Ross as HR. I use the translations of the latter with occasional changes.

[2] "*Sum ambulans,* ergo *sum ambulatio*" (AT VII, 172; HR II, 61).

[3] See AT VII, 197–204; HR II, 80–85.

[4] John Locke, *An Essay Concerning Human Understanding,* ed. by A. C. Fraser (Oxford, 1894), Bk. II, ch. i, sec. 9.

business is done."[5] Locke added this tart comment: "If such definition be of any authority, I know not what it can serve for but to make many men suspect that they have no souls at all; since they find a good part of their lives pass away without thinking."[6]

It is not true that the business is done by a mere stipulation. Descartes supported the doctrine *sum res cogitans* with proofs. But it is true that his explicit arguments do not have the force or plausibility that one would expect of the supports of a doctrine so central to his system. To many students of Descartes, tne *cogito* is both compelling and profound, but the subsequent demonstrations in his system, supposedly built on the *cogito*, are unconvincing.[7]

I will propose that Descartes's doctrine that his essential nature is thinking is based on a line of thought, not explicitly stated but suggested in various passages, which does have an impressive appearance of cogency. If we attribute this line of thought to Descartes we shall find it easily intelligible that the lucid philosopher should have drawn the conclusion that he was "a substance the whole essence or nature of which is to think."[8] I am interested in Descartes for his own sake: but also I want to understand better what it is that makes his dualism of mind and body a persuasive doctrine, despite the unsatisfactory character of his explicit proofs of it.

2. *Discovering what I am.* Having made certain *that* he is, Descartes undertakes to find out *what* he is. "I know that I exist, and I inquire what I am, I whom I know to exist."[9] He says that he will examine himself attentively.[10] "I must be careful to see that I do not imprudently take *some other ob-*

---

[5] *Ibid.,* sec. 19.

[6] *Ibid.*

[7] Speaking of Descartes and the *cogito,* Jaspers says: *"Er kann von dieser Gewissheit aus keinen weiteren Schritt zu neuer Gewissheit tun, der den gleichen Character zwingender Evidenz hätte."* See Karl Jaspers, *Descartes und die Philosophie* (2d ed.; Berlin, 1948), p. 18.

[8] AT VI, 33; HR I, 101.

[9] AT VII, 27; HR I, 152.

[10] AT VI, 32 (*"examinant avec attention ce que j'étais"*); HR I, 101.

ject in place of myself."[11] Descartes is trying to pick out, from
various candidates, that which he is. He is searching for that
which "pertains" to him or "cannot be separated" from him.[12]
In the language of the *Principles*, he is trying to discern his
"principal attribute" or "principal property."[13] Or, as Descartes also puts it, he is trying to discover his "essence" or
"nature."

Descartes does not explicitly define the terms "essence" or
"nature." He does say that "nothing without which a thing
can still exist is comprised in its essence."[14] The essence of a
thing, he is saying, contains only what is necessary for the
existence of the thing. Does the essence of a thing contain
everything that is necessary for the existence of the thing?
Descartes does not say. But one would think so, for otherwise
the essence of a thing would fail to contain something that
was essential to that thing—which seems like a contradiction
in terms. If the essence of a thing contains *all* that is necessary
for the existence of that thing, does it follow that the essence
of a thing is *sufficient* (as well as necessary) for the existence
of that thing? Apparently not. For if it were so, then the
essence of anything would imply the existence of that thing;
but according to Descartes, this is true only of the essence
of God.[15]

---

[11] AT VII, 25; HR I, 150; italics added.

[12] AT VII, 26–27; HR I, 151.

[13] "Each substance has a principal attribute" (AT VIII, 25; HR
I, 240). It is often said that Descartes uncritically assumed that the
"I" in "I think" stands for a *substance*. He defined a substance as
"a thing which so exists that it needs no other thing in order to
exist" (AT VIII, 24; HR I, 239). If he can prove that his essence
is solely thinking, and that his existence requires "no world nor
place," it would appear to follow that he "needs no other thing in
order to exist," i.e. he is a substance. Certainly we should not attribute to Descartes an unreflective assumption on this point.

[14] AT VII, 219; HR II, 97.

[15] AT VII, 68; HR I, 182. AT VIII, 10; HR I, 225. Gilson says
that, for Descartes, the essence of a thing constitutes the thing in
itself; the essence of a thing is inseparable from the thing: É. Gilson,
Discours de la Methode: Texte et Commentaire (Paris, 1947),
p. 305. There is a problem here. Descartes certainly would hold that
you and I have the same essence, namely, thinking. You can prove

3. *A criterion for determining my essence.* It is helpful to think of Descartes's procedure in terms of an analogy with sense perception. He has discovered an object, himself; and now he is studying himself attentively in order to make out what his nature is. Descartes states explicitly, of course, that this investigation of himself is not sense perception: "I shall call away all my senses."[16] What I value in the analogy is the picture of a man studying an object in order to make out what it is: "considering my own nature, I shall try little by little to reach a better knowledge of and a more familiar acquaintanceship with myself."[17]

Although Descartes would deny that the essence of a thing is sufficient for the existence of the thing (except in the case of God), he could hold that if there is an existing thing O, and if there is something E, such that if one perceives E, necessarily one perceives O and if one perceives O, necessarily one perceives E, then E is the essence of O. With regard to the existing thing, himself, Descartes could hold that if there is something x, such that if he perceives x, necessarily he perceives himself and if he perceives himself, necessarily he perceives x, then x is his essence. My hypothesis will be that Descartes did hold this view. This hypothesis will suggest a route that could have taken Descartes from the *cogito* to the doctrine *sum res cogitans.*

For my purpose it is not necessary to fasten exclusively on the verb "perceive." Some other verbs of cognition, such as

---

that your essence is thinking just as readily as I can prove that my essence is thinking. But from the fact that thinking exists it does not follow that you exist, any more than it follows from the fact that I exist. In this obvious sense, thinking is separable from you and also from me. The essence of a thing, therefore, is separable from the thing; or else thinking is not our essence.

I mention this problem only to leave it. Descartes does not discuss the question of how there can be numerically different selves with the same essence. This cannot be provided for, on his view, by a difference in bodies or by different locations in space. He did not try to set forth any criteria for the identity and difference of selves, and it is problematic whether he could have done it.

[16] AT VII, 34; HR I, 157.
[17] *Ibid.*

"be aware of" or "apprehend," can be substituted for "perceive." We must constantly remind ourselves of Descartes's frame of thought. He has proved with certainty that he himself exists. He is now going to make *himself* or *his existence* the object of his attention and study. In a striking passage Descartes says that in the *cogito* one's own existence is something known per se: one sees it by a simple act of the mind.[18] He will hold himself (or his existence) before his mental vision. As he observes himself, he will be aware of something which will be what he is, what he consists of, what he can be defined to be.

My suggestion is that Descartes employed the following principle as a criterion for determining his essential nature:

G. x is my essence if it is the case that if I am aware of x then (necessarily) I am aware of myself and if I am aware of myself then (necessarily) I am aware of x.[19]

In speaking of the perception, awareness, or knowledge that arises out of the *cogito*, Descartes sometimes calls it a knowledge of *himself*,[20] sometimes a knowledge of *his existence*,[21] and more frequently a knowledge, perception, or awareness *that he exists*. I shall take the liberty of treating the phrases "aware of myself," "aware of my existence," and "aware that I exist," as equivalent in principle G.

[18] AT VII, 140; HR II, 38. French version: *"Lorsque quelqu'un dit:* je pense, donc je suis, *ou* j'existe, *il ne conclut pas son existence de sa pensée comme par la force de quelque syllogisme, mais comme une chose connue de soi: il la voit par une simple inspection de l'esprit"* (AT IX, 110).

[19] A restriction must be placed on the scope of the variable x in this formula, to prevent a silly result. If the value *myself* were substituted for x, the result would be that my essence is myself. The term "essence" is not used that way. The value substituted for x should be something of which I could be said to "consist": I cannot be said to consist of myself. Without trying to specify further what this requirement might mean, we can at least take the precaution of stipulating that x cannot take *myself* as a value.

[20] AT VII, 28; HR I, 152. French version: *"cette connaissance que j'ai de moi-même"* (AT IX, 22).

[21] See note 18 above.

4. *If I am aware of thinking I am aware of myself.* Let us consider whether *thinking* fulfills the first condition contained in principle G. Is it true that if I am aware of thinking then necessarily I am aware of myself or aware that I exist? It should be remembered that Descartes uses the verbs *cogitare* and *penser* in a far wider sense than that in which the English verb "think" is used.[22] To feel or to seem to oneself to feel any sensation (for example, to seem to feel heat),[23] to doubt, to deny, to imagine, to will, to be actively aware of anything, would be "to think," in Descartes's broad use of *cogitare.* It should also be noted that Descartes holds that we are aware of every thought we have: "*Thought* is a word that covers everything that exists in us in such a way that we

[22] Some commentators claim that this wide usage was common in the everyday French of the 17th century and in medieval Latin. (See A. Koyré's introduction to *Descartes' Philosophical Writings*, ed. by E. Anscombe and P. Geach [Edinburgh, 1954], p. xxxvii; cf. the Translators' Note, p. xlvii.) Whether or not this is so, I can see a purely philosophical basis for Descartes's broad use of *cogitare* and *penser.* Descartes says: "Of my thoughts some are, so to speak, images of the things, and to these alone is the title 'idea' properly applied; examples are my thought of a man or of a chimera, of heaven, of an angel, or of God. But other thoughts possess other forms as well. For example in willing, fearing, approving, denying, though I always perceive (*apprehendo*) something *as the object of my thought* (*ut subjectum meae cogitationis*), yet by this action I always add something else to the idea which I have of that thing; and of the thoughts of this kind some are called volitions or affections, and others judgments" (AT VII, 37; HR I, 159; italics added). In logic and grammar *subjectum* means "that which is spoken of." It seems fair to translate *subjectum meae cogitationis* as "the object of my thought." What Descartes holds is that if I am imagining, or willing, or sensing, or feeling, etc., there is always an object before my mind, an object of direct awareness. If I *approve* of something, for example, there is an object of awareness, plus some further "attitude." The same holds for all other mental events. What is common to all of them is that there is an object of awareness. It is natural to call that state of affairs in which something is directly before the mind as an object, *thought*, or *thinking.* Thus it is intelligible and plausible that Descartes should have regarded all forms of consciousness as species of *thinking*, regardless of the contemporary popular and philosophical usage of *penser* and *cogitare.*
[23] AT VII, 29; HR I, 153.

are immediately conscious of it."[24] As a result of these two points it is true that, for Descartes, if I am aware of anything then I am thinking, and so if I am aware of thinking then I am thinking; and if I am thinking I am aware of thinking.

Does Descartes hold that whenever I think I am aware of myself (or aware that I exist)? If he does, then he is committed to holding that I am aware of myself at every moment: for he holds that I am thinking at every moment.[25] Surely it is unlikely, one will think, that Descartes would have believed that at every moment of my life I have the actual thought *I exist*. But metaphysical philosophy does not obtain its inspiration from common sense. Let us consider whether there is any evidence that Descartes did hold that every moment of my life I am aware of myself (or of my existence, or that I exist).

The evidence from his writings is not decisive. In *The Search After Truth* Polyander says: "If I did not think, I could not know whether I doubt or exist. Yet I am, and I know that I am, and I know it because I doubt, that is to say because I think. And better, it might be that if I ceased for an instant to think I should cease at the same time to be."[26] These remarks could be taken as suggesting the view that to know that one exists it is sufficient to think. In the *Second Meditation* Descartes says: "I am, I exist, that is certain. But how long? As long as I think; for it might possibly be the case that if I ceased entirely to think, I should likewise cease altogether to exist."[27] Here Descartes might be saying that as long as he thinks, and only when he thinks, is it certain that he exists. But the passage is difficult. In *Discourse IV* he says: "I saw from the very fact that I thought of doubting the truth of other things, it very evidently and certainly followed that I was; on the other hand, if I had only ceased

[24] AT VII, 160; HR II, 52.

[25] Letter to Gibieuf, 19 January 1642 (AT III, 478).

[26] AT X, 521; HR I, 322.

[27] AT VII, 27; HR I, 151–152. I follow Hintikka in reading *Quandiu autem?* as "But how long?," and *Nempe quandiu* as "As long as" (Jaakko Hintikka, "*Cogito, Ergo Sum:* Inference or Performance?," p. 129).

from thinking, even if all the rest of what I had ever imagined had really existed, I should have no reason for thinking that I had existed."[28] When he is not thinking, he "has no reason for thinking" he exists. What this suggests is that whenever he is thinking, he does have a "reason for thinking" he exists. But still, one does not actually think at every moment of all the reasons one has for believing various things; so this remark need not imply that one is always thinking of a reason for thinking one exists.

Descartes's own statements admittedly do not provide strong evidence for his having held that whenever I think I am aware that I exist. I believe it is plausible, however, that he would be drawn to accept this doctrine. This is partly because the best support for his principle "I think *ergo* I exist" is at the same time a support for the principle "I think *ergo* I am aware that I exist." I shall explain this later (Sections 14–16) and shall assume for the present that Descartes would admit that whenever I am thinking I am aware that I exist.

Assuming this to be so, thinking fulfills the first condition of principle G, namely, if I am aware of thinking I am aware of myself. For Descartes would agree that if I am aware of thinking then I am thinking, and (by our assumption) that if I am thinking I am aware of myself. It follows that if I am aware of thinking I am aware of myself.

5. *If I am aware of myself I am aware of thinking.* It is easy to see that the second condition of principle G holds for *thinking.* According to Descartes, we are aware of every thought we have. Being aware of myself would be a particular example of thinking. Therefore, if I am aware of myself I am aware of thinking.

6. *Thinking is my essence.* Thinking satisfies the two conditions of principle G and is therefore proved to be my essence. The reasoning by which this result is achieved would

[28] AT VI, 32–33; HR I, 101. For further evidence on the point at issue see note 60 below.

be very natural for Descartes, and also it appears to be rigorous.

To recapitulate: Descartes's first step in rebuilding the structure of human knowledge is to prove that a particular thing exists, namely, himself. Next he seeks to find out the nature of this thing. He proceeds to deduce by highly intuitive principles and with every appearance of cogency that what constitutes the nature of this thing (himself) is thinking. For he is aware of himself if and only if he is aware of thinking.

This method of proving the doctrine *sum res cogitans* was not explicitly formulated by Descartes, and so my attribution of it to him is necessarily a conjecture. But if we assume that this line of thought lay unclearly in his mind, it becomes easier to understand the passage in the *Discourse* where he first announces his discovery of the separateness of mind and body:

> And then, examining attentively that which I was, I saw that I could conceive that I had no body, and that there was no world nor place where I might be; but yet that I could not for all that conceive that I was not. On the contrary, I saw from the very fact that I thought of doubting the truth of other things, it very evidently and certainly followed that I was; on the other hand if I had only ceased from thinking, even if all the rest of what I had ever imagined had really existed, I should have no reason for thinking that I had existed. *From that I knew that I was a substance the whole essence or nature of which is to think,* and that for its existence there is no need of any place, nor does it depend on any material thing: so that this "me," that is to say, the soul by which I am what I am, is entirely distinct from body, and is even more easy to know than is the latter; and even if body were not, the soul would not cease to be what it is.[29]

The line of thought that I am attributing to Descartes would also help to make intelligible the otherwise puzzling passage in *Meditation* VI: "Just because I know certainly that

[29] *Ibid.*; italics added.

I exist, and that meanwhile I do not notice (*animadvertam*) that any other thing necessarily pertains to my nature or essence, excepting that I am a thinking thing, I rightly conclude that my essence consists solely in the fact that I am a thinking thing."[30]

It is evident that *body* or *my body* cannot satisfy both conditions of principle G. To be sure, if I am aware of my body (or indeed of anything) then, according to Descartes, I am aware of myself. But it is false that if I am aware of myself then necessarily I am aware of my body. It is not difficult to imagine cases in which a man is not aware of his body, or is not even sure that he has a body (suppose he has lost all sensory power and feeling): yet he can still think to himself "*Ego sum, ego existo.*" Descartes can be aware of himself even if he is not aware of anything corporeal. The criterion provided by principle G cannot give the result that any corporeal thing is his essence. Since it does give the result that thinking is his essence, and since a substance can have no more than one essence, Descartes is apparently entitled to hold that he is "entirely and absolutely distinct" from his body "and can exist without it."[31]

7. *I do not know that body pertains to my nature, ergo it does not.* In the *Preface to the Reader,* which Descartes published with the *Meditations,* he takes note of a criticism that had been made of his previously published *Discourse on the Method.* The criticism, he states, is that "it does not follow from the fact that the human mind reflecting on itself does not perceive itself to be other than a thing that thinks, that its nature or its essence consists only in its being a thing that thinks, in the sense that this word *only* excludes all other things which might also be supposed to pertain to the nature of the soul." Descartes goes on to remark: "To this objection I reply that it was not my intention in that place [the *Discourse*] to exclude these in accordance with the order that looks to the truth of the matter (as to which I was not then

30 AT VII, 78; HR I, 190.
31 *Ibid.*

dealing), but only in accordance with the order of my perception (*perceptionem*): thus my meaning was that so far as
I was aware, I knew nothing clearly as belonging to my essence, excepting that I was a thing that thinks, or a thing
that has in itself the faculty of thinking. *But I shall show
hereafter how from the fact that I know no other thing which
pertains to my essence, it follows that there is no other thing
which really does belong to it.*"[32]

Descartes gives here a wrong account of his intentions in
the *Discourse*. If one examines the passage from the *Discourse* quoted in the preceding section, one sees that Descartes was *not* asserting merely that "so far as I was aware,
I knew nothing clearly as belonging to my essence, except
that I was a thing that thinks." On the contrary he asserts,
categorically and without qualification, "I knew that I was a
substance the whole essence or nature of which is to think."[33]

But for my purpose the chief interest of the passage from
the *Preface* is to show that Descartes does maintain that
from the fact that he *knows* of nothing other than thinking
that pertains to his essence, it follows that nothing else does
pertain to it.

Arnauld acutely criticized Descartes's proof, in the *Meditations*, that his nature was solely thinking. Arnauld's main
point is that one may not *know* that y is essential to x, and
yet it may be true that y is essential to x. By reasoning that
is parallel to Descartes's, says Arnauld, a man would be entitled to argue as follows: "While I clearly and distinctly
perceive that this triangle is right-angled, I yet doubt whether
the square on its base is equal to the squares on its sides.
Hence the equality of the square on the base to those
on the sides does not belong to its essence."[34] How can it
follow, asks Arnauld, "from the fact that one is unaware
that anything else belongs to one's essence, except that one
is a thinking being, that nothing else really belongs to one's
essence"?[35]

[32] AT VII, 7–8; HR I, 137–138; italics added.
[33] AT VI, 33; HR I, 101.
[34] AT VII, 201–202; HR II, 83.
[35] AT VII, 199; HR II, 81.

If one understands Descartes's "argument from ignorance," as one might want to call it, in the way that Descartes himself states it in the *Preface*[36] and in the way that Arnauld restates it, then it is obviously fallacious. From the fact that one does not *know* of anything other than *y* that is essential to *x*, it does not follow that nothing else is essential.

If, however, we conceive of Descartes as reasoning in accordance with principle G, as previously described, then his proof is no longer obviously fallacious. On the contrary it seems flawless. And also it no longer appears to be an argument from *ignorance*. We can understand why Descartes, who sought to introduce the rigor of mathematics into metaphysics, and who believed that he had "very exact demonstrations"[37] of everything in the *Meditations*, was so confident that he had discovered his essential nature. In replying to Arnauld he says: "Although perhaps there is much in me of which I have no knowledge . . . yet *since that which I am aware of in myself is sufficient to allow of my existing with it as my sole possession*, I am certain that God could have created me without giving me those other things of which I am not yet aware."[38] Descartes was sure that he could exist with thinking as his sole possession, because his perception of thinking was seen by him to be both a necessary and sufficient condition of his perception of himself.

8. *I have a clear and distinct idea of mind apart from body*. Descartes remarks in several places that it is not proved until the *Sixth Meditation* that mind is distinct from body.[39] The proof occurring in this *Meditation* is that since he has a clear and distinct idea of himself "as only a thinking and unextended thing" (*quatenus sum tantum res cogitans, non extensa*),[40] God's omnipotence could make him exist apart from body, and therefore he is distinct from body.

[36] AT VII, 8; HR I, 138.
[37] AT VII, 13; HR I, 140.
[38] AT VII, 219; HR II, 97; italics added.
[39] E.g., AT VII, 13; HR I, 140–141. AT VII, 175; HR II, 63. AT VII, 131; HR II, 32.
[40] AT VII, 78; HR I, 190. Cf. AT VII, 169–170; HR II, 59.

It is necessary to ask what assures Descartes that he has a
clear and distinct idea (conception, perception) of himself
as an unextended thing. If this is merely a dogmatic assertion, then the proof from clear and distinct ideas has no
value. It would be unlike Descartes and contrary to his aims
to be dogmatic on so crucial a point. He needs an objective
proof that he has a clear and distinct idea of himself as an
unextended thing. On our present interpretation, this first
premise of the argument from clear and distinct ideas is
established as true by Descartes's demonstrative proof that
he is aware of himself when and only when he is aware of
thinking. Awareness of body does not come into it. This
would seem to be as good a proof as could be demanded that
he has *a clear and distinct perception* of himself as solely
a thinking thing.

9. *Why Descartes declares that the separateness of mind
from body is not proved until the Sixth Meditation.* In
support of the suggestion that Descartes employed the criterion of principle G to determine his essence, I cited evidence from the *Fourth Discourse* and the *Second Meditation.* But since Descartes declares that he has not proved
the separateness of mind from body until the *Sixth Meditation,* does not this destroy that evidence and refute my
suggestion?

No. What is delayed until the *Sixth Meditation* is the
resolution of the radical doubt as to whether our clear and
distinct perceptions (ideas, conceptions) may not be mistaken. This is a doubt as to whether there is any correspondence at all between reality and our clear and distinct perceptions. Having proved that there is a God, and that all
things depend on Him, and that He is not a deceiver, Descartes deduces, at the end of *Meditation V,* that "what I
perceive clearly and distinctly cannot fail to be true."[41]
Armed with this conclusion, Descartes can then assert, in
Meditation VI, that "it suffices that I am able to apprehend
one thing apart from another clearly and distinctly in order

41 AT VII, 70; HR I, 184.

to be certain that the one is different from the other."[42]
Since he has previously determined that he perceives himself
clearly and distinctly as "only a thinking and unextended
thing," he deduces that in reality he is a distinct thing from
his body.[43]

Our interpretation is not concerned with his radical, metaphysical doubt but only with his assertion that he has a clear
and distinct perception of himself as solely a thinking thing.
Since this assertion is made both in *Discourse IV* and
Meditation II, we are warranted in drawing evidence for our
interpretation from those texts.[44]

10. *The indivisibility of the mind.* In *Meditation VI*
Descartes has a supplementary argument for the separateness of mind and body, which would be sufficient, he says,
to prove that "the mind or soul of man is entirely different
from the body," if he had not already proved it by his argument from clear and distinct ideas.[45] His additional argument is that body is divisible and mind is indivisible. "When

[42] AT VII, 78; HR I, 190.
[43] *Ibid.*
[44] My interpretation disagrees with that of Hamelin, who says of
Descartes's position in *Meditation II,* "*S'il dit qu'il est une chose
qui pense, cela signifie qu'il n'est autorisé pour le moment à se considérer que comme une chose qui pense.*" O. Hamelin, *Le Système
de Descartes* (Paris, 1911), p. 127. We have seen that in *Discourse IV* Descartes asserts, without qualification, that his whole
essence is to think (sec. 7, above). In *Meditation II* he says: "I do
not now admit anything which is not necessarily true: to speak
accurately I am only (*tantum*) a thing which thinks" (AT VII, 27;
HR I, 152). The assertion is again unqualified. I suspect that two
things, mainly, have prevented Hamelin and other commentators
from taking these assertions literally: first, the postponing of the
final resolution of the radical, metaphysical doubt until *Meditation VI;* second, a failure to perceive how Descartes could have believed that he had proved, in *Meditation II* and *Discourse IV,* that
(leaving aside the metaphysical doubt) his nature is solely thinking.
The result is the view that in the *Discourse* and *Meditation II,*
Descartes did not assert that he really is nothing but a thing which
thinks. Descartes's own misinterpretation of the *Discourse* (see
sec. 7 above) also helps to make this view attractive.
[45] AT VII, 86; HR I, 196.

I consider the mind, that is to say, myself inasmuch as I am only a thinking thing, I cannot distinguish in myself any parts, but apprehend myself to be clearly one and entire; and although the whole mind seems to be united to the whole body, yet if a foot, or an arm, or some other part, is separated from my body, I am aware that nothing has been taken away from my mind."[46] In the *Synopsis* of the *Meditations* Descartes declares that "we are not able to conceive of the half of a mind as we can do of the smallest of all bodies; so that we see that not only are their natures different but even in some respects contrary to one another."[47]

This supplementary argument is very weak. It is true that thinking is not divisible into spatial parts. But neither is weight: yet it does not follow that weight is not a property of bodies. If Descartes were offering, as an *empirical* consideration, the claim that people who have lost some parts of their bodies have found nothing taken away from their minds, it would be unconvincing. Has someone who lost his head been aware that he suffered no loss of mind?

Descartes is saying that *I* am not divisible into spatial parts. But that is not so. I can be split in half. Descartes would reply that "I" would mean here "my body": when "I" refers only to a thinking and unextended thing, I am not divisible into spatial parts. But does "I" *ever* refer solely to a thinking and unextended thing? Descartes needs to establish that this is so: therefore he has to rely on his proof that I am only a thinking and unextended thing. Thus his "supplementary" argument is not truly a separate argument: it depends on his previous argument that I have a clear and distinct idea of myself as a thinking and unextended thing. This latter argument, we have proposed, relies on the criterion provided by principle G.

11. *What I can and cannot doubt.* Descartes employs the technique of doubting everything for which there is any possible ground of doubt in order to try to find something that

---

[46] *Ibid.*
[47] AT VII, 13; HR I, 141.

is certain beyond all possible ground of doubt. He finds that
he can doubt that he has a body but not that he exists. On
this difference he constructs still another argument for the
separateness of mind and body. In the dialogue *The Search
After Truth*, Polyander says to Eudoxus: "I know very well
that what I am inasmuch as I doubt, is in no wise what I call
my body. And more than that, I do not even know that I
have a body, since you have shown me that I might doubt
of it. . . . Yet, while entirely setting aside all these sup-
positions, this will not prevent my being certain that I exist.
On the contrary, they confirm me yet more in the certainty
that I exist and that I am not a body; *otherwise, doubting of
my body I should at the same time doubt of myself*, and
this I cannot do."[48]

These remarks contain the following argument, briefly put:

> I can doubt that I have a body.
> I cannot doubt that I exist.
> *Ergo*, I am not a body.

The same argument occurs twice in the *Principles*.[49] In the
first of these two occurrences the conclusion is, "Body does
not pertain to my nature" (instead of "I am not a body"); in
the second it is, "I am distinct from corporeal substance." In
the *Notae in Programma*, the following argument occurs: "I
wrote that we could not doubt that our mind existed, because, from the very fact that we doubted, it followed that
our mind existed, but that meantime we might doubt
whether any material thing existed; whence I deduced and
demonstrated that mind was clearly perceived by us as an
existence, or substance, even supposing we had no concept
whatever of the body, or even denied that any material things
had existence; and, accordingly, that the concept of mind does
not involve any concept of body."[50] In *Discourse IV* there is
a hint of the same argument,[51] but it is conflated with the

[48] AT X, 518; HR I, 319; italics added.
[49] Pt. I, Principles 7 and 8, and Principle 60 (AT VIII, 6–7, 29;
HR I, 221, 244).
[50] AT VIII, 354; HR I, 440.
[51] See the paragraph from the *Discourse* quoted in sec. 6 above.

test for determining one's essential nature that is described
in Section 3 above. There is a suggestion of the argument
from doubt in the *Synopsis* of the *Meditations*,[52] although
there is not much indication of it in the *Meditations*.[53]
This argument is also indicated in the *Author's Letter*, which
serves as a *Preface* to the *Principles*: "Thus in considering
that he who would doubt all things cannot yet doubt that
he exists while he doubts, and that what reasons so in being
unable to doubt of itself and yet doubting all else, is not
what we call our body but what we call our soul or
thought."[54]

12. *Criticism of the argument from doubt.* It is sufficiently evident that Descartes argued from the premise that
he could doubt the existence of his body but could not doubt
his own existence, to the conclusion either that he was not his
body, or that there was no essential connection between him
and his body. Although the argument is undoubtedly attractive, we can prove that it is invalid by constructing arguments
of parallel form that are plainly invalid. I shall not be concerned with the truth of the premises but solely with validity
—that is, with whether the conclusion follows from the
premises.

It might be true of a man that he could doubt that he is a
Grand Master of the Elks but could not doubt that he exists:
it would not follow that he is not a Grand Master of the
Elks. It might be true that I could not doubt that Bertrand
Russell exists but I could doubt that the author of the pamphlet "Why I Am Not a Christian" exists: it would not follow that Bertrand Russell is not the author of that pamphlet.

It might be objected that in these counterexamples the
conclusions are contingent propositions, whereas the conclusion of Descartes's argument from doubt was intended to be
an a priori proposition—namely, the a priori proposition that

[52] AT VII, 12–13; HR I, 140.

[53] It is worth noting, however, that Arnauld thought that the
argument from doubt does occur in the *Meditations*. See AT VII,
198; HR II, 80.

[54] AT IX, 9–10; HR I, 208.

there is no necessary connection between me and a body. It might be thought that Descartes's argument could validly prove an a priori conclusion if not a contingent one. But it is easy to construct an argument of the same form, which has an a priori conclusion, yet is obviously invalid. For example, it might be true that I could not doubt that the number of people in my living room was 17 (because I had counted them carefully) but I could doubt (because I was unconfident of my calculation) that the number of people there was equal to the only prime number between 13 and 19. The argument we are constructing will have the following premises:

> I can doubt that the number is equal to the
> only prime between 13 and 19.
> I cannot doubt that the number is 17.

Following the model of the argument from doubt, the conclusion will be either: there is no essential connection between the number 17 and the number that is equal to the only prime between 13 and 19; or: the number 17 is not the only prime between 13 and 19. Since the conclusion, in either form, is false, whereas the premises could be true, it is shown that the form of argument is invalid. The argument from doubt is not rendered *more* valid by being provided with an a priori conclusion.

Descartes's argument from doubt also makes him vulnerable to an *argumentum ad hominem*. If it were valid to argue "I can doubt that my body exists but not that I exist, *ergo* I am not my body," it would be equally valid to argue "I can doubt that there exists a being whose essential nature is to think, but I cannot doubt that I exist, *ergo* I am not a being whose essential nature is to think." Descartes is hoist with his own petard! A form of argument that he employs to help establish the doctrine *sum res cogitans* could be used, if it were valid, to refute that very doctrine.

13. *Criticism of Descartes's criterion.* Let us turn back to study the criterion that Descartes used in his most cogent-seeming proof that thinking was his essential nature. As we said, the idea behind this criterion is that he will examine

himself to find out *what* he perceives when he perceives himself. His procedure can be presented as the following deductive argument:

G. *x* is my essence if it is the case that (a) if I am aware of *x* then (necessarily) I am aware of myself, and (b) if I am aware of myself then (necessarily) I am aware of *x*. Thinking satisfies these conditions.
Ergo, thinking is my essence.

We may think of principle G as being composed of two tests, (a) and (b), each of which is to be used to eliminate candidates for what my essence is, in the sense that any candidate failing to satisfy either (a) or (b) thereby fails to satisfy the criterion of principle G. Test (a) will be thought of in the following way: When I am aware of some candidate, *x*, I will observe whether I am aware of myself (or that I exist). If I am not aware that I exist, then *x* does not satisfy the criterion.

It is not difficult to see, however, that it would be impossible for me to make the "observation" that I am not aware that I exist. Test (a) cannot serve to eliminate *any* candidates. Therefore it is not a genuine test. It is not really a method for helping to determine my essence.

14. *Self-defeating utterances.* In his brilliant article on Descartes's *cogito*,[55] Professor Jaakko Hintikka makes a case for interpreting Descartes's "I think therefore I exist" as something other than a logical inference from "I think" to "I exist." Hintikka calls our attention to the fact that although the *sentence* "Descartes does not exist" is formally consistent, it would be absurd for *Descartes* to utter this sentence in order to persuade an auditor, who knew that the speaker was Descartes, that Descartes does not exist.[56] This utterance, or statement, would be "self-defeating," as Hintikka puts it. If now we consider the sentence obtained by substituting the personal pronoun "I" for the proper name "Descartes"

[55] Hintikka, *op. cit.* (See also his *"Cogito, Ergo Sum* as an Inference and a Performance," *Philosophical Review*, LXXII [1963], 487.)
[56] Hintikka, *op. cit.*, p. 119.

(that is, "I do not exist") we see that the utterance of this sentence by anyone would always be self-defeating.[57] No speaker could, by saying those words, convince anyone (including himself) that what he says is true. Hintikka suggests that the principle "I think therefore I exist" should be conceived, in part at least, as an expression of Descartes's realization that one's attempt to say or think that oneself does not exist yields a statement that is necessarily self-defeating.

This is an illuminating interpretation of the *cogito*. Now it can be seen that if the utterance "I do not exist" is self-defeating, so is the utterance "I am not *aware* that I exist."

Sometimes a statement of the form "I am not aware that *p*" provides evidence that *p* is false. My statement "I am not *aware* of a strong odor" could be evidence, for you, that there is no strong odor. If I say to you in regard to a figure before me, "I am not aware that one side is shorter than the other," this might give you a reason for believing that one side is not shorter than the other. My not being aware of something can be evidence that the something is not so.

Suppose, however, that someone has the suspicion that I do not exist. By making the statement, "I am not *aware* that I exist," I cannot verify his suspicion. Quite the contrary. And if we imagine (absurdly) that I am uncertain as to whether I exist, my declaration to myself, "I am not *aware* that I exist," would not express anything that could be a reason for me to believe that I do not exist.

It would seem that the purpose of saying "I am not aware that *p*" is either to persuade someone (possibly oneself) that *p* is false, or to express a doubt (including noncommitment) that *p* is true. Certainly one cannot *assert* *p* and in the same breath assert that one is not aware that *p*; for example, one cannot assert: "It rained yesterday but I am not aware that it did." In saying, "I am not aware that *p*," one's attitude toward *p* must be doubt or denial.

In the special case in which "I exist" is the value for *p*, the purpose for which a statement of the form "I am not aware that *p*" is made, cannot be achieved. The statement

[57] *Ibid.*, p. 120.

"I am not aware that I exist" has to imply a denial or a doubt of the speaker's own existence—that is, it has to imply that it is possible to assert or to think "I do not exist" or "Possibly I do not exist." Now since these latter statements would be self-defeating, therefore the statement "I am not aware that I exist" has a second-order, self-defeating character.[58]

I believe that the ultimate logical truth underlying Descartes's *cogito* is the fact that the statement "I do not exist" is necessarily self-defeating. If this is so, then Descartes's most formidable argument for holding that his essence is thinking is derived from the very same foundation that supports the *cogito*.

15. *Further consideration of Descartes's criterion.* We noticed that Descartes's criterion of his essential nature can be divided into two tests. The idea of test (a) is that when I am aware of something, *x*, I should observe whether I am aware that I exist. If I observe that I am not aware that I exist, then *x* does not satisfy the criterion. We saw that the self-defeating nature of this "observation" makes it impossible for this test to have a negative result. The test will necessarily be satisfied for every value of "*x*," and so the fact that it is satisfied for the value *thinking* has no tendency to show that *thinking* is my essence.

The second test contained in Descartes's criterion is test (b): "If I am aware that I exist I am aware of *x*." Suppose I wanted to determine whether *breathing* is my essence. *Breathing* will pass test (a), since everything passes it. Let us try test (b). If I am aware that I exist, is it necessarily the case that I am aware of breathing? No. So *breathing* is eliminated. We noted previously (Section 6) that *my body* is eliminated as a candidate by test (b).

We know that *thinking* passes test (b). But why does it? This is easily explained. Awareness of anything whatever is *thinking*, in Descartes's broad use of the term (Section 4).

---

[58] For a study of various types of "self-defeating" or "indefensible" statements, see Hintikka's book, *Knowledge and Belief* (Ithaca, 1962).

So if I am aware that I exist, then I am thinking. We noted the Cartesian doctrine that if I am thinking I am aware of thinking (*ibid.*). It follows that if I am aware that I exist I am aware of thinking.

But this analysis reveals that the fact that *thinking* passes test (b) has no tendency to show that it is the essence of *myself*. In the conditional, "If I am aware of myself (aware that I exist) then I am aware of thinking," we can substitute anything whatever into the antecedent, in place of the value *myself*, and always obtain a necessarily true proposition. The particular value *myself* is irrelevant to the truth of the conditional. "If I am aware of breathing then I am aware of thinking" is necessarily true. "If I am aware of an old tire then I am aware of thinking" is necessarily true. And so on. The truth of the conditional, "If I am aware of myself I am aware of thinking," does not depend on the value *myself*.

16. *Reviewing Descartes's criterion*. Descartes's criterion for determining that thinking is my essence has the look of being airtight. Thinking is my essence if these two conditions hold: (a) when I am aware of thinking I am aware of myself; (b) when I am aware of myself I am aware of thinking.

Not only is this a plausible criterion but, furthermore, propositions (a) and (b) are both necessarily true. What more cogent proof could there be that my essential nature is thinking?

We are presented with the paradox that although thinking apparently does satisfy Descartes's criterion, nonetheless it is not established that my nature is thinking! Our analysis of why conditions (a) and (b) are true shows that this is not due to any necessary connection between myself (or my existence) and thinking. Condition (a) is true solely because the statement "I am not aware of myself" is self-defeating: this is what prevents me from making the observation that I am aware of thinking but not aware of myself. The self-defeating character of the statement "I am not aware of myself" is derivative from the self-defeating character of the statement "I do not exist," and so condition (a) has the same basis as

does the *cogito*. Condition (b) is true because the awareness
of anything is "thinking," and also because of Descartes's
doctrine that one cannot think without being aware of thinking.

This doctrine that one cannot think without being aware
of thinking could itself be justified by the self-defeating nature of the statement "I am not aware of thinking." The
statement "I am not thinking" (in Descartes's broad sense of
"thinking") is as self-defeating as "I do not exist." In exactly
the same way in which we showed that "I am not aware that
I exist" has a second-order, self-defeating character, derived
from "I do not exist," we could show that the statement "I
am not aware that I am thinking" has a second-order, self-
defeating character, derived from "I am not thinking." Thus
we can regard the metaphysical thesis *sum res cogitans* as
obtaining its *entire* support from the self-defeating nature
of the two statements, "I am not aware that I exist" and "I
am not aware that I think." This may help in understanding
why Descartes regarded the *cogito* as being so *fruitful*. For
the logical truth that underlies the *cogito*, together with another of exactly the same character, could seem to Descartes
to provide an immediate transition from the *cogito* to the
important theme that his nature is solely thinking.

We may conceive of Descartes's criterion (principle G) as
being obtained by substitution on the variables in the formula "x is the essence of y if the awareness of x is logically
equivalent to the awareness of y."[59] I am not claiming that
this formula is a logical truth, or even that it is very meaningful. Nevertheless it has a high degree of intuitive plausibility. If one's undertaking is to determine the essence of a
certain thing (for example, a triangle) and if in the process
of studying this thing one hit upon something that satisfied
the mentioned formula (for example, a three-sided plane
figure) it would be very compelling to believe that the undertaking had been successfully completed.

My criticism is that even if we assume that the formula

[59] Remembering that x and y must take different values. Cf. note
19 above.

gives a correct method of determination in *all* other cases, and even though it is a fact that when *thinking* and *myself* are substituted for *x* and *y*, the conditions (a) and (b) thus obtained are necessarily true, it is still not established that *thinking* and *myself* (or *my existence*) are essentially connected.

A statement of the form, "When I am aware of *x* I am aware of myself," is necessarily true regardless of the value for *x*. The fact that it is true when the value is *thinking* does not reveal any necessary relation between thinking and myself. Also a statement of the form, "When I am aware of *y* I am aware of thinking," is necessarily true regardless of the value for *y*. The fact that it is true when the value is *myself* does not reveal any necessary relation between myself and thinking. Neither condition of Descartes's criterion shows any essential connection between thinking and myself, although there is every appearance of the criterion's being satisfied.

It would be desirable to make explicit the sense in which the conditionals (a) and (b) of Descartes's criterion are "necessarily true." We can distinguish two senses in which a conditional can be necessarily true. In the first sense, a conditional is necessarily true if the negation of the consequent is inconsistent with the antecedent. Descartes's proof has *not* shown that the conditionals (a) and (b) are necessarily true in this sense. But this is the sense required to prove that *thinking* and *myself* are essentially connected. A conditional is necessarily true, in the second sense, if it is self-defeating to deny the consequent. The conditionals (a) and (b) are necessarily true in this sense. The seeming cogency of the proof employing the criterion of principle G may derive from a confusing of these two senses of "necessarily true."

It is worth noting that the conditional "If I think I exist" (which might be taken as a version of the *cogito*) is necessarily true in *both* senses. Hintikka's studies provide good evidence that Descartes did not clearly distinguish these two aspects of the *cogito*. Previously (Section 4) I asked whether it was credible that Descartes should have supposed that whenever I am thinking I am aware that I exist, in the sense

of having the actual thought *I exist.* I think it is credible.
For the conditional "If I think I exist" is necessarily true in
two ways that Descartes did not disentangle. The conditional
"If I think I am aware that I exist" is necessarily true in only
one of those ways. It is not implausible that Descartes should
have made the half-conscious assumption that this second
conditional, being necessarily true, has the feature (possessed
by the first one) that the consequent *follows from* the antecedent. He would thus be led to believe (mistakenly) that
since it is true that I exist at every moment I am thinking,
so it is true that I am aware that I exist at every moment I
am thinking.[60]

SUMMARY

Descartes actually states three proofs of the thesis that I
am only a thinking and unextended thing. One is the argument from doubt: I can doubt that my body exists but not
that I exist, therefore my body does not pertain to my essential nature. This argument is invalid. Another proof is the
argument from clear and distinct ideas: I have a clear and
distinct idea of myself as a thinking and unextended thing
and of body as an extended and unthinking thing, therefore
I am separate and distinct from body. This argument requires
support for the premise that I have a clear and distinct idea
of myself as a thinking and unextended thing. The third proof
is the argument from the indivisibility of myself: *I* am in-

[60] Descartes wrote to Mersenne, in July 1641, that *"il est impossible que nous puissons jamais penser à aucune chose, que nous
n'avons en même temps l'idée de notre Ame"* (AT III, 394). Is
Descartes affirming here the view that whenever I think of anything
I am aware of myself, i.e. aware that I exist? What he says is that
it is impossible for me to think of anything unless I have the *idea*
of myself (of my soul). This could mean merely that it is a necessary
condition of my doing any thinking that I should have the *concept*
of myself. It would not have to mean that whenever I think I have
an actual thought of myself. Yet if this is what Descartes meant then
why should he say that I cannot think of anything unless *at the same
time* I have the idea of my soul? This temporal specification makes
it appear that he is talking about having an actual thought, rather
than about having a concept.

divisible but my body is divisible, therefore my body does not pertain to my essence. This argument requires support for the premise that *I* am indivisible.

Descartes has another argument that is never set down in so many words, but is suggested by various passages. This argument appears to provide a complete demonstration of the doctrine *sum res cogitans,* and also to give the needed support to the second and third arguments. This new argument has an appearance of extreme rigor and cogency, although it is actually invalid. Attributing this argument to Descartes helps to explain why he thought he could make the transition from *cogito ergo sum* to *sum res cogitans:* for the seeming solidity and power of this argument is mainly derived from the *cogito* itself.

DESCARTES' MYTH

GILBERT RYLE

1. THE OFFICIAL DOCTRINE

There is a doctrine about the nature and place of minds which is so prevalent among theorists and even among laymen that it deserves to be described as the official theory. Most philosophers, psychologists and religious teachers subscribe, with minor reservations, to its main articles and, although they admit certain theoretical difficulties in it, they tend to assume that these can be overcome without serious modifications being made to the architecture of the theory. It will be argued here that the central principles of the doctrine are unsound and conflict with the whole body of what we know about minds when we are not speculating about them.

The official doctrine, which hails chiefly from Descartes, is something like this. With the doubtful exceptions of idiots and infants in arms every human being has both a body and a mind. Some would prefer to say that every human being is both a body and a mind. His body and his mind are ordinarily harnessed together, but after the death of the body his mind may continue to exist and function.

Human bodies are in space and are subject to the mechanical laws which govern all other bodies in space. Bodily processes and states can be inspected by external observers. So a man's bodily life is as much a public affair as are the lives of

From *The Concept of Mind* (London: Hutchinson's University Library, 1949, and New York: Barnes & Noble, Inc., 1960), Ch. I, pp. 11–24. Reprinted by permission of Hutchinson Publishing Group Ltd and Barnes & Noble, Inc.

animals and reptiles and even as the careers of trees, crystals and planets.

But minds are not in space, nor are their operations subject to mechanical laws. The workings of one mind are not witnessable by other observers; its career is private. Only I can take direct cognisance of the states and processes of my own mind. A person therefore lives through two collateral histories, one consisting of what happens in and to his body, the other consisting of what happens in and to his mind. The first is public, the second private. The events in the first history are events in the physical world, those in the second are events in the mental world.

It has been disputed whether a person does or can directly monitor all or only some of the episodes of his own private history; but, according to the official doctrine, of at least some of these episodes he has direct and unchallengeable cognisance. In consciousness, self-consciousness and introspection he is directly and authentically apprised of the present states and operations of his mind. He may have great or small uncertainties about concurrent and adjacent episodes in the physical world, but he can have none about at least part of what is momentarily occupying his mind.

It is customary to express this bifurcation of his two lives and of his two worlds by saying that the things and events which belong to the physical world, including his own body, are external, while the workings of his own mind are internal. This antithesis of outer and inner is of course meant to be construed as a metaphor, since minds, not being in space, could not be described as being spatially inside anything else, or as having things going on spatially inside themselves. But relapses from this good intention are common and theorists are found speculating how stimuli, the physical sources of which are yards or miles outside a person's skin, can generate mental responses inside his skull, or how decisions framed inside his cranium can set going movements of his extremities.

Even when 'inner' and 'outer' are construed as metaphors, the problem how a person's mind and body influence one another is notoriously charged with theoretical difficulties. What the mind wills, the legs, arms and the tongue execute; what affects the ear and the eye has something to do with what the mind perceives; grimaces and smiles betray the mind's moods and bodily castigations lead, it is hoped, to moral improvement. But the actual transactions between the episodes of the private history and those of the public history remain mysterious, since by definition they can belong to neither series. They could not be reported among the happenings described in a person's autobiography of his inner life, but nor could they be reported among those described in some one else's biography of that person's overt career. They can be inspected neither by introspection nor by laboratory experiment. They are theoretical shuttlecocks which are forever being bandied from the physiologist back to the psychologist and from the psychologist back to the physiologist.

Underlying this partly metaphorical representation of the bifurcation of a person's two lives there is a seemingly more profound and philosophical assumption. It is assumed that there are two different kinds of existence or status. What exists or happens may have the status of physical existence, or it may have the status of mental existence. Somewhat as the faces of coins are either heads or tails, or somewhat as living creatures are either male or female, so, it is supposed, some existing is physical existing, other existing is mental existing. It is a necessary feature of what has physical existence that it is in space and time, it is a necessary feature of what has mental existence that it is in time but not in space. What has physical existence is composed of matter, or else is a function of matter; what has mental existence consists of consciousness, or else is a function of consciousness.

There is thus a polar opposition between mind and matter, an opposition which is often brought out as follows. Material objects are situated in a common field, known as 'space', and what happens to one body in one part of space is mechanically connected with what happens to other bodies in other parts of space. But mental happenings occur in insulated fields, known as 'minds', and there is, apart maybe from telepathy, no direct causal connection between what happens in one mind and what happens in another. Only through the medium of the public physical world can the mind of one person make a difference to the mind of another. The mind is its own place and in his inner life each of us lives the life of a ghostly Robinson Crusoe. People can see, hear and jolt one another's bodies, but they are irremediably blind and deaf to the workings of one another's minds and inoperative upon them.

What sort of knowledge can be secured of the workings of a mind? On the one side, according to the official theory, a person has direct knowledge of the best imaginable kind of the workings of his own mind. Mental states and processes are (or are normally) conscious states and processes, and the consciousness which irradiates them can engender no illusions and leaves the door open for no doubts. A person's present thinkings, feelings and willings, his perceivings, rememberings and imaginings are intrinsically 'phosphorescent'; their existence and their nature are inevitably betrayed to their owner. The inner life is a stream of consciousness of such a sort that it would be absurd to suggest that the mind whose life is that stream might be unaware of what is passing down it.

True, the evidence adduced recently by Freud seems to show that there exist channels tributary to this stream, which run hidden from their owner. People are actuated by impulses the existence of which they vigorously disavow; some of their thoughts differ from the thoughts which they acknowledge; and some of the actions which they think they will to perform they do not really will. They are thoroughly gulled by some of their own hypocrisies and they successfully ignore facts about their mental lives which on the official theory ought to be patent to them. Holders of the official theory tend, however, to maintain that anyhow in normal circumstances a person must be directly and authentically seized of the present state and workings of his own mind.

Besides being currently supplied with these alleged immediate data of consciousness, a person is also generally supposed to be able to exercise from time to time a special kind of perception, namely inner perception, or introspection. He can take a (non-optical) 'look' at what is passing in his mind.

Not only can he view and scrutinize a flower through his sense of sight and listen to and discriminate the notes of a bell through his sense of hearing; he can also reflectively or introspectively watch, without any bodily organ of sense, the current episodes of his inner life. This self-observation is also commonly supposed to be immune from illusion, confusion or doubt. A mind's reports of its own affairs have a certainty superior to the best that is possessed by its reports of matters in the physical world. Sense-perceptions can, but consciousness and introspection cannot, be mistaken or confused.

On the other side, one person has no direct access of any sort to the events of the inner life of another. He cannot do better than make problematic inferences from the observed behaviour of the other person's body to the states of mind which, by analogy from his own conduct, he supposes to be signalised by that behaviour. Direct access to the workings of a mind is the privilege of that mind itself; in default of such privileged access, the workings of one mind are inevitably occult to everyone else. For the supposed arguments from bodily movements similar to their own to mental workings similar to their own would lack any possibility of observational corroboration. Not unnaturally, therefore, an adherent of the official theory finds it difficult to resist this consequence of his premises, that he has no good reason to believe that there do exist minds other than his own. Even if he prefers to believe that to other human bodies there are harnessed minds not unlike his own, he cannot claim to be able to discover their individual characteristics, or the particular things that they undergo and do. Absolute solitude is on this showing the ineluctable destiny of the soul. Only our bodies can meet.

As a necessary corollary of this general scheme there is implicitly prescribed a special way of construing our ordinary concepts of mental powers and operations. The verbs, nouns and adjectives, with which in ordinary life we describe the wits, characters and higher-grade performances of the people with whom we have do, are required to be construed as signifying special episodes in their secret histories, or else as signifying tendencies for such episodes to occur. When someone is described as knowing, believing or guessing something, as hoping, dreading, intending or shirking something, as designing this or being amused at that, these verbs are supposed to denote the occurrence of specific modifications in his (to us) occult stream of consciousness. Only his own privileged access to this stream in direct awareness and introspection could provide authentic testimony that these mental-conduct verbs were correctly or incorrectly applied. The onlooker, be he teacher, critic, biographer or friend, can never assure himself that his comments have any vestige of truth. Yet it was just because we do in fact all know how to make such comments, make them with general correctness and correct them when they turn out to be confused or mistaken, that philosophers found it necessary to construct their theories of the nature and place of minds. Finding mental-conduct concepts being regularly and effectively used, they properly sought to fix their logical geography. But the logical geography officially recommended would entail that there could be no regular or effective use of these mental-conduct concepts in our descriptions of, and prescriptions for, other people's minds.

2. THE ABSURDITY OF THE OFFICIAL DOCTRINE

Such in outline is the official theory. I shall often speak of it, with deliberate abusiveness, as 'the dogma of the Ghost in the Machine'. I hope to prove that it is entirely false, and false not in detail but in principle. It is not merely an assemblage of particular mistakes. It is one big mistake and a mistake of a special kind. It is, namely, a category-mistake. It represents the facts of mental life as if they belonged to one logical type or category (or range of types or categories), when they actually belong to another. The dogma is therefore a philosopher's myth. In attempting to explode the myth I shall probably be taken to be denying well-known facts about the mental life of human beings, and my plea that I aim at doing nothing more than rectify the logic of mental-conduct concepts will probably be disallowed as mere subterfuge.

I must first indicate what is meant by the phrase 'Category-mistake'. This I do in a series of illustrations.

A foreigner visiting Oxford or Cambridge for the first time is shown a number of colleges, libraries, playing fields, museums, scientific departments and administrative offices. He then asks 'But where is the University? I have seen where the members of the Colleges live, where the Registrar works, where the scientists experiment and the rest. But I have not yet seen the University in which reside and work the members of your University.' It has then to be explained to him that the University is not another collateral institution, some ulterior counterpart to the colleges, laboratories and offices which he has seen. The University is just the way in which all that he has already seen is organized. When they are seen and when their co-ordination is understood, the University has been seen. His mistake lay in his innocent assumption that it was correct to speak of Christ Church, the Bodleian Library, the Ashmolean Museum *and* the University, to speak, that is, as if 'the University' stood for an extra member of the class of which these other units are members. He was mistakenly allocating the University to the same category as that to which the other institutions belong.

The same mistake would be made by a child witnessing the march-past of a division, who, having had pointed out to him such and such battalions, batteries, squadrons, etc., asked when the division was going to appear. He would be supposing that a division was a counterpart to the units already seen, partly similar to them and partly unlike them. He would be shown his mistake by being told that in watching the battalions, batteries and squadrons marching past he had been watching the division marching past. The march-past was not a parade of battalions, batteries, squadrons *and* a division; it was a parade of the battalions, batteries and squadrons *of* a division.

One more illustration. A foreigner watching his first game of cricket learns what are the functions of the bowlers, the batsmen, the fielders, the umpires and the scorers. He then says 'But there is no one left on the field to contribute the famous element of team-spirit. I see who does the bowling, the batting and the wicket-keeping; but I do not see whose role it is to exercise *esprit de corps*.' Once more, it would have to be explained that he was looking for the wrong type of thing. Team-spirit is not another cricketing-operation supplementary to all of the other special tasks. It is, roughly, the keenness with which each of the special tasks is performed, and performing a task keenly is not performing two tasks. Certainly exhibiting team-spirit is not the same thing as bowling or catching, but nor is it a third thing such that we can say that the bowler first bowls *and* then exhibits team-spirit or that a fielder is at a given moment *either* catching *or* displaying *esprit de corps*.

These illustrations of category-mistakes have a common feature which must be noticed. The mistakes were made by people who did not know how to wield the concepts *University, division* and *team-spirit*. Their puzzles arose from inability to use certain items in the English vocabulary.

The theoretically interesting category-mistakes are those made by people who are perfectly competent to apply concepts, at least in the situations with which they are familiar, but are still liable in their abstract thinking to allocate those concepts to logical types to which they do not belong. An instance of a mistake of this sort would be the following story. A student of politics has learned the main differences between the British, the French and the American Constitutions, and has learned also the differences and connections between the Cabinet, Parliament, the various Ministries, the Judicature and the Church of England. But he still becomes embarrassed when asked questions about the connections between the Church of England, the Home Office and the British Constitution. For while the Church and the Home Office are institutions, the British Constitution is not another institution in the same sense of that noun. So inter-institutional relations which can be asserted or denied to hold between the Church and the Home Office cannot be asserted or denied to hold between either of them and the British Constitution. 'The British Constitution' is not a term of the same logical type as 'the Home Office' and 'the Church of England'. In a partially similar way, John Doe may be a relative, a friend, an enemy or a stranger to Richard Roe; but he cannot be any of these things to the Average Taxpayer. He knows how to talk sense in certain sorts of discussions about the Average Taxpayer, but he is baffled to say why he could not come across him in the street as he can come across Richard Roe.

It is pertinent to our main subject to notice that, so long as the student of politics continues to think of the British Constitution as a counterpart to the other institutions, he will tend to describe it as a mysteriously occult institution; and so long as John Doe continues to think of the Average Taxpayer as a fellow-citizen, he will tend to think of him as an elusive insubstantial man, a ghost who is everywhere yet nowhere.

My destructive purpose is to show that a family of radical category-mistakes is the source of the double-life theory. The representation of a person as a ghost mysteriously ensconced in a machine derives from this argument. Because, as is true, a person's thinking, feeling and purposive doing cannot be described solely in the idioms of physics, chemistry and physiology, therefore they must be described in counterpart idioms. As the human body is a complex organised unit, so the human mind must be another complex organised unit, though one made of a different sort of stuff and with a different sort of structure. Or, again, as the human body, like any other parcel of matter, is a field of causes and effects, so the mind must be another field of causes and effects, though not (Heaven be praised) mechanical causes and effects.

3. THE ORIGIN OF THE CATEGORY-MISTAKE

One of the chief intellectual origins of what I have yet to prove to be the Cartesian category-mistake seems to be this. When Galileo showed that his methods of scientific discovery were competent to provide a mechanical theory which should cover every occupant of space, Descartes found in himself two conflicting motives. As a man of scientific genius he could not but endorse the claims of mechanics, yet as a religious and moral man he could not accept, as Hobbes accepted, the discouraging rider to those claims, namely that human nature differs only in degree of complexity from clockwork. The mental could not be just a variety of the mechanical.

He and subsequent philosophers naturally but erroneously availed themselves of the following escape-route. Since mental-conduct words are not to be construed as signifying the occurrence of mechanical processes, they must be construed as signifying the occurrence of non-mechanical processes; since mechanical laws explain movements in space as the effects of other movements in space, other laws must explain some of the non-spatial workings of minds as the effects of other non-spatial workings of minds. The difference between the human behaviours which we describe as intelligent and those which we describe as unintelligent must be a difference in their causation; so, while some movements of human tongues and limbs are the effects of mechanical causes, others must be the effects of non-mechanical causes, i.e. some issue from movements of particles of matter, others from workings of the mind.

The differences between the physical and the mental were thus represented as differences inside the common framework of the categories of 'thing', 'stuff', 'attribute', 'state', 'process', 'change', 'cause' and 'effect'. Minds are things, but different sorts of things from bodies; mental processes are causes and effects, but different sorts of causes and effects from bodily movements. And so on. Somewhat as the foreigner expected the University to be an extra edifice, rather like a college but also considerably different, so the repudiators of mechanism represented minds as extra centres of causal processes, rather like machines but also considerably different from them. Their theory was a para-mechanical hypothesis.

That this assumption was at the heart of the doctrine is shown by the fact that there was from the beginning felt to be a major theoretical difficulty in explaining how minds can influence and be influenced by bodies. How can a mental process, such as willing, cause spatial movements like the movements of the tongue? How can a physical change in the optic nerve have among its effects a mind's perception of a flash of light? This notorious crux by itself shows the logical mould into which Descartes pressed his theory of the mind. It was the self-same mould into which he and Galileo set their mechanics. Still unwittingly adhering to the grammar of mechanics, he tried to avert disaster by describing minds in what was merely an obverse vocabulary. The workings of minds had to be described by the mere negatives of the specific descriptions given to bodies; they are not in space, they are not motions, they are not modifications of matter, they are not accessible to public observation. Minds are not bits of clockwork, they are just bits of not-clockwork.

As thus represented, minds are not merely ghosts harnessed to machines, they are themselves just spectral machines. Though the human body is an engine, it is not quite an ordinary engine, since some of its workings are governed by another engine inside it—this interior governor-engine being one of a very special sort. It is invisible, inaudible and it has no size or weight. It cannot be taken to bits and the laws it obeys are not those known to ordinary engineers. Nothing is known of how it governs the bodily engine.

A second major crux points the same moral. Since, according to the doctrine, minds belong to the same category as bodies and since bodies are rigidly governed by mechanical laws, it seemed to many theorists to follow that minds must be similarly governed by rigid non-mechanical laws. The physical world is a deterministic system, so the mental world must be a deterministic system. Bodies cannot help the modifications that they undergo, so minds cannot help pursuing the careers fixed for them. *Responsibility, choice, merit* and *demerit* are therefore inapplicable concepts—unless the compromise solution is adopted of saying that the laws governing mental processes, unlike those governing physical processes, have the congenial attribute of being only rather rigid. The problem of the Freedom of the Will was the problem how to reconcile the hypothesis that minds are to be described in terms drawn from the categories of mechanics with the knowledge that higher-grade human conduct is not of a piece with the behaviour of machines.

It is an historical curiosity that it was not noticed that the entire argument was broken-backed. Theorists correctly assumed that any sane man could already recognise the differences between, say, rational and non-rational utterances or between purposive and automatic behaviour. Else there would have been nothing requiring to be salved from mechanism. Yet the explanation given presupposed that one person could in principle never recognise the difference between the rational and the irrational utterances issuing from other human bodies, since he could never get access to the postulated immaterial causes of some of their utterances. Save for the doubtful exception of himself, he could never tell the difference between a man and a Robot. It would have to be conceded, for example, that, for all that we can tell, the inner lives of persons who are classed as idiots or lunatics are as rational as those of anyone else. Perhaps only their overt behaviour is disappointing; that is to say, perhaps 'idiots' are not really idiotic, or 'lunatics' lunatic. Perhaps, too, some of those who are classed as sane are really idiots. According to the theory, external observers could never know how the overt behaviour of others is correlated with their mental powers and processes and so they could never know or even plausibly conjecture whether their applications of mental-conduct concepts to these other people were correct or incorrect. It would then be hazardous or impossible for a man to claim sanity or logical consistency even for himself, since he would be debarred from comparing his own performances with those of others. In short, our characterisations of persons and their performances as intelligent, prudent and virtuous or as stupid, hypocritical and cowardly could never have been made, so the problem of providing a special causal hypothesis to serve as the basis of such diagnoses would never have arisen. The question, 'How do persons differ from machines?' arose just because everyone already knew how to apply mental-conduct concepts before the new causal hypothesis was introduced. This causal hypothesis could not therefore be the source of the criteria used in those applications. Nor, of course, has the causal hypothesis in any degree improved our handling of those criteria. We still distinguish good from bad arithmetic,

politic from impolitic conduct and fertile from infertile imagi-
nations in the ways in which Descartes himself distinguished
them before and after he speculated how the applicability
of these criteria was compatible with the principle of mechanical causation.

He had mistaken the logic of his problem. Instead of asking by what criteria intelligent behaviour is actually distinguished from non-intelligent behaviour, he asked 'Given that
the principle of mechanical causation does not tell us the
difference, what other causal principle will tell it us?' He
realised that the problem was not one of mechanics and
assumed that it must therefore be one of some counterpart to
mechanics. Not unnaturally psychology is often cast for just
this role.

When two terms belong to the same category, it is proper
to construct conjunctive propositions embodying them. Thus
a purchaser may say that he bought a left-hand glove and a
right-hand glove, but not that he bought a left-hand glove, a
right-hand glove and a pair of gloves. 'She came home in a
flood of tears and a sedan-chair' is a well-known joke based on
the absurdity of conjoining terms of different types. It would
have been equally ridiculous to construct the disjunction 'She
came home either in a flood of tears or else in a sedan-chair'.
Now the dogma of the Ghost in the Machine does just this.
It maintains that there exist both bodies and minds; that
there occur physical processes and mental processes; that there
are mechanical causes of corporeal movements and mental
causes of corporeal movements. I shall argue that these and
other analogous conjunctions are absurd; but, it must be noticed, the argument will not show that either of the illegiti-
mately conjoined propositions is absurd in itself. I am not,
for example, denying that there occur mental processes. Doing long division is a mental process and so is making a joke.
But I am saying that the phrase 'there occur mental processes'
does not mean the same sort of thing as 'there occur physical
processes', and, therefore, that it makes no sense to conjoin or
disjoin the two.

If my argument is successful, there will follow some interesting consequences. First, the hallowed contrast between

Mind and Matter will be dissipated, but dissipated not by either of the equally hallowed absorptions of Mind by Matter or of Matter by Mind, but in quite a different way. For the seeming contrast of the two will be shown to be as illegitimate as would be the contrast of 'she came home in a flood of tears' and 'she came home in a sedan-chair'. The belief that there is a polar opposition between Mind and Matter is the belief that they are terms of the same logical type.

It will also follow that both Idealism and Materialism are answers to an improper question. The 'reduction' of the material world to mental states and processes, as well as the 'reduction' of mental states and processes to physical states and processes, presuppose the legitimacy of the disjunction 'Either there exist minds or there exist bodies (but not both)'. It would be like saying, 'Either she bought a left-hand and a right-hand glove or she bought a pair of gloves (but not both)'.

It is perfectly proper to say, in one logical tone of voice, that there exist minds and to say, in another logical tone of voice, that there exist bodies. But these expressions do not indicate two different species of existence, for 'existence' is not a generic word like 'coloured' or 'sexed'. They indicate two different senses of 'exist', somewhat as 'rising' has different senses in 'the tide is rising', 'hopes are rising' and 'the average age of death is rising'. A man would be thought to be making a poor joke who said that three things are now rising, namely the tide, hopes and the average age of death. It would be just as good or bad a joke to say that there exist prime numbers and Wednesdays and public opinions and navies; or that there exist both minds and bodies. In the succeeding chapters I try to prove that the official theory does rest on a batch of category-mistakes by showing that logically absurd corollaries follow from it. The exhibition of these absurdities will have the constructive effect of bringing out part of the correct logic of mental-conduct concepts.

4. HISTORICAL NOTE

It would not be true to say that the official theory derives solely from Descartes' theories, or even from a more widespread anxiety about the implications of seventeenth century mechanics. Scholastic and Reformation theology had schooled the intellects of the scientists as well as of the laymen, philosophers and clerics of that age. Stoic-Augustinian theories of the will were embedded in the Calvinist doctrines of sin and grace; Platonic and Aristotelian theories of the intellect shaped the orthodox doctrines of the immortality of the soul. Descartes was reformulating already prevalent theological doctrines of the soul in the new syntax of Galileo. The theologian's privacy of conscience became the philosopher's privacy of consciousness, and what had been the bogy of Predestination reappeared as the bogy of Determinism.

It would also not be true to say that the two-worlds myth did no theoretical good. Myths often do a lot of theoretical good, while they are still new. One benefit bestowed by the para-mechanical myth was that it partly superannuated the then prevalent para-political myth. Minds and their Faculties had previously been described by analogies with political superiors and political subordinates. The idioms used were those of ruling, obeying, collaborating and rebelling. They survived and still survive in many ethical and some epistemological discussions. As, in physics, the new myth of occult Forces was a scientific improvement on the old myth of Final Causes, so, in anthropological and psychological theory, the new myth of hidden operations, impulses and agencies was an improvement on the old myth of dictations, deferences and disobediences.

DESCARTES'S MECHANICISM

P. H. J. HOENEN, S.J.

In many Scholastic textbooks, Mechanicism is described as if its essence consisted solely or principally in the total or partial denial of the *activity* of bodies. It is true that some Cartesians deny activity to bodies, but not Descartes himself. It is also true that some Mechanicists deny any activity except the kind found in locomotive forces. Some of them recognize only one force, which is active in the collision of bodies; for example, Descartes and—in a different way, for the phenomenal world—Leibniz. They are said to teach "rigid" Mechanicism.[1] Then there are others who recognize a number of locomotive forces. Several levels of denial can be distinguished in their modified Mechanicism, and some are rightly called "Dynamists."[2]

From *Cosmologia* (Rome: Gregorian University Press, 1949), selections from the section titled "De Mechanicismo," pp. 136–162. In this section, Hoenen deals with Greek Mechanicists—Leucippus and Democritus—as well as Descartes. He also opposes Mechanicism to Aristotelian Naturalism and offers a refutation of the former. Passages bearing on the interpretation of Descartes are included here. Translated by P. J. Crittenden and published with the permission of Libreria Editrice della Pontificia Università Gregoriana.

[1] Leibniz, for good or bad reasons, . . . is also counted as a dynamist.

[2] Contemporaneous with Descartes and under his influence, the system known as *Occasionalism* arose. This was expounded by certain Cartesians like Cordemoy and particularly by Geulincx and Malebranche. The system denies all activity not only to bodies but to every creature, and here the denial of activity really is primary. Although it has obvious connections with Mechanicism, Occasionalism must be sharply distinguished from it. It also has a totally different source. In the Middle Ages certain Arabs had defended a

This is not, however, a good description of the true nature of Mechanicism. Mechanicism does not consist primarily in the denial or restriction of the *activity* of bodies but rather in the denial of their *passivity* or *intrinsic changeability* in regard even to their qualities. Its proponents do not say, "Bodies cannot act," but rather, "Bodies cannot be acted upon—that is, they cannot undergo intrinsic change." They allow only one form of "becoming" in bodies, and that is extrinsic; viz., motion from place to place. Evidently, as a *consequence* of this, the only activity that remains is the kind found in locomotive force. The absence of changeability is not deduced from any total or partial inability to act. The very opposite is the case. The impossibility of activity is derived from the absence of changeability, and it is the latter that must be thought of as the primary and fundamental denial. . . .

A warning is necessary on another point. Among physicists (but much less so among philosophers), the view has grown up that Mechanicism is the fruit of experience, as though this system had come to be recognized because it alone could account for experimental data. It was, in fact, the only system that was used by physicists in building up their explanatory theories. (This led to errors, which were the cause of "crises" in science.) But this was only because the system was taken in an a priori way as self-evident . . . and not at all because it alone could support the theoretical explanations. . . . It was because of metaphysical reasons that doubts about the reality of qualities and especially their changes began to grow, and the qualities and changes were then rejected as unreal and relegated to the world of appearances. . . .

I. DESCARTES'S VIEW

In Part Two of the *Principles of Philosophy* Descartes sets out "the principles of material things." At the end of this Part, before applying these principles to the "visible world"

system like it, with a view to stressing the divine power. They were called *Mutakallimun*—"loquentes in lege Maurorum" in St. Thomas.

(Part Three) and the "earth" (Part Four), and as though to recapitulate the general principles of his natural philosophy established in the previous sections, he says:

> I openly state that the only matter that I recognize in corporeal things is that which is subject to every sort of division, shape, and movement—what geometers call quantity and take as the object of their demonstrations. Moreover, I consider nothing in quantity apart from these divisions, shapes, and movements; and I admit nothing as true of them that is not deduced, with the clarity of a mathematical demonstration, from common notions whose truth we cannot doubt. Because all the phenomena of nature can be explained in this way, I think that no other principles of physics need be admitted, nor are to be desired.[3]

For Descartes, therefore, the truly basic problem to be considered is the problem of becoming. He is concerned with what bodies can undergo and what changes they are subject to; and he wants to explain—to safeguard—the phenomena by means of only those changes that extension can undergo; namely, being divided, taking a shape, and moving locally. But, as we shall see, the most important of these is movement; for division results from movement, and shape from division. He does not, therefore, come to regard movement in place as the only form of "becoming" by establishing that there is no activity at all or at least no activity other than locomotive activity. Descartes arrives at the denial of intrinsic change in a different way, and that denial clearly precedes his denial or limitation of activity. (We shall see . . . why he admitted the division of matter, though it is—as the atomists were well aware—a truly intrinsic change.)

There is no difficulty, then, in extracting from Descartes's teaching the theory in which the essence of his Mechanicism consists. The essence of his Mechanicism is even more obvi-

---

[3] *Pr. Ph.* II, 64. I shall refer to the Adam and Tannery edition, giving volume and page numbers. The *Principles of Philosophy* (*Pr. Ph.*) in Latin are in Part One of Vol. VIII. References to this work will be by part and section number only.

ous when one considers its grounds. But before we go on to deal with these, it will be helpful to add some particular propositions from the teaching itself.

Matter is completely identified with extension, which constitutes its whole essence. Hence, it can undergo all things, and only those things, that extension undergoes: "We shall see that the nature of matter, or of body considered as a whole, does not consist in its being hard, or heavy, or colored, or in its affecting the senses in some other way, but solely in its being a thing extended in length, breadth, and depth" (*Pr. Ph.* II, 4). And so matter can be affected only in ways that extension can: "All the properties that we clearly perceive in it (matter) are reduced to one, viz., that it can be divided and moved according to its parts so that it is capable of all those affections that we perceive can follow from the movement of its parts" (*Pr. Ph.* II, 23). It also follows that matter is infinitely divisible, even physically, and indeed that this division is sometimes fully actuated. Thus, although Descartes holds that the world is made up of small bodies (of three different sizes), *he is not an atomist:* "We also know that atoms, or parts of matter that are by nature indivisible, cannot exist" (*Pr. Ph.* II, 20). (Certain Cartesians, however, such as Huygens, quickly reverted to atomism.)

Nor . . . does Descartes admit a vacuum. But how, in a world that is a plenum and without the admission of real condensation and rarefaction, is local motion possible? Descartes explains this by supposing that all motion is circular: "[It happens] in this way: one body expels another from the place that it is entering, and this in turn expels another, and another, and so on until the last one to be moved moves into the place left by the first at the very moment that it becomes vacant" (*Pr. Ph.* II, 33). A difficulty arises if the circle is not perfect since an actual division to infinity, which Descartes calls "indefinite," must be supposed: "Although we are not in a position to understand how this indefinite division happens, there can be no doubt that it does happen" (*Pr. Ph.* II, 35). (But clearly a division that is both actual and indefinite [even infinite] is contradictory.)

Descartes says that local motion is simply "the removal of

one part of matter, or of one body, from the vicinity of the bodies that immediately border on it and are thought of as being in a state of rest, to the vicinity of others" (*ibid.*, 25). This *movement* (and also the state of rest) is simply a *mode of body* (*ibid.*, 27). In general, a mode is what is present in a substance—in this respect it is the same as an attribute— on the basis of which the substance is classified as "such and such." (It is therefore called a "quality," but not a "real" quality.) A subject can vary with respect to a mode, and it is in this respect that a mode differs from an attribute (*Pr. Ph.* I, 56). Motion, however, has a reality such that it needed to be created by God in the beginning, and it has a definite "quantity" that is maintained through the ordinary assistance of God: "God . . . conserves the same amount of movement and rest in the totality of matter as he put there in the beginning" (*Pr. Ph.* II, 36). The quantity of motion is in proportion to the quantity of matter and its velocity (expressed nowadays in the formula: quantity of motion = mv, though it is now thought of as a "vector" not a "scalar" magnitude . . .); and one and the same quantity of motion, once created, is conserved. The quantity of motion, while remaining the same in its totality, can be distributed in different ways among different bodies. Descartes then established the following principle (later called the principle of inertia): a body of itself remains in its own state of motion (or of rest) and this motion is in a straight line (*ibid.*, 37 and 39). The particular causes that give rise to changes in particular movements are mutually colliding bodies. In these collisions, the total quantity of motion remains the same but the distribution varies, one body acquiring as much as the other loses: "All the particular causes of changes in bodies come under this third law, at least with respect to causes that are themselves corporeal" (*ibid.*, 40). . . .

Motion of this kind, which alone is clearly perceived and therefore possible, explains everything that happens in the corporeal world. It is also the cause of the division of bodies and their shapes: "All the properties that we clearly perceive in it [matter] are reduced to one, viz., that it can be divided and moved according to its parts so that it is capable of all those affections that we perceive can follow from the movement of its parts. A division that happens only in thought changes nothing. But every alteration of matter, or diversity in all its forms, depends on motion" (*ibid.*, 23). To put Descartes's propositions in Scholastic terms, local motion is not only the efficient cause of division but also its formal cause. Hence . . . the state of rest is sufficient for a single body to result from two adjacent ones, for the state of rest is the strongest of bonds, and proximity and continuity are conflated. In extended being, attention is paid not to the notion of *being* but only to the notion of being *extended*. For this reason, and for this reason alone, it is possible to admit that two things could come from one, or one from two, without the change's being seen as truly intrinsic. . . . (Cf. Descartes's reply to Burman: "It is all the same to me how others define them; I call things continuous when the surfaces of two bodies are immediately joined to each other so that both move by one and the same movement or both are at rest; things that are otherwise are contiguous.")

It is clear that Descartes's first concern is not with the denial of the activity of bodies but only with their intrinsic mutability. In addition, his teaching on Mechanicism is concerned with "becoming" as such in the natural order, which is regarded as consisting solely of local motion and its effects. But it must be added that, on a secondary level, Descartes does not deny all activity to bodies. As far as I know, there is not one text propounding such a theory. . . . On the contrary, he frequently speaks unhesitatingly of their causality, force, action, etc. It would be impossible to cite all the innumerable texts that bear this out.

Certainly he accepted the principle of causality as beyond doubt. He used it as a basis for argument, for example, in the *Third Meditation*, and he more than once claimed: "There must be at least as much in the cause as in the effect" (AT VII, 49). In the collision of bodies, a *new* effect arises in the body inasmuch as it begins to move. The reason for this is that motion, as a mode of a body, cannot migrate from subject to subject. On this Descartes wrote to H. More: "You are right in observing that motion as a mode of a body

cannot pass from one to another. But nor have I written this"
(AT V, 404).[4] There is therefore no purely passive transference of motion; in a collision, a cause must be at work. Nor
is the effect attributed to God alone, for a little before this
he had written: "The transference that I call motion is not at
a lower level of being than is shape: it is in fact a mode of
body. But the moving force can belong either to God who
conserves the same degree of transference in matter as he
placed in it at the first moment of creation, or to a created
substance such as our mind, or to any other thing to which he
has given the power of moving bodies" (*ibid.*, 403 ff.). He
does not say that this "other thing" is a body, but this nonetheless seems to be supposed. It is only on such a supposition
that the following is intelligible: "When one body *makes
another move,* it loses as much movement as it *gives* to it"
(AT V, 135—my emphasis). A little farther on in the text he
says: "it transfers its movement." All of this points to an
activity on the part of a body. The same interpretation can
be given to what he says in many places about the force of
bodies in moving and resisting, "which consists in the power
of any body to act on another or to resist the action of the
other" (*Pr. Ph.* II, 43). Moreover, "it is necessary to measure
only the degree of the forces in each, either to move or to
resist movement" (*ibid.*, 45). The same idea is found in
many other passages.

Furthermore, a body can in fact act on the soul. In the
Sixth Meditation, he argues from the passivity of the senses
that there must be an active faculty at work on the senses
and this faculty is not in the mind, nor in God nor in an
angel, but in bodies. In this way the existence of bodies is
proved (AT VII, 79; cf. *Pr. Ph.* II, 1).

Descartes is therefore not at all inclined to deny the activity of bodies. But . . . he has to restrict this activity to locomotive forces since local motion is the only change that he

---

[4] This, in my opinion, is the way in which this text is to be understood. It is made rather more obscure in that Descartes says that
even in one body motion is continuously changing; but this can also
be understood from what he adds, namely, that their *power* of moving remains the same.

recognizes in bodies. Even in this class he admits only one
form of activity, viz., the kind found when bodies in motion
collide. Thus Descartes completely rejects the hypothesis of
universal attraction put forward by Roberval: "The view that
he goes on to propose, that there is a certain property in the
individual parts of corporeal matter by virtue of which they
are borne towards one another and mutually attract one another, is most absurd" (AT IV, 401). Among other difficulties in this view, Descartes points out that knowledge of the
body that is absent would have to be presupposed in the
body that is the source of the attraction. . . .

II. BASES OF DESCARTES'S VIEW

The true nature of Descartes's teaching will be even clearer
if we consider its bases. His position on the problem of change
is not the same as that of the ancient atomists. Their view
had been followed by Aristotle's explanation of how true intrinsic change is possible, and Descartes knew that theory.
But, because he did not understand it, . . . and since he
rejected the Peripatetic view on metaphysical grounds, no
solution was left for Parmenides' problem except a mechanistic one. Hence, the most important ground of his teaching
is again metaphysical, though other reasons came to be given
as well.

Descartes rejected the elements of the Peripatetic solution,
namely, substantial forms and real qualities ("which I abhor,"
as he wrote to Ciermans—AT II, 74). But he rejected them
because he failed to understand the true Aristotelian and
Thomistic system. In this system both substantial and accidental form are not *ens quod* but *ens quo*, and it is here
precisely that a solution to Parmenides' dilemma is provided.
What is totally new after the change, viz., the substantial or
accidental act, is nothing but *ens quo*. Thus, only what is
composed of potency and act—*ens quod*—can be properly said
to *become*, and this is not so of the new form in question. If
this form existed in a proper sense and consequently came
into existence in change, then this coming into existence

would take us back to Parmenides' dilemma: it comes either from being or from nonbeing; it must therefore come from nothing, at least if we wish to avoid an impossible infinite regress. (Cf. Aristotle, *Met.* VII, 8, especially 1033 b4 seq.; St. Thomas, commentary on this text, lect. 7, Cathala 1420; *Met.* XII, 3, 1070 a2–4; St. Thomas, lect. 3, Cathala 2443. . . .) But Descartes did not understand this. He thought of substantial forms and also real qualities as beings in the strict sense, i.e. as complete substances; and in this way he confused *ens quod* and *ens quo* (though, admittedly, these terms are not to be found in his writings).

Consider the following passages. Concerning substantial forms Descartes wrote to Regius . . . :

> When we reject substantial form, what we mean is some kind of substance joined to matter and forming with it a whole that is merely corporeal; and which, no less or even more than matter, is really a substance, or a thing existing in its own right (*per se subsistens*), since it is said to be an act and matter a potency. [AT III, 402]

And he has this to say about qualities. In the Replies to the Sixth Set of Objections, real accidents are rejected on the ground that they would be substances: "Real accidents are a contradiction in terms, because whatever is real can exist separately from any other subject; but whatever can exist separately in this way is a substance not an accident" (AT VII, 434). When he gives his well-known analysis of the quality of gravity in these Replies to Objections and maintains that it would have to be a substance—in fact, a conscious soul —he describes the origin of his opinion as follows: "For example, when I thought of gravity as some kind of real quality, present in solid bodies, although I called it a *quality* in referring it to the bodies in which it was present, still I thought that it was a substance because I added the word *real*" (AT VII, 441). About qualities in general, he makes the same point: "In regard to the different qualities of bodies such as weight, heat, and the rest, although we have called them qualities, we have imagined them as real, that is, as having an

existence distinct from bodies, and consequently as being substances" (AT III, 667). . . . Cf. also his letter to Mersenne
(AT III, 648) and to "Hyperaspistes" (AT III, 430).[5]

It is therefore clear that Descartes's failure to understand
the idea of *ens quo* meant that he could not accept the
Aristotelian solution. For, in this way, the whole of Parmenides' puzzle returns: *these* forms and *these* qualities, if they
arise, can come only from nothing by means of a true creation. Descartes himself put forward this conclusion as an
insoluble difficulty for Aristotle. In the letter to Regius cited
before, he writes:

> The reasons or demonstrations of Physics against sub-
> stantial forms, which in our judgment definitely compel
> a mind eager for truth, are in the first place these a priori
> metaphysical or theological ones. It is clearly contradic-
> tory for a fresh substance to exist unless it is created by
> God. But every day we see many of these forms that are
> called substantial beginning to exist, although the people
> who think they are substances do not think that they are
> created by God. [AT III, 505][6]

Thus Descartes himself clearly indicates the metaphysical and
a priori grounds of the new opinion that rejects all intrinsic

---

[5] Gilson rightly says in regard to this opinion of Descartes's: "It
is not surprising that Descartes should have conceived dislike and
indeed horror of such a monster. But the point is well taken that
it was he himself who gave birth to it" (*Études sur le rôle de la
pensée médiévale* . . . , "La Critique cartésienne des formes sub-
stantielles," p. 163).

[6] At the same time and for the same reason, Gassendi also rejected
substantial changes. In his *Physics*, Section I, Book 7 (*Opera
Omnia*, Lyons, 1658, I, p. 467), the third chapter is entitled,
"Whether in generation there arises a form that is a new substance."
Because of many difficulties in regard to "drawing out of forms," he
rejects the Scholastic theory. He asks "whether such a form is some
new substance or substantial entity distinct from matter; whether it
is a new quality, or a new way for a substance or for matter to exist"
(p. 467). Gassendi did not understand the true meaning of *ens quo*,
which for him was only a "mode"; hence, the emergence of a substance would involve creation. Before Descartes, Gorlaeus and Basso
had done the same; and, after him, Leibniz and even some Scholastics—for example, Maignan.

change, and he is forced to adopt Mechanicism and place all "becoming" in local motion alone. But it is clear that the antinomy between this metaphysical position and experience, which testifies to qualities and their changes, remains. Faced with finding a solution to the antinomy, Descartes based his attempt on his theory of knowledge, which he then brought into play. And this is the second source, also a priori, of his Mechanicism.

We may recall that Descartes's first principle of knowledge is the principle of clear and distinct ideas:

A perception on which a certain and incontrovertible judgment can be based must not only be clear but also distinct. I describe as clear that which is present and open to an attentive mind, just as we say that we see things clearly when they are before our open eyes and have a sufficiently strong and direct impact on our vision. But I speak of it as distinct when, being clear, it is marked off and sharply defined from all others in such a way that it contains (in itself) only what is clear. [*Pr. Ph.* I, 45]

Applying this principle to corporeal things, Descartes reaches the general conclusion: "At least everything that I understand clearly and distinctly—that is, everything, generally speaking, that is included in the *object of pure mathematics* —is found in them (i.e. in corporeal things)" (*Sixth Meditation*, AT VII, 80—my emphasis). Besides extension, which would be the essence of bodies, he concludes more particularly that the following are real: parts and their position, divisibility, movements in place, to the extent that these are amenable to mathematical treatment, shapes, numbers, duration, and "the like" (*Pr. Ph.* I, 48, 55, 65, 69, and in many other places).

Our bodily feelings, appetites, and external sensations are in a different class. When, in the *Sixth Meditation*, Descartes sets out to prove the existence of bodies, it is immediately taken to be certain, on the basis of clear and distinct ideas, that at least the mathematical properties of bodies are *able* to exist: "At the very least I know that these [material things], in so far as they are the object of pure mathematics, are able to exist, since I perceive them clearly and distinctly" (AT VII, 71). . . . He then proves that these objects *must* exist as well (because nature teaches us this): he thinks that this is true in regard to the objects of the feelings in question—in regard to proper sensibles also—but only in so far as they are causes of these feelings, their nature remaining unknown. For, in regard to them, there is no clear and distinct perception. They are known in an entirely different way, if indeed they are known at all:

> Especially if we take into account that we know in one way what size is in a body which is seen, or shape, or movement (local movement at least, for, in imagining other kinds of movement, philosophers make it less intelligible to themselves), or position, or duration, or number, and the like, which as we have already said are clearly perceived in bodies; but it is in a very different way that we know what color is in the same body, or pain, or odor. . . . [*Pr. Ph.* I, 69]

This different way of knowing sensible qualities and their changes is so confused that it no longer seems right to call it knowledge. Thus, in the *Third Meditation*, he continues, after his account of mathematical notions: "But I can think of other things, such as light and colors, sounds, odors, tastes, heat and cold, and other tactile qualities, only in a very confused and obscure way, *so that I do not know whether they are true or false, i.e. whether the ideas that I have of them are ideas of real things or not*" (AT VII, 43). It is clear from what I have italicized here that Descartes denies the status of knowledge to sensations of these qualities (except for his admission that there are unknown causes of the sensations). His reason is that they are not sufficiently clear and distinct to allow for a certain and incontrovertible judgment on their proper objects. . . .

Beginning a priori with the principle of clear and distinct ideas, Descartes wishes to maintain that only the elements of the mechanistic theory, the mathematical elements, are verified in the natural order. For all real things he demands the clarity of mathematics that permits a priori knowledge to be established. He then thinks that the antinomy has been solved by denying the status of genuine knowledge to experience that seems to testify to qualities and their changes, for, in his opinion, it does not stand up to epistemological inquiry. Thus satisfied, he is able to apply the mechanistic theory exclusively to the explanation of phenomena. This is to be done by a priori knowledge; for, as Descartes often repeats, we are to know effects from causes understood a priori and not to come to know unknown causes from their effects. In this inquiry, experience is necessary only if we are to know which effects, among numerous possibilities, are in fact realized. (Cf. *Pr. Ph.* III, 4, 46, and many other places.)

It is worth noting that in the end Descartes sometimes applies the first principle of Parmenides: that to understand is the same as to be. Parmenides applied it in such a way that only what is clear both to imagination and understanding is recognized as real being; Descartes takes the same position at least in regard to the corporeal world. He differs from Parmenides in admitting infinite or indefinite extension, but in this he is in agreement with another Eleatic—Melissus. With Parmenides and against Democritus, he maintains the impossibility of a vacuum. Yet he safeguards appearances in terms of local motion by admitting circular movements, to which he thought a plenum no obstacle. . . .

We may also note that the distinction between a twofold object of sensations—proper and common sensibles according to the Scholastics, secondary and primary qualities according to modern philosophers—was clearly formulated by Descartes prior to Locke. Furthermore, we may note that this distinction arises not from physical experimentation but from the different ways in which consciousness testifies that the qualities are known. The account of the distinction that we find in many modern philosophers was accurately pointed out by ancient thinkers, and we may get a better understanding of the modern opinion from a consideration of the ancient opinion. Democritus has this to say: "There are two forms of knowledge, one genuine, the other spurious; all these belong

to the spurious class: sight, hearing, smell, taste, touch. The
genuine form is altogether different" (Diels, *Vorsokratiker* II,
55 B, fr. 11). In this passage, things that are in the senses
without the intellect having a clear idea of them—secondary
qualities—are not so much said to be obscure as they are to
be thought of as not truly knowledge. This is Descartes's position. He in fact calls them obscure, but he goes further and
denies that they have the quality of being cognitive of objects.

In Democritus (fr. 9, 117, 125), secondary qualities are
said to be only by *convention*; but atoms and the vacuum (i.e.
the elements of clear geometrical intuition), in truth, elsewhere, by nature. In the *Sixth Meditation*, Descartes says the
same:

> There are many other things which I seem to have been
> taught by *nature* but which all the same I have not re-
> ceived from her, but from a *habit* of making hasty judg-
> ments. It easily happens, then, that they are all false.
> Consider, for example, the judgment that all space in
> which there is nothing that affects my senses is a vacuum;
> or that in a body that is warm, for example, there is
> something entirely similar to the idea of heat that I
> have; that in a white thing or a green thing there is the
> same whiteness or greenness that I perceive; that in a
> bitter thing or a sweet thing there is the same taste, and
> so on for the rest. [AT VII, 83]

Descartes differs from Democritus in rejecting the vacuum,
but he is in perfect agreement with him in regard to primary
and secondary qualities, even to using terms (italicized in
the quotation) that correspond perfectly to Democritus'.

This is why, as a solution of the antinomy of Mechanicism,
objects of mathematics (extension, etc.) are admitted as true,
and secondary qualities are rejected. For the first, there are
mathematical judgments that are certain; for the second,
there is no genuine knowledge but only *putative* knowledge
based on custom (on "youthful prejudices," in Descartes's
phrase). The latter are lacking in just what the former possess—a priori knowledge based on clear judgments. . . .

[It is true that] before attempting to establish his metaphysical and epistemological principles, Descartes had been concerned for many years with the explanation of appearances by means of mathematical principles. He did this in practice, not in theory—in fact, not by right. But, once he had established and proved—as he thought—these a priori principles, he judged that he could then apply them with certainty and thereby construct the edifice of knowledge. . . . And this, it seems to me, is the origin of something that Descartes often urges in favor of his principles, namely, their suitability for safeguarding appearances. . . .

III. SUMMARY

From this historical survey, it is clear that Mechanicism is a system that is established a priori (1) from metaphysical arguments and (2) from epistemological arguments and (3) that it is applied to explain experience—to safeguard appearances. . . . What has been said about the Mechanicism of modern philosophers, especially Descartes, leads us to the assertion made before about the Mechanicism of the ancients: that its essence consists, not in the denial of the activity of bodies, but (negatively) in the denial of all intrinsic changeability and (positively) in the affirmation of the possibility of local motion alone. It is clear that the new Mechanicism is also established in an a priori way. Descartes accepts it for the following metaphysical reason: if intrinsic mutability were granted, then the new form that emerges in such a change must be supposed—falsely, however—to be *ens quod* and created therefore from nothing. There was a further influential a priori reason, perhaps in Descartes and certainly in later philosophers, taken from a theory of knowledge. According to this argument, the only real things are those which, as the objects of mathematics, belong to a priori knowledge. The Greeks also used this argument, but for them it seems to have been secondary. . . . Among modern philosophers who agreed on Mechanicism as the basic philosophical tenet of their system, disputes later broke out with regard to the activity of bodies (which it seemed at first could be only locomotive activity). The questions at issue were whether activity was to be admitted in general, and also whether, in addition to activity operating in collisions, other forms—with powers either of attracting or repelling—were necessary. But this debate is of secondary importance.

BIBLIOGRAPHY

For a comprehensive bibliography of books and papers on Descartes, see Professor Gregor Sebba's *Bibliographia Cartesiana: A Critical Guide to the Descartes Literature 1800–1960* (The Hague: Martinus Nijhoff, 1964). The references that follow, limited for the most part to writings in English, may be of some use to the reader. They represent a small proportion of the efforts expended in recent years on Descartes and the problems that he has bequeathed to us.

A. STANDARD EDITIONS

Oeuvres de Descartes, Vols. I–XII and *Supplément*, edited by Charles Adam and Paul Tannery. Paris: Léopold Cerf, 1897–1913. (The abbreviation "AT" is used in references.)

Descartes: Correspondance, Vols. I–VIII, edited by Charles Adam and Gérard Milhaud. Paris: Félix Alcan, Presses Universitaires de France, 1936–1963.

(The Pléiade *Descartes* is a convenient book containing selections, in French, from Descartes's works and letters. *Descartes: Oeuvres et Lettres*, edited by André Bridoux. Paris: Gallimard, 1953.)

B. SOME ENGLISH TRANSLATIONS

A Discourse on Method, Etc., by René Descartes, translated by John Veitch. Everyman's Library. London: J. M. Dent & Sons, Ltd., 1949.

The Philosophical Works of Descartes, Vols. I and II, translated by Elizabeth S. Haldane and G. R. T. Ross. Cambridge: Cambridge University Press, 1911–1912 and 1931. New York: Dover Publications, Inc., 1955. (The abbreviation "HR" is used in references.)

Descartes' Philosophical Writings, translated by Norman Kemp Smith. London: Macmillan & Co., Ltd., 1952. New York: The Modern Library.

Descartes: Philosophical Writings, translated by Elizabeth Anscombe and Peter Thomas Geach. Edinburgh: Thomas Nelson & Sons, Ltd., 1954.

Discourse on Method; Meditations; Rules for the Direction of the Mind, translated by Laurence J. Lafleur. New York and Indianapolis: The Liberal Arts Press and The Bobbs-Merrill Co., Inc., 1950–1961.

Descartes: Discourse on Method, Optics, Geometry, and Meteorology, translated by Paul J. Olscamp. Indianapolis: The Bobbs-Merrill Co., Inc., 1965.

C. SOME BOOKS IN FRENCH (SINCE 1945)

Ferdinand Alquié. *La Découverte métaphysique de l'homme chez Descartes*. Paris: Presses Universitaires de France, 1950.

Ferdinand Alquié. *Descartes; l'homme et l'oeuvre*. Paris: Hatier-Boivin, 1956.

Yvon Belaval. *Leibniz Critique de Descartes*. Paris: Gallimard, 1960.

Henri Gouhier. *La Pensée métaphysique de Descartes*. Paris: J. Vrin, 1962.

Henri Gouhier. *Les Premières Pensées de Descartes*. Paris: J. Vrin, 1958.

Martial Gueroult. *Descartes selon l'ordre des raisons*. Two vols. Paris: Aubier, 1953.

Martial Gueroult. *Nouvelles réflexions sur la preuve ontologique de Descartes*. Paris: J. Vrin, 1955.

Jean Laporte. *Le Rationalisme de Descartes*, 2nd ed. Paris: Presses Universitaires de France, 1950.

Henri Lefebvre. *Descartes.* Paris: Éditions Hier et Aujour-d'hui, 1947.

Roger Lefèvre. *La Bataille du "Cogito."* Paris: Presses Universitaires de France, 1960.

Roger Lefèvre. *Le Criticisme de Descartes.* Paris: Presses Universitaires de France, 1958.

Roger Lefèvre. *L'Humanisme de Descartes.* Paris: Presses Universitaires de France, 1957.

Roger Lefèvre. *La Métaphysique de Descartes.* Paris: Presses Universitaires de France, 1959.

Roger Lefèvre. *La Vocation de Descartes.* Paris: Presses Universitaires de France, 1956.

Geneviève Rodis-Lewis. *Descartes: Initiation à sa philosophie.* Paris: J. Vrin, 1964.

Geneviève Rodis-Lewis. *L'Individualité selon Descartes.* Paris: J. Vrin, 1950.

Geneviève Rodis-Lewis. *La Morale de Descartes.* Paris: Presses Universitaires de France, 1957.

Geneviève Rodis-Lewis. *Le Problème de l'inconscient et le Cartésianisme.* Paris: Presses Universitaires de France, 1950.

Jeanne Russier. *Sagesse cartésienne et religion.* Paris: Presses Universitaires de France, 1958.

Jules Vuillemin. *Mathématiques et métaphysique chez Descartes.* Paris: Presses Universitaires de France, 1960.

D. BOOKS IN ENGLISH

Albert G. A. Balz. *Cartesian Studies.* New York: Columbia University Press, 1951.

Albert G. A. Balz. *Descartes and the Modern Mind.* New Haven: Yale University Press, 1952.

L. J. Beck. *The Metaphysics of Descartes; A Study of the Meditations.* Oxford: Clarendon Press, 1965.

L. J. Beck. *The Method of Descartes; A Study of the Regulae.* Oxford: Clarendon Press, 1952.

Noam Chomsky. *Cartesian Linguistics.* New York: Harper & Row, 1966.

A. Boyce Gibson. *The Philosophy of Descartes*. London: Methuen & Co., Ltd., 1932.

Elizabeth S. Haldane. *Descartes: His Life and Times*. New York: E. P. Dutton & Co., 1905.

Harold H. Joachim. *Descartes's Rules for the Direction of the Mind*, edited by Errol E. Harris. London: George Allen & Unwin, Ltd., 1957.

S. V. Keeling. *Descartes*. London: Ernest Benn, Ltd., 1934.

Alexandre Koyré. *Newtonian Studies*, Ch. III, "Newton and Descartes." London: Chapman & Hall, 1965.

Norman Malcolm. *Dreaming*. New York: Humanities Press, 1959.

W. A. Merrylees. *Descartes: An Examination of Some Features of His Metaphysics and Method*. Melbourne: Melbourne University Press, 1934.

Richard H. Popkin. *The History of Scepticism from Erasmus to Descartes*. New York: Humanities Press, 1960.

H. A. Prichard. *Knowledge and Perception*. Oxford: Clarendon Press, 1950.

Leonora Davidson Cohen Rosenfield. *From Beast-Machine to Man-Machine: Animal Soul in French Letters from Descartes to La Mettrie*. New York: Oxford University Press, 1941.

Leon Roth. *Descartes' Discourse on Method*. Oxford: Clarendon Press, 1937.

Leon Roth. *Spinoza, Descartes, and Maimonides*. Oxford: Clarendon Press, 1924.

J. F. Scott. *The Scientific Work of René Descartes (1596–1650)*. London: Taylor & Francis, Ltd., 1952.

Norman Kemp Smith. *New Studies in the Philosophy of Descartes; Descartes as Pioneer*. London: Macmillan & Co., Ltd., 1952.

Norman Smith. *Studies in the Cartesian Philosophy*. London: Macmillan & Co., Ltd., 1902.

Marthinus Versfeld. *An Essay on the Metaphysics of Descartes*. London: Methuen & Co., 1940.

E. Articles in English (including articles since 1960).

1. Doubt concerning the Senses and the Argument from Dreaming

Virgil C. Aldrich. "DesCartes' Method of Doubt." *Philos. Sci.*, IV, 4, Oct. 1937, 395–411.

A. J. Ayer. "Professor Malcolm on Dreams." *Journ. Philos.*, LVII, 16, Aug. 1960, 517–535.

A. J. Ayer. "Rejoinder to Professor Malcolm." *Journ. Philos.*, LVIII, 11, May 1961, 297–299.

M. J. Baker. "Sleeping and Waking." *Mind*, LXIII, 252, Oct. 1954, 539–543.

O. K. Bouwsma. "Descartes' Evil Genius." *Philos. Rev.*, LVIII, 1, Jan. 1949, 141–151.

O. K. Bouwsma. "Des Cartes' Skepticism of the Senses." *Mind*, LIV, 216, Oct. 1945, 313–322.

O. K. Bouwsma. " 'On Many Occasions I Have In Sleep Been Deceived'—Descartes." *Proc. Amer. Philos. Assoc.*, XXX, 1956–1957, 25–44.

Robert L. Caldwell. "Malcolm and the Criterion of Sleep." *Austral. Journ.*, XLIII, 3, Dec. 1965, 339–352.

John V. Canfield. "Judgments in Sleep." *Philos. Rev.*, LXX, 2, April 1961, 224–230.

V. C. Chappell. "The Concept of Dreaming." *Philos. Quart.*, XIII, 52, July 1963, 193–213.

V. C. Chappell. "Critical Study: Dreaming. By Norman Malcolm." *Philos. Quart.*, XII, 47, April 1962, 178–185.

Charles S. Chihara. "What dreams are made on." *Theoria*, XXXI, 3, 1965, 145–158.

Ilham Dilman. "Professor Malcolm on Dreams." *Analysis*, XXVI, 4, March 1966, 129–134.

Donald Kalish. "Review: *Dreaming*. By Norman Malcolm." *Journ. Philos.*, LVII, 9, April 1960, 308–311.

Leonard Linsky. "Deception." *Inquiry*, VI, 2, Summer 1963, 157–169.

Margaret Macdonald. "Sleeping and Waking." *Mind*, LXII,
    246, April 1953, 202–215.
Norman Malcolm. "Dreaming and Skepticism." *Philos. Rev.*,
    LXV, 1, Jan. 1956, 14–37.
Norman Malcolm. "Professor Ayer on *Dreaming*." *Journ.
    Philos.*, LVIII, 11, May 1961, 294–297.
A. R. Manser. "Dreams." *Arist. Soc.*, S. V. XXX, 1956,
    208–228.
G. E. Moore. "Certainty." *Philosophical Papers*, 227–251.
Hans Neisser. "The Phenomenological Basis of Descartes'
    Doubt." *Philos. Phen. Res.*, XXV, 4, June 1965, 572–
    574.
John O. Nelson. "An Inconsistency in 'Dreaming.'" *Philos.
    Studies*, XV, 3, April 1964, 33–35.
L. E. Palmieri. "To Sleep, Perchance to Dream." *Philos.
    Phen. Res.*, XXII, 4, June 1962, 583–586.
D. F. Pears. "Professor Norman Malcolm: Dreaming." *Mind*,
    LXX, 278, April 1961, 145–163.
Richard H. Popkin. "Charron and Descartes: The Fruits of
    Systematic Doubt." *Journ. Philos.*, LI, 25, Dec. 1954,
    831–837.
H. Putnam. "Dreaming and 'Depth Grammar.'" *Analyt.
    Philos.*, I, 211–235.
Nicholas Rescher. "The Legitimacy of Doubt." *Rev. Meta.*,
    XIII, 2, Dec. 1959, 226–234.
Sibajiban. "Descartes' Doubt." *Philos. Phen. Res.*, XXIV, 1,
    Sept. 1963, 106–116.
F. A. Siegler. "Descartes' Doubts." *Mind*, LXXII, 286, April
    1963, 245–253.
Brian Smith. "Dreaming." *Austral. Journ.*, XLIII, 1, May
    1965, 48–57.
L. E. Thomas. "Dreams." *Arist. Soc.*, S. V. XXX, 1956, 197–
    207.
L. E. Thomas. "Waking and Dreaming." *Analysis*, XIII, 6,
    June 1953, 121–127.
W. von Leyden. "Descartes and Hobbes on Waking and
    Dreaming." *Revue Int. Philos.*, X, 35, 1956, 95–101.
Henry G. Wolz. "The Universal Doubt in the Light of Des-

cartes's Conception of Truth." *Mod. Schoolman*, XXVII, 4, May 1950, 253–279.

R. M. Yost, Jr. "Professor Malcolm on Dreaming and Skepticism." *Philos. Quart.*, IX, 35, April 1959, 142–151, and 36, July 1959, 231–243.

R. M. Yost, Jr., and Donald Kalish. "Miss Macdonald on Sleeping and Waking." *Philos. Quart.*, V, 19, April 1955, 109–124.

2. The *Cogito*

John Anderson. "The *Cogito* of Descartes." *Austral. Journ.*, XIV, 1, March 1936, 48–68.

A. J. Ayer. "Cogito, Ergo Sum." *Analysis*, XIV, 2, Dec. 1953, 27–31.

Robert N. Beck. "Descartes's *Cogito* Reexamined." *Philos. Phen. Res.*, XIV, 2, Dec. 1953, 212–220.

Arnold Berleant. "On the Circularity of the Cogito." *Philos. Phen. Res.*, XXVI, 3, March 1966, 431–433.

James D. Carney. "*Cogito, Ergo Sum* and *Sum Res Cogitans*." *Philos. Rev.*, LXXI, 4, Oct. 1962, 492–496.

Robert Champigny. "The Theatrical Aspect of the Cogito." *Rev. Meta.*, XII, 3, March 1959, 370–377.

Harry G. Frankfurt. "Descartes's Discussion of His Existence in the Second Meditation." *Philos. Rev.*, LXXV, 3, July 1966, 329–356.

Robert Grimm. "Cogito, ergo sum." *Theoria*, XXXI, 3, 1965, 159–173.

Jaakko Hintikka. "*Cogito, Ergo Sum*: Inference or Performance?" *Philos. Rev.*, LXXI, 1, Jan. 1962, 3–32.

Jaakko Hintikka. "*Cogito, Ergo Sum* as an Inference and a Performance." *Philos. Rev.*, LXXII, 4, Oct. 1963, 487–496.

Joseph Margolis. "I exist." *Mind*, LXXIII, 292, Oct. 1964, 571–574.

Richard W. Peltz. "The Logic of the *Cogito*." *Philos. Phen. Res.*, XXIII, 2, Dec. 1962, 256–262.

W. von Leyden. "*Cogito, Ergo Sum*." *Arist. Soc.*, LXIII, 1962–1963, 67–82.

Julius R. Weinberg. "*Cogito, Ergo Sum:* Some Reflections on Mr. Hintikka's Article." *Philos. Rev.,* LXXI, 4, Oct. 1962, 483–491.

3. The Truth of Clear and Distinct Perceptions and the Charge of Circularity

Edwin B. Allaire. "The Circle of Ideas and the Circularity of the *Meditations,*" *Dialogue,* V, 2, Sept. 1966, 131–153.

T. J. Cronin. "Eternal Truths in the Thought of Descartes and of His Adversary." *Journ. Hist. Ideas,* XXI, 4, Oct.–Dec. 1960, 553–559.

Willis Doney. "The Cartesian Circle." *Journ. Hist. Ideas,* XVI, 3, June 1955, 324–338.

Harry G. Frankfurt. "Descartes' Validation of Reason." *Amer. Philos. Quart.,* II, 2, April 1965, 149–156.

Harry G. Frankfurt. "Memory and the Cartesian Circle." *Philos. Rev.,* LXXI, 4, Oct. 1962, 504–511.

Alan Gewirth. "The Cartesian Circle." *Philos. Rev.,* L, 4, July 1941, 368–395.

A. Boyce Gibson. "The Eternal Verities and the Will of God in the Philosophy of Descartes." *Arist. Soc.,* XXX, 1929–1930, 31–54.

Norman Kretzmann. "On Rose's 'Cartesian Circle.'" *Philos. Phen. Res.,* XXVI, 1, Sept. 1965, 90–92.

O. A. Kubitz. "Scepticism and Intuition in the Philosophy of Descartes." *Philos. Rev.,* XLVIII, 5, Sept. 1939, 472–491.

M. J. Levett. "Note on the Alleged Cartesian Circle." *Mind,* XLVI, 182, April 1937, 206–213.

Leonard G. Miller. "Descartes, Mathematics, and God." *Philos. Rev.,* LXVI, 4, Oct. 1957, 451–465.

Roberts B. Owen. "Truth and Error in Descartes." *Studies Hist. Ideas,* I, 149–171.

Paul A. Reynolds. "Implication of Circularity in Descartes." *Philos. Rev.,* XLVIII, 4, July 1939, 423–427.

Beatrice K. Rome. "Created Truths and 'Causa Sui' in Descartes." *Philos. Phen. Res.,* XVII, 1, Sept. 1956, 66–78.

Lynn E. Rose. "The Cartesian Circle"; "Reply to Mr. Kretzmann." *Philos. Phen. Res.*, XXVI, 1, Sept. 1965, 80–89, 93.

Elizabeth G. Salmon. "The Cartesian Circle." *New Scholast.*, XII, 4, Oct. 1938, 378–391.

A. K. Stout. "The Alleged 'Petitio Principii' in Descartes' Appeal to the Veracity of God." *Congrès Descartes*, I, 125–131.

A. K. Stout. "The Basis of Knowledge in Descartes," I and II. *Mind*, XXXVIII, 151, July 1929, 330–342, and 152, Oct. 1929, 458–472.

Henry G. Wolz. "The Double Guarantee of Descartes' Ideas." *Rev. Meta.*, III, 4, June 1950, 471–489.

4. Arguments for the Existence of God

Raziel Abelson. "Not Necessarily." *Philos. Rev.*, LXX, 1, Jan. 1961, 67–84.

W. E. Abraham. "Is the Concept of Necessary Existence Self-Contradictory?" *Inquiry*, V, 2, Summer 1962, 143–157.

R. E. Allen. "The Ontological Argument." *Philos. Rev.*, LXX, 1, Jan. 1961, 56–66.

William P. Alston. "The Ontological Argument Revisited." *Philos. Rev.*, LXIX, 4, Oct. 1960, 452–474.

Kurt Baier. "Existence." *Arist. Soc.*, LXI, 1960–1961, 19–40.

Albert G. A. Balz. "Concerning the Ontological Argument." *Rev. Meta.*, VII, 2, Dec. 1953, 207–224.

T. Patterson Brown. "Professor Malcolm on 'Anselm's Ontological Arguments.'" *Analysis*, XXII, 1, Oct. 1961, 12–14.

Robert D. Carnes. "Descartes and the Ontological Argument." *Philos. Phen. Res.*, XXIV, 4, June 1964, 502–511.

Robert C. Coburn. "Professor Malcolm on God." *Austral. Journ.*, XLI, 2, Aug. 1963, 143–162.

J. N. Findlay. "Can God's Existence Be Disproved?" *Mind*, LVII, 226, April 1948, 176–183.

P. T. Geach. "Form and Existence." *Arist. Soc.*, LV, 1954–1955, 251–272.

Clyde Laurence Hardin. "An Empirical Refutation of the

Ontological Argument." *Analysis*, XXII, 1, Oct. 1961, 10–12.

Charles Hartshorne. "The Logic of the Ontological Argument." *Journ. Philos.*, LVIII, 17, Aug. 1961, 471–473.

Paul Henle. "Uses of the Ontological Argument." *Philos. Rev.*, LXX, 1, Jan. 1961, 102–109.

Desmond Paul Henry. "St. Anselm's Nonsense." *Mind*, LXXII, 285, Jan. 1963, 51–61.

W. C. Kneale. "Is Existence a Predicate?" *Read. Philos. Analysis*, 29–43.

A. M. MacIver. "A Note on the Ontological Proof." *Analysis*, VIII, 3, Jan. 1948, 48.

Norman Malcolm. "Anselm's Ontological Arguments." *Philos. Rev.*, LXIX, 1, Jan. 1960, 41–62.

Gareth B. Mathews. "On Conceivability in Anselm and Malcolm." *Philos. Rev.*, LXX, 1, Jan. 1961, 110–111.

Robert G. Miller. "The Ontological Argument in St. Anselm and Descartes." *Mod. Schoolman*, XXXII, 4, May 1955, 341–349; XXXIII, 1, Nov. 1955, 31–38.

G. E. Moore. "Is Existence a Predicate?" *Philos. Papers*, 115–126.

George Nakhnikian and W. Salmon. " 'Exists' as a Predicate." *Philos. Rev.*, LXVI, 4, Oct. 1957, 535–542.

Terence Penelhum. "On the Second Ontological Argument." *Philos. Rev.*, LXX, 1, Jan. 1961, 85–92.

R. F. Piper. "From Defect to Deity: A Restatement of Descartes' Second Argument for the Existence of God." *Congrès Descartes*, I, 118–124.

Alvin Plantinga. "A Valid Ontological Argument?" *Philos. Rev.*, LXX, 1, Jan. 1961, 93–101.

Nicholas Rescher. "The Ontological Proof Revisited." *Austral. Journ.*, XXXVI, 2, Aug. 1959, 138–148.

Jerome Shaffer. "Existence, Predication and the Ontological Argument." *Mind*, LXXI, 283, July 1962, 307–325.

Henry G. Wolz. "The Function of the Will in Descartes' Proofs for the Existence of God." *New Scholast.*, XX, 4, Oct. 1946, 295–322.

5. Substance, Mind and Body

B. M. Adkins. "The Dictum of Descartes." *B. J. Philos. Sci.*, III, 11, Nov. 1952, 259–260.

W. Ross Ashby. "Can a Mechanical Chess-Player Outplay its Designer?" *B. J. Philos. Sci.*, III, 9, May 1952, 44–57.

Edward G. Ballard. "Descartes' Revision of the Cartesian Dualism." *Philos. Quart.*, VII, 28, July 1957, 249–259.

Albert G. A. Balz. "Dualism in Cartesian Psychology and Epistemology." *Studies Hist. Ideas*, II, 85–157.

L. J. Beck. "Cogitatio in Descartes." *Cartesio nel terzo centenario . . .*, 41–52.

Henry R. Burke. "Substance and Accident in the Philosophy of Descartes." *New Scholast.*, X, 4, Oct. 1936, 338–382.

Dorothy Emmet. "Descartes on Body and Mind: After 300 Years." *Cambridge Journal*, IV, 2, Nov. 1950, 67–82.

Franklin Fearing. "René Descartes; A Study in the History of the Theories of Reflex Action." *Psychol. Rev.*, XXXVI, 4, July 1929, 375–388.

Keith Gunderson. "Descartes, La Mettrie, Language and Machines." *Philos.*, XXXIX, 149, July 1964, 193–222.

J. B. S. Haldane. "Reply to W. R. Ashby, The Mechanical Chessplayer." *B. J. Philos. Sci.*, III, 10, Aug. 1952, 189–191.

Geoffrey Jefferson. "René Descartes on the Localization of the Soul." *Irish Journ. Med. Sci.*, CCLXXXV, 285, Sept. 1949, 691–706.

Reginald O. Kapp. "Living and Lifeless Machines." *B. J. Philos. Sci.*, V, 18, Aug. 1954, 91–103.

Norman Malcolm. "Descartes's Proof that His Essence is Thinking." *Philos. Rev.*, LXXIV, 3, July 1965, 315–338.

T. R. Miles. "On the Difference Between Men and Machines." *B. J. Philos. Sci.*, VII, 28, Feb. 1957, 277–292.

Dickinson S. Miller. " 'Descartes' Myth' and Professor Ryle's Fallacy." *Journ. Philos.*, XLVIII, 9, April 1951, 270–280.

Leonard Pinsky. "Do Machines Think about Machines Thinking?" *Mind*, LX, 239, July 1951, 397–398.

M. H. Pirenne. "Descartes and the Body-Mind Problem in Physiology." *B. J. Philos. Sci.*, I, 1, May 1950, 43–59.

James B. Pratt. "Descartes and the Psychophysical Problem." *Congrès Descartes*, I, 167–172.

A. M. Ritchie. "Can Animals See? A Cartesian Query." *Arist. Soc.*, LXIV, 1963–1964, 221–242.

Jerome Shaffer. "Persons and Their Bodies." *Philos. Rev.*, LXXV, 1, Jan. 1966, 59–77.

Thomas S. Szasz. "Men and Machines." *B. J. Philos. Sci.*, VIII, 32, Feb. 1958, 310–317.

Nigel Walker. "The Definition of Psychosomatic Disorder." *B. J. Philos. Sci.*, VI, 24, Feb. 1956, 265–299.

William P. D. Wightman. "Note on Descartes and Psychosomatic Medicine." *B. J. Philos. Sci.*, VII, 27, Nov. 1956, 234–235.

Ledger Wood. "Descartes' Philosophy of Mind." *Philos. Rev.*, XLI, 5, Sept. 1932, 466–477.

6. Clear and Distinct Ideas and Method

Ralph M. Blake. "Note on the Use of the Term 'idée' prior to Descartes." *Philos. Rev.*, XLVIII, 5, Sept. 1939, 532–535.

Ralph M. Blake. "The Rôle of Experience in Descartes' Theory of Method." *Philos. Rev.*, XXXVIII, 2, March 1929, 125–143, and 3, May 1929, 201–218.

Carl B. Boyer. "Descartes and the Geometrization of Algebra." *Amer. Math. Monthly*, LXVI, 5, May 1959, 390–393.

Julian L. Coolidge. "The Origin of Analytic Geometry." *Osiris*, I, 1936, 231–250.

A. C. Crombie. "Some Aspects of Descartes' Attitude to Hypothesis and Experiment." *Travaux Hist. Sci.*, XI.

Alan Gewirth. "Clearness and Distinctness in Descartes." *Philos.*, XVIII, 69, April 1943, 17–36.

Alan Gewirth. "Experience and the Non-Mathematical in the Cartesian Method." *Journ. Hist. Ideas*, II, 2, April 1941, 183–210.

A. Boyce Gibson. "The *Regulae* of Descartes." *Mind*, VII, 26, April 1898, 145–158, and 27, July 1898, 332–363.

John Hartland-Swann. "Descartes' 'Simple Natures'". *Philos.*, XXII, 82, July 1947, 139–152.

Laurence J. Lafleur. "Descartes and Scientific Presuppositions." *Personalist*, XXXV, 1, Winter 1954, 25–31.

Jean LeBlond. "Cartesian Method and Classical Logic." *Mod. Schoolman*, XV, 1, Nov. 1937, 4–6.

James Wilkinson Miller. "Descartes's Conceptualism." *Rev. Meta.*, IV, 4, Dec. 1950, 239–246.

James Lockhardt Mursell. "The Function of Intuition in Descartes' Philosophy of Science." *Philos. Rev.*, XXVIII, 4, July 1919, 391–409.

J. A. Passmore. "Descartes, the British Empiricists, and Formal Logic." *Philos. Rev.*, LXII, 4, Oct. 1953, 545–553.

Elizabeth G. Salmon. "Mathematical Roots of Cartesian Metaphysics." *New Scholast.*, XXXIX, 2, April 1965, 158–169.

A. J. Snow. "Descartes' Method and the Revival of Interest in Mathematics." *Monist*, XXXIII, 4, Oct. 1923, 611–617.

Otis Monroe Walter, Jr. "Descartes on Reasoning." *Speech Monographs*, XVIII, 1, March 1951, 47–53.

J. N. Wright. "The Method of Descartes." *Philos. Quart.*, V, 18, Jan. 1955, 78–82.

Ledger Wood. "Descartes on the Structure of Knowledge." *Sophia*, I, 14, Jan.–June 1946, 6–20.

7. Extended Substance and Physics

E. J. Aiton. "The Cartesian Theory of Gravity." *Annals Sci.*, XV, 1, March 1959, 27–49.

E. J. Aiton. "Descartes's Theory of the Tides." *Annals Sci.*, XI, 4, Dec. 1955, 337–348.

E. J. Aiton. "The Vortex Theory of the Planetary Motions— I." *Annals Sci.*, XIII, 4, Dec. 1957, 249–264.

Carl B. Boyer. "Descartes and the Radius of the Rainbow." *Isis*, XLIII, 132, July 1952, 95–98.

Gerd Buchdahl. "The Relevance of Descartes's Philosophy

for Modern Philosophy of Science." *B. J. Hist. Sci.*, I, 3, June 1963, 227–249.

A. C. Crombie. "Descartes on Method and Physiology." *Cambridge Journ.*, V, 2, Nov. 1951, 178–186.

J. Grundy. "Descartes and Atomism." *Nature*, CLXXIII, 4393, Jan. 1954, 89.

A. Rupert Hall. "Cartesian Dynamics." *Archive Hist. Exact Sci.*, I, 2, Feb. 1961, 172–178.

S. V. Keeling. "Cartesian Mechanism." *Philos.*, IX, 33, Jan. 1934, 51–66.

B. M. Laing. "Descartes on Material Things." *Philos.*, XVI, 64, Oct. 1941, 398–411.

Peter G. Lucas. "Descartes and the Wax: A Rejoinder to Mr. Smart." *Philos. Quart.*, I, 4, July 1951, 348–352.

Anthony Quinton. "Matter and Space." *Mind*, LXXII, 291, July 1964, 332–352.

J. J. C. Smart. "Descartes and the Wax." *Philos. Quart.*, I, 1, Oct. 1950, 50–57.

A. K. Stout. "Descartes' Proof of the Existence of Matter." *Mind*, XLI, 162, April 1932, 191–207.

Patrick Suppes. "Descartes and the Problem of Action at a Distance." *Journ. Hist. Ideas*, XV, 1, Jan. 1954, 146–152.

Rufus Suter. "Science Without Experiment; A Study of Descartes." *Scient. Monthly*, LVIII, April 1944, 265–268.

John Wild. "The Cartesian Deformation of the Structure of Change and its Influence on Modern Thought." *Philos. Rev.*, L. 1, Jan. 1941, 36–59.

Henry G. Wolz. "The Will as a Factor in Descartes' Proof for the Existence of Material Things." *New Scholast.*, XXII, 2, April 1948, 209–226.

F. Wootton. "The Physical Work of Descartes." *Sci. Progress*, XXI, 83, Jan. 1927, 457–458.

J. N. Wright. "Descartes and the Wax: Rejoinder to Mr. Smart." *Philos. Quart.*, I, 4, July 1951, 352–355.

8. Comparisons

Nigel Abercrombie. "Cartesianism and Classicism." *Mod. Lang. Rev.*, XXXI, 3, July 1936, 358–376.

Nigel Abercrombie. "Saint Augustine and the Cartesian Metaphysics." *St. A. and Fr. Class. Thought*, 57–90.

E. J. Aiton. "Newton and the Cartesians." *School Sci. Rev.*, XL, 1959, 406–413.

Albert G. A. Balz. "Concerning the Thomistic and Cartesian Dualisms: A Rejoinder to Professor Mourant." *Journ. Philos.*, LIV, 12, June 1957, 383–390.

Jonathan Bennett. "A Note on Descartes and Spinoza." *Philos. Rev.*, LXXIV, 3, July 1965, 379–380.

Robert E. Cushman. "Barth's Attack Upon Cartesianism and the Future in Theology." *Journ. Relig.*, XXXVI, 4, Oct. 1956, 207–223.

Joshua C. Gregory. "Cudworth and Descartes." *Philos.*, VIII, 32, Oct. 1933, 454–467.

Ronald Grimsley. "Kierkegaard and Descartes." *Journ. Hist. Philos.*, IV, 1, Jan. 1966, 31–41.

Reginald Jackson. "The Doctrine of Substance in Descartes and Spinoza." *Austral. Journ.*, IV, 3, Sept. 1926, 205–211.

T. A. Kantonen. "The Influence of Descartes on Berkeley." *Philos. Rev.*, XLIII, 5, Sept. 1934, 483–500.

Jean-Marc Laporte. "Husserl's Critique of Descartes." *Philos. Phen. Res.*, XXIII, 3, March 1963, 335–352.

Robert McRae. " 'Idea' as a Philosophical Term in the Seventeenth Century." *Journ. Hist. Ideas*, XXVI, 2, April–June 1965, 175–190.

Robert McRae. "The Unity of the Sciences: Bacon, Descartes, and Leibniz." *Journ. Hist. Ideas*, XVIII, 1, Jan. 1957, 27–48.

James A. McWilliams. "Aristotelian and Cartesian Motion." *New Scholast.*, XVII, 4, Oct. 1943, 307–321.

John A. Mourant. "Cartesian Man and Thomistic Man." *Journ. Philos.*, LIV, 12, June 1957, 373–382.

John W. Nason. "Leibniz's Attack on the Cartesian Doctrine

of Extension." *Journ. Hist. Ideas*, VII, 4, Oct. 1946, 447–483.

Merle L. Perkins. "Descartes and the Abbé de Saint-Pierre." *Mod. Lang. Quart.*, XIX, 4, Dec. 1958, 294–302.

Leonora Cohen Rosenfield. "Peripatetic Adversaries of Cartesianism in 17th Century France." *Rev. Relig.*, XXII, 1–2, Nov. 1957, 14–40.

Leon Roth. "Spinoza and Cartesianism." *Mind*, XXXII, 125, Jan. 1923, 12–37; 126, April 1923, 160–178.

Danton B. Sailor. "Cudworth and Descartes." *Journ. Hist. Ideas*, XXIII, 1, Jan.–March 1962, 133–140.

J. E. Saveson. "Descartes' Influence on John Smith, Cambridge Platonist." *Journ. Hist. Ideas*, XX, 2, April 1959, 258–263.

J. E. Saveson. "Differing Reactions to Descartes Among the Cambridge Platonists." *Journ. Hist. Ideas*, XXI, 4, Oct.–Dec. 1960, 560–567.

Dudley Shapere. "Descartes and Plato." *Journ. Hist. Ideas*, XXIV, 4, Oct.–Dec. 1963, 572–576.

Norman J. Wells. "Descartes and the Scholastics Briefly Revisited." *New Scholast.*, XXXV, 2, April 1961, 172–190.

H. A. Wolfson. "Causality and Freedom in Descartes, Leibniz, and Hume." *Freedom and Experience*, 97–114.

Benjamin M. Woodbridge. "The *Discours de la méthode* and the Spirit of the Renaissance." *Rom. Rev.*, XXIV, 2, April–June 1933, 136–142.

John W. Yolton. "Locke and the Seventeenth-Century Logic of Ideas." *Journ. Hist. Ideas*, XVI, 4, Oct. 1955, 431–452.

9. General and Particular

E. M. Adams. "Cartesianism in Ethics." *Philos. Phen. Res.*, XVI, 3, March 1956, 353–366.

Angus Armitage. "René Descartes (1596–1650) and the Early Royal Society." *Notes Royal Society*, VIII, 1, Oct. 1950, 1–19.

Bertrand Augst. "Descartes's Compendium of Music." *Journ. Hist. Ideas*, XXVI, 1, Jan.–March 1965, 119–132.

Albert G. A. Balz. "Descartes after Three Centuries." *Journ. Philos.*, XXXV, 7, March 1938, 169–179.

J. F. Bannan. "Contemporary French Readings of Descartes." *Rev. Meta.*, XIII, 3, March 1960, 412–438.

George Boas. "Homage to Descartes." *Philos. Phen. Res.*, XI, 2, Dec. 1950, 149–163.

Émile Boutroux. "Descartes and Cartesianism." *Cambridge Mod. Hist.*, IV, 776–799.

A. C. Crombie. "Descartes." *Sci. Amer.*, CCI, 4, Oct. 1959, 160–173.

Robert Cumming. "Descartes' Provisional Morality." *Rev. Meta.*, IX, 2, Dec. 1955, 207–235.

Hugh M. Davidson. "Descartes and the Utility of the Passions." *Rom. Rev.*, LI, 1, Feb. 1960, 15–26.

Lewis S. Feuer. "Anxiety and Philosophy: the Case of Descartes." *Amer. Imago*, XX, 4, Winter 1963, 411–449.

Lewis S. Feuer. "The Dreams of Descartes." *Amer. Imago*, XX, 1, Spring 1963, 3–26.

Desmond J. Fitzgerald. "Descartes: Defender of the Faith." *Thought*, XXXIV, 134, Autumn 1959, 383–404.

Iago Galdstone. "Descartes and Modern Psychiatric Thought." *Isis*, XXXV, 100, Spring 1944, 118–128.

A. Boyce Gibson. "Descartes." *Philos.*, X, 40, Oct. 1935, 428–440.

S. V. Keeling. "Descartes." *Proc. Brit. Acad.*, XXXIV, 1948, 57–81.

Richard Kennington. "Descartes' 'Olympica.'" *Social Res.*, XXVIII, 2, Summer 1961, 171–204.

Alexandre Koyré. "Descartes After Three Hundred Years." *Buffalo Studies*, XIX, 1, 1951, 81–113.

R. E. Langer. "René Descartes." *Amer. Math. Monthly*, XLIV, 8, Oct. 1937, 495–512.

Leon Roth. "Cartesian Studies." *Cambridge Journ.*, VII, 1953–1954, 466–475.

Leon Roth. "The Discourse on Method, 1637–1937." *Mind*, XLVI, 181, Jan. 1937, 32–43.

Stephen Schönberger. "A Dream of Descartes: Reflections on the Unconscious Determinants of the Sciences." *Int. Journ. Psycho-Anal.*, XX, 1, Jan. 1939, 43–57.

Gregor Sebba. "Some Open Problems in Descartes Research." *Mod. Lang. Notes*, LXXV, 3, March 1960, 222–229.

W. F. M. Stewart. "A Survey of Work on 17th Century Rationalism, 1945–51." *Philos. Quart.*, II, 9, Oct. 1952, 359–368.

William McC. Stewart. "Descartes and Poetry." *Rom. Rev.*, XXIX, 3, Oct. 1938, 212–242.

A. E. Taylor. "Back to Descartes." *Philos.*, XVI, 62, April 1941, 126–137.

J. O. Wisdom. "Three Dreams of Descartes." *Int. Journ. Psycho-Anal.*, XXVIII, 1, 1947, 11–18.

J. N. Wright. "Kemp Smith's Descartes." *Philos. Quart.*, V, 21, Oct. 1955, 365–372.

F. ARTICLES IN FRENCH. See Sebba's *Bibliographia Cartesiana. Cahiers de Royaumont, Philosophie No II: Descartes* is an especially interesting and representative collection of papers by eminent scholars (Paris: Les Éditions de Minuit, 1957).

PRAISE FOR ALLY CONDIE'S *Atlantia*:

"Utterly captivating. A heroine unlike any I'd met before, a setting I'd never glimpsed, a story I'd never imagined. *Atlantia* is fresh, wild, and engrossing. I love Ally Condie." —SHANNON HALE, award-winning, bestselling author of *Austenland* and *Dangerous*

"A gorgeous, crumbling underwater world, a murder mystery, a sweet romance, a sinister plot, long-protected secrets . . . they're all here! But what made us love this new stand-alone from talented Ally Condie? Rio. She's a strong, brave, self-sacrificing heroine who never gives up."—*Justine Magazine*

"Condie brings tremendous depth to her world-building, finding terrific details in a culture created both to help people survive, and to perhaps keep them under control." —*Salt Lake City Weekly*

"A fast-paced fantasy adventure tale in a richly drawn dystopian future . . . this is a title that's sure to be immensely popular with teens." —*School Library Journal*

"Each mystery leads into another, and Condie keeps readers guessing to the end." —*Shelf Awareness*

PRAISE FOR THE INTERNATIONAL BESTSELLING MATCHED TRILOGY:

"This futuristic fable of love and free will asks: Can there be freedom without choice? The tale of Cassia's journey from acceptance to rebellion will draw you in and leave you wanting more." —CASSANDRA CLARE, *New York Times*–bestselling author of The Infernal Devices and The Mortal Instruments series

"A superb dystopian romance." —*The Wall Street Journal*

"The hottest YA title to hit bookstores since *The Hunger Games*." —*Entertainment Weekly*

★ "A fierce, unforgettable page-turner." —*Kirkus Reviews*, STARRED REVIEW

★ "Condie's enthralling and twisty dystopian plot is well served by her intriguing characters and fine writing. . . . Cassia's metamorphosis is gripping and satisfying." —*Publishers Weekly*, STARRED REVIEW

★ "Condie's prose is immediate and unadorned, with sudden pings of lush lyricism [and] reveals seeming to arrive on almost every page." —*Kirkus Reviews*, STARRED REVIEW

"Distinct . . . authentic . . . poetic."—*School Library Journal*

Summerlost

ALSO BY ALLY CONDIE:

Atlantia

Reached

Crossed

Matched

A novel

BY
ALLY CONDIE

DUTTON CHILDREN'S BOOKS
An imprint of Penguin Random House LLC

Dutton Children's Books
Penguin Young Readers Group
An imprint of Penguin Random House, LLC
375 Hudson Street
New York, NY 10014

Copyright © 2016 by Allyson Braithwaite Condie

CIP data is available.

Printed in the United States of America

ISBN 978-0-399-18734-6
1 2 3 4 5 6 7 8 9 10
Design by Vanessa Han
Edited by Julie Strauss-Gabel
Text set in Adobe Caslon Pro

For my hometown, Cedar City, Utah,
and in memory of my grandparents
Alice and Royden Braithwaite

Summerlost

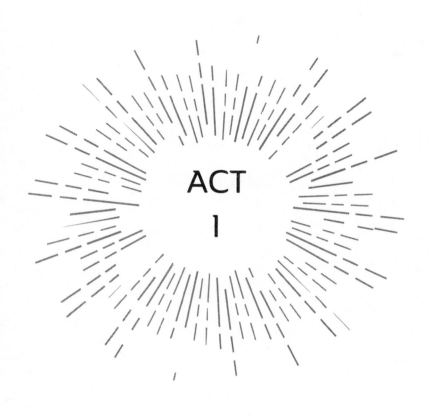

ACT
1

Our new house had a blue door. The rest of the house was painted white and shingled gray.

"Isn't it beautiful?" my mother asked.

She climbed out of the car first and then my younger brother, Miles, and then me.

"Don't you think this is the perfect place to end the summer?" Mom wanted to know.

We were spending the rest of the summer in Iron Creek, a small town in a high desert, the kind with pine trees and snow in the winter. It got hot in the day and cold at night. When a thunderstorm, all black and gray and blue, did come rolling in, you could see it a mile away.

I knew that stars would come out and rain would fall and that the days would be hot and long. I knew I'd make sandwiches for Miles and wash dishes with my mom. I knew I would do all of that and summer would be the same and never the same.

Last summer we had a dad and a brother and then they were gone.

We did not see it coming.

2

One of the things Miles and I whisper-worried about at night was that our mom could fall in love again.

It didn't seem like it would happen because she'd loved my father so much, but we had learned from the accident that anything could happen. Anything bad, anyway.

Mom didn't end up falling in love with a person, but she did fall in love with a house. We were in Iron Creek in June, visiting our grandparents—my mom's parents—when she saw the FOR SALE sign while she was out for a drive. She came home and whispered to Gram and Papa, and then they went with her to see the house while Miles and I stayed with our uncle Nick and his wife. Two weeks later, Mom used some of the money from when my dad died, the life insurance money, to buy the house. Since she's a teacher and didn't have to go back to work until the end of August, she decided we would spend the rest of the summer in Iron Creek and all the summers after that. She planned to rent out the house to college students during the school year. We weren't really rich enough to have two houses.

"It will be good for us to be around family more," she said. "Next summer we can stay for the whole time."

We didn't fight her about it. We liked our grandparents. We liked our uncle and our aunt. They had known our dad and our brother Ben. They had some of the same memories we did. Sometimes they even brought things up, like, "Remember when your dad went out in the kayak at Aspen Lake and he flipped over and we had to save him in our paddleboat?" and we would all start laughing because we had the same picture in our minds, my dad with his sunglasses dangling from one ear and his hair all wet. And they knew that Ben's favorite kind of ice cream wasn't ice cream at all, it was rainbow sherbet, and he always ate green first, and so when I saw it in my grandma's freezer once and I started crying they didn't even ask why and I think I saw my uncle Nick, my mom's brother, crying too.

"Well," Mom said, "let's go inside and choose rooms before we start unpacking."

"Me first!" said Miles.

They went in the house and I sat down on the steps.

The wind came through the trees, which were very old and very tall. I heard an ice-cream truck a few streets over, and kids playing in other yards.

And then a boy rode past on a bike. The boy wore old clothes. Not worn-out old, old-fashioned. He was dressed like a peasant. He had on a ruffly blouse and pants that ended right under his knees and a hat with a feather and he was my age. He didn't glance over at me. He looked happy.

Sad, I thought. *That's so sad. He's weird and he doesn't even know it.*

Actually, it's better not to know it. My brother Ben was different and he knew.

The trees sounded loud as a waterfall above me. "We're so lucky," Mom kept telling us when she bought the house. "The trees on the property have been there for fifty years. They're beautiful. Not many like them in the whole town."

I think she noticed the trees because my dad always loved trees.

We bought the house from a family who had lived in Iron Creek for generations, the Wainwrights. The kids had all moved away but one of them came back to sell the house when his mother died. He didn't want to live in it, but he was also kind of weird about selling it. When he ran into my mother at the real-tor's office, he told her, "It will always be the *Wainwright* home."

My mother said she nodded at him like she agreed but she didn't waste any time having the velvety green carpet torn up and the hardwood floors underneath sanded and varnished.

"I want the heart and the bones to stay the same," she said. "Anything else, we can change. *We* live here now."

She also had the front door painted blue.

I heard that blue front door open behind me and Mom came out. "Hey, Cedar," she said.

"Hey."

"Miles picked his room," Mom said. "There are still two left. Want to go next?"

Shouldn't you *go next?* I wanted to ask, but it didn't matter. Her room could be as small as ours now because she didn't have to share.

"Sure," I said, because I knew she wanted me to say *Sure.*

Inside, the house was empty, no furniture yet. Living room to the right, stairs in front of me. "Want to look around downstairs first?" Mom asked, because Miles and I hadn't spent time here yet, but I shook my head and started climbing. When I got to the top of the steps, I stopped.

"Isn't it fun?" she asked. "I left these the way they were. I couldn't help it."

Each bedroom door was painted a different color. One yellow, one purple, one green. The bathroom door was painted red. "Are the rooms inside the same colors?" I asked.

"No," she said. "Only the doors. Each room has something special about it, though."

Right then the green door opened. "I picked this one," Miles said, sticking his head out. "It has a big, big closet. Like a hideout. For me." Miles was eight, young enough to still care about hideouts.

"So green is gone," Mom said.

I didn't care which room I had but I knew she wanted me to pick.

"I'll do this one," I said, pointing to the purple door at the end of the hall.

"You can check them both first," Mom said.

"No," I said, "I'm fine. Unless you wanted purple?"

"I like them both," Mom said. "The yellow room has a window seat. The purple room has a diamond window."

That settled it. I knew Mom had always liked window seats and our real house, up in a suburb of Salt Lake City four hours away, was newish and beige and had no window seats anywhere.

"Purple," I said. "It's like a rainbow up here."

"That's what made me want to paint the front door blue," Mom said. "It was the only color that was missing."

Lots of colors were missing. Pink. Orange. Brown. Gray. But I didn't say that.

3

It turned out that a diamond window was not a window shaped like a diamond, which is what I assumed it would be. It was a big, regular-shaped window that opened outward, but instead of having two big panes of glass it had lots of small panes of glass, and *those* were diamond shaped. I couldn't see out clearly because of all the shapes and that bugged me, so I opened up the window. The wind in the trees was relentless. It sounded like an ocean outside my window so I closed it again.

Because of that stupid window, it felt like the house was a fly with those eyes that have a million parts. And it was looking at me.

I'd picked the wrong room. I should have done yellow.

Then, out of the corner of my eye, I saw something move. Something big, and black, and outside my window.

It was in the tree. I took a step closer. And then closer again.

The thing stretched its wings and settled. I could see that much, even though the window made it smeary and bleary and in diamonds.

I took another step.

I wanted to open the window to see what the thing was, but I also didn't want it to fly in.

Another step. The thing outside the window turned its head.

The purple door slammed open behind me and I spun around to see Miles. "Come on!" he said. "Gram and Papa and Uncle Nick and Aunt Kate are here! They're going to help us unpack!"

I looked back at the window but this time it only showed me trees. Something had looked away.

4

"What room would Ben have picked?" Miles asked at breakfast the next day.

Ben loved blue, he would have picked blue for sure, but there was no blue room.

And then I knew the real reason we had a blue front door.

"Maybe mine," I said. "Purple is closest to blue."

"Maybe not to Ben," Miles said, and he was right. You could never be sure how Ben would see things. He had his own kind of logic.

We were getting better at talking about Ben, but not much. Better because we did talk about him but also there was so much more to say and we were all still too fragile to say it.

After lunch I sat outside and I saw the boy on the bike ride by again, and he didn't see me that time either. And he still had on the same clothes and he still looked happy.

Next day, same thing all over again. Boy, bike, clothes, happy.

In my family we never call people names because sometimes people used to call Ben names and we all hated that.

When he was younger he didn't notice so much, but when he was nine, the year he died, he noticed every single time. You'd see his eyes flicker. He'd take it in. And then who knew what he'd do with it. Or how it made him feel.

Here is something bad about me.

I call people names in my head sometimes.

I don't do it to be mean.

I do it to label.

But I know names-to-label are bad too. Names-to-be-mean are worse, but both are bad.

Here's the name I called the boy in my head:

Nerd-on-a-Bike.

5

"Look," Miles said. "I found this in my closet." He dragged something into the middle of my bedroom. Outside, the wind blew and the sky had gone dark. A thunderstorm was moving in.

It was a box of old board games.

"Remember," I said, "you may play these games, but they will always be *Wainwright* board games."

We spread the games out on the floor. Outside the trees went crazy. The storm was almost here.

"Your room is noisy," Miles said.

"I know," I said. "It's the trees."

"You could ask Mom to trade rooms," Miles said.

But he knew I wouldn't do that. He knew I wouldn't ask Mom for anything I didn't really, really need. We both tried to be good for her and she tried to be patient with us. Sometimes I thought of the three of us as pencils with the erasers scrubbed down to the end, and the next swipe across the paper would tear through the page and make a *scree* sound across the desk.

It turned out most of the games were missing parts. But there was a very old version of Life that had everything in it. We played a few rounds before we got bored.

"Is there anything else in your closet?" I asked Miles.

"A box of old dolls," Miles said. "They're all broken up. Arms and legs sticking out. Eyes that won't close anymore."

"Are you serious?"

"No," he said. "There's only a box of old clothes. Like dress-up clothes. And some shoes. The shoes are gross. They're all curly."

"Show me," I said.

He was right. The shoes were disgusting. They looked like elf shoes, twisted up and pointy. And the dress-up clothes smelled musty. They all seemed like they were from our parents' era, except one shiny blue dress that was fancier than the rest and probably older. It had fur on the cuffs and the collar. I couldn't tell if the fur was real or fake. I hung that dress up in Miles's closet so it wouldn't be so wrinkled. It was kind of pretty.

"Want to walk to the gas station and get a Fireball?" Miles asked when I was done.

Miles was into Fireballs, the huge red kind that you get at convenience stores. Tears ran down his face while he ate them because he couldn't stand how hot they were but he wanted to suck all the way through one without stopping by the end of the summer. Since the house was in the middle of town, we didn't have to walk far to get to a gas station, which meant that Miles had learned quickly about every kind of cheap candy, like Lemonheads and Necco Wafers and gum shredded to look like tobacco. My mom wouldn't let him get the gum, or the candy cigarettes.

I liked Lemonheads best. They were so sour they made my nose sweat.

"It's raining," I said.

"It doesn't matter," Miles said. "The rain will feel good."

I decided to stay put.

I stayed put a lot, ever since last summer. My mom worried about it because she thought it meant that I was afraid to go out, because of what happened to my dad and Ben.

I walked over and opened the window. Even with the wind. Even with the rain. I felt like I might as well let all that sound surround me. I curled up on the bed and waited to see if the house would look at me again.

The black thing came back. This time, in the daylight, I could see what it was.

It was a bird.

It was a vulture.

I had never seen one up close but I recognized it from movies. Or TV. I wasn't sure how I knew, but I did.

It looked at me. It probably wasn't used to anyone living in my room, because no one had for a while. It watched me and the house watched me.

If the vulture wanted, it could fly right inside.

"*I'm not afraid of you,*" I whispered.

It cocked its ugly red head.

It knew I lied.

6

After the rain cleared up, my uncle Nick brought over an old bike that someone at his work was giving away. "I thought you kids might like it."

"We keep saying how dumb we were to leave our bikes at home," I told him. "Thanks."

"I stopped by Sports & More and got a helmet too. I knew your mom would want you to have one."

"Good call," I said. "Would you like a Fireball?" Miles had brought some back, and I had one lodged in my cheek. I almost drooled.

"Absolutely not," Nick said. He said it in a nice way though. "I didn't even know they still made those." He leaned the bike against the porch. "Where's your mom?"

"Out back," I said. "Working on the deck." My mom planned to build a deck while we were here. She'd never done anything like that before.

"I'll go say hi to her," he said.

"Will you tell her I went on a ride?"

"Sure. Where are you going?"

"I don't know," I said. That was true and also a lie. The minute I'd seen the bike I'd known what I would do, even though I didn't know where I would go.

I had decided to follow Nerd-on-a-Bike.

7

I'd never had to lie in wait for someone before. It was kind of hard. I put the bike on the sidewalk that led up to our house. Then I sat on the steps wearing the helmet so that I'd be ready to go the minute he came by. I sat behind the porch pillar just in case, even though he'd never noticed me before.

It didn't take long. As soon as he was two houses past ours I jumped on my bike and followed him.

He rode straight down the street. He stopped and waited for a light so I stopped too. I made it through after him.

He headed in the direction of the college campus. We rode past fraternities that used to be regular houses. One of them had a rope swing hanging from a tree out front, and another had a yard that was nothing but gravel.

Then we came to the best part of the campus, the forest. It was my dad's favorite part because of the pine trees that grew there. They were almost as old as the school and stood very tall and straight. The groundskeeper put Christmas lights on the tallest one every year.

The forest was big enough to feel quiet but small enough

that it didn't feel creepy. A waterfall and a couple of sculptures were hidden among the trees. And outside of the forest was a grassy quad where my mom used to play Ultimate Frisbee when she was a teenager.

Nerd-on-a-Bike turned into the forest and rode down the squiggly sidewalks under the trees.

He rode past the quad.

He rode toward the middle of campus to the theater, which looked like it got picked up out of old England and set right down in Utah. And then I realized where he was going.

The Summerlost Festival.

Of course.

I should have known.

The Summerlost Festival in Iron Creek was the third-biggest Shakespearean festival west of the Mississippi River. It happened every year on the college campus during the summertime. A big billboard told you all about it as you came into town:

LOSE YOURSELF IN SUMMER AND GO BACK IN TIME

AT THE SUMMERLOST FESTIVAL

The Greenshow they did out on the lawn before the plays was fun and also scary because they sometimes pulled people out of the audience to be part of it, and there were always crazy props. One time they had my dad get up to be a prince in a skit. He had on tan shorts and a blue polo shirt like he usually did when he was on vacation. The actors in their tights and peasant dresses surrounded him. He had to wear huge wooden shoes and stomp around on the tiny stage on a quest to rescue one of the actors, who had been cast into a deep sleep by a witch's spell. My dad had to pretend to kiss her. His face went so red. "My prince!" the princess exclaimed to my dad when she woke up.

My mother could not breathe, she was laughing so hard. When Dad sat down, he shook his head. I knew he'd hated it, but he'd been a good sport. Mom hugged him and I felt proud of him even though it had been sort of awful to watch.

Another time, a few years later, we came to see the show and Ben was having one of his hard days and couldn't stop screaming and yelling. Finally my mom took Ben away to the grassy quad and he rolled down the hill over and over, like a puppy. When he came back, happy and big-eyed and sweaty, he even sat on my lap in a kind of curly way like a puppy would have, but he was a boy.

My brother was a boy and now he's not anything.

8

"Hello," someone said, and I looked up. Nerd-on-a-Bike. He'd caught me. My face must have looked funny thinking about Ben because the boy's face changed. He'd looked as if he was going to say something to me, like he'd had all the words ready to go, and then he said something else instead.

"You live on my street," he said. He had dark hair and freckles. I expected his eyes to be brown, but they were hazel. "In the Wainwrights' old house."

"Yeah," I said.

"I was going to ask why you were following me."

"I wanted to see where you were going dressed like that," I told him. "I should have realized. The festival. Do you work here?"

"Yeah."

"How old are you?"

"Twelve."

So I could work too. The thought seemed to come out of nowhere. I didn't know I wanted a job. I didn't know *what* I wanted, except to go back to how things used to be, and that could never happen, but I wanted it so bad that it didn't leave room to want much else.

"Are they hiring?" I asked.

"We can find out," he said. "What's your name?"

"Cedar Lee," I said.

"That sounds like a movie-star name."

I almost said, *It's not. It's a tree name because my dad grew up in the Pacific Northwest and there was this huge old cedar tree in his yard and for some reason he thought that would be a great name for his first kid, boy or girl, and my mom liked it too, and he always joked that's how he knew he'd found the right person.* They fought sometimes but they were super in love, my parents. You could tell that in a lot of ways. They were the same height—my dad was short and my mom was tall—and whenever they dressed up and went out, he never cared at all whether she wore heels or not, whether she was taller than he was or not, even though that was one of those things people seemed to think they *should* care about. Without her heels they could stand together and they were exactly the same height. Nose to nose. Eye to eye.

"I *am* a movie star." I didn't know why I said that, when it was so obviously not true, but he grinned. When he did, his eyebrows went up in a very dramatic way, like a cartoon devil.

"A movie star," he said. "Like Lisette Chamberlain."

I knew right away who he meant. Lisette Chamberlain was the most famous person the town of Iron Creek had ever produced. She got her start at the Summerlost Festival and went on to star in soap operas and movies and then later died under mysterious and dramatic circumstances.

"What's your name?" I asked.

"Leo Bishop," he said.

"That's a good name too."

"I know," he said. "Come on. Let's go talk to my boss."

9

We parked our bikes out in front of the box office building, in the rack closest to the fountain. It had a pool with a geyser-like spray that went straight up, and then the water ran down like a waterfall over a pie-shaped wedge of concrete jutting out over another, lower pool. When we were kids we climbed back behind the waterfall, even though we knew we could get in trouble for it.

Leo took me around to the concessions building, which was half timbered and pretend-old-looking, like the theater.

Once we were inside, Leo introduced me to his boss, Gary, and told him that I wanted a job.

"The season has already started," Gary said.

"But we could use a few more people," Leo said. "Especially since Annie quit last week."

"Have you worked anywhere before?" Gary asked me.

"No," I said, "but I babysit a lot. And I have good grades at school. I'm very responsible." A couple of girls about my age stood watching me. I felt dumb.

Gary looked at my feet and said, "No flip-flops. *Never* again. Can you get some sandals by tonight?"

"Sure," I said. I had a pair of leather sandals at home that looked like the ones some of the other girls were wearing.

People milled around the room, all wearing peasant costumes. I saw some older people too, around my grandma's age. They were the volunteer ushers, who gave directions and instructions and helped people find their seats in the theater.

"You can train today and tonight," Gary said, "and then start tomorrow. Your mom will need to sign this because you're not sixteen. Bring it back with you tonight." He handed me a form and I nodded. I wondered what my mom would say. Would she agree to this? What was I thinking?

"You work from one to three in the afternoon and from six to eight thirty at night," Gary said. "Every day but Sunday. You're here to sell concessions before the matinees and evening performances start, and during the Greenshow. Then you come back and help clean up afterward. Payday is every other Friday."

"Okay," I said.

"Lindy," he said to one of the older ladies. "Can you go to the costume shop and ask Meg if we have anything that will fit?"

Lindy nodded and left.

"I'll have you shadow Leo today," Gary said. "He'll show you what to do. Do you have any questions?"

"I guess I have one," I said. "What do I . . . concess?"

Behind Gary I saw Leo grin again.

"We'll assign you something later," Gary said. "For now, learn from Leo."

A few minutes later Lindy came back with a peasant skirt and blouse. The blouse was white with ties at the neck. The skirt had flowers on it. They both looked big.

"It's the smallest one they had," Lindy told me.

I ducked into the employee bathroom to get dressed and I pulled out my ponytail because I'd noticed the other girls all had their hair down. I left my shorts on under the skirt but I balled up my T-shirt and put it on a chair in the bathroom, hoping no one would take it.

"That looks all right," Gary said when I came out.

Gary and Leo showed me all the things they sold out on the yard (as Gary called it). I'd seen some before when I'd been to the festival. Fresh tarts—raspberry, lemon, and cream cheese. They looked like tiny folded-up purses. I wanted to eat one. Bottled water, with the words SUMMERLOST FESTIVAL and the logo, the theater, printed on the labels. Old-fashioned candy in cellophane packages—lemon drops, horehound candy, and taffy in wax-paper twists. Chocolates. And programs. Fancy, printed-up programs. Leo took a basket of those and so I did too.

Gary had lots of final instructions. "Remember," he said, "no flip-flops tonight."

"I understand," I said.

"Take care of your costume. Delicate wash only. You don't want Meg from the costume shop mad at you. Trust me."

"All right."

"Don't forget that you're in England," he told me. "In the time of Shakespeare."

I nodded. I didn't point out that I'm part Chinese-American and so the odds that I would have been in England back in Shakespeare's time were highly unlikely.

"And," Gary said, "you're a peasant."

That part felt kind of true thanks to the outfit.

"Stay in character," he said, "but don't use an accent unless you're given specific permission. The only kid here who has permission to use an accent is Leo."

"Okay." I followed Leo toward the door.

"Where are you?" Gary called after me.

For a minute, I didn't get it, but then I did.

"I'm in England," I told him.

10

"I've actually been to England," Leo said. "That's why I can do the accent. Because I've heard it in real life."

"Let's hear it," I said.

"Oh, you will. Soon."

We walked across a brick courtyard with a big tree in the middle. A wooden bench was built all the way around the tree. "It's not as busy for the matinees," Leo said. He had a lively voice and talked fast, but not so fast that I couldn't keep up. "People don't wander around much when it's hot. They stay in the gift shop and buy their stuff there or go straight to the theater. The nighttime shows are the big ones, as far as we're concerned. That's when the real work gets done. That's when I break records."

"What kind of records?"

"*All* kinds of records," Leo said. "Most programs sold in an hour. Most programs sold in a night. Most programs sold in a week. Gary keeps track of all of it. I'm gunning for most programs sold in a single season, and I'm a lock for that if I keep up the way I'm going. But what I'm most proud of is that one night I outsold *everyone* in concessions. Do you know how much harder it is to sell programs than water? We're in the desert. But I did it. One night. One awesome night two weeks ago. And I'm going to do it again."

It seemed like Leo had more energy than anyone I'd ever met.

"So," he said. "Why did you want the job? What are you saving up for? And don't say college or a car."

"Why not?"

"That's what everyone says."

"What's wrong with wanting to go to college or get a car?" I didn't think far enough ahead for either, but something about Leo made me want to play devil's advocate.

"It's fine," Leo said, "if you're specific. Like, Jackie, one of the girls, says college, but she says UC San Diego to study marine biology. *That's* fine. And if you know exactly the type of car you want to get: also fine. But vague stuff is stupid."

"Well then, I'm stupid," I said. "Because I don't know."

Leo frowned. "You can't think of anything you want?"

I did not answer that question because right then an older lady walked by and that's when it happened.

The accent.

Leo smiled and, sounding like Oliver Twist or who knows what, called out, "Can I interest you in a program, my lady?"

I didn't know if the accent was right. I didn't know if it was real England or kid-in-a-movie England. What I did see was that Leo's face lit up and then the lady's face lit up and his smile seemed as big as the world. Like he loved the world. Like he had no idea what it could do.

She bought three programs while Leo joked with her in his maybe-real English accent and I stood watching.

"Impressed?" Leo asked me when she'd gone away.

"Very," I said, but I made it sound sarcastic.

"Let's hear you try," he said. "Next time, your turn. With an accent."

"But Gary said—"

"I won't tell Gary," Leo said. "Come on."

The next person we saw was a man, an old man, with a neatly pressed white shirt and a bottle of water in his hand. He had a nice face and big glasses, and he walked fast.

"Sir," I said, and then when he didn't hear me, I said it louder. "SIR. Could I interest you in a program?" I did not know what was coming out of my mouth, accent-wise. Maybe I was German? Or Italian? Or Irish? Australian?

He stopped and looked at me and I held out a program.

"I don't think so," he said, pleasantly enough, and then I turned around to see Leo shaking with laughter.

"What was *that*?" Leo asked.

"I'm surprised you didn't recognize it," I said. "It's from a little-known part of England. A very small province." Did they even have provinces in England? I wasn't sure. I knew they didn't have states.

"Really?" Leo said. "And what's the name of this province?"

"It's Bludge," I said, in my terrible accent, saying the first even-sort-of-British word that came to mind.

"Oh yeah?" Leo asked. "And what's the capital city of the province of Bludge?"

Did provinces have capitals? "Bludgeon," I said.

That made Leo laugh so hard that he almost missed a lady with two teenagers walking past. But then he switched right into the accent and she bought a program and smiled at him.

We were walking back along the sidewalk when some boys on bikes came through. An usher waved at them to stop but they didn't.

"They're not supposed to cut through here during festival hours," Leo said, "but they do it anyway because it's faster."

When the boys came closer, I could see that they were about our age. Spiky blond hair on one, baseball hats on all the rest. Tall socks. Shiny shirts made out of fabric that looked like plastic. Coming home from some sports practice, maybe. They were going so fast that I worried they'd slam right into us, so I followed Leo's lead and stepped over onto the grass.

As they came by, one of them knocked Leo's hat off his head and they all laughed.

"That's new," Leo said. He reached down to pick up his hat.

"Usually they just yell stuff at me when they come by." I could tell he was trying to sound like he didn't care. It was almost working. "They think they're so wild, but they're kids on bikes. It's not like they're Hell's Angels or something."

"They're like Hell's farts," I said, and that cracked Leo up hard enough that I could see the braces on his back teeth.

I smiled too.

"That's perfect," he said. "They're Hellfarts."

We walked past the Summerlost Theater, with its flags waving merrily and its dark-painted wood and white stucco. The wooden stairs outside were worn smooth-grooved with decades of people coming to get lost in lives that were not their own.

"Did you hear?" Leo asked, when he saw me looking. "The theater's coming down at the end of the summer."

"What?" I said, stunned. Did my mother know? She thought of the theater as part of the town, her childhood.

"They're remodeling some of the other buildings, but the theater's too much hassle, so they're starting over. They're tearing it down and building a new one across the street," Leo said. "Haven't you noticed?"

"I guess I haven't been over there yet."

"I'll show you after our shift," Leo said.

11

We rode our bikes over to the east on our way home.

An entire block was missing.

"There it is," Leo said. "They're building the new theater here. It's going to be part of Iron Creek's new civic center."

I knew what had been there before. A bunch of small, old houses, some of them beautiful. And a doctor's office, where I'd been once for strep throat over Christmas break. My uncle Nick ran the pharmacy and so if we ever got sick while we were in Iron Creek he'd flavor the antibiotics and also put a treat from the candy counter in the bag with our medicine.

Now, instead of the houses and the doctor's office, there was a chain-link fence and construction equipment and workers and some blue Porta Potties lined up in a row. And most of all there was the hole.

It was huge. It would have been a lot of work. Before they dug the hole, they would have had to tear everything down. Remove all the splintered boards, tear up the lawns, break up the fences, take away the glass, pull up the foundations.

And then dig, and dig.

Where did all of it go? I wondered. *Everything that used to be here?*

"But if they tear the theater down," I said, "the Summerlost Festival logo won't make sense. It's a picture of the theater. And the logo is all over the place. On the bottles, the programs, the *signs.*"

"I bet they'll keep the logo the same," Leo said.

"Even if the theater's gone?"

"It's an icon," he said. "I guess it was around for so long that it doesn't actually have to be here anymore to have meaning for people."

"It's sad," I said to Leo.

"I know."

Neither of us used our accents so I knew we both meant it.

It turned out that my mother knew about the theater coming down. She just hadn't mentioned it to us. I told her about the hole and the Porta Potties, and then about the job. I told her that there was a neighbor kid I could ride to and from the festival with so it would be safe and she wouldn't even have to worry about that or about dropping me off and picking me up.

I hadn't actually run any of that past Leo, but I'd ask him as soon as I got to work for the evening shift.

"Maybe next year," she said. "Twelve is young to have a job."

"I'm the same age as the other kids," I said. "And this is the last year that they'll have the old theater. Next year it won't be the same."

She thought for a minute, and then nodded. "All right."

That night I rode my bike over to the festival and I didn't forget my sandals. I was in England.

I'd thought Gary was dumb for saying that, but toward the end of the shift it actually felt like we were.

On the Greenshow stage, performers danced and sang and hit tambourines that had green and purple ribbons tied to them. The women had garlands in their hair. The crowd clapped along.

Leo used his accent and the lights twinkled everywhere and my skirt swished around my ankles. The tarts smelled delicious. There were a million stars, and people and music and laughing. Flags waved in the air. The trees were old, the way they were at my house, and I didn't mind so much when the wind came through and they started talking.

Maybe it *didn't* feel like England. I'd never been. But it felt different. Good.

At the end of the shift, a trumpet sounded to tell people it was time to go in to the play, and the spell was broken.

After we counted out the money (I sold fifteen programs, Leo sold fifty-six), I asked him if we could ride our bikes home together. "My mom worries," I said.

We cut through the festival's administration building to get to the bike racks on the other side. "They're making a new display over here," Leo said, gesturing to the west wing of the building. "It's called the Costume Hall, and it's going to have one costume on display for every year the festival has been operating."

"They're doing a lot of new things," I said.

"Yeah," Leo said. "The idea is that all the improvements will mean more ticket sales. I think they got the idea for the Costume Hall from this." He pointed to the wing of the administration building that led off to the east.

"The Portrait Hall," I said.

"Right."

Leo walked into the Portrait Hall so I followed him. I'd been in the Portrait Hall before. It had a painting of an actor from a play for each year of the festival.

"There she is," he said, stopping in front of one of the portraits.

I knew without looking at the plaque under the frame who he meant. Lisette Chamberlain. I'd noticed her ever since I was small. Even in the Portrait Hall, full of beautiful and interesting-looking people wearing fancy costumes, Lisette stood out. Not only was she the most gorgeous actor of all, she wore a jeweled crown in her red hair and she was looking off-camera at someone, and you couldn't tell if she loved or hated the person she saw. All you knew was that she was looking at them *significantly*. Her dress was deep purple velvet, with black brocade. And she was resting her cheek on her hand, so that you noticed her beautiful fingers and her slender wrist and her jewelry, a golden bracelet woven like a chain, a ring with three white stones.

"You know about her, right?" Leo asked.

"Yeah," I said.

"Go on," Leo said. "What do you know?"

I tried to remember everything my mom and grandparents had told me. "Lisette was born here in Iron Creek and she worked at the festival. First in the Greenshow, then she became an actor in the plays. She went to Hollywood and was on a soap opera and then in some movies but every summer she'd come back and do a one-night performance at Summerlost, which always sold out almost a full year in advance. Then she died here in Iron Creek in the hotel on Main Street."

"Right," Leo said. He seemed to be studying me. He folded his arms across his chest and tipped his head to one side. He had long eyelashes for a boy. For anyone. "I think I can work with you."

"That's good," I said, "because you are."

"That's not what I mean."

"What *do* you mean?"

"So one time my family went to Washington, DC," he said.

"And when we were there, we went on a lot of tours."

"That sounds boring," I said.

"It was awesome. You could do tours that specialized in different famous people and the places they'd lived or worked. I want to do a tour like that about Lisette. It's the twentieth anniversary of her death this summer. All the old people who came to the festival when she was alive haven't forgotten her. We could make a ton of money."

I didn't know what to say. *The anniversary of her death.* We had been through the anniversary of my dad's and Ben's deaths a few weeks ago and it was horrible. All day long, I couldn't stop thinking about what had been happening at that time the year before. When they got in the car. When I found out what had happened.

Leo reached into the pocket of his peasant pants and pulled out a piece of paper. "Here's a map I've made of possible tour sites," he said, spreading it out. "The trick is that we can't drive, so everything has to be in walking distance."

I remembered that Leo didn't actually *know* Lisette. She had been gone for a long time.

And this way at least she would be remembered.

It would be horrible if people just forgot you.

"We're going to wear either our work costumes," he said, "or all black. I can't decide. I had the idea for the tour a couple of days ago so I still haven't worked everything out."

"Gary won't be happy if he finds out we're wearing our costumes outside of the festival," I said after a second. Was I going to go along with this? I kept talking, like my mouth had decided to go ahead without me.

"You make a good point," Leo said. "Okay. We'll wear all black." He tapped the paper with his finger. "As far as the sites go, we have the theater, of course, where she performed. We also have the hospital where she was born, and the hotel where she died, and the cemetery where she's buried. It's too bad that they tore down the house where she grew up."

"Wait," I said. "The hospital is new."

"I'm talking about the old hospital. It's still around."

"That's cool," I said, picturing something old and overgrown with vines. "Where is it?"

"Two streets away," he said. "The Everett Building."

"The insurance office?"

"Yup."

"That's all you've got?" I said. "Four sites?"

Leo wasn't paying attention. "What would be great is if we could go through the tunnels."

"What tunnels?"

"There are tunnels that run under the administration building and go to the theater," he said, dropping his voice as if he were telling me a secret. I glanced over my shoulder but the only people around were the ones in the portraits. "They built them years ago so the actors could get from the dressing rooms in the basement of the administration building out to the theater without being seen by the people in the courtyards. And there's some old maintenance tunnels, too, that they don't even use anymore."

"Why would we want to go into the tunnels?" I asked.

"Because Lisette would have gone through them all the time," Leo said. "All the actors use them. They have for decades. But when they tear down the theater, they're getting rid of those tunnels too. This is our last chance to see them."

"People aren't going to let kids into the tunnels."

"Maybe we can find a way," Leo said. "For now, we have the other four places. And they're all within walking distance of each other and of our houses. It's perfect. I've done a lot of research about Lisette so I can fill you in. And I've come up with some advertising." He leaned closer. "That's another reason I want to do the programs. I can put these flyers inside without Gary or anyone noticing." He handed me a piece of shiny paper printed with a picture of Lisette Chamberlain. The lettering on the flyer read:

LISETTE CHAMBERLAIN TOUR.
FOLLOW IN HER FOOTSTEPS &
LEARN ABOUT HER LIFE.
FOR MORE INFORMATION
CALL 555-1234 between 9 a.m. and 12 p.m.
$5 per person, cash only.

"This is crazy," I said.

"We can't stay out late at night," Leo went on, "so we'll have to go early in the morning. Like *really* early, so we don't get caught. And then I'll sit by my phone every morning to make sure no one else answers it. It'll be easy. That's when my parents are at work and my brothers are at practice. I've thought it all through."

"I can tell," I said. "So what made you decide that you want a partner?"

"Meeting you," he said.

Was he flirting? Teasing? Asking me to do this because he felt sorry for me because of what happened to my family? He had to know. Everyone knew. And over the past year people did nice things for me mostly out of pity.

"I'll split the money with you," Leo said. "We'll meet at my house at six forty-five so we can walk over to the Everett Building together. That's where the tour is going to start— where she was born." Lisette stared at me from the flyer and from the portrait on the wall. "What do you think?"

"I'll do it," I said.

I wasn't sure why. But if I had to guess, I would say it was because I liked talking to Leo. He always seemed to be thinking about something. His brain was very busy.

I wanted to go along with him, tag along with his mind like a hitchhiker, so that I could keep my brain busy too.

Two days later, on the evening shift, Leo told me that he'd had three customers sign up for the tour the next day.

We were on.

When I got home, Mom wanted to know all about work and Miles wanted to play Life again and I really needed to make sure I knew where my black T-shirt and jeans were and if I'd even brought them from our other house but I couldn't tell my mom and Miles that. So I played a game of Life with Miles (he won, again) and then I started to lie to my mom so that I could leave in the morning to meet Leo without her freaking out if she found me gone.

I told her that I was going to go running in the morning sometimes. This was the story Leo and I had come up with.

"Alone?" she asked.

"With my new friend, Leo," I said. "The one from work. He wants to do the junior high cross-country team next year."

"You're spending a lot of time with him," she said.

"I know," I told her. "I'm glad I found a friend so fast. It makes everything more fun."

She smiled. "What's his last name?"

"Bishop," I said.

"His mom brought us a lasagna a few days ago," Mom said. "She seemed nice."

"Where's the lasagna?" Miles asked.

"I put it in the freezer," my mom said. "I'd already started dinner that night. We can eat it tomorrow."

"Or we could eat it now," Miles said.

We were getting away from the topic. "So you'll let me do it?"

"All right," she said. "It's light outside by then, so you should be safe. But don't go running by yourself. If Leo's alarm doesn't go off or something, come back home."

"Thanks," I told her.

When I went upstairs to go to bed and turned on the light in my room, the diamond panes reflected back at me. I found my T-shirt and jeans. I opened the window and looked out. No bird.

Then I saw something on the windowsill. A small screwdriver, the kind of thing Ben would have liked. He never really played with toys but he liked other random things, stuff that was pretty or had a certain weight to it or interested him in some way. A few of his favorites included a wire kitchen whisk, a bracelet with a round, smooth piece of turquoise in it that he'd taken from my mom's jewelry box, and a folded-up pamphlet from the mountain resort where he did special-needs ski lessons in the winter.

We called the random stuff he liked *fidgets*. He carried them around and flipped them back and forth in his hands to calm himself when he felt nervous. He took fidgets with him everywhere. I knew he'd probably had some with him in the car when they'd had the accident, but I'd never asked. I didn't go in his room after to see which ones were missing.

I held the screwdriver for a minute. It had a black handle and a silvery point. How did it get there? Had my mom been fixing my window?

But there didn't seem to be anything wrong with my window. Not earlier when I'd opened it, and not now.

I climbed into bed and put the screwdriver under the pillow. Outside I heard the wind in the trees and the rasping sound of my mom sanding boards for the deck. I thought about Lisette Chamberlain and the secret tunnels. I tried not to think about Ben but of course I did. For years I had been Ben Lee's older sister. People always thought they knew Ben but they never really did. That didn't stop them from talking *about* him.

"He's special," they'd say. "One of those special souls that don't need to worry about anything they do here on earth, they're going straight to heaven!"

Or, "He's here to teach us to be more like him."

Someone told me that they used to take away people like Ben. "My grandma's sister was like that," my friend Casey from church said once, "and they took her sister to this place. Like a hospital. My grandma hardly ever saw her after that. My mom says you guys are so lucky that we live now."

And I guess that was right, but it also seemed to me like people who said Ben was special and had no worries were as wrong as the people long ago, but in a different way.

Because that's crappy. What if this life was all Ben got? People said he was sweet and special—and he was—but he was also sad and angry. More than most people. He cried. His own body seemed to feel weird to him sometimes—he would jump and move like he wanted to be free of his skin. I could see him looking at us like *Get me out of here* and we were never sure where to take him. You can't take someone away from their own body. And that seemed unfair. Would God really do that to someone so other people could feel like they were learning important lessons in the few minutes they spent with him?

"He's healed now," they said at the funeral. "He has his perfect body. Think of how happy he must be in heaven."

I hated the funeral so much.

They were *so sure* and I was so not sure.

"And such a blessing that Ben and his father are together," someone else said. "Together when it happened, and together now. Up there waiting, the two of them."

And that stuck with me because if there was anywhere in the world Ben hated, it was waiting rooms. This was because usually scary or painful or stressful things happened to him after he'd been in a waiting room. Someone would do a blood test to make sure his medication wasn't giving him diabetes. Or he would be going to another new doctor who might be able to tell if he had something wrong with his digestive system. Or another one to see if there was something wrong with his skin.

Ben wasn't bad in the waiting room. It's not like he threw tantrums or anything. He was just *anxious*. Walking, jumping, talking loudly. Looking around, wondering where the danger was and what people were going to do to him.

So that was how I started picturing Dad and Ben. In a waiting room with beige chairs and a TV on the wall that showed a Disney movie and carpet that looked like it had bits of crayons in it but it was really colored dots they'd put in the pattern for some reason. Maybe for it to look fun. It did not look fun. Old magazines. Ben walking around worried. My dad talking to him in a low voice to try to keep him calm.

Both of them waiting for the rest of their family to die or for God to come in and say something, whichever came first.

The wind stopped blowing. My mother stopped sanding. When I put my hand under the pillow, the screwdriver was still there.

And I wondered.

Who'd given it to me?

15

I couldn't tell if our first tour customers were crazy or not.

There were three of them, all old ladies. And they had on pink shirts with Lisette Chamberlain's face silk-screened on the front.

"I like that we're doing this at dawn," one was saying to the others as Leo and I came up to them. "It feels more sacred."

"Hello," Leo said, and they jumped as they turned around.

"We're your tour guides," he said. "Are you ready to begin?"

"You're both kids," one lady said. She had gray curly hair. Another one had white curly hair and the third had a sleek red bob. The redhead looked sassier than the other two or maybe it was just the hair. I've always wanted red hair.

"Yes," Leo said, "we are. But I know everything there is to know about Lisette Chamberlain."

The ladies looked at one another. You could tell they were thinking they'd been ripped off.

"Really," said the red-haired lady. "You know, for example, what Lisette's favorite color was?"

"Purple," Leo said smoothly. "She always joked in interviews and said it was gold to match the Oscar she'd someday win, but it was actually purple."

"And the date of her wedding?" another lady asked.

"Which one?" Leo asked. "The one that hardly anyone knows about that was annulled, or the one to Roger Marin? Or do you mean Halloween? When she was a kid, she always planned to get married on Halloween and have her wedding colors be orange and black."

The redheaded lady burst into laughter, and the one with white hair joined in. The Lisette printed on their shirts went up and down with their boobs. But the gray-haired lady still looked sour.

"All right," she said. "You know your stuff. And you *do* only charge five dollars a ticket. Let's see what you can tell us."

Leo pointed at the insurance building. "Lisette's story begins here," he said.

"Wait," said one of the women. "Aren't we going to go inside?"

"No," Leo said.

"Let me guess," the gray-haired woman said. "You don't have permission to go inside, and this is private property."

"You are correct," Leo said.

"So this isn't an official tour. It's not sanctioned by the festival *at all*," she said, and now she had a grumpy look around her mouth.

"It's better that way," I said. Everyone turned to look at me. Leo raised his eyebrows in surprise. I'd told him I wanted to listen the first few times on the tour so I could learn the material. "The festival's tour would be boring."

Leo nodded. "That's right."

The grumpy woman still didn't look entirely convinced, so I added, "And there's nothing to see in there anyway. It's an insurance building now. Cubicles and office furniture and that's it. It's easier to imagine the scene if we stay out here. The outside of the building is much like Lisette's mother would have seen it as she came inside, ready to have her baby. Did she have any idea that her daughter would turn out to be one of the greatest actors of our time?" I glanced over at Leo. I was out of material, since I didn't actually know very much about Lisette other than the basics.

Leo grinned. He'd caught my cue the way my dad and I used to catch the ball when we got a good rhythm going throwing to each other in the front yard—seamless, smooth.

"We know that Lisette's mother took a list of names with her to the hospital," Leo said. "She did not know whether she was having a boy or a girl, and she had five names listed for each gender to choose from. I'm sure that the three of you already know which names were on that list."

"No," said the red-haired lady, a little smile crossing her face. "We don't."

16

The cemetery came last.

Leo and I walked away from the ladies for a minute to give them a chance to pay their respects.

"We are *so* going to get caught," I said.

"No," he said. "I swear we won't. I'm very good at reading people. I don't put the flyers in every program I sell. I only give them to people who look promising."

"What if someone drops one? Or it falls out in the theater or the courtyard?"

"The janitors sweep up the whole place right after the performances," Leo said. "It's not like they're going to look at every piece of trash. And I keep an eye out. Don't worry about it."

"All right."

"By the way," Leo said. "That was amazing. Back at the hospital. When you jumped in to help get them to stay."

"I thought about it last night. I realized they might give us a hard time because we're kids, so I wanted to have something to say if they did."

"We make a good team," Leo told me. "You think ahead. You're smart."

I fought down a smile at the compliment. "You're smart too. You know everything there is to know about Lisette. How did you find out so much?"

"I've read every interview she ever gave," Leo said. "And I read *When the Curtain Fell: The Unauthorized Biography of Lisette Chamberlain*. Some of the actors say they've seen her ghost. She appears in the tunnels, late at night, after the play ends. I've *got* to get in there."

"Can you take a picture of us?" one of the ladies called.

"Sure," Leo said.

It surprised me how much I liked giving the tour and learning about Lisette. I'd thought it might be hard, but it wasn't. She was like a character, someone I was learning about from a book or watching in a show. Long gone, far away.

When we got closer we could see that the ladies' eyes were red. From crying over someone they didn't even know, who had been buried decades before. My chest felt tight and I had to bite my lip to keep from saying something.

We walked the ladies all the way back to their car at the old hospital—about a mile, but none of them complained. They kept talking to Leo about Lisette's performances and had he watched them all and which was his favorite.

"Thank you," the red-haired lady said. Some of the insurance office workers had started to pull into the parking lot, but we stood under a big pine tree and I didn't think they could see us. "This was wonderful. I'm sorry we doubted you at first."

"No problem," Leo said. "You can make up for it by telling all your friends."

He had them wrapped around his little finger, even the gray-haired lady. They laughed and all three of the Lisettes on their shirts moved up and down.

"Here's fifteen dollars for our tickets," said the gray-haired lady, "and ten as a tip for your expertise." She handed him a twenty and a five.

We walked down the block to the bank so Leo could get the twenty-dollar bill changed to pay me. "You don't have to do that right now," I said. "You can wait until the end of the week and take care of the money all at once."

"I'd rather get it done right away," Leo said. The bank was one of the older buildings in town, made of gray stone. It looked old-fashioned, like a bank in a movie, with gold lettering on the window and an iron railing for the stairs. I started toward the front entrance but Leo motioned me to come around to the side. Then he walked right through the drive-through and took out the plastic container that takes money and checks into the bank.

"Cars shouldn't get to have all the fun," he said. He put the twenty-dollar bill in the container and put it back in the tube, where it shot through to the teller. She looked up from her spot at the window at Leo and said, "Can I help you?" in a tone that actually said, *What do you think you're doing?*

"I'd like to change this twenty into two tens," he said. "Please."

I thought for a minute she wouldn't help us, and she never did smile, but when she sent back the two tens there were also two lollipops inside the container. One red, one butterscotch.

"Which one do you want?" Leo asked me as we walked away.

"I'm too old to get candy at the bank."

Leo raised his cartoon-devil eyebrows and started opening the red lollipop. He handed me the butterscotch one and I put it in my pocket to give to Miles later.

Leo gave me one of the tens and kept the other. He also kept the five, which meant he got fifteen dollars and I got ten. Which seemed fair, since he'd done more of the work and planning.

"When you start talking more on the tours, we'll split it evenly," he said. "And maybe we should have some shirts made. Those ones the ladies had on were genius. I bet we could sell a bunch."

"You love making money, don't you," I said. Then I wished I hadn't because he also obviously liked people. It wasn't totally about the cash.

But Leo didn't mind at all. "Oh yeah. I love money. And I want to have a lot of it."

"What is it *you're* saving up for?"

"I'm saving up for a plane ticket to England."

I should have known.

"And I have to earn the money *soon*," he said. "I need to be in London in two months, and plane tickets are going to start getting more expensive the closer I get to my departure date."

"Why do you have to be there in two months?" I asked. "That's right during school."

"Barnaby Chesterfield is playing Hamlet onstage in London," Leo said. "And I need to be there to see it."

"Why?"

"He's the greatest actor alive," Leo said. "And I'm going to be able to say that I saw him do Hamlet *in person*. It's going to change my life."

Barnaby Chesterfield was a famous actor. Like Lisette Chamberlain, he had been a stage actor before hitting it big on TV and in the movies. And even though I might not know everything about Lisette Chamberlain, I did know a lot about Barnaby Chesterfield.

My dad and I used to watch *Darwin,* the show where Chesterfield got his big break, together. We both loved it because we loved science fiction and science and alternate realities, and *Darwin* was about a brilliant scientist who lived in the future. My mom and the boys weren't into it like we were, although sometimes Ben would stop and watch for a few minutes because he liked the sound of Barnaby Chesterfield's very deep voice. Ben always liked different sounds, things that had resonance.

"How is it going to change your life?" I asked Leo.

"I'll be in the presence of greatness," he said. "I think I was born for greatness too."

I wanted to laugh at him, but the truth was I used to think the same thing. Just a tiny bit, in my heart. I felt like there had to be something special for me to do. But lately I didn't think that anymore. And even when I had, I never said it out loud.

"What kind of greatness?" I asked.

"I'm still not sure," Leo said. "But I have ideas."

"That *Hamlet* has been sold out for months," I said.

"How did you know that?"

"It was in the news," I said. "It sold out faster than any other London stage show in history." It made headlines in the weeks after the accident. Every time I saw the words *Barnaby Chesterfield* I felt like I had been punched in the stomach.

"We bought the tickets last year right when they went on sale," Leo said. "With my dad's credit card. I had the money so he let me do it and we got one for him too. So I can go, and my dad's going to come with me, but I have to earn the money for my own airfare. I'm not there yet, but I'm getting close."

"And if you don't?"

"We can sell the *Hamlet* tickets to someone else, no problem," Leo said. "The theater will buy them back because the demand is so high. But the deadline my dad set for me to have the money for the plane tickets is coming up. I don't have enough money yet."

"And we don't make very much money selling concessions."

"Right," Leo said. "I need to supplement my income. That's why I came up with the tour."

We were almost to our street. "Do you want to come eat breakfast at my house?" Leo asked.

I did and I didn't. Mostly I didn't want to see him with his normal family eating breakfast together. My family ate cold cereal on our own whenever we felt like it because my mom, who used to get up super early, now got up at the last possible minute. She stayed up too late. This summer because she was building the deck; during the school year it had been lesson plans and grading. She had to tire herself all the way out, she said, before she could fall asleep.

"Thanks," I said. "Maybe another time."

"Okay," Leo said. "I'll see you at work." I watched him go the rest of the way home and walk up the steps to his house.

As soon as he'd gone inside I wished I'd said yes instead.

I sat out in the backyard eating a bowl of cereal and looking at the mess that was our deck. My mom came outside. She had her gym clothes on.

"All done running?" she asked.

I nodded. It seemed less like lying if I didn't *say* the lie. "Look," I said. The birds had started swooping around, big and dark and freaky. "Do you think they might be eagles?" I asked, even though I knew they weren't.

"Turkey vultures," my mom said. She gave me a kiss on the top of my head and said, "I'm going to be late. I'll see you soon, sweetie."

The vultures hovered for a minute more, and then they started to settle in the tree. Once they were deep in the leaves, I couldn't see them.

Every day my mom went to her exercise class and then to run errands and I was in charge of Miles.

Every day we did the same thing. We made peanut-butter-and-banana sandwiches with chocolate milk for lunch and then we watched a really bad soap opera that my mother would never in a million years have let us watch. But she didn't know. We pretended we did crafts and played games. That's what we always said we'd been doing when she came home.

The soap opera was called *Times of Our Seasons*, which didn't actually make sense when you thought too hard about it. It always started with the scene of a beautiful woman and a handsome man walking along a beach and then a ticking clock was superimposed over them.

Our favorite character was named Harley, and she had been buried alive (and I mean buried, like in a coffin in the ground and everything) by her archnemesis, Celeste. Inside the coffin, there was this walkie-talkie thing that Celeste used to talk to Harley and a tube where Celeste sent food down. That was it. Harley had to lie inside that box, day after day.

We *had* to see her get out.

Times of Our Seasons had lots of other drama too. Death and divorce and everything else besides.

You might think this would be a bad choice for two kids who had lost a parent and a sibling in an accident.

But it was so fake it was perfect.

"Hurry!" Miles shouted from the family room. "It's starting!"

I put straws in our chocolate milk and went in to sit next to him.

Harley came up on the screen. She was still in the box, wearing the white silk dress they'd buried her in when she was unconscious. Harley's long dark hair spread out on the satin pillow under her head. Her makeup was still perfect—plum lipstick, mascara, eyeliner that seemed to have sparkles in it. She beat her hands against the top of the coffin. "Celeste!" she said. "Let me out! You know this isn't fair to Rowan!"

(Rowan was the man that Celeste and Harley both loved. He was the reason Celeste had put Harley underground. Celeste wanted Rowan all to herself.)

"Do you think that this time they'll tell us how she goes to the bathroom?" Miles asked.

"Be quiet," I said. "You have to listen."

We thought today might be the day she would get out.

It wasn't.

But they couldn't leave her there forever.

19

That night at work none of the Hellfarts came by and I sold thirty-three programs, which made me so pleased that I bought myself a lemon tart at the end of the night when they went on sale for half price.

Miles waited up so he could tell me that he had sucked his way through an entire Fireball. "Mom saw," he said. "So it's documented."

"What will you do with your life now?"

"Uncle Nick told me that when he was my age he could put one Fireball in each cheek," Miles said. "And suck on them until they were both gone."

"That's insanity," I said.

"It's awesome," Miles said.

I ate Leo's mom's lasagna for dinner.

And when I went upstairs, there was something on my windowsill again.

It was a purple toothbrush. It wasn't in a package but the bristles weren't dirty.

Just like the screwdriver, the toothbrush was about the size and weight of something that Ben would have liked.

A dark shape flew past the window.

Maybe the birds are bringing them, I thought, as the breeze moved through the room. *Sometimes Mom opens the windows in the evenings to let the air in.*

I imagined the birds landing, black and swooped, on the windowsill. Looking around my room without me there to say, *Go away.*

The birds were like ghosts. Coming and going.

I'd never seen a ghost.

But some people believed they saw Lisette Chamberlain's ghost in the tunnels.

I had a weird thought. *What if Lisette Chamberlain's ghost is leaving things?*

I slowly turned around and looked at the door of the room I'd chosen. Purple. Purple was Lisette's favorite color. And I had chosen this room, even though purple was not *my* favorite color.

And our initials were the same, but in reverse. Cedar Lee, Lisette Chamberlain.

CL-LC.

You've been hanging out in too many cemeteries, I told myself. *Giving too many tours about people who are gone. And watching too many shows about people being buried alive.*

Birds or ghosts. Neither one made it easy to sleep.

But when I did, my brain kept dreaming about things I should save up for with my money from work. What if I bought boxes and boxes of Fireballs for Miles? What if I bought an entire set of silver spoons for Ben to flip back and forth? Or a brand-new baseball mitt for my father? I didn't dream about anything for my mom. Or for me.

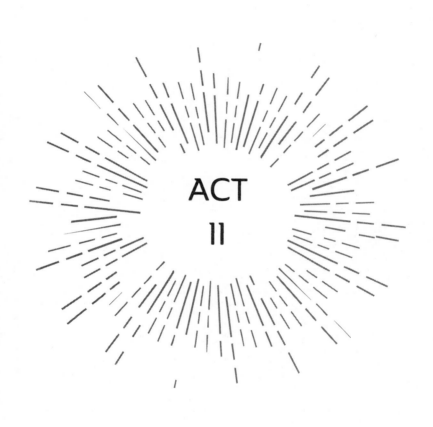

ACT
11

1.

One of the Hellfarts got a job selling concessions a few days later.

His name was Cory.

All the girls our age liked him except for me. Maddy and Samantha laughed at everything he said, even though nothing he said was funny.

"I need the money to get shocks for my bike," Cory told everyone when he first started. "This is the only place in town that will hire kids our age."

It was like he had to make sure we knew he was too cool for this job.

Cory had connections, according to Maddy.

"His dad knows *everyone*," she said.

When Cory walked by, I made *vrrt-vrrt* sounds, like he was farting with every step. I did it when he was too far away to hear. Every time I did it I kept a straight face and Leo would turn red from trying not to laugh. Leo thought I was funny. Like it was one of my main characteristics. It felt great.

It also felt great when Gary got mad at Cory for not wearing his peasant hat during part of his first shift. "You're in *England*!" he told Cory. "One more stunt like that and I'll fire you."

"I guess Cory's dad doesn't know Gary," I said to Samantha, and she laughed too. So maybe more than one person thought I was funny.

2

Leo and I were *vrrt–vrrt*ing past the concession stand when he stopped all of a sudden and grabbed my arm. "*Look*," he said. "Right over there. Daniel Alexander."

Daniel Alexander was the man who had founded the Summerlost Festival almost fifty years ago. He knew everything about the festival and was still involved with running it. Every now and then he came across the courtyard and if you were close enough to say hi to him he would always say hi back. To anyone, even though he was famous. He actually reminded me of Leo, the way his face lit up.

Leo had said hi to Daniel Alexander five times.

I had said hi to him zero times.

"This way," Leo said. "Today's the day."

"The day I finally talk to him?" I said. "Or the day you ask if you can interview him about Lisette Chamberlain?"

"The day you talk to him," Leo said.

"I can't believe you're such a chicken about this," I told Leo. "It's almost like you're scared of him."

"Oh, I'm definitely scared of him."

"But he's so nice."

"Exactly," Leo said. "It's worse when nice people get mad at you. And he'll be mad if he finds out I'm giving a tour about his friend."

"But he could probably tell you so much."

"Shut up," Leo said. "He's *right there.*"

And he was. Daniel Alexander had stopped near us to look at the signboard with the day's Summerlost Festival activities on it. I could already see people around the courtyard turning his way, preparing to swarm. Now was our chance.

"Hi," I said, and I must have said it loud, because Daniel Alexander jumped when he turned around, and his purple drink went all over my skirt and blouse.

"Oh *no*," he said. "I'm so sorry."

"Is that wine?" Leo asked.

That made Daniel Alexander laugh his wonderful laugh and more people looked in our direction. Including Cory the Hellfart. Including Gary. Oh no.

"Heavens, no," Daniel Alexander said. "It's my special health drink. I have it every morning. Tastes awful, but it's supposed to keep me young."

He reached into his pocket and pulled out a handkerchief and handed it to me. "But I'm afraid the berries in it probably stain terribly." He blinked. "Well. Nothing to worry about, my dear. You go down to the costume shop and they'll fix you right up. Ask for Meg."

I hesitated. Hadn't Gary said something about making sure to stay on Meg's good side? And wouldn't my showing up in a stained costume be a bad thing?

Out of the corner of my eye I saw Gary moving our way.

I could let Gary get mad at me or take my chances with the unknown.

"*Go,*" Leo whispered.

3

The stairwell down to the costume shop smelled old, like my dad's elementary school, which he showed us once when we went to Portland. The floor at the bottom was speckly linoleum. The ceiling felt low and the lights hummed.

I walked past doors that said WIGS and MAKEUP and kept on going toward the end of the hall and the sign that said COSTUMES. Every sound I made seemed to echo. I tried to make sure my sandals didn't squish or slap.

When I got to the costume shop doorway, no one looked up. So I stood looking in. Rows and rows of clothes on racks, all around the room. Shelves at the back. Sewing machines and ironing boards and long tables with chairs. A mini-fridge near the door. Four or five college-aged women and men moving around doing different things. One woman sitting at a computer in the corner. And an older Asian lady with short white hair sitting at one of the tables using a tape measure. She had glasses on a chain around her neck, and she wore a black apron over her blouse and pants.

She was the one who looked up first. "Can I help you?"

"I'm looking for Meg," I said.

"That's me."

"Daniel Alexander said to come see you," I said. "About my costume. He spilled his drink on it."

"Of course he did," Meg said. "Wait here. I'll find you something to wear."

She came back out with an outfit that was completely different from the white peasant blouses and patterned floral skirts. It was a deep green dress with a full skirt and ribbons woven through it.

"You can tell Gary he'll have to live with it for today," she said. "I don't have any concessions costumes left in your size. This was from the children's act in the Greenshow, years ago."

"Okay," I said. "Thank you."

"Come back tomorrow and I'll have the other one washed for you. I don't want you taking it home and doing it wrong and getting the stain set in for good."

"Okay," I said again. I resisted the urge to spin around and see what the skirt would do. The dress felt old but it didn't smell that way. And then I had an interesting thought. *If Meg had been making costumes for so many years, maybe she knew Lisette Chamberlain.*

"You're a Lee, aren't you," Meg said. "Ralph and Naomi Carter are your grandparents."

"Yes." I felt surprised even though I shouldn't. My grandparents had lived in Iron Creek for years and my mom grew up here and the town wasn't that big.

"I heard you bought a house here," she said.

I nodded. "The old Wainwright house."

"Ah," she said. "That's a house with some skeletons."

I must have looked taken aback because Meg said, "I didn't mean that literally. It's a nice house. And I bet your mom is doing a lot of work fixing it up."

"She is," I said. "She's building a deck."

"Good for her," Meg said. "What's your name?"

"Cedar."

"And you're working for Gary."

"Yes."

"We could use someone to help out in the costume shop too." Meg gestured around her at the shop, the people working in it. "We've got a lot of extra projects this summer. But we've already hired everyone we have the budget to hire. I don't imagine you're a juvenile delinquent who needs community service hours."

"No."

"I didn't think so," she said. "Bring that dress back tomorrow."

4

"Nice," Leo said when he saw me. "Are you supposed to be a princess or something?"

"Obviously," I said.

"Wow."

"They didn't have anything else in my size," I explained.

"So how was it in the costume shop?"

"Fine," I said. "Meg was pretty nice, actually. Maybe she's only scary to Gary."

"I guess it kind of makes sense that you guys get along," Leo said.

"Why?"

"She's Korean."

I stared at him.

"Like, she has Korean ancestry," he said, as if I only needed him to explain.

"*I* don't have Korean ancestry," I said. "Just because Meg and I aren't all white doesn't mean we automatically have things in common. That's a stupid thing to say."

I'd had stuff like this happen to me before. Iron Creek was a small town and even in our bigger town I'd had things said to me, usually not meant to be mean, usually just because people are stupid.

And sometimes people asked me if I was adopted, which I extra hated. I had straight dark hair like my dad's and my eyes were the same color as his. It felt like I didn't belong to my mom because I didn't look like her to people who weren't looking closely enough. Because if you do, you see that my mom and I actually look a lot alike even though she has blond hair and blue eyes.

I hated that Leo had said what he did.

"I'm sorry," Leo said. "I'm really sorry. I didn't mean to—"

I could tell he *was* really sorry because, for the first time since I'd known him—even when the Hellfarts were bugging him—he looked pale. And for the first time since I'd known him he didn't know what to say.

But I was still mad.

Right then Cory walked past and knocked off Leo's hat. "Better let your *girlfriend* get back to work," he said. I hated his stupid light eyebrows and his sunburny skin.

Leo bent down and picked up his hat. A lady came by and asked him for a program. He sold it to her without any accent at all.

I watched Leo and I realized that he also knew how it felt to be different. To want big things in a very small town. To get made fun of. He wasn't as different as I was. But he also wasn't one of those lucky people who fit in all the time. And I thought of the first time I worked with him, what I'd seen. He did like the world—that was the thing about him that I liked the best—but the world didn't *always* like him back.

"Do people think we're going out?" I asked Leo.

He looked (mostly) relieved at the change in subject. "Most people don't," he said. "I've been telling people that we're cousins so that they won't think it's so weird that we're always together."

I groaned. "Leo, that's a terrible idea," I said. "People will think we're *cousins* who are *dating*."

"That's disgusting," Leo said.

"I know," I told him. "Plus, we don't even look alike. Why would you say that?"

"We *do* look alike," he insisted. "A lot alike. We're both short. We both have dark hair and freckles. And our eyebrows are the same."

"They are?" Did mine look devilish too?

5

On the ride home we stopped by the new theater construction site.

They were pouring the foundations.

"Just big craters filled with cement," Leo said. "No tunnels there. No mysteries."

"What is it with you and those tunnels?"

"They're the only place we know Lisette went that we haven't been," Leo reminded me. "Maybe we'll see her ghost."

"You can't really believe that," I said.

"Other people say they did," Leo said. "And even if we don't, this is our last chance to know for sure. At the end of the summer, the old theater and the tunnels are going to be destroyed. *We'll never know.*"

When the policeman came to follow up with my mother about the accident, I hid out in the hallway by the living room and eavesdropped on their conversation. She asked him so many questions. Some she'd asked before. *How could this happen? Did they suffer? Why was that driver on the road?*

He said he thought it happened fast, both for my dad and

Ben and for the drunk driver who hit them, but for the rest of the questions he said, *We just don't know.*

We just don't know.

Some things are gone for good. You can't get them back. You can't know what happened. Ever.

"Meg wondered if I wanted to volunteer," I said. "Maybe if I worked in the costume shop I could find something out about the tunnels. Maybe about Lisette too. Meg's been working here for a long time."

"That would be *great*." Leo looked impressed.

I decided to take advantage of that.

"But you have to pay me equally for the tour stuff from now on," I said.

"All right."

"And never, ever say that we're cousins again."

"Got it."

"And—"

"Come *on*. Don't you think that's enough?"

"There might be more," I told him. "I'll let you know when I think of the rest."

6

My uncle Nick came over that night to help my mom with the deck. I was always glad when he did because then my mom wasn't alone out there. She wanted to finish the deck before we left for the summer and it was taking longer than she'd expected, so she often worked late, when the night cooled things off.

Nick had strung up a light in the back so they could see in the dark while they worked. I hoped it would scare the turkey vultures away but they didn't leave. Sometimes I'd hear the sanding stop and when I looked down either Nick would have gone home or he and my mom would be talking.

Ben and I could never really talk the way Miles and I did, but I got to understand Ben anyway. At first, during the earlier years, he would scream and yell and you couldn't say a lot to him. But then when things sort of evened out, when he'd had some therapy and my parents knew how to help him more, you could have short almost-conversations with him. Like he would say, "Do you want a LEGO set for Christmas?" and I would say, "No, I want a camera for Christmas. Do *you* want a

LEGO set for Christmas, Ben?" He would grin really big and say yes and I knew I'd said what he wanted me to say.

Also when we went skiing together I could tell from the look on his face that he felt the way I did. Peaceful. Good. I saw him breathing deep when we went on the trails and I knew it was because he smelled the pine trees. We looked a lot alike when his face was at rest. I had never noticed it until I saw a picture that my dad showed us from one of the days we were up on the mountain.

We didn't deal with skiing last winter. My mom didn't get out the ski rack or the skis. She wasn't as good as my dad, and driving in the snow scared her, even though she was the one who had lived in it all her life and my dad was from Portland, where it didn't snow nearly as much. We didn't even talk about going skiing. And I wasn't mad. I didn't want to go either. Maybe Miles did, but if so, he didn't say.

7

I was changing into my black jeans and black T-shirt early in the morning when I heard Miles hollering out and my mom hurrying down the hall to his room.

He didn't usually have nightmares. Not even after the accident.

I tiptoed down the hall to the room and I heard my mother soothing him and Miles saying something about Harley.

Uh-oh.

I pushed open the door. "Everything okay?"

"Miles had a bad dream," Mom said, looking shaky. "He dreamed he was buried alive."

"It's okay, Mom," Miles said. And then, before I could stop him, he said, "It's from a show that Cedar and I have been watching."

"What?" Mom asked, turning to look at me. "What kind of a show has people who are buried alive?"

"It's not real," Miles said. He was still sweating but his voice sounded back to normal. "No one is *really* buried alive on *Times of Our Seasons*. It's fake."

"You've been letting Miles watch *Times of Our Seasons*?" Mom said, and I could tell she was *mad*. "You shouldn't even be watching that. Let alone Miles!"

"I know," I said. "I'm sorry. We watched it one day and got sucked in."

"That show is trashy," Mom said. "All soap operas are. And this one sounds *sick*."

"Mom," Miles said, starting to panic now that he was fully awake and knew what he'd done. "You have to let us finish. We need to see what happens to Harley."

"Absolutely not," Mom said.

"We won't watch it anymore," I told my mom. "I promise."

"We have to," Miles said. "We *have* to see Harley get out!"

"No, you don't," Mom said. "You absolutely do not. Cedar Lee, we need to have a talk."

8

I was almost late to meet Leo. After my mother grounded me for two weeks from everything except work and running (which basically amounted to my not being grounded since those were the only places I went, but I didn't point that out), and said that she was canceling our television service *this very morning,* she did a double take. "Why are you wearing jeans to go running?"

"I'm not," I said. "I was getting dressed when I heard Miles and I threw on the first thing I found." It was a pretty good lie. I went over to my drawer and pulled out a pair of old black track pants, the kind that people wear who don't actually go running.

"You're going to be too hot," she said.

"No," I said. "I promise. I've worn these before. It's fine."

She went back to bed and I wore the track pants out the door in case she was watching from her window.

"I thought of something else I need from you," I said when I caught up with Leo.

"What?" he asked.

"My brother and I need a place to watch *Times of Our Seasons.*"

"What on earth is *Times of Our Seasons*?"

"A really trashy soap opera," I said.

"Seriously?"

"I'm very serious," I said. Miles was never going to get over this if he didn't see Harley get out of that box. And she would. I knew it.

Wouldn't she?

9

In the city where I really lived, there are some pretty fancy hotels. They had nice restaurants, and lobbies with chandeliers, and a couple of them even had ballrooms.

The Iron Creek Hotel, where Lisette Chamberlain died, was not like that.

According to Leo, it also wasn't like that back in Lisette Chamberlain's time.

"It was better back then," he told the people when he gave the tour, "but it was never, like, *fancy*. It was the best hotel in town, but that isn't saying a lot."

Still, the Iron Creek Hotel was the best stop on the tour, and a lot of it was due to Paige, the weekday front-desk clerk.

She worked from six to eleven every morning during the week and she had a crush on one of Leo's older brothers, so Leo had talked her into letting us bring the tour inside the hotel.

"What does she get in return?" I'd asked him.

"Zach's phone number," he said. "At the end of the summer."

Paige was really fun. She had long, gorgeous hair that she always wore braided in some cool way and she also had glasses and wore motorcycle boots with her hotel uniform. Her voice was really sweet but most of the things she said were not.

It was my turn to lead the hotel part of the tour.

"As you're aware," I said, to our clients (this time it was a family, with a mom who was clearly *way* more into it than her kids and husband, and also an older man, like sixty-five), "Lisette Chamberlain died in the Iron Creek Hotel under mysterious circumstances."

Someone walked into the lobby and asked Leo where the continental breakfast was.

He pointed them in the right direction.

"What mysterious circumstances?" asked one of the kids. He was about ten and had spiky hair and an attitude. "Like drugs? Suicide?"

"No," I said.

"Murder?" asked his younger brother.

"Let me show you the room where she died," I said, "and I'll finish the rest of the story."

The hotel hadn't wanted to turn the room into a shrine or anything and they needed the space, but for a while no one wanted to stay in that room because they thought it was bad luck. So the management had turned it into a housekeeping closet.

When you went inside you saw towels folded on white shelves. Bright blue bottles of Windex shining like jewels. Jugs of bleach. You smelled fake lavender, the scent of the soaps and lotions they used to stock the bathrooms. It was a huge closet.

You could definitely tell it had once been a room, and the bathroom was still one the hotel staff could use.

"This is where Lisette Chamberlain died," I said. "It didn't look like this, of course. The bed was over there, where the towels are now. But the bathroom is similar. They've changed the tile and the fixtures, but the footprint of the room is the same."

"Did she die *in the bathroom*?" the older boy asked. The younger one cracked up.

"No," I said. I glanced back at Leo and he rolled his eyes. "She died in her bed. They found her there when she didn't check out on the day she was supposed to leave."

"So how did she die?" asked the older boy. "Are you *sure* it wasn't drugs?" The old man gave him the evil eye.

"She died of a heart attack," I said. "She was all alone."

The older boy gave a big sigh of boredom. The dad checked his watch. The mom asked Leo a question about Lisette. The old man's eyes met mine, and for a second, there was that odd understanding that happens sometimes between perfect strangers.

It would be terrible to die of a heart attack, and all alone.

It's terrible to die.

Everyone filed out and Leo started telling them about our next stop, the cemetery.

I was the last one left so I closed the door.

10

"This guy is a *really* bad actor," Leo said.

"We know," Miles and I said.

"His hair is so weird," Leo said.

"We *know*," Miles and I said.

We sat in Leo's basement, on his couch. He had turned on *Times of Our Seasons* for us. We came fifteen minutes before the show started with our sandwiches and our chocolate milk. I'd made a sandwich for Leo too. He peeled off the top piece of bread and looked at the peanut butter and banana and said, "You guys are so weird," but he ate it anyway.

It was the first time I'd met some of Leo's family. His parents were at work but he had two older brothers who were both in high school and who played football. Jeremy and Zach. They were huge. They were sweaty. They paid almost no attention to us or to Leo at all after they said *Hi*. But they weren't mean or anything. They made their own sandwiches and then sat down at the table in the dining room.

"We're using the TV downstairs," Leo called out to them as we left the kitchen.

"What are you watching?" one of them, I think Jeremy, called back.

"*Times of Our Seasons*," Leo said.

His brothers started laughing.

We got the show turned on in time to see the people finish walking on the beach and the clock ticking. Miles leaned forward.

It didn't start with Harley's story. It started with another story, one about a twin who was pretending to be his brother in order to steal his girlfriend and money. His brother was on a business trip, which was really not a business trip, but something involving some kind of super-secret spy activity.

"You kiss differently," the girlfriend murmured to the twin.

"Really?" he said. "Better?"

Miles buried his face in a pillow in embarrassment and I stared straight ahead. This was mortifying. I hadn't thought about what this would be like to watch RIGHT NEXT to Leo.

But Leo didn't seem uncomfortable. He was cracking up. "This doesn't even make *sense*."

"We *know*," Miles and I said.

"We only care about the Harley storyline," I said.

The bad-twin couple finally finished kissing and then there she was. In the coffin.

"That's Harley," Miles said, pointing to her.

"I figured," said Leo.

"We still don't know how she goes to the bathroom," Miles said, and that made Leo laugh again.

"Shhhh," I hissed at them both, and they went quiet.

It was a big day.

We found out how Celeste had managed to make Harley look dead long enough to fool everyone for the funeral and everything.

Herbs.

"Wow," Miles said, sitting back when the scene had finished. "That was a good one."

"It was?" Leo asked.

"Information-wise," I said, "yes. We found out something we didn't know before."

"Harley's not a very good actor either," Leo said, and when I glared at him he put his hands in the air. "I'm just saying."

"Was Lisette Chamberlain a good actor when she was in soap operas?" I asked. "I've only seen her in her movies."

"Wait," Leo said. "You mean you've never seen footage of her actually onstage at Summerlost?"

"No," I said. "Have you? Does that exist?"

"I have and it does," Leo said.

One of Leo's brothers rumbled down the stairs and we went quiet for a second.

"You can check out the old plays from the Summerlost film archives," Leo said. "I have a card. My mom helped me get it."

"Is your family really into Lisette Chamberlain or something?"

"No," Leo said. "Only me."

"But they're really into the Summerlost Festival, then."

"Nope," Leo said. "Everyone else is really into football. I like football too, but watching it. Not playing it like Zach and Jeremy."

Leo didn't only not fit in with the kids who teased him. He also didn't seem to fit in with his own family.

We went back upstairs.

"Thanks, Leo," I said when we got to the front door.

"No problem," Leo said.

Zach came up behind Leo. "Are you the Lee kids?" he asked. "The ones who moved in a little while ago?"

"Yes," Leo said, sounding annoyed. "We *told* you that when they first came in."

"Everyone in the neighborhood is mad at your mom," Zach said to Miles and me. "Because she's going to rent the house to college kids during the year."

"It's zoned for it," I said. I sounded snotty but I didn't care. I'd heard Uncle Nick telling my mom that people were bugged that we were going to rent it out since no one else on the street did.

"I know," Zach said, walking over to the sink and dumping his dishes into it. "And there's always the chance you'll rent to girls. Hot college girls. *I* have no problem with it."

"We *are* going to rent to girls," Miles said. "Mom says they take better care of things than guys do."

"We want to come back every summer," I said, "and renting the house is the only way we can afford to keep it."

"We'll stand up for you," Leo said. "We'll try to sway the neighbors."

"For sure," said Zach. Then he rumpled Leo's hair and Leo shoved him away. But they were both grinning.

I don't know what Miles thought about while we walked home but I thought about Leo. I guess I was wrong about him fitting in with his family. And I should have realized that he would fit in because that's one thing I do know for sure. That it is possible to be different and still belong to your family. For them to love you like crazy.

Ever since the accident I've worried that Ben didn't know that. Or feel that.

I think he did.

He had to, right?

I mean, we set up our whole lives around him. All the therapy. All the going to restaurants during the not-busy hours so that he wouldn't freak out in a crowd. All the humoring him when he wanted to wear his Halloween costume for months at a time. We listened to him say the same things over and over when he got stressed out. We glared at strangers when they gave Ben dirty looks. It was hard sometimes but we all did it, for years.

It's not only the hard stuff I remember about Ben. I

remember his ruffly hair, how he screamed but sometimes laughed. I remember his eyes wild and also very, very deep. I remember him when he was a baby and a toddler and he was cute and funny and none of us, including Ben, had any idea how things were going to turn out. And how he started to talk more again that last year and liked me to hold his hand when we watched scary parts in movies. He'd let go right when the scary part was over but when it was happening he held on *tight*.

I loved him. I finally loved him again, and then he was gone.

11

When I went downstairs to the costume shop before work, Meg wasn't at the table where she'd been before.

"She's in the back," said a woman who was ironing a long piece of fabric. "I'll go get her."

The one working at the computer didn't turn around.

The room was hot. They had a fan on, and every time it rotated past me it made the garbage bag I'd used to protect the special costume crinkle and strands of my hair blow into my eyes.

Meg brought my costume out on a hanger. "It's good to go," she said, and I handed her the other dress back. The fan blew her bangs to one side. The safety pins she had stuck to the top of her apron glittered like a necklace. She had a serious face with lines around her mouth that looked like she frowned a lot but also lines around her eyes that made it seem like she laughed a lot too.

Talk, Cedar, I told myself. But it was hard.

Did I honestly want to do this? Try to find out more about tunnels and Lisette? Did I really think a ghost was leaving things on my windowsill? Did I want to spend my time in a costume shop where I didn't know anyone?

"I came in early because I thought maybe I could volunteer after all," I said.

"Perfect," Meg said. "We can use you to take over relabeling the boxes for now. That will free Emily up for other things I need her to do."

"Hallelujah," said the person at the computer. Emily.

"Okay," I said.

And so that's how I ended up typing a list that had things on it like this:

APRONS: WHITE AND OFF-WHITE

ASSES HEADS: ALL TYPES

BUM ROLLS: NO FARTHINGALES,
BUSTLE PADS, OR RUFFLES

CROWNS: GOOD MEDIEVAL CROWNS

CROWNS: PLAIN MEDIEVAL CROWNS

FARTHINGALES

HATS: STRAW

HATS: BICORN

HATS: TRICORN

HORNS

MIDSUMMER ACCESSORIES

STOMACHERS

CODPIECES: SMALL

CODPIECES: LARGE

I couldn't help it. When I got to "codpieces," I snickered.

"Is something funny?" Meg asked. I glanced at her. Her face was serious but her voice sounded dry, like she knew exactly why I was laughing.

"Um," I said. "I've finished typing the list."

"Good," Meg said. "Print them out, one label to each page. Then take them to that row of boxes and replace the old labels with the new ones."

And so I did.

I took the old labels off.

I taped the new labels on.

I laughed to myself when I got to CODPIECES.

And then it was time to go.

13

"So you didn't get to ask Meg about the tunnels," Leo said after work. We walked through the Portrait Hall on our way out and stopped in front of a painting of an old man with wiry white hair and a dull gold crown. The man held up his hands in front of him, making a dramatic gesture, and his blue veins seemed to course with blood. RICHARD SNOW AS KING LEAR, the plaque under the painting said.

Whoever had painted this portrait had done a good job. I looked at the signature. *Arlene Stecki.* The same person who did Lisette Chamberlain's portrait.

"No," I said. "Not really. I didn't talk to anyone, actually."

"Was it boring?"

"It was fine," I said. "It's sort of interesting to see all the costumes and all the work that goes into them."

"Can you come over to my house sometime?" Leo asked. "I have a show I want you to see. Something with *real* acting in it. Not that crap you and Miles have been watching."

"I don't know," I said. "I'll ask my mom."

"We could watch it on Friday," he said. "That's my mom's day off so she'll be home. If that makes your mom feel better."

"It will. But I still don't know if she'll let me come."

"Tell her it's *The Tempest* starring Lisette Chamberlain as Miranda," he said. "I got it from the festival archives."

"It sounds boring."

"It's not. I promise."

14

"Leo invited me over to watch a movie," I said Friday after work. I shoved my sandals into the basket my mom kept by the front door for shoes and pulled on my flip-flops. They felt great. I felt sorry for all the people who had lived in England.

"A movie," Mom said.

"Yes," I said.

"That sounds like a date."

My mother had a very firm NO DATES rule. Not until we were much, much older than twelve. Which was why I'd waited until the last possible minute to ask her. I was sure she'd say no.

"It's not a date," I said. "His mom will be home. And it's with Leo."

"What movie are you watching?"

"An old production of *The Tempest*," I said. "Leo rented it from the Summerlost Festival library archives. It's a classic."

"You can go if Miles goes with you," Mom said.

"Mom," I said. "He's going to be so bored."

"I'm going to be so bored," Miles confirmed from the couch. He didn't look up from his library book.

"Leo's *mom* will be home," I said again. "It's during the day. He's a friend. *Please.*"

My mom relented. "All right."

I couldn't believe it. Maybe staying up late working on the deck was making her too tired to argue.

When I got to Leo's house, his mom answered the door. She had short black hair. Her eyes were like Leo's, crinkly with laughter. She was beautiful. "Hello!" she said. "It's so nice to meet you, Cedar."

"Thanks," I said. "It's nice to meet you too."

"I need to come by and say hello to your mother again," Mrs. Bishop said. "I always think summer won't be as busy as the school year, and then of course it always is."

"We still have your pan, I think," I said.

"Oh, that's all right." She waved her hand. "You should keep it. You probably didn't want to bring all your own cooking things down for the summer."

She was right. We hadn't. We'd brought three pots, six plates, six bowls, six cups, six sets of cutlery. A couple of knives for chopping. A can opener. A cookie sheet. One pitcher. That was it. Everything else, my mom said, was too much hassle. We didn't even use the dishwasher very much. We mostly washed things right after we used them and put them back in the cupboard. Even Miles.

"Leo's downstairs," Mrs. Bishop said, "getting everything all set up. Do you want anything to eat? Or drink?"

"I'm fine, thank you."

"You can head on down," she said. "But I'll peek in on you now and then to make sure you don't need anything."

When I got downstairs, Leo showed me the T-shirts he'd had made for us for the tour. They were black and had Lisette's face on them in white, kind of pop-arty, like that picture of Marilyn Monroe you see on towels and cheap blankets and T-shirts.

"Don't let anyone in my family see it," he said, and I nodded. None of his family or mine knew about the tour.

"They look really good. Are you going to print up extra for us to sell?"

"I'm worried about liability," he said. "Plus if people wear them around, other people might ask where they got them. Which would be great publicity, but also increases the chances that the festival finds out what we're doing and tells us to stop."

"I still don't see why they would care."

"We're using their grounds for part of the tour," Leo said. "And whenever you want to do something and you're not an adult, people tell you to stop. Even when there's no real reason."

That was true.

I sat down on the couch. It felt funny to not be watching *Times of Our Seasons*. "So," I said, "*The Tempest.*"

"Yeah," Leo said. He cued up the film.

"I haven't read it before. Will I still know what's going on?"

"Yeah. If you don't, ask me. I've watched it a bunch of times."

"I'm sure you have," I said.

Leo shot me a look then, one that I hadn't seen before. It was a look that seemed hurt. I felt bad.

So I didn't say anything when the play started and it was kind of funny and old. I didn't crack a single joke about the outfits the people in the audience wore or the actors running around onstage, pretending they were on a ship that was sinking. The seats surrounded the stage on three sides, so the actors were right in the middle of their audience.

And then a woman came onstage, wearing a cream-colored dress, tattered but beautiful. You couldn't yet see her face but the dress stood out against the dark beams, under the dim lights, like a butterfly at night, a white fish in a deep ocean.

I bet Meg made that dress, I thought.

The camera went right to Lisette Chamberlain and a light bloomed around her on the stage as she spoke. Over her white dress she wore a military coat that was too big, like it had been her dad's and he'd given it to her to keep her warm. The coat was frayed and made of blue-gray velvet. She had bare feet, long red hair, beautiful eyes.

She was alive again, for now.

You could tell right away how good she was. The other actors were good too—how they'd memorized those long complicated lines, how they projected their voices out and moved their bodies—but it seemed like they were talking to us all, speaking out to the audience at large. Lisette seemed like she was talking to you. And you. And you. It felt like she spoke to everyone individually, even though she couldn't possibly look each person in the eye.

The old man playing her father, Prospero, looked familiar too. I realized it was the guy from the King Lear portrait. The way he and Lisette interacted made me think *They could really be a father and his daughter* even though I didn't understand everything they were saying. I got most of it though. Somehow, he had the power to create a storm, and she wanted him to stop it because she worried about the people on the boat.

Lisette's character might be trapped on an island, but at least she had her dad, and he was magic.

Leo stopped the play right as a dark-haired man came onto the scene, a handsome guy staggering around as more fake wind and rain sounds hammered the stage.

"What are you doing?" I asked. I'd been getting into it.

"So the interesting thing about this play," Leo said, "besides the fact that it's Lisette Chamberlain's final performance, is *this* guy. The actor playing Ferdinand, who's the love interest for Miranda."

I leaned in to look at the man on the stage.

"Roger Marin," Leo said.

"Whoa," I said. "Roger Marin." I knew the name from the tour. "The guy who was her second husband?"

"Yes."

"And this is *after* they broke up?"

"Yeah, one year later," Leo said. "Roger Marin never got as famous as Lisette did. He worked at Summerlost every summer, for the whole season. And that last year, when she came back, she starred opposite him one more time. In *this* performance. On the stage where they'd met years before."

"Wow," I said. "So she saw her ex-husband onstage the night she died."

"Yeah," Leo said. "And he visited her at the hotel that night too."

"*What?*"

Leo nodded. "The police report says that two people visited her that night after the performance. The person with the room next to Lisette's told the police that she heard knocking and the door open and close and then voices. Twice. She admitted peeking out to see who the second person was."

"And it was . . ."

"Roger Marin," he said. "The lady next door heard them talking, but she couldn't tell what they said. Then she heard him leave. She peeked out then too. She was nosy. Back then all the rumors were that Lisette had never stopped loving Roger Marin. It was a big deal that they were performing together.

That woman had actually been to the play. So she couldn't help herself when she recognized the voices. Her name was Melissa Wells and she had come all the way from New York City to see the performance."

"So Roger Marin visited Lisette at the hotel," I said. "The very night she died."

"Yup."

"But there was no evidence of foul play."

"Right," Leo said.

"But maybe Roger Marin literally broke her heart. I mean, she *did* die of a heart attack."

"Right again," Leo said.

"Why don't you include any of this information on the tour?" I asked.

"The superfans know all of this already," Leo said. "And they've got their own theories about her death. And if they get talking, they could go on for hours. Trust me. We don't want that."

"How did you get a copy of the police report?"

"It's public information," Leo said. "Anyone can ask for it. Plus it was printed in the newspapers back when she died. That's where I found it. Do you want to see?"

"Not really," I said. And I think Leo could tell from my voice that I meant *Absolutely not*. I knew there was a police report written up about the accident with Dad and Ben. I had never read it. And I never would. I knew the bits and pieces my mom told me back when it happened and that was more than enough.

"Yeah," Leo said. "We don't have to talk about it. I wasn't thinking." He sounded awkward and I could tell he had remembered about my family. He reached for the remote to start up the play again but I stopped him.

"What did Roger Marin say about that night?" I asked. "Was that in the police report too?" I didn't want to read it. But I wanted to know more.

"He said that Lisette hadn't been feeling great after the performance so he came over to check on her," Leo said. "And that she seemed fine when he left. She was going to go to sleep."

"Can *we* talk to Roger Marin?" I asked.

Leo shook his head. "He died two years ago. In Las Vegas. He worked in a show there for a long time after he stopped doing the plays at Summerlost."

The play started up again. We watched for a while. "She doesn't have a very big part," I said. "Considering it's her final performance."

"She didn't know it was her final performance," Leo said.

"Right."

"I guess that during the last few years she liked having smaller parts so she didn't have to memorize too much," Leo said. "Since she was only coming for one night."

The camera zoomed closer on Lisette, so you could see only her. I looked at that dress again, at the way they'd done her hair, loose and wavy and beautiful. And then I noticed something else.

"That's weird," I said.

"What is?" Leo asked.

"Pause it," I said.

Leo did.

"Lisette's character, Miranda, isn't married," I said. "But she's wearing a wedding ring." I pointed at her hand, which she'd lifted up. Her mouth was frozen in a funny position, like she was yowling.

"How on earth did you notice that?" Leo asked.

"I guess because of the labels," I said.

"What are you talking about?" Leo leaned in so that his face was comically close to the screen. "I don't see any labels."

"I'm talking about the labels I made in the costume shop," I said. "For the different boxes. The people in costume design pay attention to every little thing. They care about all the details. Look at this Miranda costume. It's perfect. I mean, you sort of take it for granted because it's so good, but it's exactly what Miranda would be wearing. And I know they wouldn't have given her a wedding ring to wear if her character wasn't married."

"So it's probably Lisette's own ring," Leo said.

"But Lisette wasn't married then. Right?"

"Right."

We both stared at the screen.

"So why is she wearing the ring?" Leo asked.

"I don't know," I said.

It was hard to see on the screen, but we could make out that it was a gold ring with three pale stones.

"It's the same ring she's wearing in the portrait," I said. "I'm sure of it. It's on her left hand."

"That's her wedding ring from Roger Marin," Leo said. "It's in tons of the paparazzi photographs from when she was married to him. She wore it all the time."

"Was that painting done when she was married to Roger?"

"Yeah," Leo said. "I know from the costume she's wearing in the painting. It's from the year she played Desdemona in *Othello*. But it makes sense for her to have a wedding ring on in that picture, because Desdemona is married from the beginning of the play. So they must have let her leave it on for the painting because it fits the character. And it was an old ring, the biography said. Vintage. She and Roger found it in an antiques shop in Italy when they were on vacation."

Leo really *did* know almost everything about Lisette Chamberlain.

"Maybe she wanted Roger to see her wearing it that last night," I said. "Maybe she did still care about him. Or something."

"Her character sort of gets married later in *The Tempest*," Leo said. "But she's definitely not married yet."

"Weird," I said.

"Huh." Leo reached for the remote to start up the play again but then he set it down. He frowned and scooted closer to the screen. I noticed, not for the first time, that even though his hair was very thick there were always a few strands sticking up in the back, a cowlick. It made me think of Ben.

"What's wrong?" I asked Leo.

"This ring thing is *really* weird," Leo said. "So. She's wearing the ring the night she died. But it's not listed with the items that were found in her room with her the next morning. She wasn't wearing it then."

"Are you sure?" I asked.

"Almost positive," Leo said. He ran out of the room and came back with some papers. "It's in the copy I made of the police report."

"Maybe they wrote down *ring* and weren't specific," I said.

"No," he said. "They mention a necklace and earrings. A suitcase and the contents. Shoes. Nylons. Clothing. All of that. But no ring."

I held out my hand. Leo hesitated. But I took it from him and read the list. I didn't let my eyes wander to anything else on the report.

"They were really thorough," I said.

"They were probably worried because they couldn't tell right off how she died. Plus she was famous. They wanted to do a good job."

The ring on the screen was the same one that was in her portrait. I was sure of it. Plain gold band, three pale stones.

"Rings don't fall off," I said. "Earrings, yeah. All the time. And necklaces, maybe. If the clasp breaks. But not rings. Not if they fit right. And I bet hers did. I mean, she'd worn it for all that time when she was married."

"*Weird*," Leo said. "All of it. Why was she wearing it that night? Where did it go?"

"Maybe she hid it," I said.

"But *why* would she hide it?" Leo asked. "She had a heart attack. She didn't *know* she was going to die."

"Maybe she gave it to one of the people who came to see her at the hotel," I said.

"Roger Marin," Leo said.

"Right."

"But why would she give it back?" Leo asked. "If she'd kept it that whole time."

It didn't seem likely to me either. If she cared about it enough to keep wearing it, she wouldn't hand it over to her ex-husband. And my mom still wore the rings my dad had given her, the diamond engagement ring and the wedding band. Of course, she and my dad hadn't gotten divorced. He died.

But maybe getting divorced didn't mean you stopped loving someone either.

"Lisette could also have given the ring to the first person who came to visit her at the hotel," I pointed out. "The person before Roger Marin."

"Maybe," Leo said. "But it's not very likely. In the police report the hotel maid said she came up around that time with some fresh towels that Lisette wanted. So the maid thinks she was the first person."

"It's all pretty interesting," I admitted.

"I know," Leo said.

At the end of the play I cried.

Because Lisette Chamberlain was dead?

Yes.

For the first time, she felt real to me. The play had made her real.

And I cried because of other things.

At the end Miranda's dad, Prospero, talked about how our lives are little. How they're rounded out with a sleep. And then, at the very end of the play, he was by himself. The audience was all, all around him, watching him, but he was alone on the stage and he walked off alone.

It was like he was saying good-bye to us. To the world.

"Sorry," Leo said when he noticed me crying. "Are you okay?"

"The ending is sad," I said. "How it's about dying."

"Yeah," Leo said. He sounded uncomfortable. "I'm sorry. I didn't think about that." His mouth went down and his eyes went sad. I could tell that he felt bad for me.

But he didn't look away from me the way most people do

when they say *I'm sorry*. I felt like I could say *I'm okay* or I could say something else. I felt like Leo was waiting for whatever came next.

"My brother used to like to go on drives," I said. I'm not sure why. It's what came out, what I guess I was thinking about. "Sometimes he wanted my mom or dad to take him alone and sometimes he wanted the whole family to come. We'd get in the car and back out of the driveway. He would say left, right, left. You weren't ever sure where he was going to take you but he wasn't doing it at random. He knew exactly where he wanted to go. Sometimes past the police station, or his school, stuff that made sense. Sometimes he'd have us drive past places I'd never even noticed, down streets I'd never wondered about, and then we'd come home a new way. He always knew how to get back."

"Did the accident happen on one of those drives?" Leo asked.

"No," I said. "It was on the freeway. Dad and Ben were going to another town to run some errands. The guy who hit them was drunk, right in the middle of the day. He died too."

I waited for Leo to say things. Like *I'm sorry* or *That's so sad* or *Drunk drivers are the worst*. All of those things were true.

"I wish I'd known your dad and your brother," Leo said.

"Me too," I said. "I wish that I had."

I could tell that Leo didn't know what I meant.

"I mean," I said, "I thought I knew them really well. But it turns out there was a lot more to them." And I realized I didn't only mean Ben, who was hard to know, who had his own world. I also meant my dad. I mean, he was my dad. I knew the way his face looked in the morning before he shaved and that he would read you a story almost any time you asked him to, especially on Saturday mornings. I knew that he loved to watch soccer and eat chocolate chips with a spoonful of peanut butter and I knew his favorite Christmas song was one that hardly anyone knew called "Far, Far, Away on Judea's Plains." But I didn't know lots of things. Did he believe in God and how much? When he was a teenager, who was the first girl he kissed? How long did it take him to learn how to read? What music did he listen to when no one else could hear?

"You don't have to know someone all the way to miss them," Leo said. "Or to feel bad that they're gone."

"Like you and Lisette Chamberlain," I said.

Leo looked horrified. "That's not what I meant." His face was red.

"I know," I said, "but it's true." I kind of missed Lisette too, now that I'd seen her alive. It was not the same *at all* as for my dad and Ben. But it was still missing someone. Wondering about them.

"Anyway," I said. "Thanks for letting me watch the play. You're right. She was amazing."

We went up the stairs and Leo came outside with me. The turkey vultures were wheeling around in the sky above the neighborhood. "There's those freaky birds," Leo said.

"Did they live in our backyard before we bought the house?" I asked.

"Yeah," Leo said. "They came after the Wainwrights left. But before you moved in."

That did not make me feel better.

I wanted them to be Wainwright birds.

16

Back at home I pulled Lisette Chamberlain on over my head and studied my new T-shirt in the mirror. It fit perfectly. I would have to wear another shirt over it in the morning so my mom wouldn't think it was weird that I was wearing a shirt with a dead lady's face on it to go running.

There wasn't anything on the windowsill, but it wasn't night yet. Still, it had been a little while. Maybe I was supposed to respond somehow? Like leave something back?

The things Lisette (if it was Lisette) was leaving for me were things Ben would have loved. Was she trying to help me heal?

How could I help *her*?

Did she need us to help her with something involving Roger? Did she want us to find her ring?

Maybe I should leave something purple on the windowsill so Lisette would know I was trying. Or maybe I should ask Leo what her favorite food was, and then I could leave that out for her.

And then I started laughing at how stupid I was.

Because that was what you did for Santa. Who was also not real. Like the ghost of Lisette Chamberlain was not real. Someone real had to be leaving those things.

Maybe it was Leo. Was that possible? The gifts hadn't started arriving on the windowsill until after I met him.

17

Saturday night after work there still wasn't anything new on the windowsill. But I did have a nightmare. Or maybe a dream.

Ben and I were driving. I was picking Ben up at school, which I did tons of times but I was always the passenger in real life and never the driver. In the dream I was great at driving. Perfect. I flicked my turn signal. We stopped at all the stop signs. It was like I had been driving all my life.

And then when we got home Ben stood in front of the door and wouldn't let me in because he wanted to talk to me. "Blue T-shirt," he said. "Gray pants. Orange sneakers."

And I realized he was wearing the outfit he'd had on when he died.

I hadn't remembered until the dream what he'd been wearing that day.

"It's okay, Ben," I said. "It's okay."

"Blue T-shirt," he said again. "Gray pants. Orange sneakers."

"Ben," I said.

"Blue T-shirt."

"Please stop," I said. "I remember now."

And he did stop.

Because I woke up. Crying.

18

The second stop on the tour, the theater, was always the trickiest one because Summerlost Festival employees were around early, getting ready for the day, and the box office opened for a couple of hours in the morning.

In addition to regular-priced tickets, the festival sold discounted day-of tickets to residents of Iron Creek, and those tickets were first-come, first-served on the day of the performance. The seats were only ten dollars but you had to sit on the very back row of the lower gallery, on a bench, not a theater seat. Leo told me all about it because he usually went to a bunch of the plays with the ten-dollar tickets, but this summer he was saving every bit of his money.

The idea behind the cheap day-of tickets was that they wanted to make the theater experience accessible to everyone, like the way people in Shakespeare's time could go to see the show for a penny if they were willing to stand.

It would be awful to stand for that long.

Anyway, Leo and I didn't want to run into a neighbor coming to stand in line or an employee working or, especially, *Gary*.

If we ran into Gary, it would be a one-way ticket out of England.

Because of all that, we didn't take the tour clients to the actual theater. We took them to the forest nearby.

It had rained the night before, a high-desert rain that left everything smelling good and the sky clear and enormous. Our feet crunched on the pine needles under the trees and our group murmured quietly to one another. It was a nice group of six older people, three sisters and their spouses, who had been coming to Summerlost for thirty years. Even though it was early, all three sisters were wearing sunglasses that looked so powerful it seemed like you could wear them into space.

"You can learn about the theater and the way it works on one of the official tours," I said, when we'd all gathered in one spot under the trees. "But we like to bring you here to see the whole festival below you as we talk about Lisette's career."

"All these years coming here and we've never been over to this forest," said Amy, one of the women. I knew her name because Leo and I had started giving the people on the tour name tags, and wearing them ourselves. It was easier that way for questions.

"Silly of us," said her husband, Bill. "It's nice here."

"They're talking about building an amphitheater over here," I said, "for festival lectures and things. But it would mean cutting down some of the trees."

"Oh, I don't like that idea," said another sister, Florence.

There wasn't a lot of undergrowth under the pine trees, so you could see between the tree trunks to the theater. In the cool morning light, the banner on top waved at us.

"Lisette began, of course, in the Greenshow," I said, and everyone's gaze shifted to the Greenshow stage, with its half-timbered platform. "She was eleven. She'd been watching the show for years because it was free and her family didn't have much money. They came every night. Lisette was later quoted in many interviews as saying the Greenshow was better than a movie."

Leo grinned at me. We'd been doing the tour for a few weeks now and I sounded like a pro.

I gave the same information Leo did but I said things in different ways.

"When she was eleven, the Summerlost Festival decided they wanted to do a Greenshow act with children in it," I said. This was my favorite part. "Lisette didn't audition. She didn't hear about it in time. But she watched the performances all summer long. And one day, when one of the children stayed home sick, she jumped up on the stage. In her shorts and her T-shirt and sneakers. And she did the whole dance, and then said all the missing girl's lines."

Florence clasped her hands and smiled, even though she must have already known this. I smiled back. I understood.

I loved the story because Lisette went ahead and took her chance. She decided to go for what she wanted.

And I loved the story because it reminded me of my dad and that day he'd been pulled out of the audience. Even though he and Lisette were totally different onstage. Even though she'd wanted to go up and he'd been embarrassed the whole time.

"After that," I said, "the Greenshow director wrote Lisette into the production for the rest of the summer. And that was the beginning."

Leo took over the next part because they loved it when he rattled off the dates and names of every single Lisette Chamberlain performance in less than two minutes. He dared them to time him and they always did.

"Young man!" said Ida, the third of the sisters. "That was amazing!"

Leo smiled. "What was your favorite performance of Lisette's?"

I stood, half listening, and I noticed someone walking across the courtyard stop and look over in our direction. Whoever it was raised a hand to shield their eyes.

Uh-oh. Had we been sighted? Could they see us through the trees?

Leo and I had a code in case something like that happened.

I raised my hand, which I never did otherwise.

Leo was smooth. "Ladies and gentlemen, let's discuss this more as we move on to our next stop."

They followed him out the way we'd come, through the

trees toward the parking lot near the college's science building. Away from the festival. I looked back. People still crisscrossed the courtyard, walking back and forth, but no one watched us anymore.

19

"That was splendid," Amy said. "Wonderful. We'll be sure to recommend you to all our friends."

She gave us a fifty-dollar bill even though she only owed us thirty dollars and told us to keep the change. It was our biggest tip yet.

"Wow," I said. "Thank you."

"And we appreciate your recommending us to others," Leo said. "But if you could let them know to follow the instructions on the flyer exactly, that would be great. We don't want to get into trouble with the festival. This tour isn't official."

"It may be unofficial, but it's extremely professional," Ida said. "You kids are so motivated. Are you saving up for college?"

"For a trip to London," Leo said.

"Perfect!" Florence said. "And you, dear?"

"School clothes," I said, because that was the easiest answer.

"That's wonderful," Ida said.

It didn't sound wonderful. It sounded like nothing, next to London.

Leo and I walked over to the bank again to get the money split up. "Twenty-five dollars each," I said as we took the bills and the lollipops out of the bank tube and waved at the teller through the window. "Not a bad morning."

"We have eight people signed up for tomorrow already," Leo said. "Hopefully they'll tip too."

"Eight!" I said. "That's a record."

Leo nodded but he had wrinkled his nose up in that way he did when he was worried. "So someone saw us back in the forest?"

"I think so. But it was one person looking in our direction. It wasn't like they called out to us or came over or got mad or anything."

"Male or female?" he asked. "Tourist or worker? Gary?"

"Too far away to tell," I said. "But if it was Gary, he definitely didn't recognize us, or he would have done something."

Leo still looked worried.

"How close are you?" I asked Leo. "To having all the money?"

"Not close enough," Leo said. "My dad and I counted it out last night and looked into buying tickets. They're already more expensive than I thought they'd be."

"Are you sure your dad won't cover it for you? Or can't you pay him back once you get the rest of the money?"

"That's not the deal we made," Leo said, and his jaw was set. "I'm not going to ask for that."

We walked a few steps in silence. I put the lollipop in my pocket. Root beer.

"My dad's nice," Leo said. "But he doesn't really get me. He's into football and his job and watching sports on TV and fishing. I like all that stuff fine. Especially fishing. But he's way more into it than me."

"He's going to the play with you in London," I pointed out.

"Yeah," Leo said. "And it was a big deal for him to agree so I want to live up to my part of the bargain. Not ask for help."

And then I got it. Leo wanted to go so badly because he wanted not only to be in the presence of greatness, but because he wanted to share something he thought was amazing with his dad.

"I feel like if my dad sees Barnaby Chesterfield, he'll understand," Leo said. "I mean, he will. Right?"

"Yeah," I said, thinking of my own dad, of the way we'd yell at everyone else to be quiet while we watched Barnaby Chesterfield in *Darwin*. I remembered how my dad would lean in to hear Barnaby talk, how everything he said sounded both sonorous and snipped. But most of all how it felt to be with my dad and to love the same thing so much. "He will."

That night I put the root beer lollipop on the windowsill. It was gone the next morning.

20

My next job in the costume shop was sorting buttons. Days and days of sifting through buttons to see which ones might work for repairs and which ones belonged to costumes we weren't using this season but would use again another year.

It was kind of the worst.

And also the best.

Because the buttons were super annoying, but everyone kept forgetting I was in the corner working. So sometimes I heard and saw interesting things.

Everyone went quiet when Caitlin Morrow came in, looking portrait-faced and beautiful even without a trace of makeup. Caitlin played Juliet in one of the plays and Rosalind in another. She was the biggest star of the festival this summer.

"Well," she said. "I guess you all heard what happened last night."

I hadn't. But it looked like the others had. Their faces changed from serious to trying-not-to-laugh.

"Romeo's breeches split," Caitlin went on. "Right down the back."

No way.

"I had to grab a blanket off the bed on the stage and put it around him and pull him close to me during the scene so that he didn't moon the entire audience," Caitlin said.

"You saved the show," Meg said. "And the innocence of that senior citizens' group sitting in the front rows."

Caitlin snorted. "Can you give me a guarantee," she said, "that I am *never* going to have to see Brad Murray's butt again?"

"I've been on the phone with the fabric company this morning giving them an earful," Meg said, "and I'm using our strongest material right now to make him a new pair of breeches for the next performance. They will not rip."

"*Thank* you," Caitlin said. "With all my heart." Then she paused. "I don't suppose there's any chance I can keep the Juliet costume at the end of the season?"

"No," Meg said. "Not a chance. Festival property."

Caitlin sighed. "I know," she said. "But I had to try."

"She seems nice," I said after she left.

Everyone turned to look at me and I flushed. "I haven't ever been around her before."

"She's one of the good ones," Meg said. "You should have seen Brad Murray down here earlier. He was yelling at me right and left."

"He's a jerk," said Emily.

Privately, I agreed. Sometimes Brad Murray came over before the show to get some food from concessions and he liked to walk away without paying the bill. Gary always swore under his breath when we told him what had happened but he never made Brad come back and pay.

"What's that look on your face?" Meg said to me, so I told her what I was thinking about.

"That little snot," she said. "Is he ever wearing his costume when he's pilfering food?"

"Um," I said, because one time he had been and even the fancy actors were not supposed to eat while in costume.

"Little snot," she said again. "He thinks now that he's been cast as a lead he owns the place. But I remember him when he was a bratty kid running around at the Greenshow. Trying to steal food then too. He hasn't changed."

"I didn't know he was from here," I said.

"Oh yeah," said Emily. "I'm surprised you hadn't heard. Everyone's been making a big deal about it. He's the first local cast as a lead since Lisette Chamberlain."

An icy hush fell over the room. Or did it? Maybe only I felt it. The other assistants didn't seem to think anything of Emily throwing Lisette's name out there.

"I'll tell you one thing," Meg said. "Lisette Chamberlain would never, ever have yelled at a coworker the way Brad Murray yelled this morning."

I felt brave. Daring.

"Would she have eaten food while in costume?" I asked.

Meg didn't get mad. She smiled. "Depended on the costume," she said. "And the food."

And then we all went back to work.

When I finished in the costume shop I took the steps two at a time. I couldn't wait to get to concessions and tell Leo about Brad Murray and the wardrobe malfunction. And to share the Lisette information. It wasn't much. Almost nothing. But Meg hadn't seemed annoyed when I'd asked about Lisette.

Leo was standing right inside the door of the building, looking out, with his arms folded.

"What are you doing?" I asked.

Then I saw them. The boys on the bikes. Making gestures at Leo through the glass. Cory was with them.

"Let's go somewhere else," I said. "Into the Portrait Hall. Maybe they'll be gone when we come out."

"I'm already enough of a coward for coming inside," Leo said.

"They'll leave you alone if you walk away," I said. "You have to ignore them."

"You sound like my parents." Leo sounded mad. "Like every teacher ever. That doesn't work. You can't walk away every time they bother you. Sometimes there's nowhere to go."

The boys had seen me come up next to Leo. One of them pulled up his eyes. Like he was pretending to be Chinese. Making fun of me.

I heard Leo draw in his breath.

And someone else behind me.

I turned around.

Meg.

"Those little brats," she said. "I'm going to go say something to them."

"No," Leo and I said at the same time.

"You two have to cross the courtyard to get to work," she said.

"They'll go away," I said. "Soon."

"Come with me," Meg said. And as we turned away from the window she called out to the security guard standing near the Portrait Hall, "You've got some kids on bikes out in the courtyard. Get them to clear out."

He jumped to it.

Meg took us back downstairs and to a door at the end of the hall, past WIGS and MAKEUP and COSTUMES. She opened it with a key. I saw another doorway in front of us but she had us turn to the left and opened a final door. "There," she said.

"Wow," Leo said. "Is this one of the tunnels?" Right after he said it he looked like he wished he hadn't.

"You've heard about the tunnels?" Meg asked.

"Yeah," Leo admitted.

"This is only a hallway," Meg said. "Sorry to disappoint you." She pushed the door open. "Follow it and you'll come out right by a stairwell that will take you up to concessions."

"Thank you," I said.

The hallway was full of old food trays and other concession

stuff. Boxes and boxes that had come in from shipping, printed with CUPS and CUTLERY. Things they threw back in here because people didn't pass through very often, I guessed. Lots of those tall metal racks where you could put a bunch of trays and then wheel them along. Like the kind you see in school lunchrooms sometimes. Leo pushed one out of the way and the sound made me think of lunchroom sounds, of kids talking and trays scooting. And Ben yelling.

When I was in fourth grade and Ben was in second, my parents decided to send Ben to regular elementary school instead of his special school. It lasted for three weeks. He cried every night but couldn't tell us what was wrong. The teachers said he was doing fine in class, which meant he wasn't screaming or trying to run away.

Then I went into the lunchroom one day on an errand for my teacher and I saw him sitting at a table with the other second-graders. (Lunch was one of the parts of the day where they were supposed to integrate the special-needs kids with the other kids.) Ben was not eating. He sat there, nervous, with his eyes closed. He held his wire whisk in one hand and was shaking it back and forth like he did with stuff, like the screwdriver and the toothbrush and other things. I didn't see the teachers. Maybe they were getting their lunches. But the other kids were throwing food at Ben. A fruit snack. A pea. Every time they hit him, he said, "Don't!" in a high-pitched yell, but he didn't open his eyes, he didn't stop flicking that whisk back and forth. I could tell he was trying to shut out the world. I could tell he wanted to be someplace else.

I went over and told the kids to leave him alone.

Ben opened his eyes when he heard my voice and an M&M hit him in the eye.

He cried.

I held his hand all the way to the office and told them we needed to call my mom. She came over right away and picked him up. He never went back.

That was one of the days I didn't understand Ben completely, but I also knew I understood enough. I felt like my heart was cracking. Those were always the hardest times, when I saw Ben get hurt. Until the accident. Then it felt like not only my heart hurt. It felt like even my blood did, like my broken heart was pushing pain through the rest of my body. *Beat. Beat. Beat.*

When I was small I used to pretend that I had to tell my body everything it had to do or it would stop. *Lungs, breathe,* I whispered. *Heart, beat. Eyes, focus. Tummy, digest. Legs, walk. Arms, move.* I was so glad then that everything did what it was supposed to do without any conscious help from me. But after the accident I wished that my heart wouldn't keep hurting so much. Wouldn't keep going like this without my telling it to. *Beat. Beat. Beat.*

"That was nice of Meg to let us come through here," Leo said.

"It was."

"And she basically admitted that the tunnels are real."

"She did."

As we came out of the hallway, I pretended that the whole world had secret tunnels, where people could walk straight to wherever they really wanted to be and ignore all the meanness in the middle.

I wiped my eyes on my sleeve before Leo could see.

21

The vultures in our yard weren't only roosting in the tree any-more. Now they went back into the part of the lot that hadn't yet been cleared, the corner with an old shed and a rotting fence surrounding a square of dirt that used to be a garden but was now a jumble of soil and vegetation.

"That's next summer's project," my mother said. "I've got my hands full for now with this deck."

She did. She'd been sawing and sanding in every spare moment. Whenever it rained, she ran outside to rescue her tools. Hundreds of boards leaned against the outside wall, under the porch.

She had framed in the base of the deck but it didn't look quite right. It seemed too short. Something was off.

But of course I didn't mention that. "Looks great," I said to her. She put down her sandpaper and smiled at me.

The back door swung open and Miles came out. "I got the mail."

"We actually have mail?" Mom asked. "Real mail?" All we ever got at the summer house were advertisements or bills.

"Something got forwarded to us," Miles said.

"Miracles never cease," Mom said.

Miles handed her the letter and she glanced at the envelope and then her face changed. She looked stunned. Without saying anything, she tore into the envelope and walked inside.

"*Okay,*" Miles said.

"Who was it from?"

"The return address looked like it was from a hospital," he said.

"Oh no," I said.

My mom had spent months and months dealing with medical and ambulance bills and life insurance.

Mom opened the door and came back out. "It's okay," she said, when she saw our faces.

"Miles said it looked like it was from a hospital."

"Sort of," Mom said. "But not."

We both waited.

"There's a family that wants to meet with us," she said. "A family whose son was the recipient of"—and here she swallowed—"whose son benefited from our decision to donate."

I knew right away what she meant. And it wasn't *our* decision, it was hers. She was the one who had said that Ben could be an organ donor. My dad was a donor—it was on his driver's license—so they asked her about Ben too.

"Why did they write to us?" I asked.

"I had said it would be okay," she said. "For them to contact us. If they wanted."

"I don't want to meet them," I said.

"Me either," Miles said.

"Why not?" Mom asked.

I didn't say anything. So Miles did. He spoke in a small voice. "Because it sounds too hard."

And my mom nodded. Like she understood. Like maybe she was even relieved. "Okay," she said. "Okay. Let's think about it for a few days, but I can write back and tell them no. That's fine."

"Which of them was it?" I asked. "Ben or Dad?"

"Ben," Mom said. "Ben's cornea—part of his eye—was given to another boy. It kept that boy from going blind."

For some reason that hit me like a punch to the gut. It wasn't like Ben had saved anyone's life. That boy who got the cornea wasn't going to die. He wasn't going to be able to see. That was the worst-case scenario. It wasn't like Ben had died and then that boy could live. It wasn't even as good as that.

My mom folded up the letter and Miles asked for ice cream and I went upstairs.

22

It had been so long since I'd found anything on my windowsill.

But there was something that night. Maybe the lollipop had done the trick.

It was an old pocket-size map of Iron Creek, folded up neat and small. Ben would have liked to look at the roads and think of places to drive. Last summer he was learning to read a map and to tell time. "It's seven forty-three," he would say. "At eight o'clock, I go to bed."

I lined up the things on my windowsill. The screwdriver, the purple toothbrush. The map.

They were all so specific. So tangible. And I knew it could never be Lisette Chamberlain's ghost who left them.

Leo.

It had to be.

Even though he hadn't known Ben.

Leo was the kind of person who did his research. He would have found out about Ben from someone. Maybe his mom had overheard something in the dentist's office where she worked. My grandma went there for her checkups. My grandma thought

Ben was an angel but not in the way I hated. When Ben was alive, she looked right into his eyes and saw him there.

I looked at the things again. Screwdriver, purple toothbrush, map. I thought about how Leo had helped me get a job and how he let us watch *Times of Our Seasons* at his house every day and how he listened whenever I talked about Ben and my dad but also didn't expect me to talk about Ben or my dad and how Leo always shared the lollipops from the bank with me. (And now I'd given him one back.) How he'd shown me *The Tempest* with Lisette Chamberlain as Miranda. How he'd completely understood when I'd cried after I'd seen it.

And a thought came to my mind. Even though I'd only known him for part of a summer.

Leo Bishop might be the best friend I'd ever had.

I decided it was time to do something for him. Something biggish.

What could it be?

I stood at the window, looking through the diamonds into the dark. I thought about the costume shop and bullies and Barnaby Chesterfield and England. About birds and being buried alive. I thought about everything. And then I had an idea.

23

It took me a few days to sort out my surprise for Leo but I worked it all out at last. After the tour one day, I told him I had somewhere to go.

"I have to run," I said to Leo. "I can't walk home with you today."

"You mean, you're literally going running?" he asked, because I did have on black shorts. And running shoes.

"Kind of," I said. "I have to get back fast. But I'll see you later after my mom leaves. For *Times of Our Seasons.*"

"Okay," he said, and I hoped he hadn't figured out what I was going to do.

I ran all the way over to the Summerlost Festival. It was exhausting. Also sweaty. I'd have to wash my Lisette T-shirt for sure before the next tour. My bag bumped against my side the whole way.

I'd tried to plan for everything. I'd called Leo's mom at the dentist's office to ask if he was free on a certain night and sworn her to secrecy. I'd thought she might be mad or annoyed at me for calling her at work, but she'd been a good sport about the whole thing. I'd told my mom what I wanted to do and she'd agreed to let me go. I guess because we'd be surrounded by people the whole time. She'd promised to pick us up after the play was over.

I skidded around the corner to the box office so fast I had to put my hand on the exterior wall to stop myself. The stucco scratched my palm. A couple of older people in tall socks and khaki shorts exclaimed in surprise as I hurried past them.

There was no line for same-day tickets at the box office. Either the line had moved quick this morning or they were all sold out. *Please please please*, I said to myself as I stopped in front of the glassed-in window.

"Hi," I said, breathless. "Do you have any same-day tickets left for *As You Like It*?"

"We do," said the lady at the box office, and I breathed out a sigh of relief. "Do you have proof of residency?" she asked.

"Yes," I said. I was proud of myself for remembering that I'd need something to prove I really lived in Iron Creek so I could get the discount. I pulled out one of our utility bills that showed our address and my mom's name on it. "I'm her daughter," I said.

She looked at the bill and then at me and I started to panic. What if you had to actually be the person on the utility bill? Or what if you had to be older than me? Had Leo's mom always bought his tickets for him?

"All right," the ticket agent said, and I breathed out. "And you're aware that these are the bench seats at the back, and that there are no exchanges or refunds?"

"Yes," I said.

And then when she asked, "How many tickets do you need?" instead of saying "Two," I said, "Three." I handed her thirty dollars.

One for Leo, of course. One for me. And one for Miles.

I don't know why I did it. Maybe because my mom would feel better about it not being a date if Miles came too? Or because I felt bad about *Times of Our Seasons* and wanted Miles to see something cultural and well acted instead of something that gave him nightmares?

"Nice shirt," said the box office lady. "Is that Lisette Chamberlain?"

I froze. In all my planning, I'd forgotten to bring an extra shirt to wear. "Um, yes," I said.

"Did you buy it at the festival gift shop?"

"No," I said. "A friend had it made for me."

"Very cool." She handed me my three tickets. "Enjoy the show."

I couldn't freak out too much about the shirt and possibly

blowing our cover because I still had to do the hardest part of my plan. Talk to Gary. And I wanted to do it immediately, before I lost my nerve. So I went into the bathroom and turned my shirt inside out before I went over to concessions.

"Hi, Gary," I said.

"Hi," he said. "You're here early."

"Yeah," I said. "I, um, came by to ask if Leo and I could leave early from work tonight. We're going to the play."

Gary shook his head. "You have to ask for time off two weeks in advance. And even then, it's not guaranteed." He sounded stressed and his forehead wrinkled. When that happened, he looked as old as my grandpa.

"I know," I said. "But we can't afford the full-price tickets. So it had to be a Tuesday. And I didn't know if we'd get the tickets until now." I took a deep breath. Was Gary really going to say no? Leo was his best seller. And I wasn't bad either. I should have done this differently. Asked for the day off in advance and *then* hoped to get the tickets. But it was too late now.

"You didn't follow the rules," Gary said.

"What rules?" asked someone behind us.

Meg. She must have come through the hidden hallway. "Here are the costumes you needed fixed, Gary," Meg said. "Emily mended them. And I came over to talk with you about the concessions costumes for next year. Is now a good time?"

"It's fine," Gary said. He glanced at me. "I can't give you the time off. You didn't ask far enough in advance."

"But I already have the tickets," I said. I couldn't give up that easily. Especially not in front of Meg, with her sharp eyes and her collar of safety pins and her gravelly, no-nonsense voice.

"What are you trying to get away with, Cedar Lee?" Meg asked.

"She wants to leave work early so she and her friend can go to the play," Gary said. "Tonight."

"And you're not letting them go?"

Gary looked surprised. "I can't. It's against the rules."

"But," Meg said, "this is the very *purpose* of the Summerlost Festival. To bring people to Shakespeare. Did you buy the tickets with your own money, Cedar?"

"I did."

"And you're taking your friend?"

"Yes," I said, and then for good measure, I added, "and my younger brother."

Meg raised her eyebrows at me. Did she think I was lying? I held out the three tickets so she could see. "His name's Miles," I said. "He's eight." Meg's eyebrows went down but she still had a quirk to her mouth. Maybe I was laying it on too thick bringing up Miles.

"Gary," Meg said, "I think it would be nice to let her go."

Gary frowned, thinking it over. "Okay," he said. "Meg's right. Shakespeare wanted everyone to see his plays. And you're investing your money back into the Summerlost Festival, which is good. But next time you *have* to ask two weeks before."

"Thank you," I said to Meg as Gary turned toward his office.

"You work in the costume shop every day for free," Meg said. "The least I can do is make sure you get to see one of the shows."

"Hey, Miles," Leo said. "Looking good."

The trumpet had sounded for people to leave the courtyard and take their seats inside the theater for the evening performance. I turned around and there was Miles, wearing a button-up shirt with his favorite jeans. He'd even combed his hair. His timing was perfect.

"Are you going to the play or something?" Leo asked.

I shifted my basket of programs to my other arm and waited. This was Miles's part, and he knew his lines. I could see that he was having a hard time keeping from grinning.

"Yeah," Miles said. "So are you."

"What?"

I held out the tickets. "We're all going to *As You Like It*," I said. "I got you a ticket."

I hadn't been able to think of a good way to leave it on Leo's windowsill (what if it blew away? what if he didn't see it?) so I'd decided to do it like this.

Leo didn't seem to understand. "We still have to help clean up," he said.

"Not tonight," Miles said. "Cedar talked to Gary."

"You did?" Leo asked. "Really? And he said yes?"

"Yup," I said. "But we have to go now. And we probably won't have time to change out of our costumes."

Leo's mouth and eyebrows shot up in a smile. The sunset turned his brown hair orange and his eyelashes golden. "You are kidding me."

"I'm not."

I gave one ticket to Leo and one to Miles.

The sun was behind the pine trees now, winking at us. For once, we were going inside with everyone else to see the play. We'd be part of the Summerlost Festival in a different way. I put my hand on the wooden railing of the theater as we climbed up the stairs and listened to the sound of many feet walking on the old boards. A smiling usher showed us to our seats. "Enjoy the show," she said, and I said, "I will."

"Here we are," Leo said. We slid down along the bench. Leo, me, Miles.

"Did you read that synopsis I gave you?" I whispered to Miles as we sat down.

"Um," Miles said.

"He'll catch on even if he didn't," Leo said. "It's a lot easier to understand when you're watching it instead of reading it."

"Everyone always says that," Miles muttered.

"We're going to be so tired when we give the tour tomorrow,"

Leo whispered in my ear. "But it's going to be worth it."

I don't know what it was, but my heart started racing. Being at a play with a boy? The way the lights went down but the stars were about to come up?

Blue and green leaves hung down in ribbons from dark archways on the stage. The slightest breeze sent them moving. They were meant to be the forest of Arden, but before the actors came on, it looked like the leaves could be many other things. Seaweed, for mermaids to swim through. Strips of cloth hanging over a door, for men and women to slip past as they entered a castle, a cave, a tent. The stage was dappled with blue-and-green light, like water, like precious stone.

The actors came onstage. Miles leaned forward.

I didn't recognize Caitlin Morrow for the first part of the play. I didn't even think about Caitlin Morrow being the character of Rosalind. I saw Rosalind, clever, smart. I saw the other characters, and I felt like I was with them, in the forest.

And then Miles coughed next to me, and for a moment I came back out of the woods and was me.

And I wondered if Caitlin felt the way Lisette Chamberlain did before she was *Lisette Chamberlain*. Before everyone watched to see a movie star, a celebrity, but instead saw her as the characters.

I glanced over at Leo, who had that look on his face, the one I used to see all the time when we first met and still saw a lot now, even with the bullies and the worry about money. The look of being alive. He wasn't smiling, but his eyes had a brightness. He didn't even notice me looking at him. He was still in the forest.

So I went back too.

25

When intermission came, the three of us sat there for a moment after the lights came up. Then I looked over at Leo.

"Wow," I said to him.

"Right?" he said. He looked over at Miles, who was stretching and standing up. "What do you think, Miles?"

"It's not bad," Miles said, "but my butt hurts from sitting."

"We could call Mom and have her come get you," I said. "I won't be mad. I know it's really long."

"No way," said Miles. "I'm staying for the whole thing." And even though he'd been fidgeting a bit, I wasn't surprised. Miles never wanted to seem like the young one. He would never back down. Once he started something, he did not quit.

"Let's go walk around," I said. "We have twenty minutes."

"Eighteen, now," Leo said.

We merged into the mass of people and went downstairs. The courtyard was dark, and the lights strung on the massive old sycamore tree glimmered. I'd forgotten that I was still wearing my costume until someone asked me where the restroom was, which made Leo and Miles laugh.

"I'll go get us each a tart," I said, after I'd pointed the woman in the right direction.

"No," Leo said. "You bought the tickets, I'll get the treats."

"I don't think so," I said. "You need to save your money for England."

"You can both stop arguing," Miles said, "because look what I brought." He reached into his pocket and pulled out four huge Atomic Fireballs.

"Oh man," Leo said.

We all put them in our mouths. Tears came straight to my eyes, but they were *really* streaming down Leo's cheeks. "I don't believe it," I said. "I think you're even more sensitive to this stuff than Miles." But it came out all garbled because of my Fireball.

"I can't understand you," Leo said. At least I think that's what he said. And then he pointed at Miles, who had a Fireball in each cheek. "What does he think he's doing?"

Right then another lady came up and asked me where the restroom was.

I tried to answer but she couldn't understand me.

Leo snorted and then his eyes widened in pain. He spit out the Fireball into his hands. "Fire," he gasped. "Fire went up into my nose."

"Like a dragon," said Miles, barely intelligible around the Fireballs in his cheeks, and the woman *tsk*ed in disgust and walked away.

The three of us stood there, helpless with laughter. The sycamore tree stretched its branches over and around us. We stayed like that until the trumpet sounded for us to go back in.

I noticed how chilly it was when we went back into the theater. Desert-night cold comes fast. And all three of us were dressed in short sleeves. I noticed Miles folding his arms and hunching his shoulders. I shivered.

"Slide over," Leo said, and so I did, and then our arms and legs were right together.

"Slide over," I told Miles, and so he did too.

"Of course *you* get the middle," he muttered. "Then you're the only one who gets to be warm on both sides."

On my other side, Leo shook with laughter. I could feel it.

My brother and my best friend sat next to me. My mouth was hot from the Fireball, and my hands and feet were cold from the night. On either side, I was warm.

The minute the play ended, Miles whispered to me that he had to go to the bathroom and took off. Leo and I sat there for a minute, letting the other people exit the theater.

"Thanks," he said. "That was great."

"And you were surprised, right?"

"Yeah," he said. "I was." He stood up and stretched and then stuck out his hand so that he could pull me up. "I love coming to the plays. I've really missed it this summer."

"Are you sure you don't want to be an actor?"

"I know I couldn't ever do what they do," he said, pointing at the stage where the actors had been. "But I could be the one who writes the words they say."

I started laughing.

"What?" Leo asked. "What's so funny about that?"

"It's funny because—" I said, and then I couldn't stop cracking up, but Leo didn't get mad. He raised his eyebrows at me.

"You don't want to be an actor," I said. "You want to be *Shakespeare*."

Then Leo laughed too. "I guess if you put it that way, it sounds weird."

"Not weird," I said. "Just big."

Leo had all these dreams. He had specific dreams, like seeing Barnaby Chesterfield in London. He had big dreams, like being a writer. And he trusted me so much that he told me his dreams out loud.

I'd spent the last year feeling like being alive was lucky enough. Like being alive was *hard* enough.

But I did have dreams.

There.

I admitted it to myself.

I had all *kinds* of dreams. I wanted to go skiing again and get fast and good. I wanted to go to London too someday. I wanted to fall in love. I wanted to own a bookstore or a restaurant and have people come in and say, "Hi, Cedar," and I wanted to ride a bike down the streets in a little town in a country where people spoke a different language. Maybe my bike would have a basket and maybe the basket would have flowers in it. I wanted to live in a big city and wear lipstick and my hair up in a bun and buy groceries and carry them home in a paper bag. My high heels would click when I climbed the stairs to my apartment. I wanted to stand at the edge of a lake and listen.

Leo and I found Miles in the courtyard, and then we went to wait for my mom by the bike racks and the water fountain. Miles walked down to stick his hand in the water that cascaded from the ledge, but Leo and I stayed up by the top.

The plaque in front of the fountain said CHARLES H. JOHN-SON & MARGARET G. JOHNSON MEMORIAL CENTENNIAL CELE-BRATION FOUNTAIN.

"That's a realllly long name for a fountain," I said.

"My brothers and I call it Baby Niagara," Leo said. "Because the part where it goes over the edge looks like Niagara Falls."

"Let me guess," I said. "You've been to Niagara Falls."

"Yeah," he said. "It was for a family vacation. My dad plans one every year. It's always somewhere different. This year was the first year he didn't plan a vacation. Because of the England trip."

"He must really like England," I said to Leo. "Because he's been there before, and he wanted to go again, like you."

"Yeah," Leo said.

I sat down on the rim of the pool. The moon was full above and there were always more stars here than back at our real house, because of the light pollution in the city.

"Mom's here!" Miles hollered up from below.

"I bet we can fit your bike in the trunk," I told Leo. "Sorry I didn't tell you to walk instead of ride. But I didn't want to ruin the surprise."

"I don't think it will fit," Leo said.

I looked down at my mom's car. He was right.

I'd been thinking of our old car, not the one we had now.

We used to have a minivan.

It got totaled in the accident.

And when it came time to buy a new car, my mom realized we didn't need a minivan anymore. We didn't have enough people. We could fit into a regular car.

So every time I see a minivan like our old one (which happens all the time, because a lot of people who park at grocery stores or schools or really *anywhere* have minivans), it's like a tiny punch.

"Right," I said to Leo. "Sorry."

"It's no problem," Leo said. "And thanks again. This was great."

"I'm glad. See you tomorrow."

"See you tomorrow."

Miles and I went down and got in the car.

"Doesn't Leo want a ride?" my mom asked.

"He has his bike," I said. "He's going to ride home."

"That's dangerous," Mom said. "It's night."

"We can't fit his bike in the car," I said.

"Well, we'll follow him then," Mom said.

"Because that's not creepy at all," Miles said, and I laughed.

Mom smiled and turned around to look at us. "Did you have a good time?"

"Yes," I said. "It was great."

"It was pretty good," Miles said. "Even though the seats were hard and I got cold." I slugged him in the arm.

"Thanks," he said to me. "For the ticket."

"You're welcome," I told him. "Thanks for the Fireball."

We sat in the car waiting for Leo who didn't know we were waiting for him.

Leo pulled his bike down the stairs next to the fountain. Bump, bump, bump. My mom rolled down her window and called out, "We're going to follow you! To make sure you get home safe!"

I heard Leo call back, "Okay."

He started riding down the sidewalk. Mom gave him a minute before we swung out into the street behind him. We had to make sure everyone got home safe, in our car that still seemed wrong.

I understood why Leo called the fountain Baby Niagara. Because once you see something big, you can't help seeing it in everything small.

My dad used to say that life was like turning the pages in a book. "Oh, look," he'd say, pretending to flip the pages in the air after we'd had something bad happen to us. "Bad luck here on page ninety-seven. And on ninety-eight. But something good here on ninety-nine! All you had to do was keep reading!"

For small things it used to help, him saying that. Like if you failed a test or got a bad haircut or bonked your head on the waterslide and had to go home early from a birthday party at the pool.

Of course he never slammed the book shut, which was what had happened to him. One last bad thing and then the end, for him and for Ben. No more pages to turn, nothing to get them to a better part in the story.

It could go the other way too. Sometimes you were having a perfect day and you never ever wanted to turn the page because you knew there was no way that whatever came after would be as good.

The day after we turned the page on the play, Cory kept

looking over at Leo and me and smiling. Not a nice smile. An I-know-something smile.

"Hey," Cory said to Leo and me partway through the afternoon. "After we're done with this shift, you guys should meet me in the forest over there."

"Why?" I asked.

"Because I have to talk to you."

"We can talk now," Leo said.

"No," Cory said, acting shocked. "We're *working* now."

No way was I going into the forest—*our* forest—with Cory the Hellfart. No way was I following his orders. "We need to hurry home," I said. "Sorry."

Cory shook his head. "Seriously. You guys don't want to do that. There's something I need to tell you."

"We don't have to go," I told Leo after Cory walked off.

"I think we do," Leo said.

"Why?"

"Because it could get worse if we don't," Leo said.

We watched Cory. The sun glinted off the chocolate wrappers in his concessions basket. The candy had probably gone all melty and gross in the sun.

"Look at what I found," Cory said under the trees. He held out a piece of paper. It took me a minute to recognize it.

It was one of our tour flyers.

Leo reached out to grab it but Cory snatched it away. "I *knew* this was yours," he said.

"It's not," Leo said.

"It *is*. I called the number this morning and you answered." He laughed. "*This is Leo Bishop, how can I help you?*" Cory said, pretending to be Leo, making his voice high and weird in a way that wasn't like Leo's at all.

Leo clenched his hands into fists. His mouth had gone into a straight line. "So *you* were the person who hung up."

"That's right," Cory said.

And I thought, *Why?* Why didn't Cory like us? Why couldn't he leave us alone?

Cory would have made fun of Ben. I was sure about that.

"So what," I said. My voice sounded flat. "So what, Cory."

"So I'm going to tell Gary," Cory said. "And you'll both lose your jobs."

"Why?"

"Because Gary won't be happy that you are giving tours and putting these flyers in the programs," Cory said, in a tone that said *You idiot*.

"No," I said. "I mean, why tell Gary?"

"So he'll fire you."

"Why do you care?" Leo asked. "Why do you want us fired?"

Cory grinned. "Because."

As if that were an answer. But it was, to Cory. It was all the answer he needed.

I am different and that has nothing to do with you, I wanted to tell him. *Leo is different and that has nothing to do with you. You look at us and you don't like us and you don't even know why. I've seen it before a million times with Ben.*

But my knowing this didn't change anything. Cory was still going to tell on us. He was still going to get us fired.

"So are you going to go tell Gary right now?" I asked.

"I haven't decided when I'll tell him," Cory said. "Maybe tonight. Maybe later."

I wanted to shove Cory. To smash him down into the ground so he could lie there and feel the dirt under him and be up close to every fallen pine needle and feel scared. But I didn't do that. I watched him go.

"How close are you now?" I asked Leo when Cory couldn't hear us anymore. "To having enough money?"

"Not close enough," he said. "And I've only got a week before my dad's deadline to have the money for the plane ticket."

"We can do it," I said. "We can't quit now."

"Once Cory tells Gary it's all over."

"We're being blackmailed by a Hellfart," I said. I hoped it would make Leo laugh.

Leo didn't laugh.

He also didn't cry. Which it looked for a minute like he might do. I knew that feeling. Hold your mouth tight, tell your heart not to hurt, tell your brain not to think about what might happen next.

29

It was a busy night because the festival was winding down for the summer and everyone wanted to see the plays before they closed. Every time I saw Cory, I felt my heart sink. Had he told Gary yet? At the end of the night, when we went out and unlocked our bikes, Leo said, "We don't have to meet up in the morning. No one signed up for the tour tomorrow. The only person who called today was Cory."

Everything was going wrong. "It's okay. People will call again. It's only one day."

"The only way I can make the deadline is if the tour keeps doing as well as it has," Leo said. "Every day."

"I could lend you some money," I said. "Really."

"No," Leo said. "I couldn't take that from you."

"Why not?"

"I just can't."

"You would have had *all* the money if you'd done the tour by yourself," I pointed out.

"I wouldn't have made as much money without you," Leo said.

"I don't even know what I'm saving for yet."

"But you're saving for *something*."

When Leo said that, I realized it was true. It hadn't been before. But it was now.

A season ski pass? A plane ticket?

I wasn't sure exactly *what* I wanted yet, but things had changed. Now I could at least imagine things I might want.

You're stupid, something inside me said. *Hoping for something doesn't mean you'll get to have it. There are no guarantees.*

Shut up, I told that voice. *I'm turning right past you to another page. You're right but today I don't care.*

30

"No running today?" Mom asked when I came downstairs the next morning. She was sitting at the table with a pile of lesson plans for the new school year. Everything was coming to an end.

I'm sure I looked blank for a second before I caught on. Oh. Right. Running. What I supposedly did in the mornings.

"No," I said. "I didn't hear my alarm."

"Well, you've been every other day." Mom put her hand on my head as she set a bowl on the table in front of me and reached for the cereal. "What would you like? Cheerios with bananas?"

I nodded. The sun shone through the window. I couldn't believe how long I'd slept in.

"I'm so proud of you this summer, Cedar," Mom said. "Running in the mornings. Working so hard at the Summerlost Festival. *Volunteering* at the Summerlost Festival." She brought over a plate of sliced bananas and the milk and cereal and sat down across from me. "And taking care of Miles for me too. Except for that slipup with the soap opera, you've been amazing with him. I really appreciate it."

I picked up the plate and started to slide the bananas into my cereal. I felt guilty. I'd lied to her about the tour, and Miles and I hadn't actually stopped watching *Times of Our Seasons*.

My mother beamed.

I ate my cereal.

With all the guilt, and with everything going on with Leo and Cory and the tour, you wouldn't think that I would care that the milk was perfectly cold and the bananas not too ripe, but I did. It felt nice to have something be exactly right.

31

When I got to the costume shop, Meg was having a meeting. All of the employees stood gathered around her worktable. Emily and a nice guy whose name was Nate moved over so I could see Meg, since I was shorter than everyone else.

"Today's a big day," Meg said. "We're starting to dress the mannequins up in the Costume Hall."

"*Some* of us are," said Emily, sounding grumpy. "Some of us have to stay down here and mend the costumes for tonight's show."

Meg caught sight of me. "Cedar, you can carry the pieces of the costumes up and down," she said. "You've got the youngest legs."

The first thing Meg gave me to carry upstairs was a black-and-gold-embroidered doublet. It was *heavy*. When we got up to the Costume Hall, she showed me the display cases. Each one contained a plaque (saying who wore the costume in which play), and a faceless male or female mannequin waiting to be dressed.

It was disturbing.

"Here's where we are," Meg said. "Eric Potter, *Henry VIII.*"

"He was short," I said, looking at the outfit.

"And a terrible actor, by all reports," Meg said. "They didn't have a lot of options in those first years when they were getting started. But the real Henry VIII was also fat so that, at least, was authentic." She gave the mannequin a pat on the back. "Old Eric Potter did his best for the festival."

She hung the doublet on the portable clothes rack next to her. It had a bunch of items with ERIC POTTER: HENRY VIII tags on them. "You can head downstairs now for more pieces," Meg said. "Unless you'd like to help me dress Henry."

"No thank you," I told her.

All day long I ferried up the clothes and accessories to Meg and the others and gathered the things they needed. The last thing I brought up was a Titania robe from a production of *A Midsummer Night's Dream.* It shimmered green and purple and blue and gold. I couldn't stop touching the fabric, even though I knew they'd just cleaned it.

Meg draped the robe over the mannequin and stood back to look it over. "I've always loved this one," she said. "I helped make it during my first year at the festival."

I looked at the plaque. The actress who'd worn the dress was named Philippa Page. Not Lisette Chamberlain. But I was still curious. "Did you know her?"

"Yes," Meg said. "She was a fine actor. Very reserved when she wasn't onstage, though, so I didn't know her well. I always felt a bit sorry for her because she came along at the same time Lisette did."

"And everyone loved Lisette," I said. "Right? Because she was a great actress, and she was from Iron Creek." I felt reckless talking about Lisette with Meg, especially because of the tour situation, but what did I have to lose? And what if I could find out something amazing, something that even Leo didn't know, and then I could tell it to him? Would that make him feel better? Or worse?

"Not *everyone* loved Lisette," Meg said. "But most people did. I did. She was one of my best friends."

I had so many questions. *So who* didn't *love Lisette? What was she like? How well did you know her? Did she tell you secrets? Did you see her the night she died?*

I didn't know which one to ask.

"She and I became friends the first summer I was here," Meg said. She didn't sound sad talking about her friend. She sounded happy. Remembering. "I was an assistant in the costume shop. We were doing a full dress rehearsal, and I was in the audience watching and keeping an eye on the costumes—what fit right, and how they looked under the lights. They had to take a break to fix a trapdoor and I went up to adjust someone's costume, and Lisette said something under her breath that made me laugh so hard I got tears in my eyes. No one else seemed to get the joke. She noticed. After that we spent a lot of time together. We were almost the same age and we both had big dreams."

"Was her dream to go to Hollywood?"

Meg nodded.

"Was yours?"

"No," Meg said. "I wanted to get hired as one of the costume experts at a big museum somewhere."

But she was still here in Iron Creek. She did have the Costume Hall, though, which was kind of like a museum.

Did she like it when Lisette came back? Or did it remind Meg that she'd never left?

I didn't ask that of course. But I realized something I should have thought of a long time ago. No wonder Leo liked Lisette so much. She was a kid from Iron Creek who had big dreams. And she made them happen.

I dumped out a pile of straws and pipe cleaners on the table at home and got out some Elmer's Glue and construction paper. It was a good thing my mom hadn't really looked in the craft box she'd put together for us when we first moved to Iron Creek. There were an awful lot of supplies left.

"What are you doing?" Miles asked. "It's time to go to Leo's."

"I'm going to need to talk to Leo for a while after we watch *Times of Our Seasons*," I said. "So I'm leaving Mom a note in case she comes back while we're still gone. And I'm leaving this. I want it to look like we were doing crafts."

"What were we making?" Miles asked.

"I don't know," I said.

Miles picked up a straw. "In kindergarten we cut up the straws and put string through them and made necklaces. Do we have any string?"

"Good idea," I said. I got out some string and scissors. We chopped up the straws and threaded string through them. Miles needed a haircut. His straight dark hair hung in his eyes and he pushed it away as he bent over to tie the ends of his necklace together. "There," he said. "Done."

"Nice," I said. "Thanks." The two of us had been a good team lately. If being a good team meant that we excelled at tricking our mom and eating a lot of candy and playing a lot of board games. I reached over and took the necklace he'd made from him. "Can I wear it?"

"Sure," he said, sounding surprised. I pulled it over my head. I could barely get it on, and it was shorter than I expected it to be, more like a choker than a long necklace.

"Your head's huge," Miles said.

"I know." Ben had had a big head too. You couldn't really tell from looking at us, but when we wanted to wear hats, we always had to find them in the adult section. "It's a sign of my giant brain."

"Not necessarily," Miles said. "Dinosaurs had huge heads and tiny brains."

"Not necessarily," I said back. "I heard once that some of them had a second brain, like in their tails."

"That's a myth," Miles said. "But are you trying to tell me that you have a brain in your butt?"

"Maybe." I shook my butt at him.

Miles clapped his hands over his eyes. "That's disgusting."

We left the other necklace and the supplies out on the counter, arranged theatrically.

"Do you think Mom will fall for it?" I asked Miles as we closed the blue door behind us and started toward Leo's. I walked fast. We'd taken longer than I'd meant to with our craft.

"Probably," Miles said. His mood seemed to have changed. He wasn't looking at me. He stared down at the sidewalk, a frown on his face. His flip-flops snick-snacked on the pavement extra loud.

"What's wrong?"

"Do you only bring me places so you don't get in trouble?"

"No," I said. "I like hanging out with you. Which is good because I have to do it all the time." I shoved into him.

He didn't shove back.

"What about Leo?"

"What do you mean?"

"Do you like him?"

"He's my friend," I said.

"Do you *like* like him?" Miles asked.

"No."

"He probably wishes I'd stay home instead of hang around you guys."

"That's not true," I said. "Leo likes you."

And then I realized that Leo was also Miles's best friend in Iron Creek. And that Miles was feeling left out.

"I'm just going to go home when *Times of Our Seasons* is done," Miles said. "Then you and Leo can talk *in private*."

"I need you to stay with me so Mom doesn't get mad," I said. "*Please.*"

"What do you have to talk with him about?"

"Just something."

"You don't trust me."

"I do, but I don't want you to get in trouble. Please, Miles. I'll play Life with you later, as many games as you want. Or Clue."

For a minute I thought he was going to turn around and leave. Not even watch *Times of Our Seasons*. Then I saw him take a deep breath and do that thing. You see grown-ups do it all the time. They're about to lose their patience or get mad and then instead they take a deep breath and do not lose their patience and do not scream.

It's a weird thing to see a little kid do. I used to see Ben do it and it tore me up.

It made me feel awful to see Miles do it.

"How about," Miles said, "you eat two Fireballs at the same time."

I wanted to hug him but we were almost to Leo's and so I didn't. "Fine. It's a deal."

Leo opened the door before we could knock. "Hi," I said. Miles hurried past Leo and pounded down the basement stairs. So he was still mad.

"Have you heard anything new?" Leo asked.

"No," I said. "I guess Cory hasn't told anyone yet."

"So you think we should go to work today like usual?"

"Yeah. What else can we do?" I shrugged. "Has anyone called about tomorrow's tour?"

Leo nodded. "Two people. I had to tell them that the tour was temporarily on hold. They weren't very happy." Leo slumped against the door frame and rubbed one of his eyes. "I've got to try and make some money. I knocked on all the doors in the neighborhood but no one needs me to mow their lawn." He paused. "What about Miles? Does he need a babysitter?"

I hoped my brother hadn't heard Leo's question. That would make Miles feel even worse if he thought Leo saw him as a kid to be babysat.

"No," I said. "What if I *lend* you the money? Not give it to you. You could pay me back later."

Leo shook his head.

"Can you ask Zach or Jeremy?"

"No way," Leo said.

"Let's watch the show," I said. "Maybe we'll think of something."

When Leo and I went downstairs, Miles was sitting in a chair instead of on the couch where the three of us usually sat together. He didn't turn to look at us. The straw necklace scratched at my collarbone.

"Here we go," Leo said as he turned on the television. "Maybe today will be the day."

But I knew somehow that today would not be the day.

Harley was in her box, just like she'd been all summer long.

It felt extra claustrophobic to me. It was so dark in the coffin. The camera showed us the bruises on her hands from banging on the lid. And even though she was still beautiful, her makeup looked different now. They were trying to make her seem tired.

"I feel like she's going to die in there," I said. "They're never going to let her out."

"They *will*," Miles said.

The doorbell rang upstairs right as the show was ending.

I heard one of Leo's brothers walking to answer it.

Then he came to the top of the stairs. "Cedar," Jeremy said. "It's your mom."

Uh-oh.

Leo shot a look at me and we both stood up. Miles dove for the remote control and turned off *Times of Our Seasons*.

"What do you think happened?" Leo asked.

"I told her we'd be here," I said. "In a note. She must have decided to come over."

I didn't want to go upstairs, but even more I didn't want my mom at Leo's house. It felt weird. Like seeing your teacher at the grocery store, but even more awkward.

When I came up the stairs my mom was waiting right by the front door. "Cedar," she said. "Are you all right?"

I could tell she had just gotten back from the gym and she looked worried and mad.

"Mom," I said. "Yes. I'm fine. Hi. We can come home now. Let me go get Miles."

"I got your note," my mom said. "And there was also a message waiting for me from Daniel Alexander."

Daniel Alexander? Not Gary?

This was very bad.

I heard Leo draw in his breath behind me.

Cory. That loser. He wanted to get us in as much trouble as he could. So he went straight to Daniel Alexander instead of telling Gary. We should have known.

"He said it was regarding my daughter, Cedar, and not to worry, that everything was fine," my mom said, "but that he did need me to call him back at my convenience. I tried calling but he didn't pick up. Why is Daniel Alexander calling me about you?"

Right then the door to the garage opened and Leo's dad came in. "Leo Bishop!" he hollered. "I need to talk to you." Then he saw us and stopped. "Hi," he said. "I'm Dale Bishop."

"I'm Shannon Lee," Mom said. "I'm sorry to bother you. I came to pick up Cedar and Miles. They've been hanging out here with Leo."

"Of course," Mr. Bishop said. Then he looked at Leo. "Daniel Alexander just called me at work." It was the first time I'd seen Leo's dad up close.

I looked over at Leo. He swallowed.

Leo's dad was mad but in a dad way, not a scary way. He looked exactly like Zach, only older.

I wasn't scared for Leo. But I was sad for him.

And I was sad for me.

"Mr. Alexander called me too, but I haven't talked to him yet," Mom said. "What happened?"

"The kids have been giving tours about Lisette Chamberlain," Leo's dad said. "Daniel Alexander heard about it and thought he'd better let us know. He was worried because they're so young."

"I don't understand," my mom said, tipping her head to look at me. "Why are you giving tours about Lisette Chamberlain?"

"It was my idea," Leo said. "I thought up the tour and put the flyers in the programs at the festival. I thought we could earn extra money that way. Since she had so many fans, and it's the twentieth anniversary of her death."

"The twentieth anniversary of her death," my mother repeated.

"We give the tours in the early morning," I said as fast as I could. I wanted to get it all out. "When you thought I was running. We tell people about Lisette Chamberlain and take them to the places in Iron Creek that were relevant to her life."

"So it's the two of you kids," Mom said. "And a bunch of strange adults who just show up."

"They call first," Leo said. "If they sound weird then I tell them the tour is canceled. And actually I've never had to do that. No one has sounded *too* weird."

Stop talking, Leo. I thought it and he did, but it was too late.

"I'm very sorry for Leo's part in this," Mr. Bishop said. "I thought Leo was out running too. This is the first I've heard about the whole tour thing."

"Because I knew you'd say no if I asked," Leo said.

"Cedar, you lied to me," my mom said.

"I'm sorry," I said.

"No more tours," Mom said, "ever. And you are grounded. Until we go home for the summer."

"Mom," I said, "*please.* Don't do this." We had to try to find a way to get enough money for Leo. Maybe his dad would still let him go to England.

My mom looked annoyed. And mad. "Don't be so dramatic, Cedar," she said. "You'll still see Leo at work at the festival." She glanced over at Leo's dad, like she was embarrassed. "I guess someone has seen *Romeo and Juliet* one too many times this summer."

My face went Fireball-hot with anger and embarrassment. My mom was the one who was freaking out, not me. And I'd read *Romeo and Juliet* at school but I hadn't seen the play even once this whole summer.

"We might not be able to see each other at work," Leo said. "We're probably going to get fired. Did Daniel Alexander say he was going to fire us?"

"He said that was up to Gary," said Mr. Bishop. "Daniel said the kids should go to work like usual today."

My mom was totally wrong. I didn't feel at all like Juliet. I was Miranda at the beginning of *The Tempest* asking her dad not to cause the storm. *Please don't do this,* I wanted to tell my mom. *Please don't ruin this.* But Miranda didn't know yet who she might lose if her father destroyed that boat. I did. I knew who I'd already lost and who I was about to lose.

Becoming friends with Leo had helped me feel like my own self again. Not the person I was before the accident, but like someone I recognized.

It was almost time for us to leave Iron Creek. We wouldn't find out what happened to Harley or to Lisette's ring and we would never see the tunnels and Leo wouldn't have enough money to go to England.

The summer would be lost. I could feel it slipping through my fingers.

When we got home my mom told Miles to go up to his room—
that no, he wasn't in trouble—and she made me come out with
her to the backyard to talk.

She exhaled, a long deep breath that mirrored the sound of
the wind in the trees. Pieces of hair that had come loose from
her ponytail blew in front of her eyes and she pushed them
away.

"Something bad could have happened to you," Mom said.

"But nothing did."

"I cannot have one more bad thing happen to someone in
this family," my mother said. "I cannot."

I saw that she was right.

She could not.

I wore my sandals to work. No jewelry. No watch. Not a hair out of place because I hadn't ridden my bike. My mom had dropped me off earlier to volunteer in the costume shop and she was going to pick me up after work. She said it was to keep me safe but I knew it was also to keep me away from Leo as part of my punishment.

I tried to look as perfect as possible. But it didn't matter. The first thing Gary said when he saw me was, "You've desecrated the uniform."

I looked down at my peasant costume.

"You too," Gary said to someone behind me, and I turned around to see Leo.

"We weren't wearing our uniforms when we did the tour," I said. "It had nothing to do with the festival."

"It had *everything* to do with the festival," Gary said. He shook his head. "You used places *on* the campus of the festival as some of the tour stops."

"No," I said. "We used the forest. Which is part of the college campus, not the festival."

"You put your advertising *inside* of the official programs of the Summerlost Festival," Gary said.

He had me there.

"You can't work at the Summerlost Festival anymore," Gary said.

Lindy opened her mouth as if she were about to say something, but then she closed it instead. Cory grinned and I wanted to punch him. Maddy and the other girls had wide eyes and one of them frowned at me, but it was a sympathetic frown. I could tell they felt bad for us, but I knew they probably also liked the drama.

"I understand that you have to fire me," I said to Gary, "but you shouldn't fire Leo. He's your best employee. He's the only one with a proper accent."

"It's not a real accent," Cory said.

"Of course it's not a *real* accent," I snapped at Cory. "Leo's not actually *from England*."

"He's never even *been* to England," Cory said. He sounded gloaty and glad. "He *wants* to go there but he's never been. His brother told my brother at football practice."

I turned to look at Leo. He didn't deny it. His face looked fallen. Tired.

"Whoa," said Cory. "I can't believe that *you* didn't even know that."

"I'm sorry," Leo said to me.

"You lied about that too?" Gary sounded surprised. And sad. I had never heard Gary sound sad before. "You two can go home. Send your costumes back tomorrow after you've washed them."

As if he didn't want us there for even one more minute.

"Fine," I said to Gary. It was weird, my doing all the talking instead of Leo. And I said it mean.

Gary looked stunned. I felt bad, because Gary was strict but he wasn't a bad person. But I pushed the feeling away and marched out. I heard Leo behind me.

"I have to walk home," I said to Leo when we were out in the courtyard. The heat crackled the leaves under the sycamore tree, trickled sweat down my back. "My mom dropped me off. She won't be back for a while."

"I rode my bike," Leo said. "But I'll walk with you. If that's okay."

"Yeah," I said.

I walked with him to the bike rack. The cool blue water of the fountain looked perfect to me. I wanted to climb right in and let the water go over me smooth as the velvet of Lisette's Miranda costume jacket. I'd seen it today when Meg took it out of the box to steam and repair it for the Costume Hall.

"I'm sorry I lied," Leo said after we'd walked for a while. "I told Gary I'd been to England before you even moved here so he'd let me use the accent, and then the lie kind of kept going."

"It's okay," I said.

"And I'm sorry I got us fired."

"You didn't get us fired," I said. "*We* got us fired. Both of us. I was there too."

"It was actually my mom's idea," Leo said. He looked sad. I didn't understand what he meant—it was his mom's idea for us to get fired? To do the tour? That didn't make any sense—but then he kept going, pushing his bike along with his head down and his eyes on the ground. "For my dad to go to England with me. I heard them talking. She thought it would be good for the two of us to do something like this. He came up with the idea to make me earn the money for the plane ticket. Probably because he thought that I wouldn't be able to do it."

"I don't think so," I said. "I bet he was sure you *could* do it. Because he knows you."

We walked a few more steps. The frat houses, mostly empty for the summer, had dying grass in their front yards and I could see a couple of beer cans under a bush. Everything felt white-blue in the heat, and dusty.

"Now we don't even have the concessions job," Leo said, "so it's going to be impossible for me to earn the money in time. I've been saving all year. I can't believe it came down to this. But the worst part about getting fired is now you and I can't hang out at all."

"I know," I said. "But I'll be back next summer."

It sounded so far away.

Until I met Leo I hadn't known you could understand someone so different from you so well. And we did have lots of things in common—the things we both thought were funny, especially. He made me think. He made me laugh. He loved being alive and he had big ideas and I liked being around him because of those things. And because he was a guy. The fact that he was a guy made everything sharper. A little more crackly.

"Don't worry," Leo said. "I'll make sure you still find out about Harley. I'll keep watching and take notes. I could leave them someplace for you."

"Like on my windowsill," I said, feeling bold. Why not let him know that I knew? It could be a while before we saw each other again.

Leo smiled. "I think under the doormat or mailing them might be easier," he said.

So he wasn't going to admit right out that he'd been leaving things. I smiled too.

"I've been thinking," Leo said. "What if Lisette hid the ring in the tunnels after the play the night she died? That would explain why she had it during the performance but not at the hotel."

"That's a good theory," I said. "We should both keep trying to figure it out."

"Yeah," Leo said. "Maybe we can send each other letters about that too."

But we both knew that the whole point of finding out about Lisette had been finding out about her together, and we both knew that there wouldn't be any way to get to the tunnels next summer with the theater gone.

"Thanks," Leo said when we got to my house. "For doing the tour with me even though it got us in so much trouble."

"Thanks for asking me to be part of it."

"I'm sure I'll see you around," he said.

"Yeah," I said. "You too."

It was not a great good-bye.

I stood on the sidewalk and watched Leo push his bike the rest of the way up the street. I didn't want to go inside. It felt like if I did, I would officially be fired and have no way to spend time with Leo. If I stayed outside, I could pretend like we were saying good-bye on any normal afternoon. Like we'd see each other again in the evening at the Summerlost Festival and make jokes and listen to the music and watch the night fall.

When I did go inside I walked straight through the sprinkler even though I was wearing my costume. The water spattered my blouse and skirt and made dots on my leather sandals. I opened my hands so they could get wet too. Before I went in the house, I made a wet handprint on the blue door.

"Why are you home?" Miles asked. My mom looked over from the kitchen table where she was working on more lesson plans.

"Leo and I got fired," I said. "Because of the tour."

Before either of them could ask me any more questions I headed for the stairs. I took off my peasant costume and put on shorts and a T-shirt and flopped down on the bed.

I heard someone open the door.

"Do you want to play Life?" Miles asked from the doorway.

I said yes because what else was I going to do. At least he didn't seem mad at me anymore.

Miles went and got the box from his room. We set up the game together. I took the yellow car and Miles took the red one.

"Remember how Dad hated this game?" Miles asked.

"Yeah," I said. "He thought it was all about money. And he was right. Because the person with the most money wins."

"Maybe we should make it so the person who gets the most kids wins," Miles said.

"Why not," I said.

We played four games and then Miles said, "I wish we could watch *Times of Our Seasons*. I'm sick of playing Life."

The two of us didn't even put the game away. Too many pieces—all that money, all those teeny peg people and property deeds, all the cars and cards—and the house was too hot. We both flopped down in the carpet in our pile of fake money and stared out the diamond-paned window at the trees moving beyond the glass. After a while Miles got up and left, and I went over and opened the window to see the trees better. The money went scooting and skating across the floor when the hot breeze came in.

I looked at the box lid that said THE GAME OF LIFE and I thought about how *Times of Our Seasons* was also pretend life. None of it was real.

I thought, *I'm sick of playing Life too.*

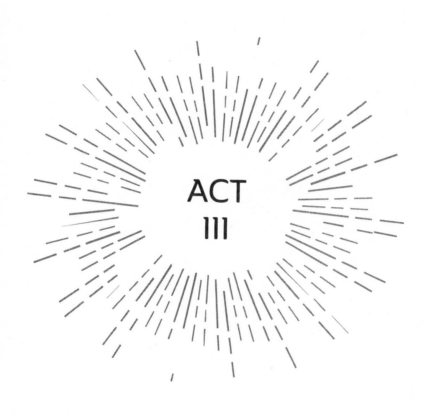

ACT
III

1

When I went into the costume shop the next morning, everyone stopped what they were doing and stared at me.

"Hello," Meg said. "I hear that you're no longer employed at concessions."

"Yes," I said.

"Gary seemed very upset yesterday," Meg said.

"He was. He told me that I'd desecrated the uniform."

"Ah," she said. "But you still plan on volunteering here."

"Yes," I said. "Unless *you* want to fire me."

"No." Meg looked at me with those sharp eyes. I knew it wasn't possible to take an X-ray of me and see the murky gray mass of sadness and frustration and anger stuck around my head, my heart, my lungs. But if anyone could *sense* those feelings, I thought it might be Meg.

Meg had to know about the tour. And Lisette was her friend. Did Meg feel like I'd been asking her about Lisette just to find out information for the tour?

At least Meg hadn't told me to leave.

Everyone was in a hurry. Meg and the others sent me on errands while they set up the Costume Hall and got the costumes ready for the day's performances. I hunted through the boxes downstairs looking for a crown made of metal filaments, then for a pair of shoes covered in fake amethysts. I walked over to the campus print shop to pick up an order of signs that Meg needed. I matched buttons that I'd sorted earlier in the summer to costumes that needed repair. At the end of my shift, Meg gave me a list with everyone's lunch order written on it. She wanted me to go out to the concessions stand and get Irish jacket potatoes and fruit salad and lemonade and tarts for everyone. *Three raspberry tarts, two lemon, one cream cheese*, the list said.

Was Meg trying to punish me by having me go face my former coworkers?

"It's the closest place and we're taking as short a break as possible today," she said, as if she knew what I was thinking. "If you want lunch too, you can add your order on to this and they'll bill it to Costumes. You've earned it. If you're tired, you can go home for the day instead."

What should I do?

I wanted to stay and eat out in the courtyard with all of them. I wanted to laugh with Meg and Emily and Nate and the others at the tables under the sycamore tree and look up at the sky and see if an afternoon storm was on its way. I wanted

Gary and everyone to walk by and see that I still had friends. I wanted to slice into the salted skin of the potato and lick lemon tart filling off my fingers.

But Leo wouldn't be there. He was stuck at home.

And I couldn't face Gary.

"I think I'll go home," I said to Meg, handing back the lunch list.

A flicker of disappointment crossed her face. Disappointment that I wasn't staying? Or disappointment that I was too chicken to take the order?

"All right," Meg said. "Run this box back downstairs and you can be finished for today."

I found the right spot for the box and slid it back onto the shelf with the others. All those labels, all those pieces to each beautiful outfit from summers long ago.

And then I knew.

Where Lisette's ring would be.

Who'd had it all this time.

I walked down the aisle, looking at the years until I came to the right one.

LISETTE CHAMBERLAIN, MIRANDA.

The date was twenty years ago.

Her dress and coat were labeled and hung up on a rack with the other costumes waiting to go upstairs, but all the accessories were still in the box. There weren't many. A few shimmery hair-pins. A packet with extra buttons for the coat. And a small velvet-covered box. I opened it.

There was a ring inside. With three pale stones.

Lisette must have given it to Meg.

And now Meg was going to put it on display. Because Lisette *did* wear it in the play that night, whether it was an intended part of the costume or not.

I took the ring out and put it on my finger.

Lisette Chamberlain wore this, I thought.

I closed the box and put it back on its shelf.

2

I knew Meg would notice that the ring was missing, eventually.

I knew that she would probably figure out it was me who'd taken it.

I knew I should tell Leo that I'd found it.

All through dinner and talking with my mom and Miles and doing laundry for our move back, the ring sat in my pocket, like a secret. A stolen secret.

Meg trusted me.

Leo trusted me.

And I stole from them.

Everything made sense. If Lisette had given the ring to anyone, as a gift or to keep it safe, it would have been her best friend. Maybe Lisette knew Roger was coming to the hotel that night. Maybe he wanted the ring back. Maybe Lisette asked Meg to keep it for that night, or for a while, or forever.

Or maybe *Meg* stole it, in which case she was in the wrong too.

I put the ring on the windowsill. It looked so small. I touched my finger to each of the three pale stones. They felt cold and smooth.

My heart pounded faster and faster. Would Lisette take it? Would Leo?

And then I realized that I hoped she wouldn't.

I didn't want the person leaving things to be Lisette's ghost, or even Leo.

I wanted it to be Ben.

When I let myself realize this—my deepest most important wish—it hurt, how much I wanted it. It hurt, how much I hoped.

Breathe, I reminded myself. *Beat.*

And my lungs did and my heart did and I hoped.

Let it be Ben.

I opened the window a crack. The wind came in but it didn't move the ring.

I decided I would stay up all night to see what happened.

I didn't have anywhere to go in the morning, anyway. The tour was finished. I'd been fired from concessions. And I couldn't go back to the costume shop after taking the ring. Everything was over.

The night was shadows and wind and the smell of a storm on the way, a night for crying until the tears were gone but the ache was left. A night for imagining that you could step out onto the windowsill and say hello to the dark, say *I am sad* and have the wind say *I know.* You could say *I am alive* and the trees would sigh back *We are too.* You could whisper *I am alone and everything ends* and the stars in the sky would answer *We understand.* Or maybe it's ghosts telling you all these things, saying *We know, we're alone too, we understand how everything and nothing ends.*

I was almost asleep when I saw him. When I heard the wind and opened my eyes and there was a boy, a kid, standing at the windowsill holding the ring.

Ben, I said, with my mouth. *Ben*, my heart beat. Right there. Messy hair. Pajamas. Face that looked gray because there was no light. Was he real or a ghost?

I didn't care.

He looked at the ring.

And then I noticed Ben's hand, the other one not holding the ring. He had a spoon, a wooden cooking spoon. He was not flicking it back and forth. As I watched, he set it on the windowsill.

Ben, I said louder.

"Cedar?" Ben said, with Miles's voice. He sounded scared.

Why would Ben use Miles's voice?

"It's me," he said. "Cedar, it's Miles."

"What?" I said.

And then he flicked on the light and I knew. It was Miles. Not Ben.

Of course it was. Of course that's who it had been all along.

"Where did you get this?" Miles asked. He opened his hand and held out the ring.

I didn't answer.

"You have to take it back," Miles said. "It looks fancy."

"Back where?" I asked, which was a stupid thing to say.

"Back where you got it," Miles said. He stood over me. He looked tall. He looked like Ben, a little.

The storm outside picked up, pushing the trees to and fro. I heard a smack of scattered raindrops against the window.

"You're the one who's been leaving things on the window-sill," I said.

Not Lisette.

Not Leo.

Not Ben.

Miles nodded. "I'm sorry if I scared you. Usually you don't wake up." He looked worried, his eyes searching mine. I'd called him Ben.

"All the things you leave," I said. I stopped. "It's all stuff Ben would have liked."

"Yeah," Miles said. He glanced over at the spoon. "And you left me that lollipop. He liked lollipops."

Right.

"So why leave those things for me?" I asked.

"Because I kept seeing stuff he would like," Miles said, "and I didn't know who else to give it to."

I scooted over in the bed. "Come here," I said. I didn't sit up, but Miles sank down next to me. He was eight and I was twelve and we were too old to snuggle like kids but we did anyway. I put my arms around him and buried my face in the back of his hair and he smelled like Miles, Ben's brother. Sweat and strawberry shampoo and clean pajamas.

The wind made a low, deep sound, one that went through my bones and every board of the house. The clouds moved and the moon came back.

And then, almost in slow motion, an enormous dark shadow went past my window.

The tree, I thought, as it creaked and ached and my heart pounded. *The tree is coming down.*

Some of its branches scratched, and I swear I saw a vulture going down with the tree, terror in the bird's glinting eyes. And then a bigger branch came in, right through the window. The diamonds, dark, shattered all over the floor.

Miles and I both jumped up.

I stood there dazed for a second, and then I remembered my mom working down on the deck.

"Mom," I said, and I ran down the stairs as fast as I could, Miles right behind me. My heart hit against my rib cage, my feet slammed on the steps. I shoved open the back door against the rain and the wind.

All I could see were branches and splintered wood. The vultures circled above us, agitated, swooping down. "Get away!" I screamed at them, and I ran out into the rain and broken branches and slippery leaves. Was she under the tree?

The whole world was a forest. How could one tree be so enormous?

"Cedar," Miles said, and his voice was a sob.

"Stay back, Miles," I said. "Stay back."

And then I heard my mother's voice.

At first I didn't understand. I thought it was in the leaves. I thought she was under the tree. I started grabbing at the wet branches. But then she called out, "Cedar!" louder, and I turned around, and she was coming toward me, the back door open, spilling light, Miles with her.

"It's all right," she said, "I wasn't outside. I went down to the basement to get more sandpaper."

One of the vultures came down and landed near the top of the fallen tree. It had crushed the shed. The vulture hopped around, upset. My mother shone her flashlight on the ground. "Oh no," she said. "They'd been nesting in here."

The shed had come apart almost perfectly along the beam, and we could see inside, where they'd built their nest. My mom shone her flashlight on the knotty nest, on the eggs. They were light purple and cream colored, spotted dark.

Every egg was broken. I could see a fluff of feathers and a shimmer of slime on one of them.

"No," Miles said. "No, no, no."

My mom put her arms around us both and we went back inside.

Things happen fast. A car hits another car, a tree comes down, an egg breaks and a bird dies. Leaves lie on the ground gathering rain instead of lifting up in the sky and turning in the wind.

3

The three of us waited in the kitchen for the fire department and animal rescue to show up. My mom had called them both and then made us hot chocolate. Miles took his to the front room to watch for the rescuers. "They said for us not to touch the birds," Mom said.

I didn't want to talk about the baby vultures. I knew there was nothing anyone could do to help them. "I'm sorry about the deck," I said to my mom.

"I wanted to prove to myself," Mom said, "that I could do this *one thing* on my own."

I understood. The deck was something my dad would have done. Not her. She could make stuff and fix things in the house and grow plants in the garden and mow lawns, but building a deck was something new.

"I learned all these things," she said. "How to measure and sand and saw. And it didn't even matter."

"It's the stupid storm," I said. "It would have been fine without the storm."

But I knew, and she knew, that I was lying.

"No," my mom said. "It wasn't working before the storm, either." She was crying. "It's not working, is it?"

She'd never said that before. I didn't know how to answer. Because it *didn't* work the same without my dad and Ben. No matter how hard we tried.

Lights flashed through the front window. "The fire department's here," Miles said. "And some of the neighbors are coming out too."

My mom left her mug at the table and went to the door with him.

This summer I'd been spending a lot of time on other people's deaths. Harley's. Lisette's. But somehow it had helped me feel alive. Because they weren't *my* deaths. The ones that were my own were too hard to face.

I heard voices outside. People had come over to help us. Flashlights flickered around, all over the backyard. I heard Leo's dad talking, and then Leo came in through the front door. His hair stuck up everywhere from sleeping. He had on sweatpants and a T-shirt. I put my head down on the table.

Leo sat down next to me, the chair squeaking across the hardwood floor as he pulled it closer. "What's wrong?" he asked. "Is something else wrong besides the tree?"

I didn't do anything. Just sat there with my head down. I couldn't even cry.

"I want to help you," he said. He sounded like *he* might be crying. "I'm your friend."

But I couldn't tell him.

I couldn't tell anyone.

I never, *ever* wanted Ben to be dead.

But sometimes I wanted him gone.

And then he was.

4

All morning long the saws hummed, cutting the tree into small enough chunks to haul away. Animal rescue hadn't been able to do anything about the nest. The vultures swung out in the sky and circled, their home gone, their eggs ruined. I saw the birds settle once in the trees by Leo's house and I watched, hoping they'd stay there, but they took to the sky again not long after.

I didn't see where they came to rest after that because I had asked my mom to take me back to the costume shop. I kept glancing over at her, at her sunglasses, the rings she still wore on her wedding finger. One diamond ring, one gold band, both from my dad. She was in the right place at the right time last night, safe inside when the tree came down.

One thing different—an extra piece of sandpaper outside when she needed it, the tree falling a bit sooner—and she would be gone. One thing different—hitting a red light instead of a green one on the way to the freeway, choosing another errand to run that day—and my dad and Ben would still be here.

It's not right that something so big, your entire life, depends on a million tiny things.

The Costume Hall was full of assistants dressing manne-quins, but I couldn't find Meg. "She's downstairs," Emily said. "Will you tell her I need Juliet's cape? Not the one from this year, the one from the production starring Hannah Crowe."

I nodded, but I didn't know if I'd have a chance to tell Meg anything once I'd given back the ring.

And then I realized, looking around, that they hadn't got-ten to Lisette's costume yet. Maybe Meg wouldn't know the ring was missing. Maybe I could slip it back into the box.

But when I saw Meg there, bent over a costume she was repairing, her shoulders hunched, she looked old, because I couldn't see her eyes. And I thought about how Lisette and Ben and my dad would never be old. About how I might be old some-day. About how Meg had lived a long time without her friend.

I came up close and put the ring on the table in front of her. "I took this," I said. "I'm sorry."

Meg looked at the ring and then up at me. "From the box for the Costume Hall display?" she asked, and I nodded.

"Why?" she asked.

Because I thought the ghost of your friend might come to my window.

Because what I really hoped was that my brother would appear. I thought he might like it. The weight, the stones.

"Leo and I noticed that she wore it in her final performance," I said. "We knew it was her ring, not the festival's, because we knew it was the one from Roger Marin. And Leo looked at the police report from the night she died and the police didn't list the ring among her personal possessions. It was a mystery."

"A mystery," Meg said. "And you wanted to be part of it."

"I'm sorry," I said again. "And I'm sorry about the tour. I know I shouldn't have done that either. I know you're probably mad at me because Lisette was your friend."

"No," she said. "I'm not mad about the tour."

Meg pushed back from her table, where she'd been leaning over something that looked like chain mail, shiny and gilded and silver. "I need to get out," she said. "I'm going to ruin my eyes trying to repair that armor. Come with me." She picked up the ring and put it in her pocket.

I followed her out into the hall. Past WIGS and MAKEUP. Up the stairs and out into the front of the building by the fountain. We stopped there, and Meg gestured for me to sit down on a bench with her. I did. The bench had a small plaque on it that said THIS BENCH WAS GIFTED TO THE FESTIVAL BY AN ANON-YMOUS DONOR.

DONOR. The words made me think of Ben, and the letter from the family of the other boy.

It felt like everything was named after someone, or was made possible by someone else. Fountains. Benches. Eyes.

"Is there something you want to talk to me about?" Meg said. "Something you want to ask me?"

What was Lisette like? How do you keep going when you miss someone so much? How do you stand getting old? Why are we all going to die?

I said something else instead. "My friend Leo and I really want to see the tunnels before they tear down the theater. Could you let us go in them?"

"Lisette's ghost doesn't walk those tunnels," Meg said. "Not in the way you think, anyway. You won't see her there unless you knew her. Unless you saw her there when she was alive. Laughing. Serious. Getting ready to go onstage or coming off it or talking to everyone in the tunnel. Then she'd be all too easy to picture."

"I'm sorry," I said.

We both watched the fountain for a moment. Meg wasn't crying but her voice had that sound voices get when you're sad and achy, too dry for tears.

I didn't know if I should keep pushing. But I had to. Because Leo wasn't going to see Barnaby Chesterfield in London, so he should at least get to see the secret tunnels of his hometown theater before they were lost for good.

"I don't really want to see the tunnels because of Lisette," I said at last. "I want to see them because of Leo."

"Leo," Meg said. "Your friend."

"Yes."

"And you're asking me to do this favor for you even though you stole a ring and gave a tour about *my* friend."

"I brought the ring back," I said. It was all I could think of besides *I'm sorry*, which I had said so many times.

Meg kept studying me.

"Also, I sorted a *lot* of buttons."

Meg stood up and brushed off the seat of her pants. "Come back to the shop tonight," she said. "Late. After the play ends and they've had time to put things away. Let's say midnight. I'll see what I can do."

5

Meg let me use her phone before my mom came to pick me up from volunteering. Meg didn't ask me who I was going to call and I didn't tell her.

I'd never called Leo's number before, but I knew it from the flyers we'd put in the programs. I prayed he'd pick up.

"Hello?" said a guy. An older guy. Zach.

"Zach, it's Cedar," I said. "Can I talk to Leo?"

"I'm afraid I can't let you do that," Zach said. "Don't take it personally. Leo's not allowed to use the phone for *anything* right now due to his poor decisions. I'm the enforcer while our parents aren't home."

"Oh," I said.

Silence for a minute. I could hear noise in the background.

"He's recording this terrible show called *Times of Our Seasons*," Zach said, "and he's got Jeremy and me hooked on it. Tell me again how this girl got buried alive?"

"Well," I said, "she fell in love with Rowan. That's the guy that her archenemy, Celeste, is also in love with. Celeste wanted

Harley gone. First Celeste tried to get Harley a job in a different state so that she'd move. Then Celeste hired a handsome man to try to get Harley to fall in love with him instead, and what ended up happening was that the guy fell for Harley and Harley remained faithful and committed to Rowan and the other guy gave all the money back to Celeste and said he couldn't be a part of this anymore and that Harley and Rowan had a love that only death could divide. And, you know, things kind of went from there."

"As they do," Zach said.

"Yeah."

Neither of us said anything. Now I could make out the voice of the bad twin in the background. I wondered if Leo knew Zach was talking to me.

"I can't let you talk to Leo," Zach said, "but I *could* give him a message."

"Um," I said.

"I can be trusted," Zach said. "I'm no Celeste."

"Okay." I didn't know what else to do. "Could you tell Leo to meet me tonight at midnight at the corner by my house and to bring his bike and a flashlight and wear all black?"

"I could," Zach said. "But what are you doing?"

"I can't tell you that," I said, "but it's safe. I swear."

"It sounded cool until you told me it was safe."

"Zach, come on," I said. "Please."

"I'll do what I can."

"This might be my last chance to see Leo before I leave for the summer."

"It's like *Romeo and Juliet*," he said. Why did everyone keep saying that?

"It's actually not," I said.

"Okay," Zach said. "Harley's coming back onscreen now. I've got to go. How does she go to the bathroom in that thing, anyway?"

"It's one of the great mysteries of our time," I said, but he had already hung up.

6

Midnight felt late, impossibly late, and strange. The houses were dark and the streetlamps not bright enough for you to be sure what street you stood on, what year you lived in. I stood to the side of the lamppost, in the shadows. The sound of sprinklers coming on made me jump and turn at the whispers of water.

Leo's house looked dark.

What would I do if Leo didn't come? Would I go see the tunnels by myself? Walk through them alone?

But then I saw him, a dark shape moving on his bike. I breathed in the smell of summer, the grass, the wind, the world warm and wide and tall and, in this moment at least, not coming down in pieces the way it did in fall and winter, leaves and snow.

"You're here," I said. "Zach gave you the message."

Leo hopped off his bike. He'd followed instructions. He'd worn all black. He stood right under the streetlamp and I could see him grin at me and his eyebrows go up.

"So where are we going?" he asked.

"To the festival," I said. "Where else?"

"We're going to get in trouble," he said. "Our parents are going to kill us."

"They might. But at least we'll die having seen the tunnels under the theater."

"*What?*" Leo asked. "We can't do that."

"We're not breaking in," I said. "That's the best part. Meg is going to let us in."

"I don't believe it," Leo said, but I could hear in his voice how much he wanted to believe me. "Meg's going to let us in? How did you talk her into that?"

"I have ways," I said.

"Wow," Leo said, and then he hugged me, fast. He felt warm and smelled good like laundry and for a second I wanted to put my head on his shoulder and stand there for a minute. *We take care of each other*, I thought. I knew.

Then it was over. Leo stepped back and I shifted my backpack straps over both shoulders. The flashlight inside felt heavy.

"So Zach knows you're with me," I said. "And I left a note on my pillow for my mom saying that we went to the festival to meet with Meg." Our parents were going to lose it if they woke up and found us gone, but at least this way they'd know where we were. "Do you think anyone heard you leave?"

"No," he said. "What about you?"

"I'm good too." I'd taken the stairs so slowly I thought I'd scream, but I hadn't made any noise. Miles and my mom both seemed fast asleep.

"All right." Leo swung his leg over his bike. "Let's go see a ghost."

7

The fountain still shone with light, but the theater and the administration building were dark.

We went to the side of the main building, and when we got close enough, we could see a faint slice of light under one of the doors. When I tried the door, it was unlocked. Once we took a few steps inside, I saw another sliver of light at the bottom of the stairs, this time in the costume shop.

I turned on my flashlight and Leo and I went down the stairs together.

Meg looked up when we pushed open the door. The fluorescent lights hurt my eyes but I could still see how tired she looked. She pulled a pin from a costume and stuck it in the strawberry pincushion on the table and I noticed that her fingers were curled in, like they had been sewing so long they couldn't go straight. I'd never seen them like that before. She was working so hard.

I wished I hadn't taken the ring.

"So you're ready to see the tunnels," Meg said. "And maybe a ghost."

I couldn't find my voice so I nodded.

"I see you brought flashlights," Meg said. "Good."

It felt strange to look around the costume room and see it abandoned; almost as strange as it had felt outside when we crossed the empty courtyard. Everyone else in the world seemed asleep. Gone.

Meg took us out into the hallway where she'd let us through to the concessions area. But this time, she went to the doorway straight ahead and unlocked it. "Be back in half an hour. That's when I'm leaving and I need to lock up."

"*Thank you*," I said.

"Thank you," Leo said.

"I'm not joking," Meg said. "If you aren't back in half an hour, I'm still going home. I'll lock up and get you in the morning. I'm exhausted from getting the Costume Hall put together and I need my sleep."

Leo looked at me as if to say *Would she really lock us in?* and I tipped my head as if to say *She could*. Even though I didn't think she would do it, there was no way I was going to be late. I couldn't disappoint her again.

"I promise," I said. "We won't keep you waiting."

8

We were finally, *finally*, in the tunnels.

The rumors weren't true about the ceilings being so low that we had to crawl, but there were times we had to duck our heads. There wasn't room for us to walk side by side. Leo shone his flashlight around on the wall when we first started and found a light switch. When he clicked it on, fluorescent lightbulbs lit up all the way down the main tunnel, but everything was still dim and gray.

I'd pictured something ancient, rotting wooden beams, packed dirt for a floor. Something that felt like a mine, maybe, or the catacombs of Paris.

But it was only a narrow hallway with other small hallways branching off it and then ending. Dirty gray paint on the walls. Cement floor, cracked in places. Pipes on the ceiling.

It was even eerier this way.

I could imagine every bad thing happening in here. Old bad things. New bad things.

I opened my mouth to tell Leo that I was afraid, but he said something first.

"Do you think we'll see her?" he asked.

I thought about what Meg had said. About how we'd only see Lisette's ghost in the tunnels if we'd seen her there in person. I knew exactly what she meant. I saw Ben and my dad so many places even though I had never *actually* seen them since they died. It was hard to explain but easy to understand if you'd lost someone you loved.

"I don't know," I said.

"This is the way to the theater," Leo said after a minute. "See?"

A black cardboard sign with gold printing said TO THE STAGE with an arrow on it. The edges of the cardboard were coming apart and looked soft, like a sponge.

"She could have hidden the ring anywhere," Leo said. "Should we stay in the main tunnel? Or go off to the side?"

"Actually," I said, "I know where the ring is. I'll tell you. When we get to the stage."

"*What?!?*" Leo said. "Tell me *now!*"

"Meg has it," I said. "I'll fill you in on the rest later."

"I guess that makes sense," Leo said after a pause.

"Let's try one of the side tunnels," I said.

We turned left and felt our way down the walls, getting dust on our fingers and flickering our flashlights around. The tunnel ended in a cement wall. "Where do you think this went?" Leo asked.

"I don't know," I said, but it looked like it had been blocked off for decades, from before Lisette's time. My hands felt smudgy with dirt.

"We don't have a lot of time left," I said. "Maybe we should go where we *know* she went. Out to the theater."

"Right," Leo said.

The actors and crew for the play would have walked back down the main tunnel only an hour or so before, when they finished the performance. But it didn't feel like that, with the dim bulbs and the cracked tile and the quiet and the creaking. It felt like no one had been there in years.

We came to a sign, gold printing on black cardboard like before.

QUIET, it said. PERFORMANCE ABOVE.

"We're right below the stage now," I said. The tunnel opened up into a bigger space, with more pipes and a ladder and a door labeled DRESSING ROOM.

"Let's try it," Leo said.

Inside we found two mirrors with lightbulbs around them, five chairs, a garbage can, a fan, and a tiny fridge. I opened it up and found bottles of festival water, a moldy orange, and a candy bar. A few lipsticks and a comb and a bottle of makeup remover had been left on the tables. The chairs looked newish, like office chairs from Kmart or something. But the mirrors looked old. I leaned in, wondering who I might see.

Only me. And Leo.

"They probably use this for some of the fast changes," Leo

said. "Since the other dressing rooms are back down the tunnel near the costume shop."

"I'm sure Lisette came in here," I said.

"Yeah."

Leo shone his flashlight on all the corners of the room. Spiderwebs. Cracks in the wall. A bobby pin, the shiny silver lid to a tube of lipstick. The empty room felt thick with memories, but none of them were ours. We could imagine, but we couldn't *know*.

Leo and I went back out into the larger space under the theater and I shone my flashlight on the ladder in the middle and the sign hanging near it.

TRAPDOOR.

"Let's go up," I said to Leo. "You first."

The ladder was made of black wood with white tape on the rungs that caught the light so you knew where your next step should be. I heard Leo push on the door at the top, and it swung open to more black. I held on to my flashlight with one hand and started to climb.

Leo was waiting for me at the top. We came out onto the stage in the dark. Without saying anything, we both switched off our lights.

Rows and rows of seats in front of us.

They could be full, they could be empty. It was too dark to see.

"The actors say that when you're onstage, the lights make it too bright to see the audience," Leo said.

So this was like that, only dark instead of light.

The breeze still smelled like last night's rain. It came in through the open roof of the theater and stirred the dark leaves behind us, the ones from the forest of Arden.

Lisette would have stood right here. It was where she stood for *The Tempest*. What did she see, if anything, in the audience that night? What did she see in Roger Marin's eyes?

"So about the ring," Leo said.

"I found it in the costume shop," I said. "In the box that had part of Lisette's costume for the display."

"And you asked Meg about it?"

I wanted to tell Leo the truth. "Yeah," I said, "but first I stole it."

"You *stole* it?"

"I took it," I said, "and I put it on my windowsill."

"Why?"

"Someone had been leaving things there for me all summer," I said. "Not every night. Every couple of weeks or so. For a while I thought it was you. But it wasn't. Anyway, that's why I took the ring. I put it on the windowsill for whoever was leaving stuff."

"Did you think it might be Lisette?" Leo asked.

"Sort of," I said. I didn't want to explain that I wanted it to be Ben. Not even to Leo.

"Did anyone come?"

What if she had come? Lisette, slipping up to my window in her Miranda dress, her eyes bright?

What if Ben *had* come, quiet, smiling, with his hair sticking up in back and his favorite blue shirt, worn soft with wear? Would I have reached out to try and touch him, or would I have been grateful just to see him?

"Yes," I said. My voice didn't work. I tried again. "Yes. Miles. He was the one leaving things."

"That was nice of him," Leo said.

"Yeah," I said. "He told me I had to return the ring. So I did."

"Was Meg mad?"

"A little," I said. "But she let us come out here."

"We should probably go back," Leo said.

"I know."

Neither of us moved.

What if we think we're alone, I thought, *but we're not, and there are creatures all, all around us, watching? Ghosts in the audience? Birds high in trees?*

I turned on my flashlight. Leo did the same. "You go first," I said, swinging my light toward the trapdoor. When he opened it up, some of the light below seeped onto the stage. He went down. I watched the top of his head. "One second," I called to him, "I'll be right there," and I shut the trapdoor and flicked off my light.

I stood there all alone onstage in the dark. I closed my eyes. "Dad," I said. "Ben."

I flicked my light back on but I didn't shine it over the seats to see who might be there. I said their names. I left the stage.

Leo and I went back and found Meg in the Costume Hall. "I decided I'd do this one tonight," she said. I looked into the case and saw Lisette's costume from *The Tempest*. The mannequin already wore the dress and the jacket. Meg smoothed down the cuff, her hand lingering on the blue-gray velvet.

"You're three minutes late," she said.

"I'm sorry."

"I designed this costume for Lisette," Meg said. "She loved it." She reached into her pocket and took out the ring, slipping it onto the mannequin's finger. I heard Leo draw in his breath.

"It's not the real ring, you know," Meg said. "It's a replica."

"Really?" I asked.

"Then where's the real one?" Leo asked.

"I sold it," Meg said. "That's what Lisette wanted me to do."

Meg let go of the mannequin's hand and closed the display case. "She took the ring off and gave it to me in the hallway right after the show ended that night." Meg smiled. "She told me to sell the ring and give the money to Gary."

"Gary?" I said.

"He's been here a long time too," Meg said. "He was work-ing concessions back then. It was his first job. His car had broken down and he didn't have enough money to fix it. He loved that car. Lisette could have gone home and written him a check, of course, but this was a grand gesture. Impulsive. In the moment. That was like her. She said at least something good would come out of her marriage to Roger."

"Roger went to see her at the hotel that night," Leo said. "Do you think he killed her?"

"No," Meg said. "I don't." She was looking at the photo of Lisette wearing the costume at the back of the display case. "He wasn't that kind of person. He was a jerk and a mediocre actor, not evil. But he didn't deserve her. And during her last trip home to the festival, Lisette finally saw that." Meg's face fell. "Once Lisette knew something, she *knew* it. I wish she'd had more time. To fall in love again. To perform again."

I watched Meg, looking at the mannequin and the photo of Lisette. How hard would it be to have to swallow down your own feelings and bring the image and memory of your friend back to life?

Meg turned away from the display case and our eyes met.

"I still sold the ring, even after Lisette died," Meg said. "But I had this replica made later, for the Costume Hall. I wanted the display to truly represent her last performance."

"Did Gary get to keep his car?" Leo asked.

"Yes," Meg said. "He was so happy. I didn't tell him where the money came from, of course. I told him it was an anonymous friend. But I think he figured it out." She frowned at me, and then at Leo. "Gary can seem uptight," she said. "But he worked very, very hard to get his job. He works very hard to keep it. He knows the festival inside and out, and he loves it. It's a place where he belongs."

While she said that, I thought about Gary, and imagined him talking about England, and the way he wanted everything to be exactly right, and suddenly I knew. What I should have known all along. My throat and eyes and heart felt like I was going to cry.

Gary was like Ben.

Not exactly. But similar. And I hadn't put it together until now because Gary was older and had come a long way and we would never know if Ben could have come that far or found a place that felt as right to him as Summerlost did to Gary. We would never ever, ever know.

I blinked and tears went down my cheeks. I wiped them away fast.

"It's like his kingdom," I said. "It's where he's the most safe."

"Yes," Meg said. She handed me a tissue, and I knew that she understood what I'd realized. I knew she must know about Ben.

"The last I knew of Lisette was that she did something nice

for her friend," Meg said. "And that she was full of life and ready to move on. It's a good way to remember someone."

I want a good way to remember, I wanted to say to Meg. *I want to stop crying. I want everything in the world to stop breaking my heart.*

10

"No ghost," I said to Leo as we rode our bikes home.

"That's okay," Leo said. He veered around something on the sidewalk that looked like a mysterious silver grenade but turned out to be a soda can.

"Would you have *wanted* to see Lisette's ghost?" I asked.

"Of course," Leo said.

I bumped over an uneven sidewalk crack that had grass growing out of it, furred and dark in the dim light.

"But I did see the tunnels," Leo said. "Thanks to you."

We stopped in front of my house. Leo's house, across the street and down a short ways, was still dark.

We were home and nearly home.

I almost said *I'm sorry about Barnaby Chesterfield* but I didn't want to ruin anything. So I asked Leo something else. "Why did you ask me to do the tour so soon after you met me? You hardly knew me."

Leo sounded embarrassed. "I thought you were cute."

The surprise of his answer made my heart beat quick. "I thought you might have asked me because you felt bad for me. Because of Ben and my dad."

"No," he said. "I mean, I do feel bad that that happened to you. But I asked you because after we met I knew the tour would work with you. It wouldn't have worked with anyone else."

"Thanks."

"I mean it," Leo said. "I had the idea for the tour, but I didn't actually *do* it until I met you."

I hadn't thought about it that way, but he was right. It made me feel good, like I had helped him too.

Leo took a deep breath. "I wanted to tell you something before you left."

"Okay," I said. "What is it?"

"Um," he said, and for a minute under the streetlamp in the night I thought he was going to tell me that he liked me.

What would I do if he did?

I liked him too. He was cute. I could picture kissing him. I could picture holding his hand.

"I wanted to say thanks," Leo said. "I have a lot of friends. You might not think that because you saw Cory and those guys bugging me at the festival. But at school, I do. And at home, I've got my family. I feel alone a lot, though. I like things they like, but I also like *different* things. So when you and I became friends this summer it was great. I feel like we get each other."

I waited for him to say something more. But he didn't. *Is that all?* I wanted to ask. He stood there on the sidewalk and I noticed that he had dust from the tunnels on his black T-shirt.

He smiled at me. I realized that what he'd said was a lot.

"I thought you were going to tell me that you liked me," I said.

"I *do* like you," Leo said.

"I mean, I thought you were going to tell me that you wanted me to be your girlfriend or something."

"Oh man," Leo said. He looked embarrassed again.

"A minute ago you told me that you thought I was cute."

"Yeah," Leo said. "I mean, I do think that. But you're not my girlfriend. You're my person."

I knew right away what he meant.

I thought he was cute and he thought I was cute but it was different than it was when people have crushes.

With Leo I'd fallen into another kind of like. I couldn't wait to tell him stuff and I loved hearing him laugh at my jokes and I loved laughing at *his* jokes. He made me feel like I had a spot in the world.

It felt as if Leo and I could like each other all our lives.

So I hugged him.

He was my person too.

11

I slept in because my room stayed dark for a long time. We'd had to board up the window until we could get a new one installed. I rolled up my blanket and pulled off the sheet to take downstairs. My last set of clean clothes sat out on the dresser.

Through the kitchen windows I saw my mom out in the backyard, wearing work gloves and pulling the smaller branches left over from the big tree cleanup into a pile. The morning was greeny-gold, end-of-summer. Our suitcases and boxes sat in the mudroom, ready to go out into the car.

I went outside to help her.

"I want to get this part of the yard cleaned up," she said. "Mr. Bishop said he can come and haul the last of the branches away and I don't want to leave him with too much to do, since he's already being so nice about it."

"I snuck out with Leo last night," I said, pulling some of the sticks into the pile. The grass was dewy and long. I didn't look at my mom. "We went over to the festival. Meg let us see the tunnels when everyone else was gone. I'm sorry. I know I was grounded. But it was our only chance." I decided to keep the part about exactly *how* late we'd been out to myself.

"I guess that's okay," Mom said. I glanced over at her in surprise. She shrugged and smiled. "Leo's been a very good friend. But the next time you break the rules like that there will be *big* trouble."

"Okay."

"So you got to say good-bye."

"Yeah," I said. "But we're going to keep in touch. Write to each other and stuff."

"Tell him we'll be back in December," Mom said. "For the Christmas break. The renters will be gone for the holiday."

"I will," I told my mom. "You know who else we should write to? That boy."

"What boy?" she asked.

"The one who Ben helped," I said.

Her eyes filled with tears.

The back door opened and Miles came out. "Hey," he said. "Didn't you guys hear the doorbell?"

"No," my mom said. "Who was it?"

"Mrs. Bishop," Miles said. "She brought this." He held up a jar of jam. "It's homemade. She said to tell you guys good-bye and that she'll keep an eye on the house while we're gone."

"That's nice of her," Mom said. She wiped her forehead with the back of her hand.

"Where's the bread?" Miles asked.

"We're all out," Mom said. "All we have left is cereal and milk. We can get a hamburger for lunch on the road."

Miles groaned. "That's too long." He went inside and then came back out with the jam and a bowl and a spoon.

"Wait," I said. "You can't eat it straight."

"I *can*," said Miles. "Do you want some?"

I looked at the jar. The jam was colored the most beautiful red. It was like bottled rubies, but better, because you could eat it. "Sure," I said.

"Me too," said my mom.

"Really?" Miles and I asked at the same time.

"Really," she said.

Miles went inside to get more bowls and spoons. He dished up the jam and handed each of us a bowlful. I turned the spoon upside down in my mouth so I could get it all. It tasted sweet and full. Like summer.

We ate every bit of the jam. I took the jar inside to wash it out. When I did, the sunlight caught the facets of the jam jar and it was like a prism, sending bits of rainbows around the room. Like my broken diamond window used to do.

I went upstairs and found the things Miles had left for me—screwdriver, toothbrush, map, wooden spoon. I took them downstairs and put them in the jam jar and brought it out to the backyard.

"There," I said.

"What are these?" Mom asked.

"Ben objects," I said. "Miles found them. He's been leaving them for me."

"Oh, Miles," my mom said.

Miles had jam on his face.

"We need something for Dad," I said.

Mom stood up and went out to the yard. She came back with a splintered piece of wood. At first I thought it was part of the deck but then I realized it was from the fallen tree. One of the old trees that my dad would have loved. It stuck out above the toothbrush and spoon and screwdriver and map like the tallest flower in a bouquet.

We put the jar in the cup holder of our car to bring it home safe with us.

"I wonder if the vultures will come back to live in our yard when everything's cleared up," I said as we backed out of the driveway. I craned my neck, looking out my window. Trying to see the birds in the sky. Or Leo in his yard.

"Maybe," my mom said. "I hope so."

The baby birds died in their nest.

Lisette died in a hotel room.

My dad and my brother died in an accident.

The end is what people talk about. How they died.

Why does the end always have to be what people talk about? Think about?

Because it's the last thing we knew of you. And it breaks our hearts because we can picture it. We don't want to, and we know we might get it wrong, but we do. We can't stop. Those last moments keep coming to our minds, awake, asleep.

At the end, everyone is alone.

You were alone.

But other times you were not.

You clomped around onstage, your face red with embarrass-ment, your knees knobby in your cargo shorts, and you looked back at your wife and kids who laughed and cheered.

You rolled down a hill. You had been crying but now you smiled. There was grass on the back of your shirt and in your hair and your eyes were bright. I put my arms around you.

Your last moment was the worst moment, but you had other moments.

And people were with you for some of them.

I was with you for some of them.

There were times when we were all, all around you.

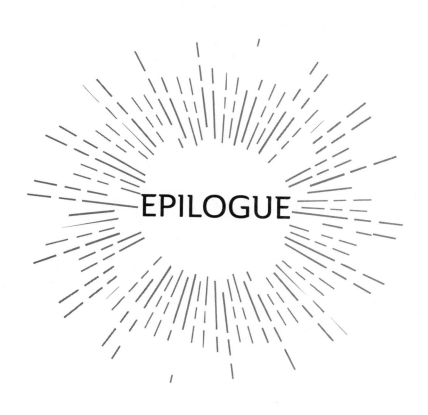

EPILOGUE

Leo wrote to me and told me that Harley got out of her box. Celeste got kidnapped by someone in the Mafia and so no one knew about Harley in the grave and things looked really dire and Harley kept getting weaker and weaker, but then Rowan had a dream that told him exactly where to go and how to find Harley. He rescued her and also resuscitated her and also kissed her, and then everything was okay. It took until November before that happened and Leo stopped watching *Times of Our Seasons* as soon as she was free. Zach still records it to watch when he gets home after school.

Leo's mom and dad gave him the last of the plane ticket money as an early Christmas present, so Leo and his dad did go to London and see Barnaby Chesterfield in *Hamlet*. Leo called me when he got back. "How was it?" I asked. "To witness greatness?"

"Amazing," he said. "But the best part wasn't the play. It was the day after we went to the play. We had no plans. We spent a whole day walking around London looking at things and eating stuff. We never ran out of things to talk about."

"That does sound great," I said, and even though I was happy for Leo my heart hurt because I wanted a day like that with my dad.

Leo cleared his throat. "But the play was pretty awesome too," he said, in his best Barnaby Chesterfield voice.

"I hope he sounded better than *that*," I said.

"He did," Leo said.

Miles and my mom and I move the jam jar around. Sometimes it's on the kitchen table like a centerpiece. Sometimes on a bookshelf. Sometimes one of us takes it into our room for a few days. When I take it into my room, I put it on the windowsill.

Meg sent me a postcard the festival had printed up to commemorate the opening of the Costume Hall. They used the Lisette costume as the picture on the front of the postcard. On the back, next to the information about the exhibits and the hours, Meg wrote, *Hope you will volunteer again next summer. We'll keep you away from the jewelry.*

That made me laugh.

The family of the boy who Ben helped sent us a letter too. My mom put it on the counter with a bunch of other mail. It's there if we want to take it out and look at it. When we're eating cereal in the morning. When we're up at night.

The boy's name is Jake and he is ten. He has brown hair and a soccer jersey for a team that my dad would have known all about, one of those European league teams. It would be a long time to go without seeing anything, if you went blind when you were ten and ended up getting to have a long long life.

I think a lot about last summer, and ones before that.

Meg, in the costume shop, sewing, remembering her friend.

Leo, leaning forward to watch a play in the theater at dusk. My mom, building a deck at night while the birds rested in the trees. Miles, eating Fireballs and playing Life and leaving things on my windowsill.

My dad, calling to me that it was time to watch our favorite show.

Ben, sitting barefoot on the back porch with a bowl of rainbow sherbet, looking up at the mountains where he liked to ski.

I have been in the presence of a lot of greatness. And people I love who loved me back. It might be the same thing.

ACKNOWLEDGMENTS

In some ways, this novel was easy for me to write, and in other ways, it was the most difficult piece of work I've done. I'm very grateful to those who made it happen.

Calvin's insightful and heartbreaking questions and comments gave me the initial idea for this story. My husband, Scott, and our four children gave me the time and heart to write it.

My grandparents, Alice Todd and Royden C. Braithwaite, were essential in helping a festival much like Summerlost grow and thrive, and in helping me grow and thrive as well. She gave me poetry to read, taught me how to bake, and had the best laugh in the world. He told me stories in his grandfather-clock voice, took me on "dates," and was often sitting on the bench outside by the roses to greet me when I came home from school. I miss them every day.

Justin Hepworth was exactly the friend I needed in seventh grade and has continued to be there for me and for my family ever since. I am also indebted to Lindsay Hepworth, one of my London study-abroad roommates, for her unwavering friendship and support.

This book wouldn't exist without Krista Lee Bulloch, friend since middle school/college roommate/guide extraordinaire, who took my oldest son and me on a tour of the tunnels and who ate Irish jacket potatoes in the courtyard with us afterward.

Fred Adams, who lived in my growing-up neighborhood in Cedar City, Utah, created the award-winning Utah Shakespeare Festival and was a good friend of my grandparents. Fred and his wife, Barbara, have given so much to our community. Fred was the festival's director for decades and continues unfailingly to work for the festival's good, and I know many people whose best summer memories include his brilliant smile and ready *hello*.

My agent, Jodi Reamer, and I exchanged many emails about Disneyland trips and the best convenience-store candy during the writing of this book. She is fierce, fun, a dear friend and a trusted mentor and advocate. Thanks also to the wonderful team at Writers House, especially Alec Shane and Cecilia de la Campa.

My editor, Julie Strauss-Gabel, said yes to this book even though it was different, and, as always, made it better with her questions and comments, her guidance and insight. It's an honor to work with her.

This is my fifth book with the team at Penguin Random House, and it is not something I take for granted. They are passionate about books and readers, and it is a privilege to be one of their authors. Many thanks to Don Weisberg, Shanta Newlin, Eileen Kreit, Anna Jarzab, Theresa Evangelista, Melissa Faulner, Jen Loja, Felicia Frazier, Rosanne Lauer, Lisa Kelly, Emily Romero, Erin Berger, Erin Toller, Carmela Iaria, and Nicole White.

The beautiful cover art was done by Jennifer Bricking, and the cover design by Theresa Evangelista. I feel very lucky to have such talented artists associated with this story.

I appreciate and love my local community of writers and readers, teachers and booksellers. Special thanks to the Rock Canyon group, Denise Lund, The King's English Bookshop, the Provo Library, the Orem Library, and Megan O'Sullivan at Main Street Books in Cedar City.

And to all my readers, everywhere—thank you for taking a chance on my stories and for writing to tell me yours. Also, thanks to Noelle Eisenhauer, who read the book to help make sure I portrayed my characters as whole and true.

I also want to express deep gratitude to all of those who work with neurologically diverse kids (particularly the incomparable Holly Flinders, Holli Child, BreAnna Moffatt, Sue Lytle, Dawn Gummersall, Ryanne Carrier, Amy Ericson Jones, Sheila Morrison, and Amy Worthington). Special thanks to Aubrey Mount, Jordan Worthington, and Kyra Ward, who are true friends and old souls. And my deepest admiration and love to all those who live with hard things every day and step up and keep going.